D1414430

Principles of Management and Organizational Behavior

The Wiley Series in
MANAGEMENT AND ADMINISTRATION

ELWOOD S. BUFFA, *Advisory Editor*
University of California, Los Angeles

Principles of Management and Organizational Behavior

Burt K. Scanlan
The University of Oklahoma

HD
31
.S326

John Wiley & Sons, Inc. New York London Sydney Toronto

INDIANA
PURDUE
LIBRARY
SEP 11 1978
FORT WAYNE

To my family, LaVon, Mike, and Kim,
and to my parents, Burt and Helen Scanlan.

Copyright © 1973, by John Wiley & Sons, Inc.

All rights reserved. Published simultaneously in Canada.

No part of this book may be reproduced by any means, nor transmitted, nor translated into a machine language without the written permission of the publisher.

Library of Congress Cataloging in Publication Data:

Scanlan, Burt K.
Principles of management and organizational behavior.

(The Wiley series in management and administration)
Includes bibliographies.
1. Management.   2. Organization.   I. Title.

HD31.S326   658.4   72-8010
ISBN 0-471-75630-X

Printed in the United States of America

10 9 8 7 6 5

Preface

The success of an organization depends chiefly on the quality of management existing within the organization. It is often acknowledged that organizational survival depends on effective management and that the main single ingredient that distinguishes a more successful organization from a less successful one is the ability to procure, train, and develop a competent management team. This is true whether the organization is public or private, profit or nonprofit. Effective management is the key factor that must be present if the organization is to exist.

This book is devoted to the study of management thought. It is designed for undergraduate and graduate students taking basic management courses, as well as for individuals who may wish to crystalize previously acquired knowledge or experience. A deliberate attempt has been made to present the material in a straightforward manner, and to provide a text that is easy to understand and to assimilate.

Historically, the study of management has been approached from the standpoint of the functions that a manager performs. Although various authors list various functions, the ones that almost universally appear are planning, organizing, directing, and controlling. In recent years, the function of decision making has also received a considerable amount of emphasis. It is this functional approach to studying management that serves as the basis for this text.

The book is divided into six parts, each comprised of several related chapters. Each chapter is followed by discussion questions and a list of related readings. The discussion questions highlight some of the more important concepts discussed in the chapter. Frequently these questions are written in the form of short case studies which require a practical application of the material. The readings are of practical value to the student and were chosen on the basis of their readability and directness. I have included a few selected references to encourage further investigation in particular areas of interest.

In writing the book, I have placed considerable emphasis on readability and practicality. Too often, management texts have a tendency to overwhelm the student in several ways. First, they present management principles and concepts in the abstract; it is very difficult for both the beginning student as well as one with some previous background or experience to relate to them in a practical way. Second, many texts contain an excess amount of discussion which does not contribute to the students' understanding. Finally, the organizational format of many books does not provide for a smooth flow of reading and an integrated view of the material being covered.

This book has been written with these traditional problem areas in mind. Specifically, an attempt has been made to present management principles and concepts in such a way that the student can relate to them and see their direct applicability. Also, I have tried to avoid using three or four sentences to say what can be said in one and have organized the material in a way which will enable the reader to follow easily the subject being discussed.

Burt K. Scanlan

Organization of the Book

This book, like most management texts, is divided into several parts, each of which is devoted to exploring a particular function of management. Part 1 introduces the subject of management and traces the historical development of management thought. Part 2 is devoted to the functions of planning and decision making, while Part 3 examines the function of organization. In recent years, the behavioral sciences have become more and more important as they relate to the study of management. For this reason, Part 4 explores the behavioral aspects of management. Parts 5 and 6 concentrate on the functions of direction and control, respectively. The table of contents will provide the reader with a detailed outline of the major subject headings in each chapter. In addition, each part is preceded by an introduction which will provide an overview of the material to follow.

Although the book follows the traditional functional approach to studying management, it is unique in that it also provides the reader with a thorough yet concise overview of current management theory and research. Another important feature of the text is its practicability. Wherever appropriate, an actual situation has been created and the principles and concepts are developed around that situation. This will hopefully enable the reader to relate more directly to what is being discussed and to see its significance.

B. K. S.

Acknowledgments

I am grateful to many people for help in writing this book. I especially thank Roger Nibler, Homer Brown, and Steve Scherling. In addition to writing the end of chapter discussion questions, Mr. Nibler contributed Chapter 7. Homer Brown contributed Chapter 24 and Steve Scherling contributed Chapter 3. I also wish to express appreciation to the many people at Wiley who worked on the book. The time and effort they spent in the various phases of editing has greatly helped the author. Finally, I thank Judy McClure, Barbara Hisey, Mercedes Nibler, and Lana Mc-Farland for typing the manuscript.

B. K. S.

Contents

staff in the organization structure, 169; Authority, responsibility, accountability, 175; Steps in organizing, 179; Power and authority, 182.

Part 1

Introduction

Part 1 gives the student a broad perspective of what management is all about. In Chapter 1, two alternative definitions of management are presented. The first emphasizes the job of the manager, working by, with, and through people to achieve results. The second definition views management in terms of the functions of management. After presenting each key managerial function, a contrast is made as to how they are performed at the executive versus the first-line supervisory level. In addition, Chapter 1 discusses the difference between doing versus managing, management as a profession, and the universality of management.

Chapter 2 views the historical development of management thought, and presents four different eras of management thought. Some of the major people involved in each era and their substantive contributions are discussed. Chapter 2 gives the student an appreciation for the evolutionary nature of management thought and an understanding of how we arrived at where we are today.

1.   Management in Perspective

Imagine that you have been an operative employee for a period of three or four years. It does not matter whether you are engaged in accounting, engineering, production, general office work, or any other type of activity. It also does not matter in what industry you work or the size of organization you work for.

One day your superior calls you into his office and explains that because of expansion and other changes which will be in effect shortly, a new supervisory position has been created. He further explains that over the past few years your general work and other aspects of your overall job performance have been observed; because of the total positive picture, you have been chosen to fill the new position if you wish to accept it.

Assuming that you are somewhat typical, the opportunity to move into a management position is something that you have aspired to as a distinct step in your career development. Let us assume that you accept the new job and the challenge which accompanies it. As you begin to function as a manager, several things will happen. First, you will notice that things look much different than they used to; what may have seemed at the time to be a small step was a giant leap. You will realize that there is a big difference between being one of several operative employees in a department and being the supervisor of that department. Your perspective broadens, your outlook and perhaps your attitude, also, change.

Second, the distinction between doing versus managing will come into sharper focus. As an operative employee you were expected to perform a series of activities or tasks and meet certain basic performance standards with respect to these tasks. You were a doer. As a manager, however, you no longer "apply your trade" in a direct sense. In fact, if you were a supervisor of production workers in a unionized plant there probably would be specific prohibitions against you or any other supervisor doing any *actual* work. Your job is now that of a manager. You are responsible for the total operation of the department and the overall direction of other people in their efforts. This distinction will be clearer when we examine the functions of management.

Finally, if you did not realize it when you started your new job, you will quickly learn that you will be successful if your employees, individually and as a group, are successful in their jobs. Your performance will be a reflection of their performance and you will be judged by what they accomplish. This leads us to an initial definition of management: *getting things done by, with, and through people.* Although this may appear somewhat simple and academic, it carries with it three very significant implications.

It stresses the importance of the *human element* in management. A manager does not get things done by himself. If he tries to do things alone, total accomplishment will be limited to just his talents and energies. In addition, those he supervises will take an apathetic and lackadaisical approach to their own jobs because they do not really have anything meaningful to do. They are left only the routine and semi-automatic details which do not utilize their skills and abilities. If people are expected to contribute and become enthusiastic about their work, they must be involved. More specifically, they must have "a piece of the action." Management cannot reduce man and his efforts to the routine status of a machine and at the same time expect him to respond positively.

The definition suggests that a manager's job is to *make things happen.* If quality is bad, he takes steps to improve it. If sales are down, he develops new customers and markets. If costs are high, he takes the initiative to find out how to cut them. Thus, management is active rather than passive; it is causal not effect oriented. The manager does more than to simply react to what is happening—he makes things happen.

The third implication of our definition is that management is a *dynamic process.* The manager transforms potential into reality. He must be an innovator and an agent for change, progress, and growth, as opposed to simply reacting or adapting passively to what is happening around him. His job is to insure that progress is indeed achieved.

The Functions of Management

Management may also be defined as involving the *coordination* and *integration of all resources (both human and technical) to accomplish specific results.* According to this definition, management is viewed in terms of the functions which a manager performs. The five basic functions which have historically formed the core for studying management are planning, decision making, organizing, directing, and controlling. This approach to viewing management will serve as a basis for the entire text. In the remainder of this chapter we will briefly examine each of the functions, developing an overall picture of what they involve. To further develop our preliminary understanding of what management is, we will contrast how each function is performed at the executive versus the first-line supervisory level, as well as discuss management as a profession and the universality of the management.

An Overview of Planning. The Planning function can be subdivided into two essential phases. The first phase is concerned with determining the overall long-range direction of the organization. This requires considerable analysis and thought. First it must be determined whether or not the industry in which the organization is centered is a growing and expanding one, a declining one, or one which is between the two. If either of the latter two situations is true, decisions must be made regarding where, how, and to what degree diversification should be undertaken. If it is a growing and expanding industry, plans must be made for the organization to keep pace. Determining the mission also involves decisions about the long-range size of the organization, where growth potential exists, the degree and extent to which the organization wants to expand in those areas, and consideration of the advantages, disadvantages, and consequences of taking or not taking certain actions. Only after decisions are made with respect to these and similar questions can shorter range specific objectives be set to insure that plans are realized.

The second phase of planning involves establishment of these specific shorter range objectives to insure that the longer range goals are realized. Part of this objective-setting process involves the determination of overall policies and procedures as well as setting forth the operational or "how to" aspects of accomplishing the objectives. Consideration must be given to taking maximum advantage of the strengths of the organization and analyzing what can be done to overcome or compensate for any factors which may detract from eventual accomplishment.

An Overview of Decision Making.   One of the most important functions of a manager and one that has received considerable emphasis in recent years is that of decision making. In many respects decision making is the function which ties together and gives meaning and depth to the other four functions. Viewed another way, the payoff in terms of much of what a manager does is in the decisions he makes. Decision making involves managerial problem analysis, developing and analyzing alternative courses of action, and decision implementation. Since the goal of all management activity is the accomplishment of certain results, the manager must continually be concerned about and sensitive to the problems which hinder that accomplishment. If accomplishment is to be realized, he cannot afford to operate on a strictly day-by-day basis, but rather must concern himself with some of the broader issues in the environment. More specifically, he must concentrate his problem analysis efforts on identifying some of the longer range factors which play a critical role in achievement. Once these major problems are pinpointed, alternative courses of action for overcoming them should be developed and analyzed in terms of their advantages and disadvantages. By stressing the need to develop alternatives, we are recognizing that there is usually more than just one path to follow in reaching a given destination. Similarly, in organizations there is usually more than one way to overcome or alleviate a given problem. Only if all the various possibilities are explored can there be reasonable assurance that the action taken is a sound one.

The final element in decision making is that of implementation. In the last analysis it is people who implement decisions, and to neglect this human element is equal to inviting limited success if not complete failure. Every decision which requires action on the part of other people must be accompanied by a plan for implementing that decision. This plan should include the necessary procedures which must be followed, a blueprint for communicating the decision to both those directly and indirectly involved, and provisions for participation.

An Overview of Organization. The function of organization involves developing a formal structure which will facilitate the coordination and integration of resources. Viewed another way, the organization structure should contribute to the efficient accomplishment of both long and short range plans. The process of organizing begins with the concept of division of work. Accordingly, a series of operating units or departments are formed with each being responsible for a particular phase of the operation. Once this departmentation is complete, the manager must concern himself with specifying the relationships among the various operating units. These relationships may take many forms, including authority relationships among people and departments, lines of responsibility and accountability, channels of communication, lines of decision making, and the complete spectrum of interrelationships that exist among the various parts. In the process of developing the total organization structure, consideration must be given to such issues as the degree of decentralization that should exist, span of control, delegation, utilization of staff departments, and chain of command.

An Overview of Direction. The function of direction is primarily concerned with the question of managerial leadership. After developing an appreciation for the fundamentals of human motivation, management must be concerned about an overall organizational philosophy about people and how the human element should be managed. Based on these two factors, an approach to management conducive to creating a motivational climate must be adopted. The issue at hand is essentially one of creating a climate where the needs of the individual are integrated with the needs of the organization; that is, a climate in which the individual can best satisfy his own goals by working toward the goals of the organization. Of particular significance in leadership is the quality of face-to-face and day-to-day interaction that a manager has with his people. Although many factors are involved in creating a "result-producing" climate, communication and participation are two key concerns. Also, the extent and degree to which a manager works with his people in a coaching and counseling capacity to help them accomplish their specific job objectives and perform at their maximum level of capability determines how successful he will be in his efforts at direction and leading.

An Overview of Control. The purpose of the control function is to insure that events conform to plans. With this in mind, control is concerned with the present, with what is happening now. As a result of planning, specific objectives have been set in all important phases of the operation. The control function, if effectively carried out, will provide the manager with continual feedback on exactly where the operation stands at a given point in time with respect to achieving these objectives. This information feedback should not only deal with the overall, but will ideally pinpoint some of the specifics. If objectives are not being achieved, or if their accomplishment is behind schedule, the manager must use available information to identify the areas that are causing problems and develop alternatives to overcome these problems. Thus, control is a four-phase process involving the presence of standards and objectives, determining how performance in each area is to be measured (criteria of successful performance), developing a reporting system, and finally taking corrective action when and where needed. Exhibit I summarizes the five basic functions of management.

How Managers at Different Levels Perform the Functions of Management

Further insight and understanding of the functions of management can be provided by comparing how managers at different levels in the organization perform these five basic managerial functions. The farther apart the various management levels, the more dramatic the difference. For this reason we compare the executive, or very top-level manager with the first-line supervisor, who is at the bottom of the managerial ladder. Exhibit II summarizes these differences.

As indicated in Exhibit II, planning at the executive level is long range. Such questions as the extent and degree of diversification, expansion by either internal growth or acquisitions, and capital procurement and mergers are significant. These issues and the decisions which are made concerning them will have an important impact over an extended period of time. Planning at this level of management is usually concerned with broad overall goals. It concentrates on such things as return on investment, sales-earnings ratios, share of the market, and product mix. Finally, executive planning requires originating. By this we mean that the decisions made and the plans formulated at this level serve as a basis for planning at each successive level in the organization.

In contrast, planning at the supervisory level is shorter range in nature. It is more likely to be on a day-to-day or week-to-week basis and

Exhibit I   The Functions of Management in Perspective

Planning Function
A. Establishing the mission or overall direction of the organization
B. Making decisions regarding mergers, acquisitions, new products, diversification, overall organizational size, growth potential
C. Establishing specific shorter range objectives
D. Determining policies and procedures
E. Developing operational plans

Decision-Making Function
A. Identifying the major problems that hinder accomplishment (problem analysis)
B. Developing and analyzing alternative courses of action
C. Decision implementation

Organization Function
A. Developing a formal structure
B. Grouping activities into departments
C. Specifying relationships between departments and operating units
D. Considering issues such as degree of decentralization, delegation, and chain of command

Direction Function
A. Developing a total organizational philosophy about people
B. Integrating the needs of individuals with those of the organization
C. Creating a motivation producing leadership climate

Control Function
A. Developing standards or objectives
B. Setting forth measures or criteria of successful performance
C. Designing a system of reporting
D. Taking corrective action when and where needed

---

carried out in a more informal way. Indeed, many aspects of the planning function are performed for the supervisor by any number of centralized planning departments. Accordingly, in a production operation a centralized production planning and control department may predetermine the supervisor's production schedule to the point of specifying which equipment will be used to perform various jobs. The supervisor's responsibility is to see that the schedule is met. Also, there may be a plan to carry out equipment maintenance work on a periodic schedule. The supervisor becomes involved only in emergencies. Similarly, a cen-

Exhibit II   How Managers at Different Levels Perform the Managerial
Functions

EXECUTIVE LEVEL	SUPERVISORY LEVEL
Planning	
A. Long range	A. Short range
B. Broad overall goals	B. Specific and precise
C. Originating	C. Derivative
Decision Making	
A. Broader long-range issues	A. Concerned with immediate issues
B. Establish direction for the total organization	B. More likely to be firefighting in nature
Organizing	
A. Overall formal structure	A. Coordination of men, machines, and materials on a short-range basis
B. Lines of authority, responsibility, and accountability	
C. Lines of communication and decision making	
D. Degree of decentralization	
E. Relationships between departments	
Direction	
A. Establish total organizational philosophy and approach toward managing people	A. Deal with operational employees
B. Long-range development of people	B. Emphasis on getting the work out
C. Organize wide programs to motivate the human element	C. Overall leadership style and specific leadership techniques important
Controlling	
A. Long-range overview	A. Specific day-to-day factors affecting results
B. Setting overall requirements	B. Removing immediate obstacles to accomplishment
C. Scope broader	C. More immediate in scope

tralized cost control unit may plan and predetermine a cost budget for his department. They keep the necessary records and provide feedback, and the supervisor is charged with making needed adjustments to meet the budget. These phenomena lead to our second observation that the further down in the organization the more specific and precise planning tends to become. Plans at lower levels necessarily must be concerned with the details that affect accomplishment of broader goals. Thus, planning at these levels is derivative rather than originating in nature. They are an outgrowth of decisions made at higher levels. They deal more with the "how to" as opposed to the "what."

Organizing. Decisions involving organization at the top level are directed toward determining what the overall formal organization structure should be. They must consider such questions as what the basis for departmentalizing work will be. Should activities be grouped on a functional basis such as production, marketing, and personnel management, or should the basis for organizing be in terms of products, territory, or types of customers. These various forms of organization will be explored in Chapter 8. Also of concern to the executive is the question of how much decentralization should exist. The decentralization issue includes the question of facilities or physical decentralization as well as decentralization of decision making. Finally, a part of developing an overall organization structure involves establishment of lines of authority, responsibility, accountability, communications, and decision making. Of critical importance will be the relationships between line and staff departments, particularly in terms of the provisions for integration and coordination of effort between them.

Organization at the supervisory level deals almost exclusively with the day-to-day coordination of men, machines, and materials to accomplish specific results. In an organizational sense, the supervisor is more concerned with the relationships among things than he is with relationships among people. His place in the total structure has been determined from above and he must operate within that framework.

Direction. As in the functions of planning and organizing, the executive-level manager's concern with the direction function is broader in scope than that of the first-line supervisors. It is the responsibility of the top-level administrators to develop and promote throughout the entire organization an overall positive philosophy and approach with respect to how they feel the direction function should be carried out.

Beyond this, the executive level must see to it that managers at all levels receive whatever training is necessary to make them effective leaders and developers of men. It is not enough simply to verbalize what should be. The example must be set from above. To a degree, how a manager directs his people in general and his specific approach to leadership is a mirror of his superior. Managers tend to manage as they themselves are managed. Beyond the issue of laying the groundwork for effective approaches for day-to-day supervision, the executive level will also become involved in developing organizational wide motivation programs. Also of concern to the higher level executive is the longer range development of people in the enterprise to insure a continued supply of qualified personnel.

Rather than managing other managers, the first-line supervisor is responsible for the efforts of operative employees. Although his ultimate goal is to get the work out, he must be particularly concerned about his overall style of leadership and the specific leadership techniques that he uses to create a motivational climate. To the operative employee the first-line supervisor represents the total organization and his perception of that organization is a reflection of his perception of his supervisor. The ability to relate to people individually and to be sensitive to them as individuals are key elements of effective first-line supervision.

Controlling and Decision Making.   Because of the very close tie among the functions of planning, decision making, and control, the distinction between the executive and supervisory levels in terms of performance of these functions is very similar to those cited earlier. The executive level is more likely to focus on the longer range issues which are somewhat broader in scope. They will be more concerned with setting forth standards or goals to be achieved and reviewing information to assess where the organization as a whole stands. Unless high-level issues are involved, they will leave the details of corrective action to lower level administrators. Also, their emphasis will focus on the major functional areas of the organization such as production, marketing, finance, and personnel management. The supervisor will center his control efforts on specific factors which influence day-to-day results and removal of immediate obstacles. Although not always true, he is more likely to become involved with immediate crisis.

With respect to decision making, the same general observations are true: the executive level focuses on broader long-range issues which establish direction for the organization while the supervisor is more concerned with the immediate day-to-day operating problems.

Doing versus Managing

A number of years ago two engineers with essentially the same educational background, experience, and tenure in a large organization were placed in management positions at about the same time. As opposed to being paid for performing their technical specialty they were now paid for being technical administrators, or managers of departments in which engineering work was accomplished. At the end of the first six months one of them was experiencing considerable success and enjoying his new managerial job. The other was not so successful. He was experiencing problems in meeting schedules and project deadlines, there was a degree of unrest among the engineers in the department, and he himself was becoming discouraged, disillusioned, and frustrated. In the second case higher level management was also becoming very concerned about the situation.

The first man had obviously adapted to his new role very well. He realized that in a way he was embarking on a new and different career with the organization and had adjusted accordingly. More specifically, whether it was because of his own personal insight or because he received help from his superior, he perceived his role and function to be different from what it used to be. Among the many things he did after being appointed a manager was to first take inventory of the department in terms of the work that had to be done and the people he had available to do it. In the latter area he not only concerned himself with the number of people available but also with their individual skills and abilities and strengths and weaknesses. He reviewed the present status of work in the department and using this as a base formulated some priorities and schedules for completion of various projects. Through individual and departmental meetings, he communicated to his people the place and importance of the department as a whole in the total organization as well as the reason behind, and purpose and objectives of the various projects in which they were involved. In addition, he gave his engineers a clear picture of where the total department stood with respect to what was expected and the present status of completion of work. He shared and discussed with them his perception of some of the problems which he thought were inhibiting better departmental performance and obtained their ideas on what could be done to improve things. Beyond this, he took an active interest in each man individually and worked with him in a coaching capacity to set goals, help him improve his own performance, and gain more satisfaction from his job. In other words, he *managed.* He planned, organized, directed, controlled, and made decisions.

The other man became somewhat overawed by his new role. As soon as he realized he was no longer expected to do actual engineering work, confusion set in. He had to spend his time some way so he began by making a point of checking everything every engineer did before it left the department. When he found errors, which he was bound to do being technically competent himself, he was quick to call it to the attention of the engineer in question. The corrections he made himself. After finding a few such cases he became convinced that more checking of work was needed; it almost became a challenge to find something wrong. This series of events led him to spend more and more time watching over his people's shoulders to make sure things were done right. There were also projects upon which the organization had placed high priority and which were known to be very strategic. These projects he felt demanded his personal attention so he had his drafting table moved into his office and worked on them himself, very often until late at night and on weekends. Because he became so involved in working alone on these special projects, certain other things did not get done. Progress reports on other projects were not filed on time. At a central unit meeting with other managers he was unable to give an adequate breakdown of the status of the entire department's work and projected completion dates for various jobs. In addition, his people assumed less and less responsibility for their work. They became passive. One of the better and more experienced engineers resigned, and two others filed transfer requests. This man was *not managing;* he was *doing.* He was doing what he had always done, practicing his technical specialty. In management he had found something strange and different to which he could not adjust. He was not able to become a supervisor and gain satisfaction in the accomplishments of others. He could not let go of the slide rule, the "T" square, and all the other tools with which he worked. Eventually he failed as a manager of others and returned to his specialty. Whether the problem lies in bad selection or in inadequate training is not our concern here. Rather, the point is that managing is a distinct activity which requires a unique set of skills, abilities, knowledge, and attitudes. Not everyone can be a successful manager nor can one necessarily be successful at higher levels in the organization. Doing and managing are distinctly different activities.

Management as a Profession

The preceding discussion helps to illustrate that management today is a profession and requires a professional to do it. In the past, many writers have debated the pros and cons of this viewpoint but we have reached a point in time at which such debates seem redundant. Developments over the past few years leave little or no room for considering management as anything but a profession.

In prior years, when a manager was needed, the common practice was to look around the organization or department and spot the best operative employee. He was then appointed the manager. The assumption was that since he was good at whatever operative job he held, he would automatically make a good manager. Accordingly, the best drill press operator, accountant, engineer, or salesman was the prime candidate for a management position. There were undoubtedly many employees desiring to move into management who believed that superior performance and competence on their present job was the key to the door.

We have come to learn that this type of direct relationship does not represent the real world. As stated previously, management requires a completely unique set of knowledge, skills, abilities, and attitudes on the part of the individual. If he is to be successful, he must develop the necessary knowledge, skills, and abilities. It is certainly true that some people probably have more innate or inborn talent to be effective managers than others, but it is also true that these skills and abilities can be learned and developed. This point is evidenced by the fact that organizations are spending millions of dollars each year on various types of management development programs. Also, there are few organizations of any size which do not either have a separate management development department, or one person who devotes a major share of his time to management development activities.

Universality of Management

The word management evokes in most people the thought of profit-making business and industry. Much of the impetus for developing a unified body of knowledge about management and a professional approach to performing the management function has come from needs created by our free enterprise system. One will usually find that the quality of management is the key factor in determining the degree of success or failure of an organization. But it would be a mistake to assume that the only place management takes place or that management skills are needed is in a profit-making enterprise. Anytime that two or more people are involved in a joint effort, management is required. The activity being undertaken may be as informal as a bowling team or three or four men going on a hunting trip, or as highly formal as in a business. The point is that whether it be a hospital, a university, the military, a health clinic, or a branch of the federal government, the management functions discussed in the preceding section must be performed effectively if objectives are to be achieved successfully. Earlier we noted that there is a considerable amount of time, effort, and money being devoted to management development efforts today. It is also interesting to note that some of the greatest concern in this area stems from outside the confines of profit-making business. By way of example, the United States Postal Service Institute headquartered at the University of Oklahoma graduates over 6000 managers annually in their two week management development programs. Similarly, the Extension Division of the University of Wisconsin has a separate area which devotes its efforts exclusively to management development programs for hospital administrators. This illustrates that the concern for professional management is universal and that management is indeed a universal process.

Summary

This chapter introduced the student to the field of management. Management was first defined as getting things done by, with, and through people. This definition stressed the importance of the human element in management, the idea that the manager's job is to make things happen, and the fact that management is a dynamic process.

A second definition proposed was that management involved the coordination and integration of all resources (both human and technical) to accomplish specific results. This definition stresses the idea of viewing management in terms of the functions a manager performs. The five basic managerial functions which were discussed include those of planning, decision making, organizing, direction, and control. Planning involves establishing the overall direction of the organization, determining shorter range objectives, developing policies and procedures, and setting forth day-to-day operational plans. Decision making is concerned with problem analysis, developing and analyzing alternatives, and decision implementation. The function of organization encompasses the creation of a formal structure within which the actual work will take place. The matters of departmentalizing the work, determining the relationships between departments, and such things as the degree of decentralization, delegation, and chain of command are all significant issues in organization. The direction function is concerned with managing the human assets of the organization. Development of a management philosophy about people, the process of motivation, and leadership strategies are significant aspects of direction. Finally, the objective of managerial control is to insure that events conform to plans. Standards must be set, measures of successful performance must be developed, a system of reporting events as they occur must be established, and provision must be made for corrective action, if needed.

In addition to surveying each of these managerial functions, their performance at different management levels was explored. Exhibit II summarizes this comparison.

Key Concepts

Doing versus Managing.   Although there is always a certain portion of physical work that a manager does, it must be emphasized that his prime responsibility is to manage the work of others and of his department as a whole. His job is to coordinate the total effort and to furnish assistance, and support to his people as they work toward accomplishing the objectives.

Management as a Profession.   Management is a distinct profession and requires a professional to do it. The higher one goes in the organization the more this becomes true. Management requires a unique set of skills and abilities which everyone does not necessarily have, and everyone cannot develop to the same degree of proficiency.

Universality of Management.   Many times the word management is linked exclusively with profit-making business and industry. Such is not the case. All organizations, whether they be public or private, profit or nonprofit, require effective management. Thus, a church, a university, a fraternity, or an organization such as VISTA need good management as much as a large corporation does.

Discussion Questions

1. Assume that you are in a first level supervisory management position and have just been informed that you will shortly be promoted to a second level managerial job. You have been asked to pick a successor to your present job. After considerable thought you settle on Alex Tompkins, one of your better employees. Much to your surprise, when you inform Alex of the situation he shows some hesitancy to accept the job. During your conversation he asks the following questions: "What does the job of management and supervision really involve?" "If I become a supervisor, what things will I find different?" How would you answer Alex Tompkins?

2. Just as there is a distinct difference between being an operative employee and a supervisor there is also a difference between performing the management job at the higher versus the lower management levels. In terms of the functions of management, contrast the job of a president with that of a supervisor.

3. Management was initially defined as getting things done by, with, and through people. The concept of doing versus managing was also discussed. What relationship do you see between these two?

Selected Readings

Barnard, Chester I., *The Functions of the Executive*, Harvard University Press, Cambridge, Massachusetts, 1938.

Boyd, Bradford, *Management Minded Supervision*, McGraw-Hill, New York, 1968, pp. 3–22.

Brown, David S., "POSDCORB Revisited and Revised," *Personnel Administration, 29* (3), May–June 1966, pp. 33–39.

Donham, Paul, "Is Management a Profession?" *Harvard Business Review, 40* (4), September–October 1962, pp. 60–68.

Fox, William McNair, *The Management Process: An Integrated Functional Approach*, Chapter 1, Richard D. Irwin, Homewood, Illinois, 1963.

Learned, D. P., D. N. Ulrich, and D. R. Boor, "The Role of an Executive," *Executive Action*, Graduate School of Business Administration, Harvard University, Boston, 1951, pp. 53–63.

McLennan, Kenneth, "The Manager and His Job Skills," *Academy of Management Journal, 13* (3), September 1967, pp. 235–245.

Megginson, L., "The Pressure for Principles: A Challenge to Management Professors," *Journal of Academy of Management*, August 1958, pp. 7–12.

Sonthoff, Herbert, "What Is a Manager?" *Harvard Business Review, 42* (6), November–December 1964, pp. 24–36.

Stewart, Rosemary, *Managers and Their Jobs: A Study of the Similarities and Differences in the Ways Managers Spend Their Time*, McMillan, London, 1967.

———, *The Reality of Management*, William Heinemann, London, 1963. Part II.

2. Historical Development of Management Thought

As in all fields of study, the development of management thought has been evolutionary in nature. Therefore, in order to better understand and appreciate where we are today, it helps considerably to know from whence we have come. The purpose of Chapter 2 is to explore the historical development of management thought. Our objective is not to expose the reader to such a vast amount of material that he qualifies as a completely competent management historian. Anyone so qualified could readily point to certain gaps in our discussion in terms of the people referred to and the stages or areas involved. Indeed, the subject of the history of management thought is of such magnitude that whole books have been written on it and complete courses are taught which deal with nothing else.

Our objective is more modest in nature. Specifically we will concern ourselves only with building a base or a foundation which will give the reader an appreciation of how we arrived at where we are today and the evolutionary nature of management. For purposes of discussion, four principle eras will be covered.

1. Scientific management era
2. Human relations era
3. Behavioral sciences era
4. Management science era

In discussing each era, some of the more significant contributors will be referred to.

Scientific Management Era

The scientific management era was marked by the contributions of Frederick W. Taylor and Frank and Lillian Gilbreth. For his original pioneering work in the early 1900s Taylor is historically referred to as "the father of scientific management." Taylor originally received training as a machinist in the early 1870s and eventually became a machinist foreman. Young and ambitious, he wished to establish his department as a top producing one. With this objective in mind, Taylor quite naturally was very much concerned with the efficiency with which machinists performed their jobs. More specifically, he knew that the key to better productivity was greater efficiency. Having been a machinist himself, he was also convinced that there was a substantial amount of inefficiency present in the performance of all tasks at the shop level.

Taylor believed that the remedy for curing this inefficiency lay in scientifically designing jobs. Under Taylor's approach each job, operation, or process was studied to determine the one best way of completing it ("best" meant requiring the least number of motions on the part of the man and the least amount of time) and then workers were thoroughly trained to follow this method. Thus, according to Taylor's thinking there were certain laws, principles, rules, and concepts that could be applied to designing all jobs and thereby increase the efficiency of the person doing it.

To actually determine what constituted the "one best way," Taylor broke down each job or task into sets of individual elements. Each element constituted a small but distinct part of the total. With a stop watch he timed how long it took a man to complete each element of the job. Making some allowances for unavoidable delays and brief rests, as well as a judgment about how much effort the worker was expending, he could then add the individual element times to arrive at the total time that the job should take. According to Taylor, it was thus possible to scientifically determine a standard of worker performance which constituted a "fair day's work." A very integral part of Taylor's approach was also to study the motions themselves and how the tools were used with an eye toward simplification. He found that in most cases the same end result could be achieved with fewer or shorter motions. Thus, Taylor provided the impetus for the growth of time and motion study.

One of Taylor's implicit assumptions was that the worker was paid to produce and should be willing to follow the instructions and methods which were specified by those in authority. To promote this cooperation, he introduced the concept of a "differential piecework" plan for wage payment purposes. Under this plan two piece rates were established. If a man produced at "standard," he would receive one rate for each piece he produced, say $.20 per piece. If he exceeded "standard," however, he would receive $.25 per piece and this second higher rate would apply to *everything* he produced, not just those pieces which exceeded standard. Taylor believed that management could afford this arrangement because of higher productivity, and the wage incentive would encourage workers and management alike to respond positively.

Industrial engineering was not Taylor's only concern. He was also an advocate of drawing a sharp line between those things that a supervisor did as opposed to what an operative employee did; that is, the supervisor should plan the work while the operative employee concerned himself only with physically doing it. Prior to Taylor, it was common practice for each man to plan his own work. Through observation and experience he developed his own approach to the job on a hit or miss basis. The supervisor told him *what* to do but not *how* to do it. In line with this idea of separating management planning from operations and increasing efficiency through specialization, Taylor also advanced his concept of functional foremanship. Under this plan a worker would have several supervisors, each a specialist in a given line of work. If he was doing a job that required drilling, grinding, and lathe work he would get three sets of "how to" instructions; one from each supervisor who dealt only in his specialized area. Thus, he would have three different supervisors.

What Taylor sought was a reshuffling of management and worker thinking. He believed that there was no reason why the two could not and would not work together cooperatively toward the achievement of common goals. He further believed that the key to achieving this cooperation was to offer incentives for superior production. With this opportunity available, the worker would be willing to follow management's methods and directives. From management's standpoint, he argued that the increased productivity would more than offset the cost involved.

Frank and Lillian Gilbreth.   The second major contributors to the scientific management era were Frank and Lillian Gilbreth. After completing high school, Gilbreth became a bricklayer's apprentice and, like Taylor, he was very much interested in his career development. He began by developing a series of shortcut motions for laying bricks. While Taylor was concerned with both the time it took to do a job and the method of doing it, Gilbreth concentrated primarily on the latter area. He went beyond Taylor in that he concerned himself not only with the method requiring the fewest and simplest motions but also placed considerable emphasis on the work area and the positioning of tools and workers themselves. As he applied his ideas to the bricklaying trade, he designed better rigging and scaffolding and positioned things so as to eliminate excessive stooping, bending, and wasted time out. Eventually Gilbreth went in business for himself and later became a consultant.

While Taylor did much to stimulate interest in the application of principles of motion economy, Gilbreth was the one who refined the whole concept. The system Gilbreth developed broke the job motions down to seventeen basic elements. He called these elements "therbligs" and together they furnished a basis for a very fine breakdown of work for purposes of studying and then simplifying it. The seventeen elements were (1) search, (2) find, (3) select, (4) grasp, (5) position, (6) assemble, (7) use, (8) disassemble, (9) inspect, (10) transport, (11) preposition, (12) release, (13) empty, (14) wait, (15) avoidable and unavoidable delays, (16) rest, and (17) plan. Using these elements as a base, a thorough "therblig analysis" could be made of any job.

Another of Gilbreth's very significant contributions was the introduction of process flow-charting which enabled one to scientifically study a whole operation as opposed to a single task or one operator. The process flowchart provides a written record of what is done in producing or processing something. The various steps are diagramed in terms of operations, transportation, inspection, delays, and storage. The total can then be studied with the objective of eliminating, shortening, or combining some steps.

Results of Scientific Management.   Before getting to the specifics of the impact and results of the scientific management era, it is important to note two things which apply not only here but also will apply to our discussion of the results of the other eras being covered. First, as we noted in our earlier discussion the development of management thought has been and will continue to be evolutionary in nature. This observation has in turn two important implications. For purposes of clarity in study we are discussing each era separately and independently of the others as if to imply that there are finite breaking points in terms of the time at which they occurred. This obviously is not the case and indeed would conflict with the evolutionary idea set forth in the preceding discussion. In fact and practice the eras blend into one another. Thus, the division into eras is simply recognizing that because of social, economic, and other changes, we merely experienced a shift of emphasis in terms of the overall issues that were of concern. It is also important to note in this respect that the contributions of the men in one era did not all of a sudden cease to be of significance and lose their validity. Just as Taylor's work was a stepping stone for Gilbreth, the scientific management era in total was the forerunner of the human relations era and both of them together provided the foundation for the behavioral sciences. In the future we will find another distinguishable development emerging on the horizon.

A second major point that deserves emphasis is that the student of management must realize that because the eventual application of any given individual's ideas or those of a total era were not all favorable and did not in practice turn out the way they were conceptualized should in no way be interpreted to mean that they were unsound all along. Rather, as conditions change, approaches to management must necessarily change in terms of new points of emphasis. Ideally, past experience furnishes us with the basis for entering a hopefully more productive future. With these observations in mind, we can summarize some of the results and impact of scientific management as follows.

1. Considerable new emphasis was placed on achieving output and efficiency. In a sense these two things became the bywords of industry.

2. There was a move toward reducing jobs to their least common denominator. It was believed that the more a job could be specialized and routinized the greater would be the worker's productivity. Accordingly, in many instances what was done by one man was now done by two or three, that is, each one performed only a small part of the total. The idea was that if a man repeated over and over again only one small segment of work he would become very proficient at it.

3. The above approach led to reducing the worker and his

efforts to the status of a machine. It neglected the human element and human aspects of work.

  4.   The belief that money was the worker's reward for compliance, and incentives would stimulate him to higher production to get it fell short of the mark. Instead, in many cases there was open resistance to incentive systems. This took the form of restriction of output and sabotage of equipment, for example.

The results of scientific management can perhaps best be summarized by saying that the cooperative revolution that Taylor envisioned between labor and management never materialized. The reasons for this are not necessarily found in anything that was or was not directly or indirectly related to the scientific management itself. Rather, numerous things were happening in society in general and in our industrial development in particular, which caused the gap between labor and management to grow continually larger. Notwithstanding this, the developments of this era are still with us today and we are still benefiting from much that happened.

Human Relations Era

At the same time that the underpinnings of scientific management were being developed, the human relations era was beginning to take shape. The principal people involved were Elton Mayo, a psychologist and Fritz Rothlesberger, a sociologist. They were primarily concerned with the link between the physiological aspects of work and productivity, or more specifically the effect of working conditions on productivity. Beginning in 1924, a series of experiments were begun at the Hawthorne branch of the Western Electric Company in Chicago. The experiments continued over many years, lasting into the early 1930s, and took on many aspects. The results of the total study are best summarized however, by the findings related to the assembly of telephone relays by a group of women. Each relay consisted of a number of parts which the women assembled into the finished product. Output depended on the speed and continuity with which the women worked. The conditions which existed at the beginning of the experiments were that operators were grouped together in numbers of about 100 and incentive pay was awarded to individuals on the basis of the total group's performance. With their consent five girls were selected to participate in the experiment. For a period of time before the experiment began production records were kept so that the effect of various changes on subsequent productivity could be assessed. Over a period of time and with adequate controls and precise record keeping, the following changes were introduced in sequence:

1. The five girls were moved off the main assembly floor and into a separate assembly room by themselves.

2. The incentive was changed so that each girl's extra pay was based on the output of the five rather than on the output of about 100, as before.

3. Two rest periods (one in the morning and one in the afternoon) of five minutes each were introduced.

4. The rest periods were later extended to ten minutes.

5. Later, the rest periods were again reduced to five minutes, but the number of such periods was extended to six.

6. There was reduction to two rest periods of ten minutes each but in the morning coffee or soup was furnished along with a sandwich; an afternoon snack was also provided.

7. The morning period was extended to fifteen minutes with the same arrangements as above.

8. Changes in the work day were introduced at various times, such as cutting an hour off the end of the day and eliminating Saturday work.

9. Lighting, ventilation, and similar things were changed.

Before each change was introduced, the operators were consulted and it was discussed with them. They had an opportunity to express their viewpoints and concerns with the supervisor; their ideas and suggestions were sought, and in some cases they were actually allowed to make decisions concerning the experiment. In addition, the supervisors of the girls were connected with the experimental team and tended to take more of a personal interest in the girls than did the previous supervisors.

As each successive change was introduced during the course of the experiment, an increase in productivity occurred. In addition, it was found that absenteeism was much lower than on the main assembly floor, less actual supervision was required, and morale was generally higher. After several years had elapsed and everyone was fairly convinced that there was a very definite link between productivity and the various factors being adjusted, the experimenters decided to return everything to its original status. In other words, no breaks, no coffee, and poor lighting. Much to their surprise, productivity once again took a jump and stayed there.

Results and Impact of the Human Relations Era.   This development caused a considerable amount of redirection in thinking. The Hawthorne studies pointed out the fact that there was more to productivity than just money and working conditions. Specifically, the type of supervision given (understanding as opposed to authoritarian) was important. The effect and influence of the group on the individual is significant and group solidarity and cohesiveness are factors. The opportunity to be heard and to participate has its effect. These findings served to refocus attention to the social side of work and man as opposed to just the economic and technical aspects.

At the same time that these "new discoveries" were being unveiled, other developments were emerging on the industrial scene. Principal among these was the very strong move toward extensive unionization, and a great deal of resultant strife between labor and management. While supervision before and during the 1920s could be characterized as primarily authoritarian in nature, in the 1930s it began to swing in the opposite direction. In short, more of a "be nice to people" and keep them happy philosophy began to appear. The latter, of course, was equally as ineffective as the former. Undoubtedly the findings of the Hawthorne studies *in conjunction with the economic and social developments taking place* helped bring about this switch in management strategy. The problem lay in the fact that to a degree there was a *misinterpretation* of what good human relations really involved. Management read things into the findings and drew some conclusions which were never there in the first place. This is perhaps understandable considering the pressures many firms were under and their desire to find ready answers to labor problems. By the middle 1940s the words "human relations" were capable of eliciting some strong negative responses from practicing managers. Since then we have considerably refined our insights into what was really discovered at Hawthorne and we have also refined our application of these things.

Behavioral Science Era

The behavioral science era can be divided into two phases, the human behavior school and the social system school. Since the contributions of the men involved in both these phases will be dealt with in greater detail later in the text, they will be only briefly summarized here. The human behavior school began about 1940 and centered its attention on the principle of understanding people and interpersonal relations. The emphasis was on the psychology of the individual in terms of his needs and motivations. It also concentrated on the manager as a catalyst to triggering the motivational potential in people.

The human behavior school was primarily triggered by Abraham Maslow and his development of a need hierarchy to explain human behavior. Following Maslow's original contributions the work of such people as Herzberg (see Chapter 17), McGregor (see Chapter 18), and Likert (see Chapter 19) took on increasing significance.

A later development in the behavioral science era was the social systems school. According to this view, organizations are seen as a social system or a system of cultural interrelationships. This approach to viewing organizations leans heavily on principles of sociology and emphasizes groups, their interrelationships, and the need to build a total integrated system. Such men as Chester Barnard, Edgar Schein, Chris Argyris, and Warren Bennis, have been significant contributors.

Results and Impact of Behavioral Science Era. As contrasted with some of our earlier thinking, the work of the behavioral sciences has served to point up all of the following:

1. Management cannot be viewed as a strictly technical process (rules, procedures, principles).

2. Management cannot be haphazard and the approach used cannot be left to chance.

3. The organization as a whole and the individual manager's approach to supervision must fit the situation.

4. Although the job must be done, it does not get done by means of exercising pure authority over people. An approach which results in the worker's commitment to the goals of the organization is needed.

In addition to these findings, some of the more specific ideas which have come out of behavioral research are that:

1. The human element is the key factor in determining the success or failure of achieving objectives.

2. Today's manager must be thoroughly trained in the principles and concepts of management.

3.   The organization must provide a climate which is conducive to offering people an opportunity to satisfy their full range of needs.

4.   Commitment can only be achieved through participation and involvement on the part of employees.

5.   A man's job must be structured in such a way that it is meaningful and significant. He must be able to get a sense of achievement and self-satisfaction from work.

6.   Patterns of supervision and management control must be built on the basis of an overall positive philosophy about people and their reaction to work.

Management Science Era

At about the same time that the behavioral scientists were making their contributions to management thought, the management scientists emerged on the scene. Whereas the behavioralists are concerned primarily with the human aspects of organization and management, the management sciences concentrate their attention on the need for a more scientific approach to analyzing the complicated problems of management.

The management sciences had their beginning during World War II and, since then, there has been a great increase of interest in applying the scientific method to management problems. This increased interest was evidenced by the formation of new societies in the United Kingdom (Operations Research Society), the United States (Operations Research Society of America), and throughout Europe, Asia, and Australia (for example, Société Francaise de Recherche Opérationelle). It is also evidenced by the large number of universities which have instituted both undergraduate and graduate programs in the management sciences. The terms operations research, decision theory, and organizational theory are often used interchangeably with management science since all are concerned with the same basic objective, that is, the application of scientific methods to solving complex problems. For our purposes the term management sciences encompasses all of these areas.

Management Sciences Defined.   To define the term management sciences in one or two sentences would not do justice to the concept itself nor an understanding of it. With this in mind, the following excerpts are drawn from the Encyclopaedia Britannica to provide the reader with an insight into what the management sciences are all about.

"The management sciences are bound together by more than a common intellectual interest; they also share a common philosophy of method: namely, the need for more rigorous analysis of the complicated problems of management. This need can often be satisfied by the use of mathematics or of carefully controlled observation and experiment. Opinions about the importance of mathematics vary among those who recognize themselves to be management scientists, but most if not all would admit that science connotes among other things the attempt to become as precise as possible and that mathematics is one of the chief resources of the mind in this endeavor. Differences of opinion usually reflect different judgments about the possibility of reaching refinement of language in specific projects, and the relative importance of research problems. Sometimes the management scientists try to characterize their aims in terms of 'quantification' of managerial activities, because they feel that this term connotes the refinement and rigour they aspire to, and not because they feel any importance attaches to numbers as such."[1]

This definition stresses several things. First, it indicates that the management sciences believe that decision making should be as precise as possible. Second, to accomplish this, a heavy reliance is made on the use of mathematical and statistical techniques to quantify as many of the variables involved in a decision as possible. Third, it stresses the need for viewing any situation in terms of its total rather than in terms of a series of individually segmented parts. In other words, the emphasis is on the interrelationship between all the elements of a problem, the total organization, or a particular segment of the organization.

A Preview of Some Management Science Techniques. In Chapter 7 several specific techniques which the management scientist might use are explored in detail. The following is a brief description of some of the more familiar of these techniques.

Linear Programming. Linear programming is a mathematical and graphical technique used to determine the best allocation of scarce or

---

[1]Encyclopaedia Britannica, William Benton, Publisher, 1971, Vol. 14, p. 749.

limited resources. For example, assume that a manufacturer produces three different types of power tools: a drill, a handsaw, and a sander. Each product sells for a different price but the manufacturing process for each is similar; component parts must be fabricated, assembled, and tested. In a given period of time, perhaps a week, the company could devote all of its time to the manufacture of one, two, or a combination of all three products. However, the number of hours it takes to complete a unit of product will vary for each of the three stages of manufacturing. The problem for the firm is to determine the quantity of each product which should be produced in order to maximize its revenue. Linear programming can be used to solve this problem.

Breakeven Analysis.   Cost analysis goes beyond simply gathering cost data from accounting records. It is concerned with the behavior of certain costs with regard to various alternatives that are available. Breakeven analysis analyzes the behavior of pertinent costs as the volume of operation fluctuates. It can be used to determine the point at which income and costs are equal. Operating below the breakeven point will result in a deficit, and operating above it results in profits of various size.

Queuing Theory.   Queuing theory, often referred to as "waiting line" theory, is concerned with the build-up waiting lines as they relate to a need to receive service. An example would be a cafeteria where the number of customers coming through the line must be balanced against the number of service workers and checkout stands. Queuing theory is a way of forecasting the length of the waiting line and the waiting time. By balancing the costs of waiting for service and the costs of providing service facilities, total cost can be minimized. Some of the other problems where queuing theory is applicable include how many men should be used to service a tool crib where workmen are waiting to check out special tools, and how many men should be available to service incoming airplanes. Queuing theory enables us to determine a minimum total waiting time cost.

These three quantitative techniques which, with several others will be discussed more fully in Chapter 7, are not intended to be fully representative of the entire management science field. They should, however, provide the reader with an insight into what this particular specialized phase of management thought encompasses. The preceding discussion makes it readily apparent that the process of time, change, and research all combine to make management a developing field of study and practice. We are constantly getting new insights which, when blended with the old, result in a continually growing body of knowledge. Any new era will always carry over and utilize those most valuable ideas developed in previous years. That is why in management today we are still effectively using the concepts developed by men such as Taylor, Gilbreth, Mayo, and Rothlesberger. The past will always influence the present and the present will furnish the base for the future.

Summary

The development of management thought has been and will most likely continue to be evolutionary in nature. In this chapter we have discussed four principle eras as they relate to the evolution of management thought. These four eras include scientific management, human relations, behavioral sciences, and management sciences. The scientific management era was concerned with the application of the principles and concepts of industrial engineering to designing and structuring work. Through the use of time and motion study, as well as other techniques, the one best way of performing various jobs was determined and workers were then trained accordingly. It was anticipated that since management was willing to pay incentive wages for above average production there would be a cooperative effort between labor and management. Taylor described this anticipated cooperative effort as a mental revolution. In fact, it never occurred.

The human relations era emerged as a result of the Hawthorne studies, conducted at Chicago's Hawthorne branch of the Western Electric Company. Originally these studies were designed to investigate the effect of working conditions on productivity. The end result, however, was to focus attention on the importance of the social aspects of work; also studied were the influence of the group, the role of supervision, communication, and the opportunity to participate, as they relate to productivity.

Beginning in the early 1940s the behavioral science era began to crystalize. The human behavior school which emerged initially placed emphasis on the psychology of the individual as related to his needs and motivations. This was followed by research and investigations as to how the organization and individual manager could trigger the motivation potential in people. The social systems school viewed organizations as systems of cultural interrelationships. It leans heavily on the field of sociology and places emphasis on groups and the need to build a total integrated system. The result of this era was to place more emphasis on the human element in organizations.

The management sciences had their beginning during World War II. They are concerned with the application of mathematics and the use of scientific method in making managerial decisions. Over the past 20 years a variety of very sophisticated approaches to solving management problems have been developed and their applicability has increased extensively.

Discussion Questions

1. Applying your knowledge of United States history and the information given in this chapter, discuss some of the reasons Taylor felt that man was motivated primarily by economic (financial) incentives. Does this type of motivation exist today? If so, cite examples of situations where Taylor's assumptions of worker motivation might apply.

2. Why do you think the human relations era failed to provide management with a sound theory of worker motivation? From your own experience, cite examples where you did not necessarily work hard for a supervisor or teacher who was "nice" to you. Why did you fail to respond to this "be nice" motivation? Do you think that your reasons would apply to other people if they were in your situation? Is it possible that the findings of such people as Mayo and Rothlesberger have been misinterpreted? What were the really important ideas which they uncovered?

3. Two of the basic concepts of the behavioral science era are as follows:
    (a) Commitment can only be achieved through participation and involvement on the part of the employees.
    (b) A man's job must be structured in such a way that it is meaningful and significant.

What is meant by commitment, involvement, and structured in these concepts? How are each of these concepts applied? Be specific and illustrate with an example.

4. In your own words define what is meant by the term management sciences. In terms of its point of emphasis how do the management sciences differ from the other three eras of management thought which were discussed?

Selected Readings

Boddewyn, J., "Frederick Winslow Taylor Revisited," *Journal of the Academy of Management*, August 1961, pp. 100–107.

Dale, Ernest, *Readings in Management*, McGraw-Hill, New York, 1970, pp. 137–145.

Hoagland, John H., "Management Before Frederick Taylor," proceeding from the *Journal of the Academy of Management*, December 1955, pp. 15–24.

Kelly, Joe, *Organizational Behavior*, Richard D. Irwin, and the Dorsey Press, Homewood, Illinois, 1969, pp. 69–87.

Landsberger, Henry A., *Hawthorne Revisited*, New York School of Industrial and Labor Relations, Cornell University, Ithaca, New York, 1958.

Petit, Thomas A., "A Behavioral Theory of Management," *Academy of Management Journal, 10* (9), December 1967, pp. 341–350.

Spriegal, William R., and Clark E. Myers (eds.), *The Writings of the Gilbreths*, Richard D. Irwin, Homewood, Illinois, 1953.

Suojanen, Waino W., "Management Theory? Functional and Evolutionary," *Journal of the Academy of Management, 6* (1), March 1963, pp. 7–17.

Tannenbaum, Robert, Irvin R. Weschler, and Fred Massarick, *Leader-*

ship and Organization: A Behavioral Science Approach, Chapter 15, McGraw-Hill, New York, 1961.

Taylor, Frederick Winslow, *The Principles of Scientific Management*, Harper and Row, New York, 1947.

Urwick, Syndall F., *The Pattern of Management*, Chapter 3, University of Minnesota Press, Minneapolis, 1956.

Part 2

Planning and Decision Making

Part 2 is devoted to an examination of the managerial functions of planning and decision making. Chapter 3 gives an overview of the planning process. After establishing the role and importance of planning as it relates to organizational effectiveness, a systems approach to planning is explored. The four phases of the system include establishing goals, formulating policies, developing short-range plans, and developing procedures. Each of these major phases is discussed in terms of the inputs required, the process involved, the output or result produced, and the feedback. The last two sections in the chapter deal with an integrated approach to planning and to an example of corporate planning.

With the overview of planning as a background, Chapter 4 examines a management-by-objectives approach to departmental planning. After discussing the relationship between objectives and both individual motivation and departmental efficiency, management by objectives is defined and the operational implications of the definition are given. The remainder of Chapter 4 is devoted to outlining and illustrating with examples a step-by-step approach to installing a management-by-objectives program at the departmental level.

Chapter 5 presents the managerial problems and prerequisites to installing a successful management-by-objectives program. Five major potential problem areas are identified and discussed, and guidelines for overcoming each of these problem areas are suggested. The chapter also points out five key areas to be considered when adopting a management-by-objectives approach to planning and concludes with a summary of ten specific guidelines that need to be followed.

Chapter 6 is devoted to a discussion of managerial problem analysis and decision making. The decision making process is divided into four essential phases: problem analysis; developing alternatives; analyzing alternative solutions; and implementing decisions. Each of these phases is discussed in detail and an analytical framework or systematic approach toward each is developed. The final section of the chapter identifies some potential barriers to effective decision making.

Chapter 7 examines some of the quantitative techniques which the manager has available to aid him in his decision making efforts. Included are: correlation analysis; breakeven analysis; linear programming; PERT (program evaluation and review techniques); CPM (critical path method); and queuing theory.

3. Planning

Planning is the first and a very important function of management. Before any other managerial function can be undertaken, the direction, objectives and means for achieving them must be determined. Luther Gulick[1] describes the duties of an executive as POSDCORB, or planning, organizing, staffing, directing, coordinating, reporting, and budgeting. Earnest Dale[2] classifies them as: planning, organizing, staffing, direction, control, innovation, and representation. Koontz and O'Donnell[3] list the following as functions of an executive: planning, organization, staffing, direction, and control. The lists vary, but they all include planning, which is always placed first. This is because all other functions of management are dependent on planning.

Planning allows us to design for an uncertain tomorrow with some assurance of meeting our goals. This assurance is described by Dale as "bridging the gap"[4] between what is desirable and what can be

[1]L. Gulick and L. Urwick, eds., *Papers on the Science of Administration* (New York: Institute of Public Administration, 1937), p. 13.

[2]Earnest Dale, *Management Theory and Practice* (New York: McGraw-Hill, 1965).

[3]Harold Koontz and Cyril O'Donnell, *Principles of Management: An Analysis of Managerial Functions* (New York: McGraw-Hill, 1968).

[4]Earnest Dale, *Management Theory and Practice* (New York: McGraw-Hill, 1965), p. 383.

accomplished. Managements of most organizations can be divided into three groups according to their ability to "bridge the gaps." McConkey[5] has classified organizations as the pussycats, the fat cats, and the tigers.

The pussycat organization operates under the mistaken assumption that today and tomorrow are reflections of the past. This organization is content to ride the waves and follows others only after success is assured. Its business-as-usual approach results in small profits and little enthusiasm on the job. Opportunities are missed or probably never seen because the pussycat organization's own capabilities and resources have been neglected. Management is thoroughly convinced that it can meet tomorrow's challenges with yesterday's talent and resources. Change in other words, has little meaning to the pussycat organization. Their soft purr almost lulls them to sleep.

The fat cats, to some extent, have shed the complacency of the pussycats. The realization that the future is not just a projection of the past leads to some positive initiative. The fat cat management still does not stick its neck out too far, but achieves higher growth and profit by more efficient management of its present resources. It is still content to follow the leader and engages in little innovative management. The fat cat is a step up from the pussycat, but is far from being "top cat."

To the tigers, the future is what you make it. This organization continually monitors the environment for new ideas and developments. Its primary concern is with bridging the nebulous gap between the present and the future. To accomplish this the tiger not only efficiently manages its present assets, but adds new investments, expands into new operations, acquires other organizations, and develops its employees and resources to the fullest. The tiger organization is thoroughly committed to change and recognizes that change is the path to success.

Although there are many factors which distinguish a tiger from the other two managements, one of the most critical is the amount of planning involvement. Results don't just happen, they are planned. In its simplest form, planning involves establishing objectives and organizing all efforts to meet them.

Peter Drucker[6] defines long-range planning as "the continuous process of making present entrepreneurial (risk taking) decisions systematically and with the best possible knowledge of their futurity, or-

[5]Dale D. McConkey, *Planning Next Year's Profit* (American Management Association, 1968), pp. 151–155.

[6]Peter Drucker, *Long-Range Planning Management Science.* Vol V (April 1959), pp. 238–239.

ganizing systematically the efforts needed to carry out these decisions against the expectations through organized sytematic feedback."

Planning then, can be thought of as a system which begins with objectives, develops policies, plans, and procedures, and provides for feedback information in order to adapt to a changing situation.

Systems Approach to Planning

The planning function can be divided into four phases, which will enable us to better understand the function and also to provide a framework with which to implement the function. These phases are:

PHASE I   Establishing the goals and objectives of the organization.

PHASE II   Formulating policies to carry out the objectives.

PHASE III   Developing intermediate and short-range plans to implement the policies.

PHASE IV   Statement of detailed procedures for implementing each plan.

Each phase must be completed and interrelated for efficiency in planning. The development of departmental plans, which make up the total plan, will guide the organization toward its desired goals.

This planning process stresses the "systems concept." A system is "an organized or complex whole; an assemblage or combination of things or parts, forming a complex or unitary whole."[7] A system, therefore, is defined as a continuing process of certain elements which are themselves systems, each having been functionally and operationally united in the achievement of an objective.

The system approach to planning organizes the objectives, policies, plans, and procedures to provide a framework for planning implementation. "The whole is greater than the sum of its parts" indicates that the systems approach to planning provides a network of subsystems and interrelated parts which together form the planning function.

Each system is made up of four elements. These four elements will

[7]Johnson, Kast and Rosengiveig, *The Theory and Management of Systems,* 2d ed. (New York: McGraw-Hill, 1967), p. 4.

be used in each phase of the planning function. Each phase is in *itself* a system which, when combined, forms the planning function.

The elements of any system are:

1.   *Inputs* are the resources that initiate the system.

2.   *Process* is defined as the mechanism that transforms inputs into outputs.

3.   *Outputs* are the inputs transformed.

4.   *Feedback* is output rechannelled as input.

The relationship of inputs, process, outputs, and feedback is illustrated in Exhibit I.

Exhibit I The Systems Approach

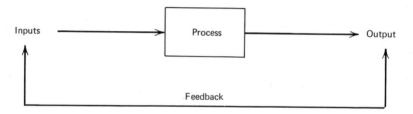

In summary, planning can be thought of as a system of interrelated phases. Each phase is itself a system which interreacts to contribute to the total planning function. The phases follow in sequential order beginning with objectives and ending with procedures.

Phase I.   Establishing the Goals and Objectives of the Organization

Objective setting is the first and most important phase of planning to be considered. The right direction must be clearly defined in order to accomplish the desired results.

Objectives are the goals, desires, missions, or targets, that an organization must closely approximate for continuing existence. The identification of these objectives requires careful consideration by top management.

The objectives of the organization are a function of a number of variables which will be described as the *inputs* to the top management decision-making *process*, which in turn determines the objectives as *output.*

Inputs to Establishing the Goals and Objectives of the Organization

1. *Profits* are widely recognized as a major requirement for corporate existence. It is essential that this goal be accomplished in order to meet other goals. Profit goals are usually the most explicitly stated goals of an enterprise. They not only make other goals possible, but provide an evaluating and decision-making technique.

As an evaluating technique, profits form many of the standards by which managers and employees are measured. Division managers of many firms are paid, promoted, and fired according to rate of return earned on their investments. Boards of directors and presidents have been "proxied" out of office as a result of dissatisfied stockholders. Finally, many employee wage plans are directly related to the amount contributed toward company profit.

As a decision-making technique, profit is one variable in determining the selection among alternative investments. Although there are many qualitative factors involved, those projects with the highest net present value are often selected for development.

Maximizing the profits of a firm is generally not considered a realistic objective. A number of reasons account for this.

(a) Perfect knowledge is an impossibility under present accounting methods. Microeconomic theory tells us that maximum profits are achieved where marginal cost equals marginal revenue. This information, along with demand and price information, is not always available.

(b) Perfect decision-making ability would be required in order to maximize profits. Human limitations and the uncertainty of the future prevent us from making perfect decisions.

(c) Other variables which influence the objectives of a firm, such as the government, social responsibility, and personal goals, will prevent the enterprise from maximizing profit.

Therefore, it is generally recognized that a firm will set a "satisfactory" profit level as its objective.

2.   The second input consideration is *social responsibility*. Chester Barnard,[8] in discussing authority, said there was a "zone of indifference" beyond which the individual would no longer accept direction from above. This same idea can illustrate a "zone of indifference" on the part of stockholders and the general public toward United States corporations. Just as the individual is no longer accepting complete rule from superiors, the general public is speaking up and demanding more socially responsible corporations. Both the individual's and the public's "zones" have narrowed considerably in the past decade.

What is social responsibility? Adam Smith, in 1776, argued for economic freedom on the premise that if the individual maximized his self-interest, this would provide a maximum of social benefits to the total society. Smith's "invisible hand," which was pure competition in the marketplace, would assure proper allocation of resources for the individual and society.

Today's marketplace is far from that envisioned by Smith. The giant corporations and holding companies have turned the marketplace into one of monopoly, oligopoly, and monopsony. The "invisible hand" can no longer provide a guiding hand. As a result the government since the turn of the century, and the general public in the last decade, have been calling for more socially responsible firms.

Social responsibility can be defined as an obligation on the part of business toward society. These obligations can be very complex and are continually being debated today. The obligations may be: government and community service, educational and philanthropic grants, or environmental control.

It is top management's responsibility to perpetually review its objectives. In recent incidents, stockholders and the general public have been dissatisfied with management's consideration of its social obligation. In the past, it was accepted practice to sell one's stock in a corporation which wasn't measuring up. Today's "social involvement movement" is causing many to voice their opinions in the running of the firm. Top management is often finding that the demands of the public and employees must be given more consideration.

3.   Personal objectives influence decision making. Constituent democracy is a new emphasis, stressing the objectives of stockholders, employees, and managerial personnel. These individuals have a major stake in the successful operation of the firm; their interests should therefore be considered in objective setting.

Among and within the above groups, the personal goals differ and

8C. Barnard, *The Functions of an Executive.*

at times seem to conflict with one another. Each group would desire to receive the maximum amount of remuneration possible, and have a significant voice in policy setting.

Within each group, the goals also differ. Stockholders' interests vary from high pay-out ratio to high stock appreciation through retentions. Young employees desire high salaries, while older employees place more emphasis on fringe benefits. Young managers want an aggressive firm, and older managers are more cautious in accepting new ideas and strategies.

The objectives of the firm and the individuals, while not in complete conflict, are not usually in complete harmony. Only with full recognition of these personal goals, and a conscious effort to integrate them with the enterprise goals, can we hope to achieve both. One set of goals cannot be achieved without the other.

4.   Federal, state, and local governments all have a major impact on corporate objectives. Their influence is felt in such areas as minimum wages, working hours, safety regulations, pricing policies, antitrust regulation, collective bargaining, taxes, and accounting procedures. The list is endless and significant.

5.   Union representation has grown significantly in the last 25 years. Not only blue collar workers, but white collar and professional people are joining unions in increasing numbers. Their demands for better wages, working conditions, safety procedures, and fringe benefits, present top management with yet another factor to consider in setting its objectives.

There are many other variables that management considers in determining its objectives. A few of the most important have been presented to illustrate how they influence management's thinking in setting objectives. Management is unable to simultaneously satisfy every variable input. At times, some variables will be emphasized more than others, and it remains top management's responsibility to assess changing conditions and make the necessary adjustments in its goals.

Process and Outputs as they Relate to Establishing the Goals and Objectives of the Enterprise.   There is no set process by which management feeds these variables into and receives as output the organization's stated objectives. All these variables must be analyzed with consideration to industry factors, individual firm characteristics, external factors, and the ethics of top management. The framework of the "scientific method" is utilized in deciding on the objectives.

The objectives of the firm are therefore a function of a number of variables (profit, social responsibility, personal goals, government influence, unions, and others), which top management analyzes using the scientific method to arrive at the objectives. The system is illustrated in Exhibit II.

Exhibit II   Phase I.   Establishing Goals and Objectives

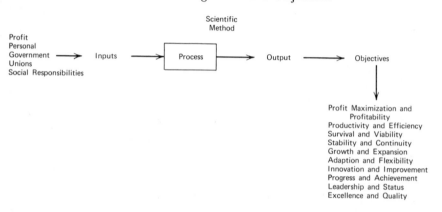

Phase II.   Formulating Policies to Carry Out the Objectives

Formulating company policy is the second step in the systems approach to planning. A number of policies may be developed in order to carry out any one objective. Policies are more detailed than objectives, and allow us to interpret each objective and provide a framework for the development of plans.

Nicolaidis[9] has defined policy as the following.

"Policy is a rule for action, manifesting or clarifying specific organization goals, objectives, values, or ideals and often prescribing the obligatory or most desirable ways and means for their accomplishment. Such a rule for action established for the purpose of planning, guiding, or directing organizational activities, including decision-making, intends to provide relative stability, consistency, uniformity, and continuity in the operation of the organization."

[9]N. G. Nicolaidis, *Policy Decision and Organization Theory* (University of California, 1960), p. 74.

Other definitions of policy which are close to the above are:

"A business policy then, is essentially a principle or group of related principles, with their consequent rules of action that condition and govern the successful achievement of certain business objectives toward which they are directed."[10]

"A policy is a definition of common purpose for organization components of the company as a whole in matters where, in the interest of achieving both component and overall company objectives, it is desirable that those responsible for implementation exercise discretion and good judgment in appraising and deciding among alternative courses of action."[11]

Policies can generally be considered as guides for administrative action. They set the boundaries within which managers can act. Chase Manhattan Bank states the following usefulness of properly stated policies.[12]

· It secures consistency of action throughout the undertaking.

· It acts as a basis for future action and decision.

· It insures coordination of plans.

· It requires control of performance in terms of the corresponding plan.

· It provides a means by which authority can be delegated, thus contributing directly to one of the most important principles of organization.

· It preserves the morale of employees when they know the declared policy of the undertaking, particularly if the policy is ethically sound and strictly followed.

· It stimulates the staff to greater efforts and sustains loyalty in difficult times, with beneficial effect upon labor turnover.

---

[10]Ralph C. Davis, *The Fundamentals of Top Management* (New York: Harper and Brothers, 1951), p. 173.

[11]General Electric Company, *General Electric's Organization,* Book II, *Professional Management in General Electric* (New York: General Electric Company, 1953–1955), p. 15.

[12]M. Valliant Higginson, *Management Policies I* (American Management Association, AMA Research Study 76, 1966), p. 10.

- It maintains sound relations with customers and agents.
- It enhances prestige and reputation in the eyes of the public.

Inputs for Formulating Policies to Carry Out the Objectives.   The formation of policy is based on several input factors. The stated policies of a company are developed at two levels of management.

1.   The primary stated policies are those developed by top management in carrying out the stated objectives of the firm. These are the most clearly stated and communicated of all policies. They can originate from the board of directors, executive presidents' offices, or the upper management group. These top management policies are broad in nature, usually leaving to lower management the task of developing operational policies and procedures.

2.   Policies also arise from less structured areas of the firm. In the day-to-day operation of the firm, managers are confronted with situations requiring decisions with no previous policy guidance. Their analysis of the situation and decision may become future policy. Excess policy formed in this manner indicates little foresight on the part of top management in developing guidelines. Policies developed in this manner must be clarified or else confusion due to a lack of coordination can arise.

3.   The other major source is that of externally imposed policy. The government, unions, professional associations, and industry practices impose certain policies on the firm.

These three areas: top management objectives, middle managerial, and externally imposed policies provide the variables that management must consider in developing effective corporate policies.

Process for Formulating Policies to Carry Out Objectives.   In formulating busines policies, the *process* is loosely defined. But, the scientific method does provide us with a framework for approaching policy development. Each area needing policies should be set forth, and pertinent information concerning them should be gathered.

This information comes from stated company objectives, industry practices, government requirements, trade associations, unions, and other sources. Once the information has been assembled, top management, together with the entire firm, should work on drafting the policy statements. In order to assure effective policies, the operative employee should participate in their development.

Exhibit III illustrates some guidelines for policy development.

Exhibit III Guidelines for Preparing Statements of Policy[13]

---

1. Briefly define the subject matter so that there may be a common understanding of what the policy covers. This is particularly necessary when technical or other terminology can have different meanings.
2. State the overall policy clearly and concisely.
3. Establish the areas of authority, including levels of approval.
4. Include brief references to supporting policies if necessary.
5. Confine procedures to the practical minimum. An absolute minimum for company policies can be a reference to the executive whom the president holds responsible for administering or coordinating the policy, and reference to coverage in any supporting manuals such as the insurance manual, the accounting manual, employee relations manual, etc.

In preparing policies along the above lines, observe the following:

1. Explain in transmittal letters the purpose of a new policy or change in policy. A clear picture of the reasons will aid understanding.

2. Leave as much room as possible for interpretation by the individual who must apply the policy. Make it clear where people may exercise discretion and which points are mandatory.

3. Be realistic. A policy should offer a practical course of action in recognizable situations.

4. Provide for change. Policies should be subject to periodic review to keep them up to date and timely.

5. When suggestions are made for changing drafts of policy statements, as part of the clearance routines make sure that there is a feedback before the final policy is released, particularly when suggestions are not fully adopted.

To be effective, policies must be communicated and not filed away

---

[13]Reprinted by permission of the publisher from AMA Research Study No. 76, *Management Policies I* © 1966 by the American Management Association, Inc.

in the policy manual, never to be seen again. In communicating policies, the written statement seems to be the most efficient. In written form, policies can be referred to when future situations call for action, and if a particular policy is new or complex, analysis of it is made easier.

Oral communication can also be used in releasing policies. This form of communication is best used when introducing and explaining new policies, and should be supplemented at a later time in written form.

Formulating policies is a continuing process. Changes in technologies, government requirements, union demands, customer wants, and top management, require constant policy review and appraisal. Management must continually analyze these changes in adjusting its policies.

Output from Formulating Policies to Carry Out the Objectives.
Upon processing the inputs, certain major policies are developed by every company. These policies exist in the following areas: administration, finance, employee relations, public relations, marketing, distribution, purchasing, production, engineering and research. Policies are developed in each of these areas to give management consistent guidance in decision-making. Exhibit IV indicates some of the policies needed in each of these areas.

Exhibit IV   Types of Policies Used in Corporations[14]

Administration. Acquisitions, antitrust, authorization, centralization, decentralization, confidential information, conflict of interest, contracts, control, corporate symbol, coordination, diversification, evaluation and appraisal, growth, interdivisional transactions, international operations, location management responsibilities, meetings, mergers, organization, planning, policies, products, real estate, relations with competitors, reporting, security, travel and transportation use of consultants.

Finance. Accounting, assets, auditing, banking, billing, budgets, capital appropriations, capitalization, collection, cost control, credit, depreciation and amortization, dividends, expenditures, expense accounts, expenses, financial reporting, forecasting, funds, incentives, insurance, leases, loans,

[14]M. Valliant Higginson, *Management Policies I* (American Management Association, AMA Research Study 76, 1966), p. 63.

payment of suppliers, payroll, pensions, profits, reserves, return on investment, securities, surplus property, taxes.

Employee relations. Absenteeism, appraisal, benefits, compensation, complaints, discharge, education, equal employment opportunity, federal and state employment regulations, hiring, hours, leaves, loans, manpower utilization, medical examinations, outside employment, pensions, promotion, recreation, recruitment, retirement, selection, seniority, sickness, termination, training and development, transfer and relocation, unions, vacations, working conditions.

Public relations. Associations, communication, community relations, conferences and conventions, contributions, educational activities, gifts, government relations, institutional advertising, legislative activities, meetings, membership, participation in public affairs, political activities, press relations, public speeches, publications, release of information, stockholder relations, tours, visitors.

Marketing. Advertising, branches, brands, business inquiries, competitor relations, complaints, contracts, credit, customer relations, discounts, expenses, exporting, forecasting, freight charges, intracompany sales, inventory records, market research, markets, new business, new products, packaging, pricing, proposals, reciprocity, return of goods, sales promotion, sales to employees, services to customers, territories.

Distribution. Freight, inventory levels, labeling, materials handling, product shipments, receiving, stock shipments, traffic, warehousing.

Purchasing. Buying for employees, centralized purchasing, conservation, contracting, control of material, gifts, interdivisional purchasing, inventory control, inventory levels, investment, make or buy, material purchase, procurement, reciprocity, standards, supplier relations.

Production. Contracting, cost estimates, equipment, facilities, inventory, maintenance, plant protection, plant tests, process specifications, product specifications, production control, quality control, quantity, safety, scheduling, standards, time studies, tooling, utilities.

Engineering. Bids and quotations, construction, contract services, design, equipment replacement, job orders, leasing, patents, product engineering, product reliability, projects, quality, rental, safety and security, standards, technical ideas, technical services, testing, value engineering.

Research. Applied research, basic research, coordination, copyrights, development, inventions, laboratory, patents, payout of projects, product development projects, royalties, secrecy agreements, security, selection of projects, trademarks.

The following are a few concrete examples of company policies.[15]

Marketing

1.   To price each item with full awareness of that item's competition.

2.   To place marketing emphasis on company brands and, most especially, company premium quality brands.

3.   To develop a sound scientific research program on marketing policies and methods in order to minimize unit costs and increase market effectiveness.

Corporate Growth

1.   To grow in a carefully selected combination of directions and methods which give balance to the total company operation.

Personnel

1.   To delegate authority and accountability commensurate with responsibility, and to recognize that the three are inseparable.

2.   To handle all company-employee relationships with understanding, honesty, and courtesy, recognizing the employee's individuality and dignity.

Finance

1.   To extend credit, after satisfactory investigation, in line with sound credit principles.

2.   To continually evaluate our risk exposures, controls, and ability to absorb losses; and in light of this evaluation, to assume risk or purchase insurance accordingly.

Production

1.   To plan production to meet approved quantity and quality goals at the lowest possible cost.

2.   To provide prompt shipping service at the lowest possible cost consistent with high-quality packaging and distributor requirements.

The policy formation phase of planning is represented in Exhibit V.

---

[15]M. Valliant Higginson, *Management Policies I* (American Management Association, AMA Research Study 76, 1966), pp. 80–82.

Exhibit V Phase II. Formulating Policies to Carry Out Objectives

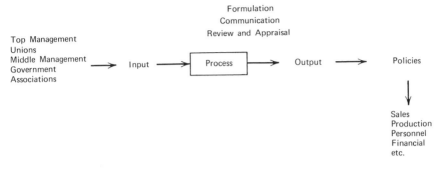

Phase III. Developing Intermediate and Short-Range Plans

Plans are the extension of company objectives through the incorporation of company policies. Intermediate and short-range plans will be developed for sales, production, personnel, and finance. Although top management is involved in developing these plans, the middle management group is primarily responsible for their formulation and implementation.

Most managements prepare three types of plans. They vary in time, horizon, and detail.

1. Strategic plans determine the major objectives of an organization and the policies and strategies to achieve those objectives. Strategic plans are long-run and give general guidance to the firm. The subject matter covered includes profits, pricing, capital expenditures, production, marketing, personnel, and others. This type of plan may not be in written form and may merely exist in the thinking of corporate officers.

2. Intermediate-range plans are detailed plans for carrying out and coordinating the functions of a firm. These plans are usually five years in length and are mainly concerned with implementing the strategic plans. For example, the strategic plan may call for a certain growth rate in the firm, and the intermediate plan will provide the means, through acquisition, merger, and new product development, to fulfill this requirement.

3. Short-range plans are one year plans for carrying on the actual

work. They are very detailed and include some of the following: inventory replenishment, working schedules, advertising budgets, dispatching rules, salesmen's quotas.

Inputs to Developing Intermediate- and Short-Range Plans to Implement the Policies. In developing plans to accomplish the firm's objectives, the manager must continually analyze (1) the company policies and objectives, (2) external economic conditions, and (3) the industrial outlook of the firm and the firm's position in that industry. Each of the factors is constantly shifting, causing past planning to become partially or wholly inadequate.

The changing external environment reveals the importance of population growth and changing patterns of distribution, increasing education and skill level, the rapid growth rate of technology and new production methods, the growing role of federal government purchases, and the expansion of union membership.

The industry outlook determines the individual firm's future profitability. A declining industry cannot expect to continue supporting healthy firms. The nature of an industry's product or service can greatly affect its demand and thus the company's plans. A product's or service's demand is influenced by the number of uses it has, its durability, the number of substitutes it has, and the type of customers who seek to use it. The cost side of the industry should also be analyzed.

Labor costs, material costs, taxes, and the capacity of the industry will have a major influence on the profitability of the firm. The analysis of the industry outlook will indicate the setting in which a company must conduct its operations.

The final information needed to develop plans and forecasts is the firm's position within the industry and its ability to capitalize on future developments. Key factors to consider would be the reputation of the company and its products, percent of company sales to total industry sales, the efficiency of equipment and plant, and the ability of management.

Process and Outputs as They Relate to Developing Intermediate- and Short-Range Plans to Implement the Policies. Providing detailed answers to each of these questions is only a start. Thorough analysis and good judgment are essential for future success. There is no set process for developing plans, but the scientific method again provides a framework within which to approach plan development. The outputs will be both short- and intermediate-range plans in each of the functional and support areas of the firm, and will be closely related to each policy area.

This third phase is illustrated in Exhibit VI.

Exhibit VI Phase III. Developing Intermediate- and Short-Range Plans to Implement Policies

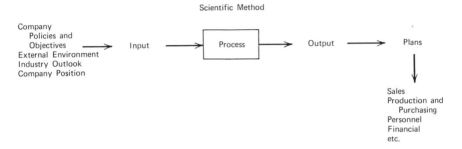

Phase IV. Statement of Detailed Procedures for Implementing Each Plan

Developing procedures is the last step in the systems approach to planning. Procedures are the sequence of steps and rules that should be followed in implementing the plans developed in Phase III. Procedure development is not to be separated from development of plans, and should be done concurrently.

Each plan will have a different set of procedures for its implementation. For example, a production policy may call for a high-quality product. One of the plans a manager could develop would be a statistical quality control plan. This plan would include sampling, inspection, and running statistical techniques on incoming raw material, in-process production, and final finished goods. The statistical technique may have the following procedure.

1. Select a random sample of 50 items of each incoming lot.

2. Inspect each item and replace each defective item with a good item.

3. If the number of defects found exceeds three, subject lot to 100 percent inspection and replace each defective item.

4.   If the number of defectives found is less than three, accept the lot and calculate average outgoing quality limit.

Every other area within the firm will have similar sequences of procedure for carrying out their plans.

In analyzing the procedural system, then, the input is each individual plan, the process is the formulation of a sequence of procedures, and the output is the procedure itself.

This fourth phase is illustrated in Exhibit VII.

Exhibit VII   Phase IV.   Statement of Detailed Procedures for Implementing Each Plan

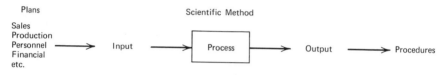

Integrative View of Planning

Each phase of planning is not to be isolated from the others. Management must consider each phase as influencing every other phase, but these four phases do provide a framework for systematically approaching management's most important function. An integrated view of this total framework is presented in Exhibit VIII.

The framework emphasizes the following points.

1.   There are four phases in the systems approach to planning: objective setting, policy formation, plan development, and statement of procedures. Each phase has such factors as inputs, a managerial decision-making process, and an appropriate output.

2.   Top management has full responsibility for each phase, but successively lower levels of management are delegated the authority for developing and implementing each phase.

3.   The setting of objectives is the most important and abstract of

these four phases. Therefore, they have the greatest impact upon the firm. The other phases become more and more detailed.

4. Every phase is influenced by every other phase, and feedback from each phase allows management to continually adjust to changing conditions. Planning is therefore a continuous process.

5. This framework can represent a division or department approach to developing its plans. Combining these plans results in a "hierarchy of plans" representing the enterprise plan.

This chapter has presented a conceptual model representing business planning. A conceptual model presents a framework for implementing an idea. The operational model may vary for individual firms, but the underlying framework of progressively planning firms is similar to the one presented here.

Exhibit VIII   Integrated View of Planning

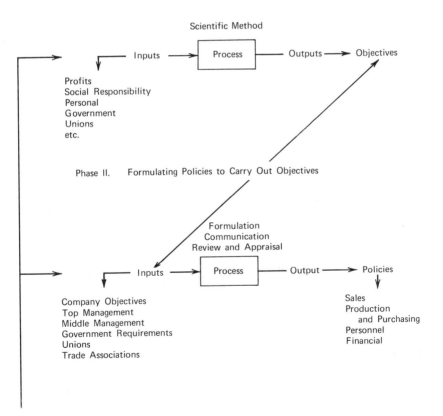

Phase I.   Establishing Goals and Objectives

Scientific Method

Inputs → Process — Outputs → Objectives

Profits
Social Responsibility
Personal
Government
Unions
etc.

Phase II.   Formulating Policies to Carry Out Objectives

Formulation
Communication
Review and Appraisal

Inputs → Process — Output → Policies

Company Objectives
Top Management
Middle Management
Government Requirements
Unions
Trade Associations

Sales
Production
  and Purchasing
Personnel
Financial

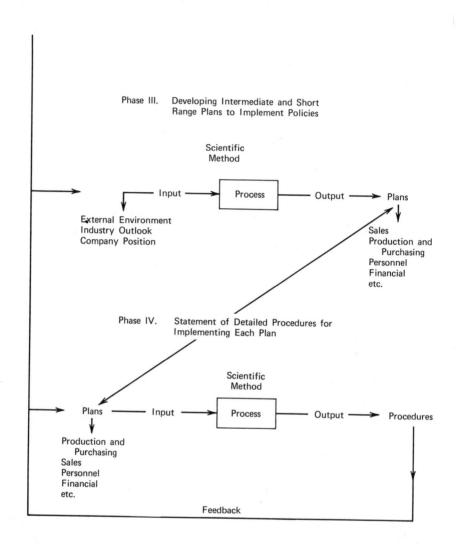

Corporate Example of Planning

Every firm will have a different operational approach to carrying out the planning function. While the conceptual model presented has been abstract in order to highlight the essential factors involved in planning, its basic premises can be seen underlining any good corporate planning process.

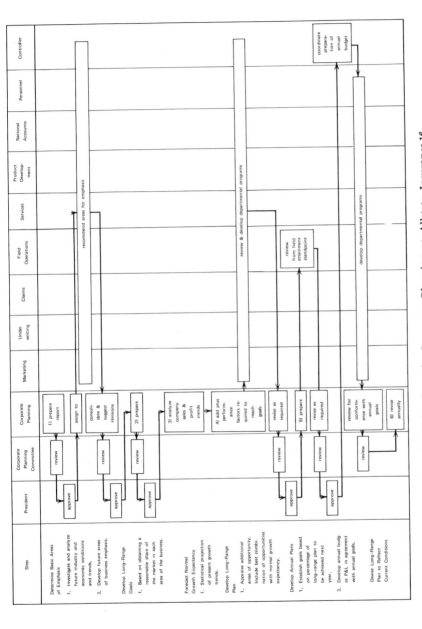

Figure I. Major Steps in Corporate Planning at Allstate Insurance.[16]

16George A. Steiner, *Managerial Long-Range Planning*, McGraw-Hill, 1963.

Allstate Insurance Company Planning. The scientific method was the *process* utilized in each of the four phases. This method provides a general approach to solving or handling any problem, since each firm's approach is different, this general methodology was used to describe each process. Figure I illustrates in flowchart form, Allstate's major steps in corporate planning and its decision-making process. The six major steps are represented along the vertical axis and the decision-making process along the horizontal axis. Starting with step 1 and following the arrows reveals the decision process for each step.

Summary

The planning function can be divided into four phases. In each phase there are certain inputs which management must consider in making decisions. These inputs are processed and decisions are made; these decisions constitute output. The first phase of planning is that of establishing goals and objectives. To do this the inputs of profit, social responsibility, personal, government, unions, and others must be considered. These factors are all processed, decisions are made, and the end results are the organization's objectives.

The second phase is concerned with the formulation of policies to carry out objectives. The inputs for policy making include the objectives which have been set, top management, middle management decisions, government requirements, union influences, and trade associations. Again, these factors are processed and policies are developed in all key areas of the operation such as sales, production, personnel, and finance.

The third phase of planning concerns the development of intermediate- and short-range plans to implement policies. In this case the inputs to be considered include the external environment, industry outlook, and company position. As with policies, plans are then developed for all key functional areas.

The final phase of planning is a statement of detailed procedures for implementing each plan. These procedures constitute the "how to" of carrying out plans.

Key Concepts

Objectives. Objectives are the goals, desires, missions, or targets that an organization must achieve in order to continue in existence.

Policies. A policy serves as a guide for decision making within the organization. Policies are principles or groups of principles which constitute rules for action that contribute to the successful achievement of objectives.

Procedures. Procedures are the sequence of steps and rules that should be followed in implementing plans. They are guides to action.

Discussion Questions

1. What are the approaches to planning of the fat cat, pussycat, and tiger organizations? Which type of planning approach is most likely to be successful in the electronics industry? Why?

2. Briefly describe the four phases of the systems approach to planning and the four basic elements of any system. In your own words, describe the systems approach to planning.

3. Is the objective of maximizing profit a sound objective for a business firm? Explain why or why not.

4. Briefly describe what you think are the three most important variables in determining a firm's objectives.

5. In your own words, define policy and describe how policy is related to objectives.

6. What guidelines should be followed if policies are to be effective?

7. Briefly describe the three types of plans.

8. In your own words, describe procedures. What function do procedures play in the planning process?

9.   Describe the scientific method of planning. Use a flow diagram to show how the outputs of one system become the inputs of another. What are the four major points which should be emphasized in this framework?

Selected Readings

Ansoff, Ilgor H., *Corporate Strategy,* McGraw-Hill, New York, 1965.

Ewing, David W., "Corporate Planning at the Crossroads," *Harvard Business Review, 45* (4), July–August 1967, pp. 77–86.

Higginson, Valliant M., "Management by Rule and by Policy," *Management Policies,* American Management Association, New York, 1966, pp. 95–103.

————, *Management Policies I: Their Development as Corporate Guides,* AMA Research Study 76, American Management Association, New York, 1966.

Kline, Charles H., "The Strategy of Product Policy," *Harvard Business Review, 33* (4), July–August 1955, pp. 91–100.

Koontz, Harold, and Cyril O'Donnell, *Principles of Management: An Analysis of Managerial Functions,* Part II, McGraw-Hill, New York, 1972.

McConkey, Dale D., *Planning Next Year's Profits,* American Management Association, 1968.

Newman, William H., "Shaping the Master Strategy of Your Firm," *California Management Review, 9* (3), Spring 1967, pp. 77–88.

Phillips, Charles, F., Jr., "What is Wrong With Profit Maximization?" *Business Horizons, 6* (4), Winter 1963, pp. 73–80.

Redfield, J. W., "Elements of Forecasting," *Harvard Business Review,* 2 (6), November 1951.

Reilley, Ewing, "Planning the Strategy of the Business," *Advanced Management,* December 1958, pp. 8–12.

Steiner, George A., "How to Assure Poor Long Range Planning for Your Company," *California Management Review,* 7 (4), Summer 1965, pp. 93–94.

———— ed., *Managerial Long Range Planning,* McGraw-Hill, New York, 1963.

4.   Establishing a System of Departmental and Individual Job Objectives

It is virtually impossible today to pick up a management periodical or book without running across specific reference to the concept of "results management" or "management by objectives." Similarly, it is almost always included as a topic for exploration in management development seminars, whether they are of an in-company or public variety. Without question, the philosophy concerning how an organization should be run and how individuals should be managed represents some of the most dynamic and exciting thinking in the area of management that has taken place in many years. It is an approach which, when properly applied, offers management an opportunity to realize the maximum productivity potential from all its resources.

In the literature, reference and discussion can be found relating to all of the following.

    1.   Results management as a way of coordinating and giving direction to overall company activity.

    2.   Results management as a way of planning, organizing, and

controlling work for an individual manager in his own department or functional area.

3.   Results management as a way of insuring maximum utilization of individual talents and strengths.

4.   Results management as a means to insure maximum levels of achievement for individuals, departments, and the total organization.

5.   Results management as it relates to more effective performance evaluation and appraisal.

6.   Results management as a system for better and more equitable salary administration.

7.   Results management as a basis for coaching and developing subordinates.

8.   Results management as a system for insuring continued analysis, improvement, and growth.

9.   Results management as an approach to releasing the motivational potential in people.

The purposes of this chapter are:

1.   To review the importance of setting objectives as they relate to individual motivation and total departmental efficiency.

2.   To present a framework for establishing objectives within a department and for individual jobs.

3.   To discuss the importance of participation in setting departmental and individual objectives.

Objectives and Individual Motivation

The tie between the concept of management by objectives (MBO) and motivation is a strong and basic one. Much of the rationale of the concept is rooted in the idea that it is a way of unleashing the full motivation potential in people so that they are making a maximum contribution to departmental and organizational objectives. This high degree of individual motivation is triggered by structuring the work situation so that people can best satisfy their own needs as they work toward the objectives of the unit. Let us look at the total picture in more detail by first summarizing some of the basic ideas about motivation, which will be expanded in Chapter 17.

1. People adopt given patterns of action and behavior in order to satisfy certain needs which they have.

2. In addition to the commonly recognized economic needs which can be satisfied by wages, people also have social, psychological, and self-fulfillment needs.

3. In order for maximum-level motivation to occur an opportunity for the worker to satisfy his needs in these three areas must be built into the work climate.

4. More specifically, it has been found that some of the strongest job motivators include such things as a sense of achievement, opportunity to assume responsibility, growth, advancement, recognition, accomplishment, and a feeling of doing important and significant work.

5. When these things are present in the work environment the man becomes ego-involved in his work; he is not only physically, but also mentally and emotionally involved.

6. This type of involvement is a necessity if there is to be full commitment and motivation.

Although there are many facets to providing the climate in which employees can satisfy some of the above-mentioned specific needs, clear-cut objectives are a first and basic requirement for developing and maintaining high levels of satisfaction and motivation. Without definite objectives, a man lacks a sense of accomplishment. His job becomes one of putting out fires so that the status quo can be maintained.

Furthermore, without clearly defined objectives, the man finds himself constantly on the defensive. Since it has not been agreed where he should be heading, he is likely to be criticized because he has not reached the point where second guessers have decided he should be. This is both unfair and frustrating and is directly responsible for lowered morale.

On the other hand, when clear-cut objectives are established the employee has a constructive purpose in his work. Some of the very direct benefits can be summarized as follows.

1. He sees clearly where he wants to go and can strike out purposefully to get there. When a man's job is defined solely in terms of the activities he must perform it tends to reduce the man and his efforts to the same status as a machine. The job seems to lack purpose and his individual efforts lack meaning. Defining jobs in terms of results to be accomplished as well as activities adds vitality to otherwise neutral

statements. Objectives give direction to a man's effort and make them both purposeful and meaningful.

2.   As he progresses toward his goals he gets a rewarding sense of accomplishment. In addition to knowing that their activities have a purpose, employees like to feel a sense of accomplishment. Without specific goals toward which to work this sense of accomplishment is very difficult to gain, at least on any regular basis. Continual motivation requires a continual opportunity to meet challenges. Objective setting, therefore, is a way to build into the job climate on a rather automatic basis both the required challenge and the subsequent satisfaction which comes from meeting this challenge.

3.   He knows that he is doing what his superiors, associates, and subordinates expect him to do and he can look forward with confidence to the recognition that will result when he reaches the established goals. When objectives for the department as well as for each individual job have been established, coordinated team effort is substituted for otherwise random individual activity. Each man begins to see himself as an integral and important part of the total operation with success of the operation depending on how well he carries out his role. He also begins to develop a sense of obligation to carry out his role adequately. As a result, and in return for his performance, the man knows that he will obtain the esteem of his fellow workers and receive recognition for his performance.

4.   As a result of this, personal morale will be high. Reasonable and clearly established objectives and high motivation go hand in hand. As indicated by the above comments, clearly defined objectives give purpose, meaning, vitality, and direction to the work that people do. They contribute significantly to mental and emotional involvement and foster the type of personal commitment desirable for each man.

The Role of Objectives in Achieving Departmental and Overall Organization Efficiency

In addition to the influence of objectives on individual motivation, there are also some general departmental-related advantages to objective setting. First, when a manager sets departmental objectives he is taking a step toward making things happen that might otherwise not occur. For the same reason that a navigator on an airplane must develop a flight plan to help guarantee a safe and on-schedule arrival at his destination, a manager must set objectives if he expects the department to accomplish its mission.

Second, objectives serve to focus attention on results. They direct the stream of total effort toward achievement of concrete goals and restrict the area of freedom for purely random activity and ad hoc decisions. Without objectives there is likely to be a tendency for the total operation to lack direction.

Third, the presence of objectives encourages efficiency and economic operation. Costs are minimized because of the emphasis on consistency. Joint effort is substituted for uncoordinated piecemeal activity; an even flow of work replaces an uneven flow, and deliberate objective decisions take precedence over snap judgments.

Finally, objectives facilitate control and serve as a yardstick against which to measure accomplishment. The purpose of control is to insure that events conform to plans, and to make things happen that might otherwise not occur. Clearly defined objectives aid in keeping the department "on track" by providing definite direction on a continuous basis, and also by providing a yardstick against which to measure progress continually, as well as to evaluate contemplated actions.

The full effect of management by objectives on departmental efficiency may be summarized as:

1. A way of *coordinating and giving direction* to department activity.

2. A way of *planning, organizing,* and *controlling* work for an individual manager in his own department or functional area.

3. A way of obtaining maximum *utilization* of individual *talents* and *strengths.*

4. A system for insuring continued *analysis, improvement,* and *growth.*

5. A system for more effective performance *evaluation* and *review.*

6. A basis for more equitable *salary administration.*

7. A basis for *coaching* and *developing* subordinates.

From the standpoint of total organization there are also some very significant advantages which develop from a results management approach. Research on the installation of such programs has uncovered the following benefits.

1. *A higher degree of purpose.* Objectives give the organization

more specific direction. There is less tendency to operate on a day-to-day or week-to-week basis and otherwise drift aimlessly. Rather, they begin working toward something more precise and tangible.

2.   *A higher degree of manager motivation.*   As with the organization as a whole, objectives also channel the efforts and energy of the individual manager toward specifics. As he begins to experience the series of successes which are associated with the achievement of objectives, continued motivation becomes somewhat of a self-generating process.

3.   *More self-direction and control on the part of employees.*   As will be pointed out in the next section, when employees are aware of the actual results they are expected to achieve in terms of specific objectives, and receive continuous feedback concerning where they stand in relation to those objectives, they are then in a position to direct and control their own performances as opposed to the manager having to exercise close direction and control. This in turn allows the manager to spend more of his time in overall planning and coordination of the total work effort.

4.   *More demanding organizational tone.*   The presence of objectives throughout the entire organization tends to create a more demanding and accomplishment-oriented tone throughout the entire organization. Once again, this is because everyone in the organization is striving toward some commonly agreed upon goals. The emphasis is on achievement and accomplishment of specifics as opposed to merely operating on a short-term basis.

5.   *Better communication and cooperation among managers.*   A final advantage which organizations installing a results management approach have found relates to the improvement in coordination of effort between various managers within the organization. To the extent and degree that the objectives of each unit or department in the organization relate to and are part of a total scheme, and also to the degree that the concept of coordination of effort to achieve total results is stressed, there tends to be a greater degree of cooperative interplay among managers.

Management by Objectives Defined

Management by objectives is a system of management whereby every department and every individual has defined and is working toward achieving certain results in key areas of job accountability during a specified period of time.

    A. It assumes that certain basic performance requirements are met on a continual basis in all key areas of the job.

    B. It emphasizes continual analysis of the operation with the purpose of improving results either in total or by specified individuals.

    Thus, rather than operating on a day-to-day, week-to-week, or year-to-year basis and at the end of a period simply looking back to see what happened, management by objectives suggests that we determine ahead of time what we want to happen and then make sure it happens. Whether it be the organization as a whole, a particular department or individual, management by objectives implies that we are initiating results and not just reacting to what has happened in the past.

    The definition also stresses the need for balance in performing the management job. Thus, it is not a system which emphasizes crisis points at the expense of everything else. As stated in part *A* of the definition, it assumes that certain basic performance requirements are met on a continual basis in all key areas of the job.

    Some additional important assumptions should be understood. First, the definition assumes that the manager has identified the areas of the job or departmental activity where certain results are sought; there will typically be anywhere from four to seven such areas. Second, the definition implies that for each specified area of accountability, certain minimum acceptable levels of performance have been set and that these are met on a continual basis. (The difference between standards and objectives will be discussed later in the chapter.) Finally, there is the assumption that a concerted effort is always made to reach new levels of achievement by identifying and overcoming problems that hinder accomplishment.

Setting Objectives for a Department

    The development of departmental objectives is a step-by-step process with each succeeding step being an elaboration and refinement of what was done previously. Outlined below is a six step procedure which, when followed, can result in a meaningful departmental plan for accomplishment and future growth. It should be cautioned, however, that what appears on paper to be a rather simple and straightforward process is, in actual practice, a very time-consuming and difficult one. The old adage, "easier said than done," most assuredly applies with respect to objective setting.

1.   A General Statement of the Overall Mission of the Department. As an organization grows and develops there is a tendency for individual departments as well as major functional areas to become entities in themselves. Specifically, two things happen. First, the relationship between departments in terms of their interdependency to accomplish maximum results becomes obscured. To some degree, there is an informal tendency for a series of independent operating units to develop. Each unit or department becomes engrossed in meeting its particular schedules, budgets, quality standards, and in order to do this it must overcome a variety of operational problems.

In practice the great majority of these problems do not reflect departmental effectiveness in itself but rather they are a reflection of how departments interrelate with one another in total. In other words, they are interdepartmental problems in nature.

Often too little attention is given to solving problems on this scale. Managers frequently spend their time fighting the immediate crises which are hindering accomplishment while the bigger issues go unsolved. In short, the need to accomplish results becomes a pressure force which hinders the process of interdepartmental cooperation and integration of effort.

This situation cannot improve until each department of the unit analyzes its reason for existence in terms of how it relates to the total organization and other closely allied departments.

Accomplishment from the standpoint of each individual department must be phrased in terms of, and reflect the department's relationship to, other specific units as well as the whole. Step one in the objective setting process is designed to lay the groundwork for the necessary integration of effort.

The rationale behind the formulation of such a statement is twofold. First, it crystallizes in a general way the overall function, purpose, or service of the department as it relates to both the organization as a whole and to other specific departments with which it is closely allied. An organization is a complex of many units or functional and subfunctional areas. In order for the whole to be effective, each unit must be effective in making its contribution to the whole as well as to what might be thought of as "closely allied units." The formulation of the general statement of the purpose, function, or service that a department is engaged in forces (perhaps for the first time) a department to look at itself in terms of two very basic yet important questions: "Why are we here?" and "If this is why we are here, then broadly speaking, what should be accomplished?" As individual departments begin to go through this type of questioning process their relationship to each other and to the whole becomes crystallized. Second, the groundwork for the integration of effort between departments is laid and also the basic guidelines for interdepartmental activity begin to take shape. Depending on the type of operation, this general statement will vary in detail and length. The following examples illustrate the statements of the mission of specific departments.

Overall Mission—Personnel Department

1. To analyze, formulate, and recommend to management personnel-related programs and procedures that will contribute to the effective utilization of human resources and company profitability.

2. To give support and provide the maximum service possible to all departments in all important phases of personnel management.

3. To engage in all the necessary activities that will assure the company an adequate and qualified labor force for the present as well as the future.

4. To continually research, evaluate, and report on the results and effectiveness of all personnel-related activities in relation to their contribution to company goals as well as to the specific objectives of the program itself.

Overall Mission—Design Engineering Department

1. To build a climate conducive to creating maximum levels of motivation as well as continual growth, development, and progress of individuals on their jobs.

2. To contribute to the growth, development, and profitability of the enterprise through analysis and recommendations for product improvement, new product development, and improved manufacturing methods.

3. To provide maximum level of assistance to other functional areas, such as sales and manufacturing, in overcoming specific problems and implementing changes and improvements.

Overall Mission—Production Planning And Control

1.   To establish, administer, and give direction to a system of production planning and control which will contribute to company profitability by providing a smooth and continuous flow of work within the plant as well as maximum utilization of all equipment and personnel.

2.   To continually work with and support line personnel in identifying and overcoming any problems that relate to departmental or interdepartmental flow of work and scheduling.

3.   To provide departmental staff with a satisfying and meaningful work experience with opportunities for growth.

Overall Mission—Line Manufacturing Department

1.   To make a definite and meaningful contribution to the profitability of the firm.

2.   To complete and supply to the main assembly line all the required components within the various established requirements.

3.   To provide a satisfying work experience for employees.

It will be noted that two of these examples contain statements relating to the creation of a climate conducive to motivation. This is because of the important role which the individual usually plays in achieving productivity. Having such a statement as part of the general mission serves to focus the manager's attention on the climate which exists and encourages him to evaluate the degree to which this climate acts as a stimulant to maximum individual achievement.

Another important aspect of formulating this statement of the general mission is that the manager can refer to it frequently and determine whether or not the department is undertaking specific programs or activities that relate to each phase of it. If not, the mission either needs to be revised or something must be introduced to fulfill that part of it.

These examples as well as all others in this chapter are not designed to be perfect finite statements; rather, their purpose is to illustrate each of the steps discussed.

2.   Specific Areas of Responsibility Which Must Be Met if the Overall Mission Is to Be Accomplished. What Work Does the Department Do? In What Activities Does the Department Engage?   The second phenomenon which hinders maximum accomplishment of a growing organization is the defensiveness which each unit takes concerning its activities.

Because there is constant pressure for results and because departments are interdependent in order to accomplish their objectives, natural points of friction occur. Specifically, the manager of one production department says he cannot meet his schedule unless another department does a better job of supplying him with the components parts he needs. The manager of the unit supplying the components, in turn, extends this same argument and line of reasoning to other departments which are closely associated with him and on which he depends, and the chain reaction has begun. Various departments fence with one another while everyone does his best to meet emergencies and get the work out. Among line managers, who by necessity must cooperate to some degree, this fencing is usually carried out with blunt swords. When it comes to line-staff relationships, the points of the swords may become sharper as charges, countercharges, and defenses are parried by the parties!

An example of this phenomenon occurs when programs and procedures which cut across departmental lines exist. Very often such programs are administered by one department but affect the operation of other departments. When problems develop, as often happens, friction begins to appear and the lines are drawn. Instead of working to solve specific problems to the benefit of all, considerable energy and creativity is expended in solidifying individual positions. Consequently, the procedure in question becomes an end in itself, rather than a means to accomplishing desired results.

As noted above, step one lays the groundwork for the necessary integration of effort by forcing each department to analyze its own contribution in relation to other departments. Step two carries this a little bit further, particularly in the case of line-staff responsibilities.

Part of the procedure in detailing the department's major areas of responsibility is to identify those areas where overlap does and should occur. Indeed, in the analysis process the manager should deliberately seek to identify certain areas of activity which play a significant role in his ability to accomplish results, yet which he may have considered as part of someone else's sphere of operation. An example will illustrate this concept.

One key area of responsibility for everyone in production is quantity, with success or failure usually measured in terms of some predetermined production schedule. In order to meet the schedule, however, the department must receive the necessary raw materials, components, and subassemblies within the required lead time. If lead times are not observed, then logically the manager should not be held responsible (in a formal sense) for meeting his schedule. This situation, of course, does not remove him from constant pressure. Carrying the analysis further, the job of coordinating production on an interdepartmental basis is the responsibility of a centralized production planning and control department, and not of the individual department supervisor. Therefore, to the extent that schedules are not met due to lead times, the fault lies with centralized staff units. These units, not the line production manager, are charged with the responsibility of developing a system which provides for coordination on a plant-wide basis.

But this is exactly the type of logic and thinking which leads to conflict, continued fire-fighting tactics, and unsolved major problems. To the extent that they are responsible for quantity, the line cannot absolve itself from the production planning and scheduling function. They have a responsibility for constructive evaluation and analysis of the present system; only the line manager is in a position to determine which lead times are not met, how frequently this occurs, the size of gap between scheduling and receiving, and how much man and machine time is lost. Only when this information is available can the staff unit begin to look at the present system in terms of its effectiveness, and fulfill its obligation to design an adequate system.

The job of the staff unit is to devise a system which solves the major problem and difficulties which confront the line. If they do not, they are failing in one major area of their total mission. Therefore they have a responsibility to evaluate critically the present system on a continual basis as to whether or not it is solving the problem it was designed to correct. In fact, the specific system, as well as overall department effectiveness, should be measured in these terms. This forces the staff unit constantly to be concerned and sensitive to its relationship with the line. Similar examples could be given in any number of areas.

The point is that accomplishment of results rests on developing an integrated team effort whether it be in terms of line-line, line-staff, or staff-staff relationships. In order to insure that this integration takes place each department must look at its major areas of responsibility in broad perspective. This approach will facilitate mutual objective setting, discussed later.

Moving from the general to the specific becomes a difficult and somewhat detailed task because it involves a thorough analysis of the departmental functions. The manager must ask himself: "If we are to accomplish our general mission what are all the specific functions this department must engage in?" Essentially, the major areas where the manager must concentrate his own managerial efforts in a planning,

organizing, directing, and controlling sense are delineated, and the major areas of performance accountability are identified.
Example from a staff personnel department:

1. To provide an adequate and qualified labor force requires:
   (a) Job analysis to determine job requirements.
   (b) Estimating labor needs.
   (c) Determination of sources of supply.
   (d) Selection.
   (e) Placement.
   (f) Training.

2. Maintenance of adequate labor force which is productive requires:
   (a) Performance evaluation.
   (b) Transfer and promotion.
   (c) Communications.
   (d) Wage determination (job analysis).
   (e) Employee benefits and services.
   (f) Morale development and appraisal.
   (g) Grievance handling.
   (h) Employee motivation.
   (i) Health and safety.

3. Management development requires that the personnel department:
   (a) Measure and evaluate present conditions.
   (b) Predict future conditions and events.
   (c) Evaluate effects of current policies, programs, and activities.

4. Functional control requires that the personnel department:
   (a) Establish uniform procedures to be followed with respect to various activities.
   (b) Set forth specific objectives for all programs.
   (c) Establish criteria for judging performance.
   (d) Devise a system of records and reports.
   (e) Analyze records and reports in light of desired objectives.
   (f) Make provision for corrections as needed.

5. Counseling top management on such subjects as organization

structure, line-staff relationships, labor-management relations, organization planning, etc., requires:

(a)   Study of existing organizational problems.

(b)   Clarifying lines of authority and responsibility.

(c)   Development of a basic philosophy concerning dealings with unions, as well as recommending specific policies and courses of action.

(d)   Study of future organizational needs for personnel on all levels.

Example from line production department supplying components to main assembly line:

1.   Cost control.   Under this area should be delineated the major cost items that require consideration. Examples might include such items as downtime, direct labor, and material costs.

2.   Quality.

(a)   Determining points of control.

(b)   Detail of inspection.

(c)   Complete versus partial inspection.

(d)   Establishing quality standards and/or tolerances.

3.   Quantity.

(a)   Production planning and scheduling.

(b)   Work flow.

(c)   Man and machine scheduling.

(d)   Machine and individual work standards.

(e)   Raw material control.

4.   Safety.

(a)   Analysis of conditions.

(b)   Devising safety procedures and setting safety standards.

(c)   Continuous program to promote safety consciousness.

(d)   Accident frequency rates.

(e)   Accident severity rates.

5.   Training and development.

(a)   Job and man analysis to determine needs.

(b)   Developing training schedules and programs.

(c)   Programs for employee upgrading.

6. Employee performance control.

(a) Develop individual job standards.

(b) System to measure performance as it's happening.

(c) Procedure for feedback and corrective action.

7. Work methods and layout.

(a) Familiarity with present methods and processes.

(b) Knowledge of capabilities.

(c) Systematic approach to analyzing present procedures and developing new ones (work simplification).

The reader will note that what has been done is first to set forth the area of responsibility or accountability and then under it to delineate the specific activities which are or should be carried out as they relate to that area. Listing these specific activities has the advantage of clarifying why certain things are done and also making sure that some activities that should be carried out are not omitted.

3. Specific Quantifiable Measures or a Series of Statements Which Describe the Conditions That Will Exist When Each Area of Departmental Responsibility Is Met.   For each major area of responsibility specific measures of successful performance should be established. Where possible these measures should be quantifiable in terms of numbers, percentages, time, or some other type of figure. In most cases *it is possible* to develop this type of measure. This is true even for areas which, historically, have been considered unmeasurable. The preciseness may, of course, vary, but some measure is better than none at all. The important point is that the manager recognize where various degrees of objectivity exist and weighs his evaluation of actual performance accordingly.

Where no quantification of any kind is possible, then it is desirable to develop a series of specific statements which describe the general conditions that will exist when the area of responsibility has been adequately performed. The process of measuring various phases of departmental activity is not a major problem from the standpoint of technical feasibility, but it is as far as getting people to accept the idea that performance can be measured accurately and that there are both organization and individual advantages to such a system.

These comments emphasize two key points. First, in most situations there is some type of quantifiable data which can be used to measure performance with regard to various aspects of either individual or departmental performance. The fact that these quantifiable measures are not 100 percent precise or that the man may not have complete control over that phase of the work should not deter their use. They are still better than nothing. Second, where specific quantifiable measures are not available the problem can be solved via a series of statements which precisely describe the conditions that will exist when that area of responsibility is adequately performed.

The diagram below depicts this situation.

Statements describing conditions that exist now	Activity or area of responsibility	Conditions we want to exist as a result of improved performance
1. _____	1. _____	1. _____
2. _____	2. _____	2. _____
3. _____	3. _____	3. _____
4. _____	4. _____	4. _____
5. _____	5. _____	5. _____

On the left is a series of specific statements that would describe conditions as they now exist. In the middle is the area of activity or responsibility with which the manager is concerned. On the right is a series of statements describing the conditions we would like to have prevailing as a result of adequate performance of these activities. Deviations between what exists on the left versus what is desired as stated on the right represents a gap in performance.

The process of formulating such statements (quantifying what was heretofore only qualifiable) is illustrated below.

In the line production department example shown previously, quantifiable measures of performance can be established without too much difficulty.

Area of Responsibility	Measure of Performance
1. Cost	1. Production budget of standard cost data.
2. Quantity	2. Production schedule or specific output standards for various machines and/or jobs.

3. Quality	3.	Rejection rate, tolerance standards, or scrap.
4. Safety	4.	Accident frequency and severity rates.
5. Individual Job Performance	5.	Standard output data.

However, results in the areas of training and development may seem to defy measurement at first. Here is where the concept of developing a series of statements describing the general conditions which will exist when the responsibility is performed adequately can be applied. For the training and development area these statements might read as follows. The department as a whole will have performed its training and development responsibility adequately when:

1. New employees are able to progress to jobs requiring a higher degree of skill within certain specified periods of time (to be determined for each situation).

2. There are at least two people in the department capable of performing any given job or operation.

3. All employees are producing at a level consistent with the minimum standard required.

4. New employees are able to reach standard performance in the normal expected period of time. These times would be based on past experience for the average employee.

5. Qualified candidates for new or upgraded jobs can be chosen from the ranks.

In the area of work methods the following criteria of successful performance might apply: A department will have done a satisfactory job when, in any given year, at least two jobs or processes in the department have been studied and improved through the introduction of new methods, revised layout, or new procedures. To be significant the improvement must meet at least one of the following or other similar criteria.

1. A decrease of at least 10 percent in the amount of time involved.

2. A decrease of at least 10 percent in the cost as measured by such factors as downtime, scrap, and direct labor or material costs.

3.   A 10 percent increase in quality, measured by fewer rejects, less rework, reduced scrap, and so forth.

Another example of quantifying the qualifiable might be a case where something such as creativity is considered to be an important aspect of successful job performance. Following the concept of developing a series of statements, specific examples of creative behavior could be described as:

1.   Creativity is exhibited when an engineer develops an improved method of manufacturing.

2.   When the manufacture of a product or part is simplified by elimination of an unnecessary or nonfunctional part or component, creativity has been exhibited.

3.   When a new design improves the physical operation of a product, an engineer will have made a creative contribution.

4.   When an engineer overcomes a particular problem relating to an assigned project he has demonstrated creativity in his job.

With this or any other list of specific examples of creative behavior, the extent, degree, and frequency to which an individual has demonstrated creative talent in performance of his job can be pinpointed. Through cost- or time-saved figures, a numerical value can be placed on his creative contribution. Also, certain minimum requirements of creative behavior can be set, for example, in the course of a year; an engineer should have at least six instances of creative contributions. To be considered as such, each must meet at least one of the conditions specified above, and also be quantifiable through such factors as cost saved or time saved.

As a final example, suppose that new employee orientation is considered a key factor in reducing turnover, building motivation, and thereby increasing the overall level of productivity. The following series of statements might be developed and used to describe the conditions which will exist when a supervisor has adequately carried out this phase of his job responsibilities.

1.   After reporting for work, the employee is interviewed for a minimum of 15 minutes, during which time the following subjects are covered:

(a)   A check of the previous steps carried out by the personnel department and the new employee's understanding and comprehension of them.

(*b*) A review of some pertinent personal data to establish rapport.

(*c*) An explanation of the department's work, how it relates to other departments and to the company.

(*d*) An explanation of his job, its significance, and importance.

(*e*) A review of his previous job history and significant relevance to the new job.

(*f*) A preliminary tour of the department and necessary facilities.

2. After reaching a reasonable level of efficiency, he is given a more detailed tour and explanation of the department itself, closely related departments, and the total operation.

3. Within one month he is interviewed concerning the following:

(*a*) Key areas of departmental performance accountability and how the department as a whole is doing in these areas.

(*b*) An explanation of possible progression as it relates to his job and procedures relating to progression.

(*c*) Feedback on how he is doing in his job as it compares to a "typical" new employee (this should cover strengths, areas for improvement, etc.).

(*d*) A check of his questions, concerns, problems, impressions, and level of job satisfaction.

4. At designated times additional interviews are held relating to all of the above (at least two per year).

5. A brief yet specific log is kept concerning all the above areas. This would include a summary of the supervisor's impressions, specific things discussed, and action taken.

4. Analysis of the Present Status of the Operation as it Relates to the Major Areas of Responsibilities. Once the conditions for ideal accomplishment have been described, the manager must determine exactly where his department stands. He must pinpoint specifically the results he is presently achieving, and at the same time determine where the biggest problem areas are and where the biggest payoff would be if improvement could be effected. Essentially, this is an inventory of the present "status quo." There will be some areas in which present achievement is very close or equal to what seems the maximum level. In these cases the important question is whether the performance level as outlined reflects the maximum possible or just an adequate level. (To say that performance in a given area is maximum indicates that there can be no significant further improvements in results and methods.)

Usually there will be gaps of varying size between actual versus desired levels of performance in the key areas of responsibility. Also, there may be some areas of responsibility and accountability which have been neglected. These would most likely occur in areas of line-staff overlap.

5.   Picking Out Key Area Where the Manager Would Like to See Improvement Made and Writing Specific Objectives.   The actual writing of objectives is a highly critical step and certain guidelines should be followed. The essential ingredients of a well-written objective include:

1.   The actual result being sought should be set forth in quantifiable terms.

2.   The way in which actual performance will be measured should be clearly indicated.

3.   The time period should be specified.

Effective objective writing can best be illustrated by such examples as:

Example 1.   To reduce the average amount of time lapse between testing and the test engineers' written reports from six weeks to three weeks during the next three months.

Example 2.   To reduce the accident frequency rate in department 81 from a level of 5.31 to a level of 4.25 during the next six months.

These examples are fairly simple and straightforward. Somewhat more complex are the following examples:

Example 3.   To improve production efficiency at work station 25 by developing new methods and a relayout of the station. This objective will have been accomplished when the following conditions are met within the next 2½ months:

(*a*)   Downtime at subsequent work stations due to shortages in subassemblies produced at station 25 is completely eliminated.

(*b*)   The average level of efficiency for all types of subassemblies completed at station 25 is raised from 110 percent to 120 percent of a standard.

(c) The individual worker's average incentive earnings are increased by 10 percent.

Example 4. To improve the work of the design engineering department in estimates of cost savings and of the amount of time various projects will take. This objective is operative for the next six months and will be accomplished when the following conditions are met:

(a) Cost savings estimates are within 7 percent of actual savings for 90 percent of the projects worked on.

(b) The actual time spent on projects is within 3 days of the estimated time in at least 95 percent of the cases.

Example 5. To improve the service rendered to line production managers by production expediters during the next eight months. Accomplishment of this objective will be measured by the following:

(a) We are able to pinpoint at least 10 items whose late delivery into production departments collectively accounts for 20 percent of the downtime due to parts shortages.

(b) After these major difficulties have been spotted, we are able to make preliminary adjustments which reduce the downtime due to shortages of these items by half.

(c) Specific recommendations for permanently alleviating the difficulties are made.

6. Developing Plans and Programs Designed to Achieve the Desired Results. Once the specific objectives have been set the question of how to achieve them becomes paramount. Achievement does not occur by accident but rather is the result of well-formulated plans and programs. In developing plans to accomplish results the following steps are suggested:

1. Identify the problems or areas of difficulty which must be overcome for better achievement. In terms of some of the above example objectives, questions such as the following must be asked: What are the things that cause delays in test reports? Based on analysis of previous accidents, what are some of the major or significant causes of accidents in the department? What in the present work station layout and methods are causing the delays, bottlenecks, and excess time? What factors make it difficult to come up with cost savings estimates

and estimates of project times? What are the delays occurring which result in late delivery of certain materials?

2.   Having identified the problem areas the manager must now determine what might be done to overcome these difficulties. This analysis must take place with respect to each major problem mentioned in order to develop a list of all possible solutions without regard to their feasibility or who would do them.

3.   From this list of what might be done, it can now be determined what will be done. Which things are key factors? Where will the biggest payoff be if effort is concentrated? This recognizes that there is a limit to the amount of attention and effort that can be given to one phase of the total operation and also that there must be some degree of correlation between effort and eventual payoff.

The list of what might be done to overcome a given problem often can be divided into two parts: those things that involve adjustments in other departments, and those over which the department itself has control. Initially, the latter should receive the attention. It is easy for the manager to say that achievement of results is out of his control, but this is seldom altogether true. Although the reaching of the maximum level of accomplishment may depend on the interdependent action of several departments, there is usually a considerable amount that can be done on an intradepartmental basis.

When more than one department must be involved, it is desirable to set a shorter-range objective—reflecting what can be achieved with improvements within the department itself—and a longer-range objective which would reflect the results desired if cooperative action is taken. Definite plans and target dates should then be set to achieve the shorter range goals while laying the groundwork for longer range achievement.

Guidelines for Individual Objective Setting

1.   The Number of Objectives on Which Each Man Should Concentrate in a Given Period Should Be Limited.   This not only prevents frustration but insures a thorough and organized effort toward achievement. With too many objectives for a given period, it is easy to lose perspective as to which are most important.

2. Objectives Should Be Specific. In the methods example cited above, the general criteria for judging a man's performance in that area of responsibility are as outlined. In any given period, however, the manager should set specific objectives which relate to this area of responsibility. Accordingly, at the beginning of the period of measurement he would look at the jobs and processes in his section and pick out those which, if some improvement could be made, would have significant impact. Having identified the jobs or processes to be analyzed, specific objectives would be written for each one.

Following the previously described procedure these objectives would go beyond stating that a new method or procedure would be developed. It would outline specifically the conditions which would exist when the new method or procedure is a good one. These conditions should reflect both the problem situations which will be removed as well as some type of quantitive measurement such as time saved, quantity increased, or cost lowered.

3. Individual Objectives Should Be a Blend between the Objectives of the Department as a Whole during a Given Period and the Man's Personal Situation. For example, during the next six months major departmental objectives may have been set in the areas of reducing overtime and improving the safety record. These are areas in which every member of the team is expending a unified effort and has specific objectives set for his section which tie in with those of the department. In addition, one supervisor may have a personal objective relating to upgrading the skill level of the people in his department, while another may be concerned with reducing cost in given areas of the budget.

4. Balance Must Be Maintained. Achievement of results in one area should not be at the expense of performance in other areas. Thus, to increase quantity at the expense of quality is obviously not conducive to progress. This means that during certain periods of time given areas of a single individual's job are going to receive emphasis in terms of the improvement sought. At the same time, however, there is an implicit assumption that previous levels of accomplishment in other areas will be maintained.

5. Objectives Should Be Reasonable and Yet Offer a Challenge. They Must Be Tailored to the Man and Reflect Previous Levels of Accomplishment. Some managers feel that the best way to get high performance is to put pressure on subordinates by asking for much more than they actually or reasonably expect to get; because of this pressure people will push a little harder and more will get done. Although this approach may work effectively for a short time it does not have much potential as a permanent system. People quickly catch on to the pattern and make adjustments accordingly. They develop a defensive approach to their work and always have reasons and justifications when these "pie in the sky" targets are not met; they undertake little constructive analysis which might result in an improved, smoother running, more efficient operation; finally, a padding effect develops as people overestimate in order to cushion in advance the effect of unreasonable targets.

Reasonable and challenging objectives offer an opportunity to gain a rewarding sense of achievement and are a spur to future performance. Both departmental and individual objectives are reasonable and challenging when (1) they promote continued critical analysis of the present operation in order to achieve better results, and (2) the results actually achieved through the objective setting process reflect progressively better levels of accomplishment. There are, of course, some areas of departmental and individual responsibility where present levels of accomplishment are maximum. These then become a fixed standard until such time as conditions change and it no longer reflects maximum. The difference between standards and objectives will be discussed later.

6. Even Though a Man or Department Does Not Have Complete Control Over a Given Area, That Area Should Not Be Avoided. Objective setting is a derivative process in the sense that accomplishment on a total basis requires cooperation and integration of effort between departments.

By setting objectives and forcing some degree of accountability for areas of performance where the department and individuals do not have complete control, but which are strategic in terms of accomplishing the general mission, the necessary integration of effort will be achieved.

7. It May Be Desirable to Set Different Levels of Accomplishment. In order to distinguish between levels of actual performance for people in similar jobs it is sometimes desirable to set different levels of accomplishment for certain strategic and common areas of accountability. Accordingly, the conditions describing satisfactory, above average, and exceptional performance as they relate to a specific area would be outlined.

The Importance of Feedback

A special advantage of a system of objectives is that it allows the man to exercise self-direction and self-control over his work. In order for this advantage to be operative, however, he must receive continual feedback on the results which he is achieving. Ideally this feedback should come to him in some other way than from the manager himself so that self-direction can, in fact, be a reality. The manager's role in controlling individual job performance should be restricted to those circumstances in which the man does not adjust his own performance in response to deviations from predetermined standards. This does not mean the manager abdicates his control function. Rather, his role changes from that of an authoritative one to more of a supportive one. Within broad limits of policy and procedure he guides and coordinates the efforts of the total group, at the same time as he coaches individuals.

The Manager as a Coach

The process of establishing a system of departmental and individual job objectives tends to change the superior-subordinate relationship to one of team effort with everyone working to accomplish common goals. In short, the manager becomes less of a "boss" and more of a coach and coordinator. He works with the individuals in his department several ways:

1.   He reviews the progress being made toward accomplishing the desired results.

2.   He helps the man to evaluate the effectiveness of plans and strategies, and to formulate new ones.

3.   He gives support and whatever other assistance he can to help his people achieve the results they seek.

4.   He sets new goals which are realistic and yet offer a challenge.

5.   He formulates plans which provide for the man's continued growth and development.

Some General Observations Concerning Objective Setting versus Standards

The process of managing by objectives is a dynamic, continuing, and changing one. It is not a process which takes place once and then is all over. The manager who adopts it, analyzes and challenges all phases of his operation. He sets objectives or goals in a given area which, when achieved, represent significant accomplishments; develops plans, strategies, and programs to achieve them; sets target dates; and evaluates progress on a continual basis.

Thus, there is a difference between the concept of management by objectives and ordinary standard setting. Some of these differences can be summarized as follows:

1.   Standards are static; once set, they tend to remain fixed. Objective setting is dynamic in that new goals are constantly set and some additional improvement is always sought.

2.   Objective setting tends to cut across the whole spectrum of departmental functions rather than just a few areas.

3.   Standards often reflect levels of performance which are adequate but not necessarily maximum. Objectives call for the best that a department or an individual can give.

4.   Objectives are accompanied by plans for their achievement. They are concerned with making things happen that might otherwise not occur. Standards are usually used to measure performance after the fact.

Participation in Objective Setting

In order for a result-oriented operation to be effective, employees must have an active and integral role in both its initial establishment and its subsequent functioning. Objective setting, whether it be for an entire department or a specific job, cannot be done by the manager alone.

The success of the system depends on the degree to which the people are committed to it. Their commitment in turn is a function of how actively they are involved in it. In other words, involvement and commitment go hand in hand.

When people participate in the objective-setting process they become mentally, emotionally, as well as physically involved in their jobs. The job itself begins to take on more importance as they see how it is related to the total department. Their efforts become more meaningful as they see tangible results in accomplishment. The individual's sense of his own significance and worth is enhanced. In addition, he is given the opportunity to grow and develop to the full extent of his skills and abilities. The result is not only one of personal motivation as far as each individual is concerned, but also one of being able to realize the full potential of our human resources.

In establishing a system of management by objectives, the people should be involved from the very first step all the way to setting personal goals. Any attempt at forcing the system by dictating individual job goals is likely to meet with less than full success. At different times the manager must exercise varying degrees of control and authority, but the general climate must be a highly participative one.

The establishment of a system of management by objectives is not an end in itself, but rather a means to an end. From the standpoint of the total organization or department it is a system which, when properly functioning, will result in maximum productivity. Built into the mechanics of the concept is the opportunity to integrate the needs of the individual —such things as achievement, responsibility, growth, recognition, and a sense of significance—with the goals and objectives of the firm. The advantages of the system can be summarized as follows:

1. Clarifies departmental activity as it relates to:

(a) Total organization.

(b) Other departmental units.

2. Gives long- and short-range direction to the stream of effort within a department.

3. Provides a basis for detailed analysis of major areas of responsibility so that the department may accomplish its mission.

4. Establishes a framework for in-depth analysis of present procedures in terms of their effectiveness.

5. Creates a climate in which continuous improvement is emphasized and attainable.

6.   Fosters maximum contribution to the whole and other units by integration of efforts.

7.   Creates conditions which lead to maximum levels of individual motivation.

The key to implementing an MBO program is desire and dedication on the part of the manager. He is the one who must give leadership and direction and generate enthusiasm for the system and its potential. To be sure, it is not something that can be accomplished overnight. Jobs cannot simply be defined in terms of areas of accountability and measuring results. Success requires participation on the part of subordinates, experimentation with ideas, and constant refining as experience is gained. The benefits of maximum levels of departmental achievements, mutual trust and confidence, and high levels of individual motivation are the culmination of a results approach. The manager who does not want to implement the concept can and will find many reasons why it will not work. These reasons include the facts that performance for this type of work cannot be quantifiably measured, that people won't accept it, and that it is just another gimmick. For the first objection, quantification is possible. With respect to acceptance, people will experiment with such a system as long as they can participate in a non-threatening climate. On the third point, it is not the system itself which is bad, but the way it is implemented and administered.

Summary

In this chapter we have explored a concept of management which in recent years has seen tremendously widespread application. It is being implemented extensively not only by private business but also in the health services, local, state, and federal government agencies, and organizations of all types. The reasons for the popularity of management by objectives lie in what it can accomplish in terms of increasing organizational and departmental efficiency as well as contributing to individual motivation.

A management-by-objectives approach implies that the organization establishes a hierarchy of objectives which run from the top of the organization to the bottom. The objectives at each successive level and for individuals in that level are derived from and complement those at the previous level. Once this hierarchy of specific objectives is established all efforts are directed and all resources mobilized toward their accomplishment. In addition, the objectives in question serve as a focal point for continually evaluating the present status of operations and for making needed adjustments to insure their achievements. The organization that is not using an objectives approach is more likely to be operating on somewhat of a loose or haphazard basis. Also, they are more susceptible to the environment controlling them instead of their, to a degree, controlling the environment.

The steps involved in order for a given department to successfully implement an MBO program include determining their overall mission, identifying their major areas of responsibility, establishing measure of performance for each area of responsibility, analyzing the present status of the operation, writing specific objectives in areas where improvement can be made, and then developing plans designed to achieve the desired results. Once departmental objctives have been set they should be translated into objectives for each individual within the department. The manager's job then becomes one of working with his people individually and as a group to achieve the objectives which have been set.

Key Concepts

Management by Objectives. A system of management whereby the organization as a whole, every department, and every individual has defined and is working toward achieving certain results in key areas of accountability during a specified period of time.

Objectives. Objective setting implies that the manager is continually analyzing various phases of his department's operation with an eye toward improving the present level of achievement. In this sense it is a dynamic process.

Standards. Standards differ from objectives in that once set, they tend to remain fixed. Thus, they are to a degree static in nature. In addition, standards many times reflect levels of performance which are adequate but not maximum. As opposed to this, objectives reflect the best that a department or individual can give.

Participation. If people are expected to be committed to the achievement of certain results they must have an opportunity to participate in determining what those results are to be. A key ingredient to a successful MBO program is participation.

Discussion Questions

1. Briefly define and explain the concept management by objectives.

2. What are the possible disadvantages that might result if a manager does not use a management-by-objectives approach in motivating his subordinates?

3. What are some of the benefits available to a manager who uses management by objectives in motivating his subordinates?

4. What are the departmental advantages available to a manager who uses a management-by-objectives approach?

5. Briefly describe each of the steps of the six step procedure for a departmental plan of establishing management by objectives. Explain the key considerations involved in each step.

6. Assume that you are vice-president of sales for a manufacturing firm which sells to retailers in the southwest region of the United States. Set up a possible overall mission for your department. Repeat this procedure for the remaining five steps of the objective-setting process.

7. What are the essential ingredients of a well-written objective? Discuss each of the guidelines for establishing individual objectives.

8. What is the importance of being able to *quantify* objectives?

9. What is the importance of employee participation in objective setting?

Selected Readings

J. D. Batten, *Beyond Management by Objectives*, American Management Association, 1966.

Peter F. Drucker, "The Objectives of a Business," *The Practice of Management*, Harper and Brothers, New York, 1954.

Charles H. Granger, "The Hierarchy of Objectives," *Harvard Business Review*, May–June 1964.

Walter Hill, "The Goal Formation Process in Complex Organizations," *The Journal of Management Studies*, May 1969.

George S. Odiorne, *Management by Objectives—A System of Managerial Leadership*, Pitman, New York, 1965.

Phil N. Scheid, "Charter of Accountability for Executives," *Harvard Business Review*, July–August 1965, pp. 88–98.

Edward C. Schleh, *Management by Results*, McGraw-Hill, New York, 1961.

Stanley E. Seashore, "Criteria of Organizational Effectiveness," *Michigan Business Review*, July 1963, pp. 26–30.

Walter S. Wikstrom, "Management by Objectives, or Appraisal by Results," *Conference Board Record, III* (7), July 1966, pp. 27–31.

———, *Managing By—and With—Objectives*, Personnel Study No. 212, National Industrial Conference Board, Inc., 1968.

5. Managerial Prerequisites to Installing a Management-by-Objectives Program

In Chapter 4 we examined a management-by-objectives approach to planning at the departmental level. Early in the chapter the observation was made that MBO represents one of the most dynamic developments in management thought to occur in recent years. This point deserves further emphasis at this time. All indicators point to the fact that each day more and more organizations turn to the MBO approach. It is also fairly safe to observe that in the very near future one might be hard pressed to find any progressive organization which to one degree or another is not operating with this concept. Interestingly enough, a great deal of the impetus for MBO is coming from more than just business and industry. More specifically, there has been considerable interest and implementation of MBO principles in the health services, federal, state, and local government, and private institutions.

It is the purpose of this chapter to discuss some of the problems associated with the introduction and implementation of MBO, and suggest some guidelines for overcoming these problems. Ideally, such information should provide managers with a basis on which they can anticipate problems and can plan alternative courses of action for their resolution.

Although several of the problems associated with the introduction and implementation of MBO are interrelated, the following problem areas will be discussed separately for conceptual clarity: (1) top management support, (2) training for the implementation of MBO, (3) meaningful employee participation, (4) the paperwork problem, (5) feedback for self-direction and self-control, and (6) other considerations in implementing MBO.

Top Level Management Support

The presence or absence of top level management support is a critical factor in determining the degree to which an MBO program will be successful. The concern which the operating manager has for this facet of effective implementation is reflected in the following comment which was made by an administrator[1] of a large, southern hospital: "The administrator . . . not only must do an internal selling job on this philosophy but must also sell the Medical Staff and Board on the usefulness of the theory and the practical value of the written document itself as an indicator of what will be going on during the coming year in the various departments."

The potential problem of lack of support was also pointed out in a study by Tosi and Carroll.[2] In response to a question concerning the problems and disadvantages associated with MBO, "not used in full potential" was the second most frequent mentioned item. In addition, when asked the question, "How would you improve the program?" the respondents focused, with only one exception, on items relating to the way their superior was implementing it. Thus, the issue of top management support, use, and reinforcement is strategic and has an impact on how subordinates react to MBO.

With these general observations in mind, one of the very critical factors in effective MBO implementation can be pinpointed. It must be a *way of managing on a day-to-day basis* rather than an academic exercise of writing objectives once a year. The manager has the responsibility of (1) periodically discussing with each subordinate the

[1]James N. Kulpan, Personal correspondence with Stanley Sloan, July 24, 1967, p. 3.

[2]Henry L. Tosi and Stephen J. Carroll, "Managerial Reaction to Management by Objectives," *Academy of Management Journal,* December 1968.

objectives that were set, (2) evaluating progress made in achieving those objectives, and (3) assisting and supporting the subordinate by removing obstacles that hinder accomplishment. In short, an MBO program is not an end in itself, but rather a means to an end. Research has shown that management support for using objectives to plan and control work on a continuous daily basis increases the probability of a successful program. Without continual emphasis the system will deteriorate and enthusiasm for it will wane.

Training for the Implementation of MBO

A second critical factor in implementing MBO is the existence of some type of training program for people who will be operating under it. In the Tosi and Carroll study, cited previously, there was some evidence to support the idea that "attempts to introduce and initiate the program did not substantially affect the attitudes and knowledge of the managers about the program." This statement would seem to suggest that employees may be uncertain about the reasons for which MBO is being undertaken. Although reports of open resistance and antagonism toward MBO are infrequent, it must be recognized that people tend to fear what they do not understand. This fear can lead to suspicion and mistrust which in turn, undermines employee enthusiasm which is very important during the initial stages of MBO. According to one consultant[3]: "The importance of orientation and training should not be overlooked . . . I think it is important when you move into a program like this, if you are starting from scratch, that people understand why and how you are developing the program. Sometimes there is a certain amount of fear involved when a program of this kind is introduced." As one hospital administrator[4] notes: ". . . I would say that the single most difficult obstacle to overcome is the problem of developing real understanding and commitment on the part of the management group for the MBO theory. At least in our experience this in itself has been such a major problem that the program would have been dropped long ago had I not been so personally committed and equally hard headed about the matter." Also, they should be given a clear specific picture as to why the organization

---

[3]J. B. Joynt, "Basic Concepts of Management by Objectives," *Management by Objectives in Retailing* (New York: Personnel and Store Management Groups, National Retail Merchants Association, September 1967), p. 58.

[4]James N. Kulpan, Personal correspondence with Stanley Sloan, July 24, 1967, p. 3.

is using it. Subordinates should be told the potential benefits of using MBO, the problems associated with its use, how to overcome those problems and how the program will operate. As Edward D. McDougal,[5] Director of Managerial and Professional Development at the New York office of The Equitable Life Assurance Society of the United States, cautions, ". . . it must be very easy to get off on the wrong foot in introducing the concept of managing by objectives, and that perhaps more emphasis needs to be put on the difficulties that should be anticipated and avoided, when we begin using this approach."

A second type of training that is needed involves the development of specific skills that are necessary for the successful implementation of MBO. The first and most obvious of these skills is the ability to write objectives that are: (1) realistic, (2) challenging, (3) explicit, (4) guides to action, (5) suggestive of methods of measuring performance, (6) related to objectives at higher and lower organizational levels, and (7) cognizant of organizational constraints. A considerable investment in time is necessary in order to write objectives that possess these characteristics. Although this investment is necessary and advantageous in terms of the potential benefits that can be derived from it, some individuals have considerable difficulty in translating their thoughts into a systematic, formalized written document. Part of this difficulty is psychological. As one executive[6] comments, "Most of us, when asked what our responsibilities are, find it difficult to describe them to someone else's satisfaction. Sometimes, we even privately squirm at having to answer the question at all. . . ."

Writing meaningful objectives is neither an easy nor semiautomatic process; it is a distinct skill that requires substantial training followed by subsequent practice. The problem of writing objectives is partially a result of the formality of MBO. However, the potential benefits of MBO seem to outweigh the costs of doing this paperwork. The importance of writing formalized objectives in a systematic way should not be underestimated. David E. Babcock,[7] Vice President of Organization Planning and Development at the May Company in St. Louis states: "I

[5]Edward D. McDougal, "Setting a Personnel Department's Operating Objectives," *Management by Objectives in Retailing* (New York: Personnel and Store Management Groups, National Retail Merchants Association, 1967), p. 90.

[6]Herbert A. Leeds, "Today's Problems and Tomorrow's Challenge," *Management by Objectives in Retailing* (New York: Personnel and Store Management Groups, National Retail Merchants Association, 1967), p. 7.

[7]David E. Babcock, "Standards of Performance—a Vital Part of Management by Objectives Program," *Management by Objectives in Retailing* (New York: Personnel and Store Management Groups, National Retail Merchants Association, 1967), p. 80.

want to say flatly, and will challenge anyone on this point, that you cannot carry on management by objectives in an informal procedure. If you want to obtain the kind of real results which can come from this kind of program, it must be procedurized. You must discipline yourself to follow and live within procedures, or you have nothing but 'pot luck.' "

The written objectives themselves provide the nonemotional, result-oriented basis of discussion between the supervisor and the subordinate. Another aspect of training concerns the auxiliary management skills which are also critical for effective implementation of an MBO program. Properly interpreted, MBO is more than a program of setting objectives in a technical sense. MBO is a philosophy of managing human resources on a daily basis. The objective setting process provides a vehicle for superior-subordinate interaction within a setting that is not threatening to the subordinate's feeling of self-worth. Here the role of the superior changes from one that may have historically relied on authority, exerting pressure when needed, and judging, to a more supportive role. The superior becomes a coach and counselor. He is a catalyst, stimulating the subordinate to identify problems that hinder accomplishment and to develop plans to overcome them. The manager must advise and guide the subordinate so that the subordinate's objectives are challenging, yet reasonable. Such objectives should provide the subordinate with ample opportunities for the subordinate's growth and self-development. The basis for superior-subordinate interaction in an MBO system may require that the superior himself develop or acquire the appropriate coaching and counseling skills. If training in these areas is not provided, the MBO system may never live up to its potential.[8]

Meaningful Employee Participation

Success with MBO requires a commitment on the part of each individual involved in this type of system. Their commitment, in turn, is a function of their identification with and participation in the system. In order for the individual to identify himself with MBO it is critical for him not to view the approach as just another method his superior is using to control his performance and to "check up" on him. One way to avoid this undesirable perception is to encourage the subordinate to play an

[8]For an excellent discussion of the relationship between management development and management by objectives see Henry L. Tosi, Jr., *Management Development* and *Management by Objectives.*

active role in the preliminary phases leading to the actual writing of objectives. One component of the subordinate's role should include (1) the identification of important areas of accountability for his job, (2) the determination of mutually agreeable performance measures, and (3) the identification of this present performance level. After the individual submits his proposed objectives and they are approved, he must also participate to the degree that he develops and plans for their achievement with the help of his superior. Here, the individual has some control over achieving the goals he set. By enlisting the subordinate's participation during the early phases of MBO, the manager can increase the probability that the subordinate will be committed to MBO and will feel that he is a vital part of a team effort.

There are also some broader, more indirect, subtle aspects of participation. Tosi and Carroll[9] found that satisfaction with MBO was related to the subordinate's perception of his superior, the organization's interest in the program, and how much time he spends on it. "It is only when all levels of management reinforce the use of the program by subordinates by using the system themselves that benefits can be obtained." Thus, true participation means that a climate of constant use and involvement in the MBO program must be created at all levels.

A final aspect of participation revolves around the subordinate's perception of the total program. To the degree that he feels the goals that are set are significant in terms of their relationship to his own needs and that their importance is made clear, he will tend to be more committed.

The manager seeking to implement MBO should be cautioned that research has shown a tendency for participation to decrease as MBO is implemented at lower organizational levels. More specifically, by the time the supervisory level is reached, there seems to be a very insignificant amount of participation.[10] Since it is frequently at this level where the "make or break" issues arise, extra care to elicit involvement is needed.

The Paper Work Problem

One possible reason for the decreased participation at lower levels in the organization may be a lack of desire. That is, MBO involves sub-

[9]Henry L. Tosi and Stephen J. Carroll, "Managerial Reaction to Management by Objectives," *Academy of Management Journal*, December 1968, p. 424.

[10]Anthony Raia, "A Second Look at Management Goals and Controls," *California Management Review*, Summer 1966.

stantial paper work. As one executive[11] observes, "The first major difficulty is the amount of time it takes to set up objectives and goals for a company or a department. The initial effort to get under way often is said to take so much time and energy that there is little left for subsequent follow-up and use of the goals that have been prepared. The time problem may be made worse by having such a complex procedure that the whole program bogs down under red tape." Indeed, most researchers[12] have found that paper work is a major problem associated with MBO. As one manager in a public organization, reflected, "It's a hell of a lot of work if you do it in a way that will benefit you. It's the kind of work that is tough because you have to sit down and think about it."

Perhaps it is reasonable to expect that during the initial stages of implementing MBO substantial paper work must be tolerated. This expectation, however, signals a note of caution to any organization wanting to keep its MBO program operating effectively. If working with the system on a daily basis becomes too cumbersome, two possible adverse reactions may occur. First, enthusiasm for the program may be significantly dampened. The individual manager may begin to perceive MBO as an academic exercise of report filing or a more sophisticated system of control through paper work. A second possibility is that MBO participants will begin taking shortcuts. To fulfill the paper requirements, individuals may put their thoughts into writing in a hurried way, just to "get the damn thing done." There is also the greater possibility that once completed, the written documents will simply be filed away and the manager will revert to managing work itself in his traditional way, rather than managing to achieve specific results.

Feedback for Self-Direction and Self-Control

One of the strongest arguments for operating under an MBO system, and also one of its major potential advantages, is that within this system a man can direct and control his own performance. In essence, a man who has performance objectives and knows how well he is achieving them knows "where he stands" and "where he's going," particularly if

[11]Edward D. McDougal, "Setting a Personnel Department's Operating Objectives," *Management by Objectives in Retailing* (New York: Personnel and Store Management Groups, National Retail Merchants Association, 1967), p. 91.

[12]Anthony Raia, "A Second Look at Management Goals and Controls," *California Management Review*, Summer 1966.

he can make necessary adjustments to achieve the desired results *on his own.* This assumes, of course, that he gets appropriate, meaningful, and timely feedback from his superior. One critical role that the superior plays in this context is that of providing ample opportunities for the subordinate to make appropriate adjustments in his objectives and in the methods he uses to achieve them. The vehicle for these adjustments is the continual, two-way feedback system in which the superior and subordinate discuss progress and problems.

Feedback under MBO should take two forms. First, the individual should get periodic reports on where he or his department stands on an overall performance basis. A manager's role as a source of feedback and information is particularly significant when the subordinate requests his help.

A second type of feedback which is necessary is the periodic counseling and appraisal interview. As stated earlier, under MBO the manager becomes an advisor and a coach. His job is to offer support to his people and to help *them* accomplish results. This means he helps to evaluate progress, to identify problems, and to offer planning suggestions. Without periodic meetings this function will disappear and many of the potential benefits of MBO, in turn, will not be reaped.

Other Considerations in Implementing MBO

In addition to the considerations discussed above, there are several other factors that can influence the eventual success of a program. To the extent that those responsible for implementation are aware of these potential problems, provision can be made in advance for preventing their occurrence.

Restrictive Objective Setting.   Most of the research studies cited previously have shown that in the initial stages of a program, objectives are set over a wide range of job responsibilities and areas of accountability. This is as it should be. One of the potential advantages of MBO is that it should cause the individual or the department to examine its activities in a broad sense and to develop a comprehensive picture of what its function really is and should be.

However, research findings suggest that by the time the second round of setting objectives occurs, some of these areas of accountability "drop off" and are neglected. More specifically, there may be a tendency for the manager to concentrate on those three or four areas which are traditionally very quantifiable in nature (and historically have received the most emphasis) and to neglect the others.[13] Part of the rationale of installing the system in the first place is thus defeated because a balanced approach to viewing the job disappears. The only solution, of course, is for the man's superior to make sure that the initial analysis of the job encompasses all key areas of accountability and then to make sure that goals set are representative in subsequent periods.

Conflicting Objectives. One of the inescapable results of an MBO program is that to a degree it builds a competitive climate. (It should be noted that this is not necessarily bad as long as it does not go to extremes.) If there is no central coordination, however, departments or functional areas may end up setting competing objectives. The purchasing department, for example, may have the perfectly legitimate objective of lowering unit and procurement cost by purchasing items or material in larger lot sizes. Accomplishment of this objective may create problems in the warehousing department. The warehousing department may face increased handling and storage costs in order for the purchasing department to accomplish its objective. Similarly, a production department supplying components to a main assembly line may have an objective of increasing quantity or output. If this is achieved at the expense of some quality, however, labor and reject costs in assembly may increase significantly.

The point is that accomplishment of results in organizations today largely requires interdepartmental cooperation and integration of effort. Every department and functional area must ask itself why it exists and what it should be accomplishing from the standpoint of the total organization. Moreover, each department must also ask itself these same questions with respect to how it interrelates with other departments or units. The persons responsible for implementing MBO must be certain that this analysis occurs and that competing objectives are not set.

Implementing MBO at Lower Organizational Levels. If the full benefits of MBO are to be realized, it must be carried all the way down

---

[13]For a discussion of quantifying qualitative areas of accountability see Burt K. Scanlan, *Results Management In Action,* Management Center of Cambridge, Cambridge, Massachusetts.

to the first-line level of the organization. Research findings seem to suggest that this is not always the case. There is a tendency for active participation in objective setting itself and for periodic feedback and review to diminish the further down the management ladder the program gets. To the degree that this happens the program may lose some of its impact, and serious blocks to accomplishing overall objectives which are set higher up the line will be encountered.

Organizational Paraphernalia. Historically we have built into our organizational structures various policies, procedures, and control mechanisms to insure that people perform their job and behave as we would have them behave. Many of these are, of course, an absolute necessity, but some are a throwback to a negative philosophy about people and their normal reaction to work. Management by objectives, however, presupposes a "Theory Y" philosophy (that is, most people want to work and to accomplish results on the job, and conditions can be such that they will be committed to accomplishing results).

In a management-by-objectives climate, therefore, everything possible must be done to make sure that excessive restrictions are not placed on the individual. He must have the maximum freedom possible to achieve results without undue burdens of reporting and meeting otherwise unnecessary procedural requirements.

Salary Decisions and MBO. Perhaps the most elusive aspect of MBO has been the difficulty of in fact, not just in theory, tying the organization's compensation system into the MBO program. Although this issue may not come forward initially it will eventually become a big "bone of contention" and if not confronted can eventually break the system. In short, if the accomplishment of results is emphasized people will eventually expect to be paid on the basis of what they achieve.

This is not a simple problem, and may well be the most difficult of all. First, there is the problem of equating the degree of difficulty to the achievement of various objectives. This is particularly true when comparing departments or functional areas. Second, there is always the unconscious tendency for the superior to stress most heavily those two or three things that seem to represent the most tangible areas of performance. Subordinates must have in advance a clear understanding of the weight various things will be given in the final evaluation.

A third difficulty concerns the degree to which the opportunity does or does not exist to reward *significantly* (dollar wise), the superior performer. If the dollar difference between the superior and the average performer is not perceived as being significant, the superior performer will lose enthusiasm to continue his outstanding performance. Fourth, minimal increases for average performers can also be discouraging. They may be doing their best work (which, by the way, may not be too bad; *someone* must be average), and getting only a minimum increase may be perceived as punishment.

There is also the difficulty of equating what the man expects with what he actually gets. Based on his own analysis of his performance he may quite reasonably and justifiably anticipate an eight to nine percent salary increase. There are always practical limits to how much total money can be allocated, however, and ideally everyone must get a reasonable share of the total. Although the superior performer receives one of the biggest percentage increases, it may fall two or three percentage points short of what he expected. Again this is a very difficult situation. The experience of one personnel department[14] is particularly relevant here.

". . . our Personnel Department did attempt to use our operating objectives and goals as a basis for decisions on salaries. We found that this created resistance among our people to using the objective and goal setting process effectively for operating purposes. Why this was, I don't know . . . At any rate, we now separate appraisals of performance for salary purposes from our cycle of objectives and goal-setting and review."

These are only a few of the difficult problems associated with trying to integrate the compensation plan with the MBO plan. They are, of course, very real, and unfortunately there are no ready answers. Schrieber and Sloan discuss MBO as a basis for an incentive compensation system in more detail.[15]

Suggestions for Installing an MBO Program

On the basis of the experience of several organizations that have confronted the previously discussed problems in their MBO programs, the

[14]E. D. McDougal, "Setting a Personnel Department's Operating Objectives," *Management by Objectives in Retailing* (New York: Personnel and Store Management Groups, National Retail Association, 1967), p. 95.

[15]D. E. Schrieber and S. Sloan, "Incentives: Are they relevant, obsolete, or misunderstood?" *Personnel Administration,* 1969.

following summary suggestions for installing a program are recommended.

1.   The individual(s) responsible for introducing MBO must be certain that the top level of management is willing to support actively managerial practices consistent with MBO. Mere tolerance for or acceptance of MBO is insufficient for effective implementation. Top management must provide ample opportunities for MBO participants to practice and test their newly acquired knowledge and skills and must provide earned recognition and reward for managerial behavior consistent with MBO.

2.   The MBO participants should receive extensive training in the methods of implementing MBO. Such a training program should be carefully designed to provide the participants with a thorough knowledge of (a) the motivational underpinnings of MBO, (b) the specific skills necessary to implement MBO, such as writing objectives and reviewing performance, (c) the potential benefits and problems of MBO and ways to resolve those problems, and (d) the types of leadership styles, managerial attitudes, and managerial behavior that are consistent with the MBO philosophy.

3.   Subordinates must participate completely in the MBO process to satisfy their own needs while simultaneously satisfying organizational needs. MBO is not a gimmick or facade to disguise an authoritarian approach to managing human resources. The keynote here is the subordinate's self-direction and self-control. Managers must avoid the temptation of unilaterally setting objectives and then convincing or coercing the subordinate to agree to achievement of these objectives. Instead, managers must advise, guide, and listen to the subordinate, but must also provide ample opportunities for the subordinate to fulfill his need for recognition, advancement, growth, and self-actualization. The manager's role is that of coach, not judge, and he must allow room for the subordinate to test his limitations and to make mistakes.

4.   Because the amount of paperwork necessitated by MBO is substantial, it seems advisable to initially keep the paperwork within tolerable limits. If this is not done, the MBO participants may become discouraged at the very time when their enthusiasm for the program is critical in providing an impetus for its implementation.

5.   The MBO participants should always "know where they stand." One of the important components of an MBO system is an explicit, clearly understood method of regularly reviewing the achievement of objectives, setting new objectives, coaching subordinates, and solving

problems confronted by the subordinate in the achievement of his objectives.

6. Both the superior and the subordinate should be sure that all the subordinate's key areas of responsibility have been analyzed and discussed as a basis for establishing a priority of objectives. Some areas of responsibility are naturally more critical than others. More value or priority should be placed on achievement of objectives in the critical areas of responsibility. Furthermore, the subordinate should ask himself: "If I fulfill all of these areas of responsibility, will my total job be accomplished?" If the subordinate cannot truthfully answer this question positively, he has neglected one or more key areas of responsibility that must be fulfilled in order for him to do his job.

7. In order to attain optimal efficiency in achieving individual employee and organizational goals, objectives at *all* levels of the organization must be mutually compatible and reinforcing. If this is not the case, then the achievement of certain objectives at one level in the organization may impede the achievement of other objectives in the same or different organizational level.

8. For an organization to reap as many benefits from MBO as possible, it is desirable to accentuate the thrust of MBO throughout the organization. One way to accomplish this is to carefully develop a plan to implement MBO through and across all levels of the organization. When MBO is first introduced into an organization, it may be helpful to initiate the system into several departments which seem to have a high probability of successfully implementing MBO. If these departments do succeed, other department heads will be anxious to apply MBO in their department. The enthusiasm generated by success provides the momentum that is vital for implementation of MBO throughout the organization.

9. To facilitate progress within an MBO system, it is desirable to remove as many organizational barriers as possible. Such barriers include excessively restricting organizational policies, procedures, practices, and informal group rules and norms. These barriers frequently may inhibit the employee's desire to experiment and innovate; fulfillment of this desire is important in an MBO system.

10. Managers should be very cautious in their attempts to base salary decisions on the achievement of objectives. It should be noted, furthermore, that financial compensation for the achievement of objectives is only one form of reward. Earned recognition in the form of nonmonetary rewards may have more of a positive motivational effect on the employee than material rewards.

Summary

Much of the recent management literature about MBO has focused upon the potential advantages of using this approach. As more and more organizations have turned to MBO, however, it has become apparent that several critical problems inherent in MBO must be overcome if the potential benefits are to be reaped and installation of the program is to be successful.

In this chapter problems related to top management support, training for implementation of MBO, meaningful employee participation, the paperwork problem, and feedback for self-direction and self-control have been discussed briefly. Other considerations in implementing MBO include restrictive objective setting, conflicting objectives, implementing MBO at lower organizational levels, organizational paraphernalia, and salary decisions. In addition to these potential problem areas the concluding portion of the chapter outlined 10 guidelines to overcoming these problems.

Discussion Questions

1. What are the three basic responsibilities to his subordinate of the manager who installs an MBO program?

2. Briefly describe the nature of the following basic problem areas which are often encountered when an MBO program is established: top management support; training for the implementation of MBO; feedback for self-direction and control; and meaningful employee participation.

3. If you were installing an MBO program, what steps would you take to reduce the paper work problem?

4. Under the heading "Other Considerations in Implementing MBO" the author discusses five key points. Summarize what is involved in each of these.

5. Briefly describe the ten suggestions for installing a management-by-objectives program.

Selected Readings

Peter Drucker, *The Practice of Management,* Harper and Row, 1954.

H. F. Leavitt, and R. A. H. Mueller, "Some Effects of Feedback on Communication," *Human Relations,* 1951.

Douglas McGregor, "An Uneasy Look at Performance Appraisal," *Harvard Business Review,* May–June 1952.

Anthony P. Raia, "Goal Setting and Self Control," *Journal of Management Studies,* February 1965, pp. 34–53.

————, "A Second Look at Management Goals and Controls," *California Management Review,* Summer 1966.

Robert D. Smith, "MBO: A Management Strategy for the Emerging Generation," *ASTME Vectors, 4* (6), November–December 1969, pp. 13–19.

Henry L. Tosi, and Stephen J. Carroll, "Managerial Reaction to Management by Objectives," *Academy of Management Journal,* December 1968.

6. Managerial Problem Analysis and Decision Making

The factor that weighs most heavily in the success or failure of a manager is his decision-making ability. True, there are a multitude of specific skills which he must possess to guarantee results, such as organizational ability and the capacity to plan. All of these, however, require that effective decisions be made.

These comments may sound like an overstatement of fact so it might be well to dwell on them for a moment. The manager's job is usually described either from the standpoint of the functions he performs, that is, planning, organizing, directing, and controlling, or in terms of his specific duties and responsibilities such as cost control, training, and quantity and quality of work. Specific knowledge of basic concepts, principles, and procedures in each of these areas is essential but the knowledge by itself is passive—it must be used, applied, and put in motion. It must be made active in terms of applying it to the everyday operation. This requires decision-making skill within the context that it will be developed.

A second reason for stressing the very strategic role of decision making-skill lies in the changing environment in which today's manager manages. The era of management by objectives, automation, and electronic data processing is here to stay. It calls for today's manager to put his decision making on a rational basis. No matter what functions he performs or activities in which he engages, the end result—the payoff—is based on the decisions he makes. Decisions based solely on intuition and past experience are becoming less effective in dealing with organizational problems because things are changing at too rapid a pace and because yesterday's experience does not always mirror tomorrow's problem.

For these reasons it becomes necessary to look at decision making as a rational process and to attempt to find an approach which, when applied, can sharpen significantly the manager's ability to make effective decisions. The approach which will be developed is designed to foster analytical thinking and an objective approach to problem solving.

Decision Making—Four Essential Phases

On paper the decision-making process can be fundamentally and simply stated. The problem lies in the actual implementation. It is too often either forgotten completely or poorly executed. The four essential phases are:

1. Analysis of the problem.
2. Developing alternative solutions.
3. Analyzing alternatives.
4. Implementing the course of action to be followed.

The purpose of this chapter is to examine each of these phases to effective decision making in considerable detail. The full ramifications of each step will be explored by discussing the basic principles and concepts and developing a systematic approach.

Problem Analysis—A Systematic Approach

If the doctor diagnoses appendicitis and the problem is ulceration, the treatment will inevitably fail. So it is in organizations. If the manager fails to identify correctly and completely the real problem, one of two things happens to the decision he makes: the solution fails completely, or it puts out the fire only temporarily.

Complete problem analysis can be broken down into five basic steps which, if followed, provide the manager with a practical and systematic approach to problem solving. This discussion identifies and explores the ramifications of each of the five steps. Two cautions are in order at the outset, however. First, although discussed separately, the steps are a long way from being independent of one another. There is considerable overlap among them in terms of one being an extension and refinement of the preceding one. Second, the approach to problem analysis which is described is not intended to be, nor should it be allowed to become a straitjacket. It serves as a tool or an analytical framework which, when used, in time develops in the decision maker a systematic approach. In some situations which arise the answers to the five steps are so clear-cut and straightforward that little conscious attention need be given to the analysis process. In others it may be both desirable and necessary to return in a very formal sense to the procedure outlined. In any case, the manager who wishes to improve his decision-making skill will find it helpful to consciously consider and write out all the steps in the early stages of training. Once the pattern or approach is firmly established and becomes more or less automatic, adjustments can be made.

Statement of What Is Wrong. The first step in problem analysis involves stating specifically what is wrong, the situation where improvement is needed, or the area where results might be better. Often it is a situation which is quite obvious. For example, machine number 256 may be producing defective parts, Jim Smith may have an excessive number of absences, or department 40E is not meeting its budget. Such incidents come to the attention of the manager rather automatically. These are basic deviations from well-defined standards which usually receive prime consideration. For this reason, they present little difficulty in this step of problem analysis.

It should be noted that many managers never get beyond these basic deviations in their decision-making activity. In other words, they make decisions but they do not solve problems. They put out fires but only temporarily. Viewed another way, the manager who is continually concentrating on *just* basic deviations is dealing with *effect* rather than *causal* problems. The same or similar types of crisis situations will always reappear. It is not until he identifies the causal or real problem that action can be taken which will permanently eliminate the appearance of these basic deviations.

The real challenge comes in the more nebulous situations. The manager just feels that results could be better or that something might be wrong. For example, the output of machine 256 is adequate but not as high as it could be, the employees in a given department are meeting the standards but there seems to be a degree of negativism present, department 40E seems to be always "under the gun" in keeping up with its schedule, or a given employee is doing his job but not performing to his full capability. Unlike the earlier examples, these situations are not fires, but only sparks. They are *symptoms* of larger problems. Too often they are overlooked completely or perhaps just ignored until they become basic deviations. To identify them as situations that need improvement requires that the manager have three things. First, he must have a full and exact awareness of the specific standards of performance and capabilities for all equipment and personnel under him. High productivity of an operation requires maximum performance from all the various elements. Whether or not maximum performance is being achieved requires a standard against which to measure actual results. Second, the manager must have a keen insight into the actual level of performance in his department in relation to specific standards. He must know what is going on and then pinpoint the deviations as situations needing improvement before they develop into crises. When quantitative things are concerned this is not too great a problem. Beyond these, however, there must be a sixth sense. From the standpoint of quantity production, a situation of generally poor morale among workers may not show up. Yet, if not sensed by the manager, it could become the basis for serious trouble.

Finally, the manager must be "maximum results oriented." He must be able to look beyond the obvious difficulties which demand immediate attention to those deeper and more hidden things which can later lead to primary difficulties.

Also of importance are those instances where a number of things (on the surface appearing to be unrelated) seem to be wrong. In short, there are several phases of the operation which do not seem right. Schedules are not being met, raw materials or component parts are not available when needed, supervisors constantly have to adjust to meet emergencies, people are overworked, and the job is generally one of constant pressures. All of these are situations needing improvement but are not problems in themselves. Rather, they are situations reflecting a much more complex difficulty, for example, the absence of an effective system of work planning and control. As long as effort continues to center on the individual circumstances and difficulties as they arise on a day-to-day basis no permanent relief will be found. It is not until someone reviews the total operation, and identifies the *real problem* (lack of an effective planning and control program) that some permanent solution can be found. The distinction between situations needing improvement and real problems will become more obvious after step three is studied.

Getting the Facts. The second essential step in problem analysis is getting the facts. This step is the key to making the transition from the first step to the highly important third step. Its importance can perhaps best be illustrated by means of a story which was told in a management training session.

Shortly after a rather bitter and hard-fought organizing campaign (which the union won), one of the first-line supervisors came across a worker sitting on a box cracking hickory nuts with a micrometer. When questioned by the supervisor as to what he was doing, the worker replied "eating hickory nuts," whereupon the supervisor immediately discharged him for loafing on the job, insubordination, and destruction of valuable equipment. He received support from management and the case went to arbitration. In the arbitration hearing the following facts were brought out by the union attorney. First, the worker was on his own time, not company time. His shift did not start for 20 minutes after the incident occurred and he had not yet punched in. Second the micrometer was one which the tool crib was discarding and he had asked the supervisor in charge if he might take it home for his children to play with. Finally, the hickory nuts were his own.

A little exaggerated? Perhaps, but too often decisions are made and action is taken before getting all the facts. When this happens, rather than a proper solution being determined, two things usually result. The real problem is not correctly identified and the decision which is reached falls short of accomplishing objectives.

In a given situation some of the facts which are needed to make a decision are both obvious and easy to obtain while others may be neither of these. Of particular importance in fact gathering is a questioning attitude. What exactly are the complete facts surrounding the situation outlined in step one? It is not enough to say that machine number 256 is producing defective parts, or that department 40E is not meeting its budget. These statements must now be sharpened considerably. What specifically is defective about the parts? Is it that the holes are being drilled off center or that they are not being reamed properly? In what account classification is the major trouble with the budget located? When is the particular situation occurring? Do the budget discrepancies occur all the time or just during rush periods or when certain types of work are being performed? Are the parts bad regardless of machine speed or just when it is stepped up beyond a certain point? Where is it happening? Are the defective parts coming off all shifts or just one particular shift? Is the same operator on the machine all the time? Are other departments within the plant or the same department in other plants experiencing difficulty with the same phase of the budget?

This step attempts to distinguish or identify all the *key factors* surrounding the situation which was generally described in step one. The fact-gathering process should enable the manager to crystallize his statement of the situation considerably. He should now be able to say most of the discrepancy in department 40E's budget can be accounted for because of excessive downtime, that this account is particularly high about every other day, and there is at least one other department in the plant doing similar work with a similar situation. As to the defective parts, the manager might say that the holes are being drilled off center, they are appearing on the second shift only, the number of those drilled off center is about the same as those done correctly, a new operator is on second shift, and the machine speed is faster.

As stated earlier, this fact-gathering process appears, on the surface, to be a rather simple and somewhat academic project. If effective decisions are to be made, however, the manager must take a completely analytical and rigorous approach to this step. He must go beyond the obvious and immediately available facts in an effort to uncover all pertinent information which may help explain and clarify the situation. This approach will help insure that a proper decision is made.

Investigation of Possible Causes and Identification of the Real Problem.   The third step to effective problem analysis is basically inseparable from the first two. It involves investigation of possible causes and identification of the real problem. The particular event or occurrence which arouses the manager's attention initially is often a factor, but not the real problem. The key to the trouble usually has a deeper root. As long as only the apparent difficulty is dealt with, only temporary relief will be experienced. The real problem (not being solved) will cause the same symptom(s) to reoccur later or perhaps it will be manifested in a completely different symptom.

For example, there may be an unusual number of complaints or grievances coming out of a department. Each one is dealt with and solved on the basis of the complaint itself. Not until much time has elapsed and many adjustments have been made is it discovered that the real problem all along was the attitude and approach of the supervisor toward his men. Very often a whole series of symptoms which on the surface may seem unrelated have as a common root the same basic problem. As long as each symptom is treated independently or as a problem in itself, the total situation will not improve.

The process of investigating possible causes must be approached with caution. Whenever a situation needs correcting there is usually pressure for quick action. Because of this pressure the tendency to jump to conclusions and to take hasty action is always present. Often the first plausible piece of evidence available is labeled as the cause, and action is taken. Very often the result is frustration and failure.

Effective decision making also requires in-depth thinking and insight. The manager must consciously ask himself what are all the possible things that could have caused the situation to arise, and then, in the light of the facts available, determine which actually apply. Sometimes the cause of a particular situation will be suggested by the facts as they have been uncovered and subsequent "testing" will, in fact, verify this. Other times, however, the facts may suggest a cause which does not get at the real problem, or a possible cause which the decision maker develops may be refuted by the facts. The former case very often arises when there are a number of seemingly unrelated situations all of which stem from a common deficiency. The illustration cited earlier of the department with excessive grievances is a good example of this. The facts surrounding each grievance will suggest a cause for that particular grievance, but not until the decision maker opens his mind to the supervisor as being the possible cause is the real problem uncovered. In the example of machine number 256 cited earlier, the facts may indicate that the second shift is producing the bulk of the defective parts and that a new operator is running the machine. It may develop, however, that the real problem is not the operator but the fact that the machine speed has been turned up on the second shift and at that speed it will not hold tolerances. In the budget example the initial implication may be that the supervisor is not doing a good job of controlling excessive downtime of his men or that the men are not performing up to standard. The real problem however, may lie in the fact that the material being worked is defective and causes machine jams. Some key questions which will help in this step include the following.

1. Has a procedure or policy been violated?
2. Is there a lack of procedure?
3. Have changes been introduced?
4. What is different now compared to before the situation arose?
5. Is there something not being done which should be done?

Only after the cause has been specifically and precisely pinpointed can the real problem be identified. In simple cases this statement of the real problem may be nothing more than restatement of an already identified cause. The manager with insight will always look beyond this point. He will ask himself, "If I solve this problem, am I completely putting out the fire or might there be some sparks left to start another? Is there any relationship among the various situations with which I have to deal which might point to a problem that is larger in scope than that suggested by any specific incident?"

Requirements of a Satisfactory Solution Stated as Objectives. The fourth step in the problem analysis phase of decision making is the requirements of a satisfactory solution stated as objectives. The rationale behind this step has three dimensions. First, it insures that the remainder of the process has direction. The end purpose of any decision should be to accomplish certain results. It is axiomatic that if the manager does not first specify what results he is after, any decision that is made is likely to be somewhat haphazard.

Second, this step serves as a focal point for getting additional facts. Setting forth the results desired will suggest those areas where additional fact gathering is needed. Very often, of course, the requirements of a satisfactory solution can and will be derived from the statements of situations needing improvement; that is, the decision eventually made should remove these situations as areas of difficulty. Therefore, the relationship is a derivative one.

Finally, this step insures objectivity in the development and analysis of alternatives.

Restrictions or Limits on a Solution.   Finally, problem analysis requires that any restrictions or limits to what otherwise might be an acceptable solution be noted. Examples of some typical restrictions include cost, personnel, and facts which cannot be changed. It does little good to extensively probe and mentally debate solutions which, although good, cannot be implemented. This is not meant to imply that new ideas and new approaches for doing things should be stifled and cut short without first carefully weighing and analyzing them. If critical limitations are set forth initially, however, the decision-making process can be simplified and speeded.

The approach to problem analysis described previously must be systematized (at least at the initial stages of use) if it is to be translated into actual use by the individual manager. To aid in developing decision-making skill the worksheet depicted in Exhibit I can be valuable. It is a visual reproduction of the key steps discussed.

Developing Alternative Solutions

Once a problem has been clearly defined, the decision maker develops and analyzes the desirability of various alternative courses of action. The old saying that "there is more than one way to skin a cat" most certainly applies to solving business problems. There are usually several different approaches which can be taken to overcome a given difficulty, with each having its peculiar set of advantages and disadvantages.

It would appear (on the surface, at least) that this step in the decision-making process is a relatively simple one compared to that of problem identification. In actual practice this is often true, mainly because managers are expected to be good decision makers already. When faced with a problem they pride themselves in having a ready answer. After all, this is, to a large extent, what they are being paid for. Thus, developing and analyzing alternatives may appear to be a somewhat semiautomatic process because in fact and in practice, managers often do not really develop or analyze alternatives; therein lies the difficulty. Just as surely as a weak link can cause a break in the chain, a lax approach to this phase of the decision-making process can result in less than fully effective decisions.

The Importance of Alternatives. A number of years ago there was a television program about a company which was trying to decide which of a group of four engineers should be hired. To aid them in the selection process they presented the group with an actual problem being experienced on the assembly line and gave them two days to work out a solution. The intent was to award the job to the engineer who came up with the best solution. The problem involved a bottleneck which was created by the need to manipulate a very bulky and heavy part as it came down the line in order to perform all necessary operations. All the engineers except one went to their drafting boards and began to devise various types of handling equipment which might be installed. By the end of the first day three of the candidates had made fairly extensive preliminary sketches of their ideas. The fourth had nothing to

Exhibit I Problem Analysis Worksheet

Specifically what is wrong, situation needing improvement or area where results might be better (symptoms)	Specific facts surrounding the situation	Possible causes stated and evaluated	The real problem	Requirements of a satisfactory solution stated as objectives	Restrictions or limits on a possible solution
	What? Where? When?				

show for his efforts. When the second day had elapsed each of the three was putting the finishing touches on his plan while the fourth still had nothing. On the third day each man was to make a presentation to an executive committee. The first three were indeed impressive. They included elaborate drawings and cost estimates. When the fourth man entered the room to make his presentation it was obvious that he was not prepared. Immediately the man responsible for his being considered in the first place began to berate him for such lack of interest and initiative. When the young engineer finally had a chance to speak he explained that he had spent considerable time watching the operation being performed in the plant; he suggested that the operation could be speeded up significantly and the bottleneck relieved by placing left-handed men on one side of the line and right-handed ones on the other. This would eliminate the need to be continually turning and positioning the part. A quick inspection at the assembly line quickly illustrated the validity of his approach.

Although this seems somewhat unrealistic and exaggerated, it illustrates a point. The quality of the eventual decision depends to a large extent on whether or not there are some good alternatives from which to choose. A lack of alternatives has important ramifications as far as the decision maker is concerned. If he fails to develop and analyze various alternatives he is necessarily restricting the course of action. He is, in a sense, saying that there is one and only one way to solve this problem. For most problems this simply is not true. We have the option of following a number of paths to reach a given objective. Some will be shorter and more economical, but in the long run, less effective than others. Some may be more effective but also less economical and longer. Only if a number of alternatives are considered can there be assurance that the decision eventually made will be a good one.

Developing Alternative Solutions to Problems. When faced with the need to develop alternative solutions to problems the manager has two directions in which to turn: his own past experience and those experiences and practices of other managers. Let us consider each of these in turn.

The most logical and undoubtedly the most widely used approach to solving problems is to draw on one's own past experience. This method is adequate in the majority of cases. Faced with a given situation the manager compares it with similar occurrences which he may have experienced and successfully solved at an earlier time. Noting the circumstances which are peculiar to the present case he can then follow a course of action similar to the previous one, but with the necessary adjustments made. Of course, the more depth in experience which he has had the better off he is in two respects. First, he can rely on his experience to solve a bigger variety of problems, and second, his experience will suggest more possible alternatives, both those likely to work and those not so likely to work.

Today's world is a world of change, however. The modern-day manager is continually called upon to solve problems and face challenges which go beyond what has been experienced in the past. The decisions which solved yesterday's problems are not always adequate for those of today. New and fresh approaches are needed. For these reasons it often becomes both desirable and necessary for the decision maker to look beyond his own experience when developing alternatives and see how others are handling problems and what ideas they might have. Supplementing our own experiences in this way can contribute significantly to both the number and quality of alternatives developed.

Past experience, whether it be the manager's own or that of others, can never be fully sufficient in developing alternatives to solve problems. It serves its most useful purpose when used as a guideline. Because of the dynamic nature of problems a certain degree of creativity is needed. Using both past experience and knowledge the modern-day decision maker must be able to come up with new ideas and new approaches to problem solving. Thus, a second procedure that must be guarded against is that of always taking the "easy road." There is a real need in organizations today for the thinker, or explorer, the man who can bring things together and come up with something fresh.

Analyzing Alternative Solutions

The analysis of alternative solutions involves setting forth the advantages and disadvantages of each possible course of action and then weighing each course as to how effectively it will accomplish the objectives or requirements of a satisfactory solution which were stated in the problem analysis phase. The analysis of advantages and disadvantages may range all the way from being relatively simple and straightforward to being a very complex and detailed procedure. The analysis may necessitate gathering and interpretation of extensive cost data and the use of various statistical techniques, or, this type of factual data may not have to be used. The more comprehensive the problem the more difficult the analysis becomes.

Setting Forth Advantages and Disadvantages. In considering the advantages and disadvantages that apply to each alternative, the decision maker will do well if he goes back and reviews thoroughly each step in the problem analysis phase. Specific attention should be given to the following questions:

1. Will the alternative in question eliminate reoccurrence of the situation(s) which was originally identified as needing improvement?

2. Will the alternative meet the requirements of a satisfactory solution stated as objectives?

3. Does the alternative meet any restrictions or limits that have been set forth?

4. What other specific benefits apply to the alternative?

Perhaps the most difficult step in analyzing alternatives is the identification of the disadvantages or consequences of each alternative. This is particularly true in cases where either consciously or unconsciously a favorable "mental set" toward a particular course of action has already been formed.

The consideration of disadvantages is extremely important. Many otherwise good decisions fail in the implementation stage simply because potential difficulties and shortcomings have not been spotted and provisions have not been made for dealing with them in advance. Consideration of disadvantages is a two-step process. First, just as each alternative has explicit advantages, it will usually have disadvantages, and these must be identified and precisely pinpointed. To the extent that this is done the decision maker will not find himself expecting results that do not appear, nor will he be caught short because the decision had an impact in an area he did not anticipate.

Having considered the direct consequences of a given course of action, the decision maker must also give some thought to areas where difficulties may be encountered in implementing the decision and the ease with which these might be overcome. Both potential technical and human problem areas should be considered. This additional step serves a very important purpose. It insures that an otherwise good alternative will not be rejected on the basis of a disadvantage which can be easily overcome. It also provides a stepping-off point for making plans to implement or put the decision into effect.

A Systematic Approach to the Analysis of Alternatives. Having arrived at this point, it becomes necessary to summarize everything that

Exhibit II Analysis of Alternatives

Results Expected or Objectives in Order of Priority	Restrictions on Acceptable Solutions
1.	1.
2.	2.
3.	3.

Alternative	Disadvantages		Advantages		Areas of Difficulty in Implementing Decision; Things to Consider in Implementing Decision	Specific Action Needed to Remove
	very important	mod. important	very important	mod. important		
I	a.		a.		a.	
	b.		b.		b.	
II	a.		a.		a.	
	b.		b.		b.	
III	a.		a.		a.	
	b.		b.		b.	

has been done so far. Exhibit II calls first for listing the objectives of the decision in priority of order. This is done at this time for several reasons. By now the decision maker is undoubtedly much more familiar with the problem and all of its ramifications than he was originally. He should have a rather thorough understanding of just exactly what needs to be accomplished and which considerations must receive the most weight. Also, it is seldom possible to find a course of action which will accomplish all objectives with the same degree of effectiveness. In the earlier analysis some very necessary objectives may not have been thought of at all, while one which was given heavy consideration may now appear to be secondary. It is necessary to be quite positive at this point that any decision that is made will, at a minimum, enable us to achieve the more important goals that were set forth. The top priority objectives will, of course, be those which most closely relate to the real problem and the symptoms which need to be corrected. Second, Exhibit II calls for a restating and changing, if necessary, of any restrictions on an otherwise acceptable solution. Column 1 provides a space for briefly stating the alternative. In column 2 the disadvantages of that alternative are listed and rated as to whether they are very important or just moderately important. This rating is a judgment on the part of the individual manager, but it should be made with consideration to the priority of objectives. Column 3 is a repeat of column 2, but it lists advantages. In columns 4 and 5, areas where possible difficulties may arise in implementing the decision and the action needed to remove them are considered, respectively.

Exhibit III is an extension of Exhibit II but provides for final evaluation of each alternative. Each alternative is evaluated in terms of whether or not it accomplishes each of the objectives fully, partially, or is unacceptable. By comparing where the checkmarks fall in relation to priority of objectives the manager can get a good visual picture of what appears to be the best choice. Finally, a check is made to determine whether or not the alternative violates any restrictions.

Implementing a Decision—A Plan for Action

To make a good decision is one thing but to transform that decision into a plan of action or an effective approach to solving a problem is quite another. Managers who have experienced the frustration of seeing an otherwise sound decision fail or falter in the implementation stage should be keenly aware of the importance and significance of this, the

Exhibit III Analysis of Alternatives

	Objective									Restriction Violated
	Number One			Number Two			Number Three			
	Fully Acceptable	Partially Accepted	Inadequate	Fully Acceptable	Partially Accepted	Inadequate	Fully Acceptable	Partially Accepted	Inadequate	
1. Alternative										
a.										
b.										
2. Alternative										
a.										
b.										
3. Alternative										
a.										
b.										

final phase in the decision-making process. Every decision requires a well-conceived plan for implementing it.

In actual practice the various steps involved in effective implementation are (or should be) carried out as part of or in conjunction with the other phases of decision making discussed previously. The three essential steps involved in effective implementation are:

1. A questioning attitude concerning every detail of the decision and the development of necessary procedures.

2. A plan for communicating the decision to those involved and affected by it.

3. Participation.

The first of these three steps deals with the technical aspects of decision implementation, while the last two concern themselves with what might be termed the human aspects.

A Plan of Action for Effective Decision Implementation. Up to this point the problem or area(s) where improvement is needed have been concisely presented, the objectives or goals to be reached have been explicitly set forth, and a proposed course of action has been decided. The procedures which are now developed for making the decision operative form the core of a plan for action and are indeed as strategic as the decision itself. They specify in precise detail the steps or actions which must be performed, the sequence in which these actions must be carried out, the specific duties and responsibilities of the various individuals involved, and provisions for follow-up and control. The decision maker must consider and list what must be done, when or in what order must these things be accomplished, who should do them, how they can be most effectively completed, and why they are necessary. The thoroughness of this questioning process can be assured to the extent that the decision maker also asks himself what difficulties may be encountered, or, what could go wrong. Provision should, of course, be made for handling these difficulties when and if they do appear. This process of attempting to pinpoint potential problems as they relate to implementing a decision before they appear can save considerable trouble at a later time.

Communicating a Decision. In the last analysis it is the human being who determines whether or not a decision is effectively implemented; to neglect this human element is tantamount to inviting complete failure or, at the least, considerable difficulty in implementing a decision. Every decision and every plan for action must have a plan for communicating it to those directly involved and also those indirectly affected. The literature is replete with examples of organizations and managers who have found this out the hard way. On paper the decision is a sound one and from the technical standpoint no stone has been left unturned. Yet something goes wrong and frustration begins to set in.

To insure effective implementation the decision maker must ask himself several questions.

What Should Be Communicated?   Much of the difficulty in obtaining cooperation in implementing decisions stems from a lack of understanding on the part of individuals as to how the decision will affect them. With a little effort most of the vital questions which employees have can be answered before they are asked. What is the reason for the action called for by the decision? Whom will it affect and how? What are the benefits that are expected to result from the standpoint of the individual, the department, and the company? What adjustments will be required in terms of how the work will be done? What specifically is each individual's role in implementing the decision? What results are expected from him? When does the action called for by the decision go into effect? Communicating answers to these questions can head off many of the difficulties that otherwise might be encountered.

When Should It Be Communicated?   Communication is most effective when it precedes action and events. When approached in this manner it can help to accomplish a very important function. It insures that events conform to plans; that the things which are supposed to happen actually do happen in the way they should happen and when they should happen. Advance communication also helps insure that the manager is not always fighting fires or correcting things that went wrong.

To Whom And How Should We Communicate?   Anyone who is directly involved in the implementation of a decision or who is indirectly affected by that decision should receive communication concerning it. Only by doing this can there be a reasonable degree of assurance that the decision will be accepted and have the necessary support.

How to communicate depends on the type and nature of information to be given. The more comprehensive it is, the more need there is for using multiple methods such as oral, written, individual communications, and meetings.

Participation. There are two very basic and sound reasons for using participation in decision making. First, and from a technical standpoint, the manager who employs participation is utilizing the potential of his subordinates to a fuller extent. He is supplementing his own ideas and experience with those of other people and thereby guaranteeing maximum exploration, investigation, and analysis.

A second reason for using participation in all phases of the decision-making process is that it fosters commitment on the part of the people who must implement the decision. As suggested earlier, even though a decision and a corresponding plan for action are in themselves sound, they can fail to achieve the desired result if they do not have the active support of everyone involved. It is human nature for people to want to have a voice in those things which affect them and when given that opportunity they are more likely not only to accept the decision but also to work actively and positively toward the desired objectives.

The degree and the type of participation that are appropriate depend on any number of considerations. These include the nature of the problem, past managerial practice, the experience of subordinates, the manager's own skill and attitudes, and the time available. In some situations actual participation may be negligible while in others it will be maximum. Douglas McGregor outlines in five points the full range of possibilities in terms of the degree of participation.[1]

1. "Let us suppose that a manager has made a decision which will affect his subordinates. The circumstances are such that he feels that he cannot permit them to share in making this decision, but he is concerned to have them accept it with the best grace possible. He might hold a discussion in which he would inform them of the decision and reasons for it, and give them an opportunity to raise questions about it. His purpose would be to test the decision to see if it is acceptable. If he finds that it is strongly resented, he may be tempted to modify it rather than to risk the possibilities that it may be sabotaged. If it is not strongly resisted, his subordinates have at least had an opportunity to understand why he has made the decision and to clarify any aspects of it which are obscure. Such a discussion as this—when held under circumstances that permit genuine interaction—involves a limited degree of participation.

2. "A slightly different situation might arise when a superior, having made a decision, would discuss with his subordinates the best

[1]From *The Human Side of Enterprise* by Douglas McGregor. Copyright 1960, McGraw-Hill Book Company. Used by permission of McGraw-Hill Book Company.

way of implementing it. Often the implementation of a decision can occur in various ways, and it may make relatively little difference to the superior which of these alternatives is chosen, so long as the decision is carried out. The subordinates can have a voice in this matter which under some circumstances can be quite important to them. Such a situation involves somewhat more participation.

3. "A third example involving still more participation would be the situation in which the superior discussed a pending decision with his subordinates before making it final. Under this condition he would be ready to consider modifying his proposed decision or substituting another for it, depending upon the considerations which arose in discussion. The decision would still be his to make, but he would make it in the light of the discussion.

4. "A still greater degree of participation would be involved if the superior were to present to his subordinates a problem facing him with the request that they help him find the best solution to it. He would not necessarily commit himself in advance to accepting any solution agreeable to them, but the understanding would be that if they could find a solution which he felt to be workable he would accept it.

5. "Finally, there are some situations in which it is a matter of relative indifference to the superior which of several alternative decisions are made. These may be ones in which management has only a small stake and subordinates have a large one. Under these conditions the superior might say to his subordinates, "I will accept any decision which is agreeable to you."

Regardless of which of these approaches is employed the manager will do well to first clearly establish in his own mind exactly what degree he plans to use and why, and also make sure that his subordinates understand the extent to which they are to influence the decision.

Barriers to Effective Decision Making.   Before leaving the matter of decision making it would seem desirable to point out some of the barriers to an effective approach. First, there is the tendency to become preoccupied with just the immediate crisis. Stated another way and in terms of our earlier discussion, managers are too often trying to deal with only a symptom of some much larger and more complex problem. Countless hours are spent each day in meeting emergency situations and taking action to counteract these emergencies. The result is only temporary relief. Not until someone in the organization begins to look at the total picture with the objective of precisely pinpointing the *real* problems does anything in terms of long progress begin to take place.

Another important barrier can be one person in a group who will not allow investigation. He has a problem to solve *now* not later. He has a solution which is "A" perfect. He doesn't need any more facts. It is a clear-cut situation! He is a good decision maker already.

Also, there is the time barrier. Thorough, analytical thinking takes time and, as a sidelight, it is also hard work. Ironically, however, if more time were spent making quality decisions it is possible that less time would be spent fighting the crises which arise every day.

Finally, there is the attitude that the area in question is someone else's responsibility even though it affects the manager's own ability to get results, makes his job hectic, and results in the job running him instead of him running the job. True, the corrective action needed may lie in someone else's territory but analysis of difficulties and fact gathering should not be passed off.

Summary

Managerial problem analysis and decision making can be divided into four phases: problem analysis, developing alternatives, analyzing alternatives, and decision implementation. A systematic approach to the problem analysis phase has five distinct steps associated with it. The first step involves an initial statement of what is wrong, the situation that needs improvement, or the area where results might be better. Once this initial statement has been presented the decision maker must gather the facts, investigate possible causes and identify the real problem, set forth the requirements of a satisfactory solution, and specify any restrictions or limits on a solution.

In the second phase of decision (developing alternatives) the manager has three primary directions in which he can turn. He can rely on his own past experience, utilize the experience of others, and use creativity. Although past experience is valuable and also the most logical direction in which to turn in developing alternative solutions to problems, it should be noted that in today's changing world it is usually not adequate by itself. Ideally the decision maker will use a combination of all three approaches to developing alternatives.

Analyzing alternatives involves setting forth both the advantages and disadvantages of each alternative as they relate to accomplishing the objectives of the decision as outlined in phase one. Setting forth the potential disadvantages is particularly important since they may point out problems that could occur in the implementation phase. Many times provision can be made beforehand for overcoming these problems if and when they do appear.

The final phase of decision making, decision implementation, involves developing a plan of action, communicating the decision, and participation. In developing a plan of action the questions of what must be done, in what sequence must it be done, who should do them, and how can they be most effectively accomplished must be answered. The decision must also be communicated to everyone who is directly or indirectly affected by it. This communication along with giving people the opportunity to participate in various phases or steps in the total decision-making process is what determines the degree to which the people who must implement the decision will be committed to having it carried out successfully.

Key Concepts

Basic Deviations.   Basic deviations are those things which are obviously wrong with the operation. They are analogous to what might be termed "glaring mistakes." They are the immediate crises which come to the attention of the manager automatically and usually receive his prime consideration.

Symptoms.   Symptoms refer to events or things which are present in an operation but have not yet developed to the point of emerging as basic deviations. They are sparks as opposed to fires which if overlooked or ignored will become basic deviations.

Effect Problems.   When a manager deals with effect problems he is taking action which will give only temporary relief. It is likely that the same or similar occurrences will reappear.

Causal Problems.   Dealing with the causal problem gets to the "root" of the trouble. It prevents the occurrence from reappearing at a later date.

Discussion Questions

1. Discuss the three essential phases of the decision-making process in terms of what each involves and the key considerations.

2. What are the key questions a manager should ask when he attempts to identify the *real* problem in a situation?

3. When considering the advantages and disadvantages which apply to alternatives, what are the three questions a manager should ask in evaluating these alternatives?

4. What are the three steps involved in the effective implementation of a decision?

5. What is the importance of communication and participation in the decision-making process?

6. What are the barriers to effective decision making?

Selected Readings

Stephen H. Archer, "The Structure of Management Decision Theory," *Academy of Management Journal, 7* (14), December 1964, pp. 269–287.

Chris Argyris, "Interpersonal Barriers to Decision Making," *Harvard Business Review, 44* (2), March–April 1966, pp. 84–97.

Chester I. Barnard, "The Environment of Decision," *The Functions of the Executive,* Harvard University Press, Massachusetts, 1938, pp. 89–198, 201–205.

Peter F. Drucker, "The Effective Decision," *Harvard Business Review,* January–February 1967, pp. 92–98.

Robert C. Ferber, "The Role of the Subconscious in Executive Decision Making," *Management Science, XIII* (8), April 1967, pp. 519–526.

Charles H. Kepner, and Benjamin B. Tregoe, *The Rational Manager: A Systematic Approach to Problem Solving and Decision Making,* McGraw-Hill, New York, 1965.

G. L. S. Shackle, "Business Men on Business Decision," *The Nature of Economic Thought: Selected Papers,* Cambridge, England, Cambridge University, 1966, pp. 45–159.

Herbert A. Simon, *Administrative Behavior,* The Free Press, New York, Collier-MacMillan Limited, London, 1957.

Charles S. Whiting, "Operational Techniques of Creative Thinking," *Advanced Management,* October 1955, pp. 24–30.
pp. 150–164.

Charles Z. Wilson, and Marcus Alexis, "Basic Frameworks for Decisions," *Journal of the Academy of Management,* August 1962,

7. Quantitative Tools for Decision Making

Today's manager is making greater use of quantitative methods in solving many problems which were previously solved by intuition or trial and error, if they were solved at all. Quantitative tools rely quite heavily on mathematics and model building methods. When applied to real-world problems these techniques can become rather sophisticated. The application of electronic data processing (EDP) via the use of large-scale or even small computers, however, has served to lessen the often cumbersome task of performing the myriad of calculations associated with many of today's problem-solving techniques.

The purpose of this chapter is not to show the sophisticated and complex aspects of quantitative techniques. Indeed, few managers are qualified enough in mathematics and model building to effectively perform these techniques. Instead, they rely on experts to handle the details so that they can be free to perform their job . . . MANAGING. However, in order to effectively manage and communicate with the quantitative-oriented staff specialist, the manager must have at least a *basic* understanding of these techniques and must be aware of their advantages as well as their limitations.

In this chapter, then, a brief description will be given of some commonly used quantitative tools which include models, PERT and CPM, and queuing theory. The reader will also be exposed to selected quantitative techniques used to solve certain types of specialized problems. he techniques to be discussed include correlation analysis, sum of squares, break-even analysis, and linear programming. A basic understanding of algebra is all that is necessary to understand the techniques presented here. The main point is for the reader to gain a basic understanding of the nature of these techniques and be aware of their application.

Models

The word model is often used in conjunction with quantitative techniques. In fact, almost all quantitative techniques can be classified as models. The actual definition of a model can be simply stated as being anything which in some way represents something else. Thus, a complex series of mathematical formulas representing the growth of the United States economy can be classified as a model. The model consists of mathematical equations. A simple example of a mathematical expression which could be classified as a model is given in Exhibit I.

Exhibit I   Simple Mathematical Model

It takes two units of raw material A and five units of raw material B to manufacture the final product C. The cost of A is $3.00 per unit, and the cost of B is $8.00 per unit. With the above information, a general cost model can be established to illustrate the relationship between A, B, and C, such that:

$$2A + 5B = C$$

The cost of producing C can be easily determined by substituting the cost figures of A and B into the model. Thus, the cost of producing C becomes $(2)(3) + (5)(8) = 46. The above model is then established as a cost-predicting model for the production of C. If the cost of either A or B changes, or if the amounts of A or B required to produce the product C change, then the effect on the cost of C can be determined by substituting the changed variables into the model and performing the necessary calculations.

All the quantitative tools presented in this chapter are models and are of the same type as prepared above in that these models can predict an occurrence in the real world. The usefulness of models lies in their relatively low cost (as opposed to actually having to manipulate real-world occurrences), and their convenience. It should be noted, however, that models only represent something and they can vary considerably in the degree to which they can actually represent real-world occurrences. Although a given model may not be entirely accurate, it still may have widespread use because its predictive capabilities are often greater than alternative methods such as intuition, trial and error, or guesswork.

PERT and CPM

PERT (program evaluation and review technique) and CPM (critical path method) are two closely related techniques which are often used in management planning models. CPM was developed in 1957 by Morgan Walker of Dupont and James Kelly of Remington Rand. PERT was developed in connection with the Polaris weapons system.

Although each of these techniques has its unique terminology, they conceptually differ only in that CPM attempts to systematically determine the expected times of completion of the total project and subprojects (tasks) which comprise the total project, whereas PERT goes further and attempts to estimate the time variances associated with these expected times of completion. Therefore, PERT deals more directly with the problem of uncertainty with respect to time than does CPM.

Exhibit II illustrates how a PERT chart is drawn to represent the tasks that must be completed before the total project (represented by ①) can be completed. The critical path is illustrated by the heavy line that runs through the sequence of tasks that has the longest expected time of completion. In Exhibit II, the unique terminology of CPM is not used, but is adapted to show how closely CPM relates to PERT.

The total expected time to complete a given task is determined by examining all the Te task alternatives prior to that task and selecting the *largest* total leading to that task. For example, task ③ cannot begin until tasks ④ and ⑤ have been finished. No matter how early task ④ is completed, the project must still wait until task ⑤ is completed before task ③ can begin. According to expected times, it will take *longer* to complete task ⑤ than task ④. Thus task ⑤ is selected as the *critical*

Exhibit II   Pert and CPM Flow Diagram for a Four-Task Project

O = Task number which must be completed before the next task can begin

Te = Earliest expected time to complete the task (days, hours, weeks, etc.)

TE = Total expected time to complete a given task

V = Variance in time associated with the completion of task

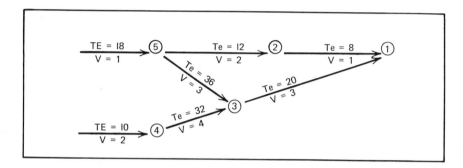

task leading to task ③, and the total expected time to complete task ③ is 54 because 18 + 36 is larger than 10 + 32. This method is continued until the total project ① has been reached. The total expected time to complete the project is 74 (18 + 36 + 20), and the time variance associated with the completion of the project is 7 (1 + 3 + 3). The time variance in this example means that the project could be completed seven days earlier (74 − 7 = 67) or seven days later (74 + 7 = 81) than the total expected time. The critical path method, however, is concerned only with the total expected time to complete the project and not the time variances associated with the project. Thus, PERT is broader in scope than CPM.

Queuing Theory

Queuing theory is used in those situations in which something (people, cars, ships, airplanes, for example) must wait in line before receiving service. It is especially applicable to those situations where the units which are to be provided service arrive in a random fashion, and the time required for service follows some type of predictable manner. If the costs associated with the time lost waiting in line and costs involved in providing service can be accurately identified, then queuing theory becomes a most useful model in determining the optimum number of service facilities which should be made available to accommodate the queue (waiting line). Queuing theory then, attempts to establish a balance between costs incurred through waiting in line and costs involved in providing additional service facilities to reduce the waiting time. Some real life situations which are applicable to queuing theory are given below.

1. Mechanics paid on an hourly basis must wait in line before receiving tools from a tool crib. They must be paid whether they are working or waiting in line. Additional service facilities also cost money, but can reduce the mechanics' waiting time. Queuing theory is used to determine an optimum balance between costs involved in mechanic time lost through waiting, and the cost of having additional tool crib services.

2. Large service stations can use queuing theory to determine the optimum number of pumps and attendants such that the costs involved in providing additional service facilities and the loss of trade resulting from impatient customers going elsewhere are optimally minimized.

3. Banks are now beginning to use queuing theory in the manner described in the above examples, such that costs associated with disgruntled customers who must wait in line, and the costs of providing additional service facilities are optimally minimized.

Selected Quantitative Techniques

The quantitative techniques presented below will permit the reader to gain some familiarity with the actual manipulations involved in solving typical specialized managerial problems. The techniques to be discussed include break-even analysis, correlation analysis, sum of squares, and linear programming.

Break-Even Analysis. Break-even analysis is used to determine the number of units of a product which must be sold at a given price so that the firm will incur neither a profit nor a loss. The break-even point, then, represents the number of units which must be sold if costs and revenue are to be equal. Sales above this break-even level will yield a profit and sales below the break-even point will result in a loss.

The concept of break-even analysis centers around the fact that the profit which a firm earns during any given period can be determined by subtracting its total costs from its total revenue. Thus, if a firm earned a total revenue of $27,000 during a given period (usually a year) and its total costs were $25,000, then the firm would enjoy a profit of $2000 ($27,000 − 25,000). Similarly, if a firm earned a total revenue of $20,000 but incurred total costs of $26,000, then the firm would incur a loss of $6000. The total revenue can be calculated by multiplying the selling price per unit by the number of units sold. Therefore, if the selling price was $10.00 per unit and 75 units of the product were sold, then the revenue would be ($10)(75) = $750.

The total cost incurred by a firm can be divided into fixed costs and variable costs. Fixed costs are those costs which do *not* vary within a given range of units produced; (they are costs which cannot be *directly* associated with a *given* unit of output). As an example, suppose a manufacturing firm hired a superintendent on a full-time salaried basis. The superintendent's salary becomes a fixed cost for the company because they must pay him whether the company produces 2 or 2,000,000 units of product. The superintendent's salary, then, could be identified with the production of each unit only at the *end* of the production period by dividing the number of units produced into the salary. In break-even analysis, however, the manager is more interested in knowing what the break-even point will be at a given future date. Therefore, the method by which fixed costs are converted to variable costs (costs per unit) is of little concern in determining the break-even point. Moreover, the conversion of fixed costs to variable costs often include estimates which are subject to error. So, for purposes of break-even analysis, fixed costs are treated as a *constant* figure, and are not associated with the number of units produced.

Variable costs are those costs which can be conveniently and accurately associated with a given unit produced. For example, if the manager of a potato chip packaging firm pays $0.02 for each empty package, then the cost of $0.02 can be directly associated with each unit of the final product, that is, packaged potato chips. If the cost of the potato chips per package is $0.35, then the total variable costs are $0.02 + $0.35 = $0.37. The total variable costs can be determined by multiplying the variable costs per unit by the total number of units.

The equation for the profit of the firm can now be expressed as:

Profit = Total revenue minus total costs
 = (Selling price per unit) (number of units) minus fixed costs minus (variable cost per unit) (number of units)

Because the break-even point is the number of units at which the firm neither makes a profit or loss (profit is equal to zero), the basic equation for the break-even point becomes:

0 = (Selling price per unit) (number of units) minus fixed costs minus (variable costs per unit) (number of units)

Using algebraic manipulation, the equation for the break-even point can be reduced to:

$$\text{Break-even point} = \frac{\text{fixed costs}}{\text{selling price per unit minus variable costs per unit}}$$

To illustrate the break-even point, suppose a firm can produce 800 units of a product during a year and incurs a fixed cost of $5000. The variable costs are $5 per unit and the firm can sell all these units for $10 per unit. What is the break-even point? Can the firm make a profit during the year?

$$\text{Break even} = \frac{\$5000}{\$10 - \$5} = 1000 \text{ units}$$

In the above example, if the firm sells 1000 units it will reach the break-even point; however, because it can only produce 800 units, it would be impossible for the firm to make a profit under the above-stated conditions.

This example illustrates the powerful analytical tool provided by break-even analysis, because under the above-stated conditions the manager should now realize that he must either reduce the fixed costs, increase the selling price, reduce the variable costs, or work on all three variables if he wants to at least break even. The only other alternative would be to go out of business. A graphical illustration of the above problem is given in Exhibit III.

Linear Programming.   Linear programming is used extensively in solving many complex business problems and also has extensive application in areas such as economics and engineering. Not all types of problems can be solved by linear programming, however. The problems which can be solved by this method must have the following general characteristics.

Exhibit III   Break-Even Analysis

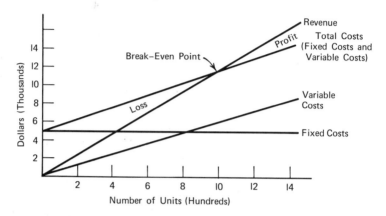

1.   The variables in the problem must involve relationships that are linear; the ratio of change in one variable to the change in another variable must be constant. Expressed mathematically, linear programming must involve variables which can be expressed solely in the first degree. Thus, $X + Y = Z$ is a linear expression because all the variables (X,Y,Z) are expressed in the first degree. It should be noted that a variable which is not explicitly raised to a particular power is assumed to be raised to the power (degree) of one, thus $X = X^1$. The expression $X^2 + Y^3 = Z^{\frac{1}{2}}$ is not a linear expression. In some cases, nonlinear expressions can be manipulated mathematically into linear expressions; in other cases, some nonlinear expressions are close enough to being linear that they are expressed in a linear manner, even though a slight error occurs when this is done. In many other cases, though, the major variables cannot be expressed in a linear fashion, and these types of problems cannot be solved via linear programming.

2.   Something must be minimized or maximized, and this something is usually referred to as the "objective function." Examples of objective functions which are to be minimized include costs, number of personnel required to perform a job, and time lost through inefficient allocation of resources. Examples of maximized objective functions include profits, number of units produced, and number of sales contacts per day.

3.   Certain conditions called "constraints" must be satisfied. These constraints are mathematically expressed in a manner similar to the objective function. A verbal example of a constraint in a linear pro-

gram would be to have an objective function which is to maximize profits. If there were no constraints then the profit would necessarily be extremely large. But certain constraints such as size of the market and cost of raw materials always seem to keep profits from reaching this very large amount. In order to determine what the maximum profit is, however, it is important that those conditions which constrain the objective function are expressed in a linear manner.

There are two models commonly associated with linear programming: simplex and transportation. The simplex model has far more applications and can solve all problems that can be solved by the transportation model, although the simplex method is more complex. The simplex model determines the optimum maximum or minimum objective function by beginning with a feasible solution and then systematically evaluating all the other feasible solutions until the optimum solution is found. When examining more than three variables, the simplex method can become quite laborious if the calculations must be performed by hand. But the use of EDP has greatly increased the application of linear programming toward certain types of complex problems. Some real-life applications will be given later in this chapter. The technique of linear programming is explained in the following paragraphs using an example that could be found in a real-life situation.

The lathe shop of a large manufacturing firm consists of 90 machines. Each machine requires a daily preventive maintenance of five minutes and a weekly preventive maintenance of 15 minutes. Machines which have undergone the weekly maintenance do not require the daily maintenance on the day that the weekly maintenance is performed. The shop employs two maintenance men who are each able to spend six hours per day on machine maintenance.

The shop foreman wants to have the weekly maintenance performed as early in the week as possible in order to be prepared for any emergency maintenance which may be necessary later in the week. The foreman realizes that it would be rather inefficient to have the mechanics perform the daily maintenance on all machines, and then spend an additional 15 minutes on the same machines which must undergo the weekly maintenance. Instead, he wants to schedule daily maintenance on a limited number of machines and then have the *remainder* of the machines undergo the weekly maintenance, so that the full six hours of each man's time are utilized as efficiently as possible during the early part of the week for the weekly maintenance.

PROBLEM: How many machines should receive daily maintenance, and how many machines should receive weekly maintenance each day in order that the weekly maintenance can be performed as early in the week as possible?

Developing the Mathematical Relationships. This is a typical resource (labor is the resource) allocation problem. It consists of two variables which are the number of machines to be maintained daily (X), and the number of machines to undergo weekly maintenance (Y). The total of these two variables obviously must equal 90; therefore, the first relationship can be mathematically expressed as $X + Y = 90$. This equation represents the objective function because the objective in this case is to service all the machines either in a daily or weekly manner.

A second relationship between the two variables is based on the fact that (6 hours) (60 minutes per hour) (2) = 720 minutes are available for maintenance each day. Because the daily maintenance time is five minutes and the weekly maintenance time is 15 minutes, the second mathematical relationship can be expressed as $5X + 15Y = 720$ minutes. This equation is called the constraint function because the number of machines which can receive daily and weekly maintenance is limited by having only two maintenance men, each available for only six hours per day. Observe that it is important that each side of the equation is expressed in the same units. This is why the total number of hours available for maintenance were converted to minutes.

SOLUTION: The problem has now been expressed in a mathematical relationship consisting of two unknown variables in two different equations. There are many mathematical methods available to solve this linear programming problem, but the one selected here is the determinant method because it is often the basic method used by computers to solve linear programming problems. The computers, however, are capable of solving problems which often consist of hundreds of variables and equations. The complete mathematical logic behind the determinant method is rather complex and is beyond the scope of this chapter. Instead, a simplified step-by-step method is presented below.

1. Align the equations in the following manner.

$$X + Y = 90$$
$$5X + 15Y = 720$$

2. Arrange the coefficients as shown below (note: a variable which does not explicitly have a coefficient in front of it is always assumed to have a coefficient of 1).

$$\begin{vmatrix} 1 & 1 \\ 5 & 15 \end{vmatrix} \quad \begin{matrix} 90 \\ 720 \end{matrix}$$

3. Calculate the base of the determinant by multiplying the top

left coefficient by the bottom right coefficient and subtracting it from the product of the top right coefficient and the bottom left coefficient.

$$(1)(15) - (1)(5) = 10$$

4. Calculate the X determinant by first substituting the coefficient column outside the box in step 2 for the X column, and then performing the same step as given in step 3.

$$\begin{vmatrix} 90 & 1 \\ 720 & 15 \end{vmatrix}$$

$$(90)(15) - (720)(1) = 1350 - 720 = 630$$

5. Solve for X (number of machines for daily maintenance) by dividing the base into the X determinant.

$$X = \frac{630}{10} = 63 \text{ machines}$$

6. Calculate the Y determinant by using the same procedure as given in step 4, except now substitute the coefficient outside the box in step 2 for the Y column.

$$\begin{vmatrix} 1 & 90 \\ 5 & 720 \end{vmatrix}$$

$$(720)(1) - (90)(5) = 720 - 450 = 270$$

7. Solve for Y (number of machines for weekly maintenance) by dividing the base into the Y determinant.

$$Y = \frac{270}{10} = 27 \text{ machines}$$

8. Verify the solution as a check against mathematical or procedural errors by substituting the value of X and Y into the original equations.

$$63 + 27 = 90$$
$$(5)(63) + (15)(27) = 720$$

The solution is verified and the most efficient allocation of maintenance under the conditions described is to perform daily maintenance on 63 machines and weekly maintenance on the remaining 27 machines. All the machines will receive their weekly maintenance at the end of $90/27 = 3.3$ days, thus allowing for additional time at the end of the week for emergency maintenance.

The above problem, although relatively simple compared to other real-life linear programming problems, should give the reader at least a basic methodology in setting up the problem and the methodology used to solve these types of problems. Other real-life linear programming problems are given below.

1.   A major midwest university uses linear programming to determine class sizes, times of the classes, and who should teach the class by setting up a series of equations consisting of such variables as the students' desire to enroll in a particular class, number of students and professors, and hours available to hold the classes. The information is fed into a computer, and after a few hours of calculating, the entire enrollment for the university has been determined.

2.   Major oil refineries are able to determine the optimum amounts of gasoline, lubricating oils, and other special purpose products that should be extracted from a given grade of crude oil by taking into account the cost of extraction of each product, current market demands, and other factors. A system of linear equations aids refineries in determining the optimum quantities of these products to produce.

3.   Feed lot managers, realizing that hay and other feed from different localities can vary significantly in mineral, vitamin, and other nourishment quality, are able to determine the optimum quantities and qualities of each type of food to purchase. Linear programming aids them in this food selection.

Correlation Analysis.   Correlation analysis is a useful quantitative tool that mathematically expresses the association of one variable with another variable. This mathematical expression is called the Pearson Product Moment Coefficient of Correlation, and ranges in value from $+1$ to -1. The greater the extent that one variable moves in the same direction as another variable, the closer the correlation coefficient approaches $+1$. When two variables move in opposite directions from each other, then the correlation coefficient will tend to approach -1. If two variables do not have any relation to each other, then the correlation coefficient will be zero.

To illustrate the correlation coefficient with an example of two variables which move in the same direction, suppose the manager of a sporting goods store has observed the sales of fishing tackle per month and the number of rainy days during each month for a period of six months. The sales of fishing tackle per month will be designated as variable X, and the number of rainy days per month will be designated as variable Y. The data are tabulated in Exhibit IV. Observe that the larger variable X is, the larger is variable Y, thus both variables move in the same direction.

The equation for the correlation coefficient and the calculation of this coefficient for the example in Exhibit IV is given below.

Exhibit IV   Data for Sales of Fishing Tackle and Number of Rainy Days per Month

Month	Sales of Fishing Tackle in Thousands X	Number of Rainy Days Y	$(X)\,(Y)$	X^2	Y^2
January	16	8	128	256	64
February	12	5	60	144	25
March	19	11	209	361	121
April	24	15	360	576	225
May	20	11	220	400	121
June	15	10	150	225	100
	$\Sigma 106$	60	1127	1962	656

Note: Σ = Total
N = Number of observations = 6 months

$$\text{Correlation coefficient} = r = \frac{(N)[\Sigma(X)(Y)] - (\Sigma X)(\Sigma Y)}{[\sqrt{(N)(\Sigma X^2)} - (\Sigma X)^2][\sqrt{(N)(\Sigma Y^2)} - (\Sigma Y)^2]}$$

$$= \frac{(6)(1127) - (106)(60)}{[\sqrt{(6)(1962)} - (106)^2][\sqrt{(6)(656)} - (60)^2]} = +.81$$

The correlation coefficient may be evaluated in the following general manner.

1. .90 or higher means that a high correlation exists.

2. Between .80–.90 indicates a good correlation.

3. Between .60–.80 indicates a small correlation.

4. Between .30–.60 indicates only the possibility of a correlation.

5. Less than .30 indicates that probably no association exists between the variables.

The previous example in which $r = +.81$, then, indicates that a good correlation exists. Another way of interpreting the correlation coefficient of $+.81$ is to state that 81 percent of the variation in the sales of fishing tackle is explained by the variation in the amount of rain. In short, on rainy days the sale of fishing tackle increases.

The type of correlation coefficient presented here is for two variables that are assumed to have a *linear* relationship with each other. If this is not the case, then a different equation must be used to determine the correlation coefficient.

There are several mathematical tests that can be applied to determine if two variables follow a linear relationship, but these tests will not be presented here. A rough approximation can be made to determine if a linear relationship exists between the variables by plotting each of the variables on a graph and observing if they follow a straight line. Exhibit V is a graph plotting the variables of the fishing tackle example.

Exhibit V   Graph Test for Linearity

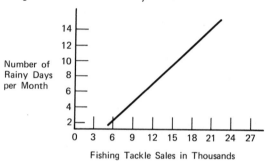

Fishing Tackle Sales in Thousands

In Exhibit V, although the relationship is not perfectly linear, it should be noted that a straight line, properly drawn, will come *close* to all the points on the graph, therefore, a linear relationship is assumed to exist.

Nonlinear relationships will generally follow some type of *curve* when plotted on a graph. An example of a nonlinear relationship which often occurs is shown in Exhibit VI.

Exhibit VI   Nonlinear Relationship

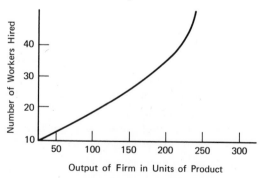

Output of Firm in Units of Product

When using the equation given previously to determine the correlation coefficient it is best to first test for a linear relationship.

At this point it is most essential to point out that the correlation coefficient does *not* in any way *establish* a *cause and effect* relationship between the two variables. But, unfortunately, many people attempt to use the correlation coefficient as "proof" of a cause and effect relationship. An interesting example of this attempt occurred in the 1940s and early 1950s when a group of people distributed leaflets showing a positive relationship between the annual consumption of soft drinks and the yearly incidence of polio. The correlation coefficient between these two occurrences was + .75, but it is highly doubtful that a cause and effect relationship could be established. Also, it should be noted that even if a cause and effect relationship were established, the question of which variable causes the effect on the other variable still remains to be answered. Thus, to state that soft drinks cause polio is just as absurd as to state that increased incidence of polio causes people to consume more soft drinks. The manager then, must always be careful of how he interprets correlation analysis. The correlation coefficient merely shows the *degree* of association between two variables.

The usefulness of correlation analysis stems from the fact that if two variables have a high correlation between each other and one variable can be reliably predicted whereas the other cannot, then the reliably predicted variable can be used to predict the approximate value of the other variable. The technique in which this is done is called the sum of squares.

Sum of Squares. The sum-of-squares method is a useful extension of the correlation coefficient in that once a high correlation has been established between two variables, the sum-of-squares method can be employed to determine the predicted value of one variable once the value of the other variable has been found.

The method is called the sum of squares because of the mathematical method used to derive the equation that predicts the value of one variable from another. The concern here, however, will not be to derive the equation, but to show the student how to work with the equation.

Essentially, the sum-of-squares equation (called the regression line) is an equation for a straight line that is derived from the value of the two variables. The basic components of this equation are given in Exhibit VII.

The fishing tackle example given earlier can be used to illustrate how the sum-of-squares method can be applied. Suppose the weatherman has a reputation for being extremely accurate in his predictions of the

Exhibit VII   Equation for the Sum-of-Squares Technique

$$X = a + (b)(Y_p)$$

X = Variable to be predicted

Y_p = Value of the predictable variable

N = Number of observations

$$a = \frac{\Sigma Y}{N}$$

$$b = \frac{\Sigma(X)(Y)}{\Sigma X^2}$$

Note: If sales volume were the *predictable* variable, then a and b would have different values.

---

number of rainy days during a given month, and he predicts that the coming month will have seven rainy days. Based on this information, what should the sales volume of fishing tackle be for that month? The calculations for this prediction, using the sum-of-squares method, would be:

$$X = a + (b)(Y)$$
$$Y_p = 7$$
$$a = \frac{60}{6} = 10$$
$$b = \frac{1127}{1962} = 0.573$$
$$X = 10 + (0.573)(7) = 14 \text{ or } 14{,}000 \text{ sales}$$
volume because the sales figures in Exhibit IV are given in thousands

When using the correlation coefficient and the sum-of-squares method, the following procedure should be used to gain maximum benefit from these techniques.

1. Align the data in the manner given in Exhibit IV.

2. Plot the data on a graph.

3. Derive the sum-of-squares equation in the manner given previously by selecting one variable and predicting the other variable from it.

4. Plot this point on the graph and carefully mark it.

5.   Mark the value of *a* on the respective axis.

6.   Draw a straight line between the two points in steps 4 and 5 above.

7.   Observe whether the plotted points tend to lie near the straight line. If they do, then a linear relationship can be assumed to exist between the two variables.

8.   If a linear relationship exists, then determine the correlation coefficient to determine the degree of predictability of the two variables.

9.   Calculate the value of the desired unknown variable, and use the correlation coefficient as an indication of the confidence of the prediction.

In the above example the correlation coefficient was + .81, thus the predicted value of $14,000 sales volume based on seven rainy days can be made with more confidence than if the correlation coefficient were only + .15.

Advantages and Limitations of Quantitative Models

The manager must be aware of the advantages and the limitations of the quantitative techniques in order to have a conceptual understanding of their application toward decision making.

Advantages.   For those decisions that lend themselves to mathematical expression, quantitative techniques provide a means whereby a rational and systematic approach can be applied in solving problems. The use of quantitative techniques requires clear and explicit assumptions. Other approaches to decision making which rely on a large amount of judgment, whim, and caprice often produce inferior decisions. Quantitative techniques encourage disciplined thinking about many of the problems which a manager faces.

Another advantage of quantitative techniques lies in the fact that the human mind can evaluate only six or seven variables at one time. Quantitative techniques do not have this limit and in many cases can simultaneously evaluate the interrelationship of thousands of variables. Linear programming and correlation analysis are examples of techniques which are able to do this.

Limitations.   The most basic limitation of quantitative techniques has to do with the nature of the mathematical models. Assumptions are incorporated into the derivation of a mathematical expression and in many cases these assumptions may not realistically portray occurrences in the real world. A nicely presented formula allegedly showing the relationship among the variables in a problem can be rendered useless if the assumptions underlying the problem are false. Linear programming is a good example of this limitation. In many cases, some of the variables do not exist in a linear relationship. But, if the assumption is made that these variables do exist in a linear manner in order to fit them into the linear programming model, then the effectiveness of the model is reduced.

Many managerial problems involve intangible or nonquantifiable factors and these nonmeasurable factors can greatly reduce the effectiveness of the quantitative techniques. To illustrate this point, a large bank used queuing theory to solve its waiting line problem, and additional tellers were added to reduce waiting times. But the bank was heavily patronized by men who were content to wait in a long line in order to visit with a rather attractive female teller.

Summary

The purpose of this chapter has been to introduce the student to several different quantitative techniques which can be of value to management in their decision-making activities. Quantitative methods rely heavily on mathematics and model building. Each of the various techniques has unique value in solving particular types of problems. CPM (critical path method) and PERT (program evaluation review technique) are two closely related techniques which are used for management planning and scheduling purposes. CPM is used to determine the expected time of completion for subprojects and total projects. With this information at hand a better job of coordinating the various phases of production can be done. PERT is somewhat more comprehensive than CPM in that it also takes into consideration the time variances that may occur with respect to subprojects as well as the total project. Since it is not always possible to pinpoint the exact time of completion due to uncontrollable factors, PERT lends a degree of sophistication to planning and scheduling. Knowing the possible time variances enables management to make advance provision for them.

Queuing or waiting line theory is used in situations where something must wait in a line before receiving service. It enables management to balance the costs of waiting in line with the cost of providing additional service and thus achieve an optimum cost level.

Break-even analysis is used to determine the number of units of a product which must be sold at a given price such that the firm will incur neither a profit nor a loss. Based on available information concerning the costs of producing a product, it can be determined how many units must be sold to break even. If anticipated sales at a given price will not generate sufficient revenue to cover the costs, the firm knows that it must either lower production costs, raise the price, or sell more units.

Linear programming is a quantitative technique that has a variety of applications in terms of the types of problems it can be used to solve. One of the more common applications is that of determining how to allocate scarce resources between alternative uses. Given the proper background information management can determine how to gain maximum benefit from the resources at its disposal.

Correlation analysis and sum of squares are two additional useful quantitative techniques. Correlation analysis expresses the association of one variable with another variable. If, as one variable changes the other variable moves in the same direction, there is a high correlation. The opposite is also true. It should be emphasized that correlation analysis *does not* show a cause and effect relationship but only the degree of association between two variables.

Sum of squares is an extension of correlation analysis in that once a high correlation has been established between two variables the sum-of-squares method can predict the value of one variable once the value of the other variable has been found.

Key Concepts

Critical Path Method.   Attempts to systematically determine the expected times of completion of subprojects which comprise a total project.

Program Evaluation Review Technique.   Attempts to determine not only expected times of completion but also the variances associated with these times.

Queuing Theory.   Is used to balance the cost of something or someone waiting in line with the costs of providing additional service facilities.

Break-even Analysis.   Is used to determine the number of units of a product which must be sold at a given price such that the firm will balance its revenue with the cost of producing the product.

Linear Programming.   Is used to determine the best allocation of scarce resources between alternative uses.

Correlation Analysis.   Is used to determine the relationship between two variables. In other words, as one moves in one direction does the other move in the same direction? It does not show a cause and effect relationship.

Sum of Squares.   If two items are highly correlated it can be used to predict the value of one if the value of the other is known.

Discussion Questions

1. A professor once stated that he thought the ideal student was one who was able to stay awake during one of his lectures. Is this an example of a model? Explain why or why not. Give two original examples of a model which include a mathematical formula and a drawing.

2. How do PERT and CPM conceptually differ from each other?

3. Explain how queuing theory might be useful in a grocery store check-out counter. What conditions are necessary in order for queuing theory to be an effective model?

4. A company produces 7000 units of a product and sells them for $18 per unit. They incur a fixed cost of $7600 and their variable costs are $9.50 per unit. What is the break-even point? How much profit will they make if all units are sold?

5. What are the three characteristics of linear programming?

6. A retirement home has 120 rooms and employs three maids who each work eight hours per day. Part of the cleaning duties include daily room "make ups" in which a maid makes the bed and changes the towels. The time required to do this is seven minutes. Other cleaning duties include the weekly "room changes" in which the maid changes the linen, vacuums, changes the towels, and performs general tidying activities. The hotel manager wants the rooms to be changed as early in the week as possible in order that the maids can work at other duties. What is the optimum number of rooms which should be made up only and changed such that the maids' time is spent as efficiently as possible?

7. The data in the table below are figures for the yearly sales volume of a company and the number of salesmen who contact their customers by phone.

Yearly Sales Volume in Thousands	Number of Salesmen Who Contact Customers by Telephone
25	5
30	4
20	7
15	10
35	1

(a) Do the above two variables appear to have a linear relationship? Verify your answer by plotting on a graph and comparing to the regression line.

(b) What is the correlation coefficient? What does the negative sign in front of the correlation coefficient indicate?

(c) If the sales manager gave permission for three salesmen to contact customers by telephone this year, what would you predict the sales volume to be?

Selected Readings

BOOKS

Charles R. Carr, and Charles W. Howe, *Quantitative Decision Procedures in Management and Economics*, McGraw-Hill, 1964.

C. West Churchman, Russel L. Ackoff, and E. Leonard Arnoff, *Introduction to Operations Research*, Wiley, New York, 1951.

Robert Schlaifer, *Introduction to Statistics to Business Decisions*, McGraw-Hill, New York, 1961.

Herbert A. Simon, *The New Science of Management Decision*, Harper & Row, New York, 1966.

ARTICLES

C. West Churchman, "Operations Research: An Evaluation," *Advanced Management*, April 1954.

Robert A. Hammond, "Making O.R. Effective for Management," *California Management Review*, Summer 1965.

Edward B. Roberts, "New Directions in Industrial Dynamics," *Industrial Management Review*, Fall 1964.

Harvey M. Wagner, "Practical Slants on Operations Research," *Harvard Business Review*, May–June 1963.

Part 3

Organization

The five chapters comprising Part 3 deal with the managerial function of organization. Chapter 8 traces the development of an organization from its beginning to the point at which it develops into a large-scale enterprise. More specifically, through a case example, both vertical and horizontal growth are illustrated and explained. In addition, this chapter will introduce the reader to the concepts of line and staff units within the organization, the chain of command concept, and other significant material dealing with the function of organizing.

In Chapter 9 the concepts of line and staff are looked at in more precise detail. The various types of staff authority that can exist are explained and some of the problems that can arise in the day-to-day functioning of the organization are reviewed. Chapter 9 also discusses the concept of span of control and points out some of the more important principles of organization.

Decentralization is the subject matter of Chapter 10. The overall purpose of this chapter is to provide the reader with a picture of how large-scale enterprises are organized and how they operate in total. Among other things the chapter covers subject areas such as why organizations decentralize, advantages of decentralization, the profit center concept, and an example of an organization in operation.

In Chapter 11 the emphasis is on the subject of delegation. Delegation is the thing that enables people to contribute positively to the organizational goals. In addition to discussing why delegation is important and the role of delegation in achieving results, a step-by-step results approach to delegation is developed. What delegation is not and why managers do not always delegate is also covered.

The final chapter in Part 3 is devoted to a discussion of bureaucracy and enterprise. It is hoped that this chapter will create an appreciation for some of the more subtle aspects of having an effective functioning organization. The material contained in Chapter 12 should provide the student with a basis for critically examining an organization and evaluating it in terms of its operational efficiency.

8. Organization Through Departmentation

As indicated in the previous section, planning is primarily a mental activity and does not result in any physical accomplishment of desired results. Organizing, the second of the managerial functions, is in this same category. Having determined a particular course of action designed to solve a problem or to meet an objective, the manager must organize so that people who are to do the work may execute their task with maximum efficiency and effectiveness. Organizing as such does not result in any actual physical accomplishment. Rather, organizing sets the stage upon which the activity will take place. It involves the process of establishing a formal structure which will provide for the integration and coordination of all the necessary resources (both human and technical) to accomplish desired objectives. The emphasis in organizing is on creating a structure which will result in maximum efficiency and effectiveness.

Elements in Organizing

The necessary activities as set forth by the plan constitute the foundation for organizing. Thus, the primary basis for organizing is the *work* that has to be done. Put another way, the whole purpose of organizing in the first place is to accomplish some objective. The accomplishment of that objective requires that certain specific activities be carried out. By necessity then, these activities must receive primary consideration when organizing. But work alone is not a sufficient basis for building an organization structure.

The people who will do this work constitute the second basic organizational element. The work that is to be done must be considered in relation to the skills and abilities of the people who must perform these activities. The work to be performed must be grouped into units, each of which one person can accomplish. The manager must always remember that people are indivisible factors in performance. When organizing, work must be grouped into jobs consisting of a series of activities that one person can do. Work assigned to people without regard to how much or how little the people can do or without regard for the abilities of the people involved will necessarily be performed at less than maximum possible efficiency. One of the purposes of organizing is to determine the proper relationship between the work to be done and the people who will do the work.

The final element that must be considered in organizing is the *workplace*. This refers not only to the specific location in which the work will be done but also all the physical factors necessary to the performance of this work by the people involved. The workplace includes machines, materials, tools, space, lighting and heating, automobiles, selling materials, and report forms. It includes everything necessary to implement the work. Just as people constitute the *animate* element in organizing, the workplace includes all the *inanimate* elements. The environment in which the people are to accomplish the necessary work is just as important an element in organizing as the first two.

In organizing the manager must consider these elements in the order in which they are named. First, he must determine the basic work activities involved in the plan. These fundamental work activities must be clearly defined and broken down until it is possible to regroup them into jobs. At this point in the process, the people enter the picture as the work activities defined must be matched on a unit-for-unit basis with the people who are to perform this work. Then the organizer must establish the proper relationship between the people who are to accomplish the work and the environment in which they must work. As can be seen, the process of organizing follows a fundamental sequence. The manager's objective is to achieve a balance among all three basic elements. This balance will result in the best possible performance of the plan.

The Basic Functions of Any Organization

Consider the situation of a man who intends to start a small business. It does not really matter whether he is making a product or performing a service, nor does it matter whether he does all the work himself or hires people to perform the work. In order to provide a product or service which customers will purchase there are three basic functions that he must perform. In fact, these functions are characteristic of any organization whether it be profit or nonprofit, or service or product oriented.

A Utility Must Be Created. Something of value in form or service must be brought into existence. In the manufacturing concern, for example, a product will be fabricated or assembled; in a retail store the means for distribution will be created; in an airline a time and place utility will be created through the procurement and maintenance of airplanes and of facilities which will make traffic possible; in an integrated petroleum company, oil must be produced and refined. Any organization must perform this basic function of creating a value The value which is created constitutes its primary reason for existence. In defining work which is to be done for the purpose of organizing, the manager must always ask himself "What basic utility does this work create?" If there is any objective at all to the work which is to be done, this question will have an answer. If it cannot be answered, the work is unnecessary.

A Means For Distribution. Next, *this good or service of value which has been created must be distributed to users.* The first function has only served to create a value which is potentially useful to people. The organization however, must make this good or service available to users. In a manufacturing or processing concern this function is sales; in a retail store it is usually called merchandising. In all cases this function is concerned with the exchange of that which has been created for some other value, usually money. In our example of a retail store, the first function made possible the merchandising function by creating a place in which goods could be made available to customers when they wanted them.

Financing.   *Finally, both of these first two basic activities must be financed.* That is, the capital necessary to create some good or service and to distribute it must be acquired and maintained if the organization is to survive. This necessary element in business enterprise, therefore, includes not only the gathering together of capital to make the organization possible in the first place but also all of the accounting and record-keeping activities necessary to the maintenance of capital.

Because these three functions *must* be performed regardless of what type of organization we are considering they are known as *line* functions. No organization will ever be found that in one way or another does not perform them.

All other activities that are often associated with organizations are auxiliary or supporting in nature and are classified as *staff* functions. They result in the growth of the organization beyond these three basic functions and arise as a result of the growth in complexity of the line functions. By way of example, the personnel function is, of course, a necessary and strategic one, but only arises when managers of line functions can no longer handle all the details of personnel management. Hence a specialist is brought into the organization to relieve them of certain activities as well as to offer expertise. The same can be said of purchasing, production planning, and many other areas. Exhibit I depicts the basic functions of an organization.

The Development of an Organization

As an illustration of the manner in which the three basic functions increase in scope and complexity as an organization grows, consider the case of a man who has just gone into business for himself manufacturing a new and revolutionary card table in his basement. His many friends predict that the market will be large. The table is light in weight, the legs pop into place at the touch of a button, and another button releases them for easy folding. He supplies his own capital to begin the business, and in its first stages, he performs all three basic functions. He produces the tables through purchase of materials and fabrication in his basement; he sells them on a door-to-door basis, and he keeps his own financial records.

As friends predicted, the demand for the product soon exceeds his capacity for production. He puts in longer and longer hours in the basement manufacturing the tables, but the backlog of orders grows

Exhibit I   The Basic Business Functions

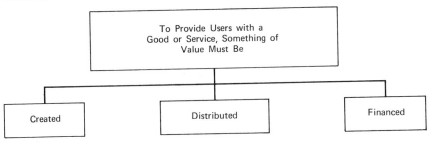

daily. His selling activities are quite limited as word-of-mouth advertising alone is bringing in more orders than he can handle. The rest of the family helps out with the production and delivery of the tables, but it soon becomes apparent that major adjustments are needed to relieve the situation.

The proper answer to this problem is, of course, to secure additional help. In a case like this, the owner-manager should hire someone who can be made responsible for one of the three basic activities so that the total work load of the business can be handled.

In the case at hand, let us assume that the owner-manager wishes to retain control over finance. Also, since orders for the table are coming in without much sales effort being expended he decides that the logical area in which to get help is that of production. Accordingly he hires several people to help him produce the tables. Now his organization has developed to the point shown in Exhibit II.

Exhibit II   An Organization Begins to Develop

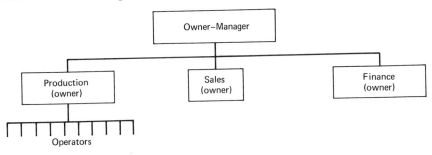

The owner still directly supervises all three basic functions but he has hired workmen to do the actual physical production. His activities in this area are thus limited to supervision.

As demand for the product and therefore the work load increases still further, the process of splitting up the three basic functions continues. More specifically, assume that over a period of time, more and more production workers are added. In addition, the owner finds that he must devote more time to selling his tables and the financial aspects of the business are demanding more time. In short, once again he finds himself overburdened with work and in need of help. This time he decides to hire a production foreman to supervise that function as well as some people to help in selling. The expanded organization is shown in Exhibit III.

Exhibit III The Expanded Organization

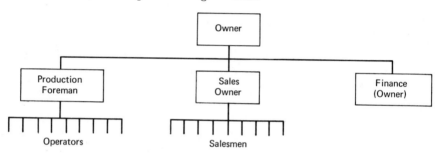

At this point the owner is still handling all financial matters and directly supervising the salesmen, but has turned over the direct supervision of production to someone else.

If all goes well and the business continues to grow it will eventually become necessary to modify the organization even further. Some possible future developments may include the following.

1. Appointing a sales manager to directly supervise the salesmen.

2. Adding an additional production foreman and putting one in charge of fabrication and one in charge of assembly.

3. Adding an additional sales manager and putting each one in charge of a given territory.

If these changes took place the organization would appear as shown in Exhibit IV.

Exhibit IV   The Enlarged Organization

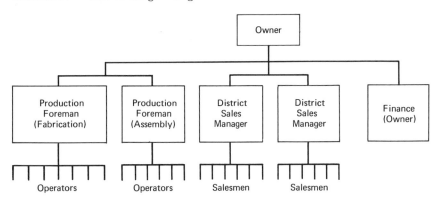

Vertical Organization Growth. As can be seen by Exhibits II–IV, the growth of the organization in these first stages is vertical in nature, that is, the organization is getting taller. This is explained by the increased volume and necessary expansion of the basic line functions. The organization grows downward as activities are split off following the three basic lines. This vertical growth will continue as long as the work load keeps increasing.

Since the organization has grown considerably past the one-man stage and since the three basic activities have been first split off by themselves and then broken down further through the addition of another level to the organizational structure, it becomes important to determine the way in which the work which must be done can be grouped into jobs. That is, *it is always necessary to define the work which must be performed and then to arrange that work into units which one man can perform.* In the production division, the various operations which must be carried out to manufacture the table could be arranged on the basis of the manufacture or assembly of component parts. They might, however, be arranged on the basis of production methods involved or the type of machines or materials used in the production process. They might even be grouped on the basis of their location. In any case, the amount of work involved in the various operative activities necessary to production would have to be grouped into work units which constitute full-time jobs.

The same thing could be said concerning the sales division. As salesmen were added to the organization because of increased work load in sales, the basic sales work would have to be grouped on some logical basis into full-time jobs. Since in this case a single product is involved, the logical basis for grouping would be some geographical division into territories. Each salesman would perform the same kind of activities as all others in each of the defined territories. If more than one product were involved, it would probably be feasible to confine each salesman's activities to a particular product or line of products. In the case of an organization with multiple products where a very large territory had to be covered, it might be feasible to use both product and territory as the basis for grouping the work of the salesmen. Another basis for grouping work in the sales division might be by type of customer. Any or all of these bases may prove feasible and reasonable in a particular situation.

In the organization which is under consideration, the owner-manager retained the third basic function—finance—in order to supervise this area as closely as possible. As the organization grew still further and the work necessary to plan, organize, motivate, and control the organization as a whole became greater, it would soon be necessary for him to delegate the responsibility for finances to someone else and operate on one level only. Very often in the beginning or early growth stages of organization, as functions begin to be split off downward but before they become full-time jobs, we find people occupying positions on two different levels. This should be regarded as a temporary expedient only and not to be desired for the best possible organizational structure.

In some other situation the owner-manager might prefer to retain the top sales or production position depending on his inclination, ability, and capacity. In any case, sooner or later he must relinquish these second-level positions and confine his activities to overall management of the enterprise on the top level if he is to accomplish his objectives efficiently and effectively.

Scalar Chain of Command.   A second phenomenon is that a scalar chain of command or a hierarchy of formal relationships is being established. Viewed another way, vertical growth results in a series of superior-subordinate relationships, where one delegates to another, and so on, forming a line from top to bottom. The line of authority so formed has three important advantages.

1.   It is clearly understood.

2.   Each member knows from whom he receives orders and to whom he reports.

3. Decision making is expedited since each member has complete authority in his area and need only consult with his superior when necessary.

In addition to setting forth these superior-subordinate authority relationships, the scalar chain serves to define the lines of formal communication and decision making, indicate who is accountable to whom, and the responsibilities of each person in terms of what work he does.

The Line Organization Structure.   When only line authority is employed the organization structure is line. It is primarily used in small enterprises and the principal advantages are quick decision making and authority relationships.

Its principal disadvantages include the fact that executives are overloaded with too many duties, specialization is not practiced, it is difficult to find managers because so much overall knowledge is needed, and insufficient time is given to planning, research, and control. To overcome these disadvantages, several kinds of staff authority are employed. Before discussing staff authority, however, let us examine the matter of horizontal organization growth and the resultant line-staff organization structure.

The Growth of Staff in the Organization Structure

Horizontal Growth.   As the enterprise continues to expand, the work load at the upper levels becomes greater and greater. The managers at the heads of the three basic lines find it increasingly necessary to split off more and more activities and delegate more and more responsibility downward. There is a limit to the number of different activities to which a man can pay attention in his work; therefore, it soon becomes necessary for the people at the next lower level to begin delegating their work downward. *As the activities which are performed become more and more complex the organization tends to grow downward at a rapid rate and the complexity of the activities being carried on at each successive level increases greatly.* For example, in the production division, when the stage of having a production manager and several producing departments is reached, it is found that department foremen must perform many different kinds of activities. It is also found that these activities are the same for each foreman. Each one must secure materials and supplies, plan and schedule work, train and place personnel, and keep records.

One of the first of these common activities to be noticed by the personnel in the card table company was the increasing burden of paper work. Manufacturing records, sales records, order processing, ledgers, journals, correspondence, and all the essential paraphernalia of modern business increase by leaps and bounds. Duplication of work is occurring in each of the three basic functions. Record keeping, files, and correspondence constitute a large portion of the owner's and foreman's work, and it is soon apparent that something must be done to relieve the line managers of this routine clerical work.

Since clerical work can be better performed by a specialist, the solution to this problem would be to hire someone proficient at office work and place him in a position where he can serve each part of the organization. This could only be done, of course, if all the office work which was being done by the line managers equaled a full-time job. Also, it could only be done if the performance of this work in one place by a specialist resulted in a greater economy of operation for the organization as a whole. The major objective of evolving a specialist's activity is to relieve the line executives so that they can devote more time to the primary work activities. In this case, a clerk-typist would probably be hired and constitute the beginning of an office force to serve the organization. The organizational position of this new activity is shown in Exhibit V.

Exhibit V   Organizational Position of Office Force

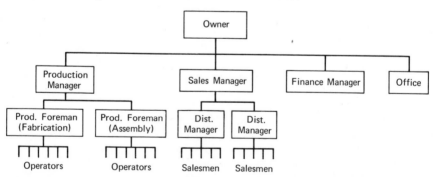

This structure preserves our three basic lines of organization and attaches the specialist who will serve all three lines at the point where they join. The organization has expanded, but the expansion has taken on an entirely different character than in the first stages of growth. Up to this point the growth of the company was only vertical, following the three basic organizational lines downward. Now, rather than let the line continue to grow only downward, necessitating the addition of the same kind of specialists in each segment with consequent duplication and overlapping of work, the organization is allowed to grow outward. Horizontal rather than vertical growth of an organization is achieved in this way.

All management specialists which service the entire organization arise in this fashion. The line executives are relieved of responsibilities which can be performed more economically by specialists. With the introduction of specialists or staff personnel vertical growth with its ever-lengthening primary chains of command is slowed down. A line executive in one of the three major activities does not have to become a "jack of all trades"; rather, he is allowed to concentrate on his major function and is helped by advice and assistance from management specialists.

For example, the personnel function found in modern business enterprises evolved in a manner similar to that just described. It is necessary to procure, place, and maintain personnel for each of the three basic activities of production, distribution, and finance. With only vertical growth in organizational structure, this function would have to be handled in each of the three primary chains of command. It should be apparent that this kind of growth can quickly lead to duplication of effort, to overlapping of responsibilities, and to unnecessary and even wasteful competition within the company for personnel. Before this situation can develop to the point where it contributes to inefficiency, such a common activity should be taken out of the three basic lines and centralized in a single personnel function which will service the rest of the organization. In this way economy of effort can be achieved and the line executives can be relieved of responsibilities, thus allowing further growth of the company without waste or inefficiency in the use of human effort.

This kind of growth does not necessarily occur only at the top level in a company but may occur at any managerial level. Specialists become necessary when the line must be given assistance in technical or coordinative activities which are common to any particular level. Consider, for example, the sales division of the card table company after it has grown to the point where it serves a relatively large geographic area which has been broken into several districts. With strictly vertical growth, the organization might appear as in Exhibit VI.

Exhibit VI   Vertical Growth of the Sales Organization

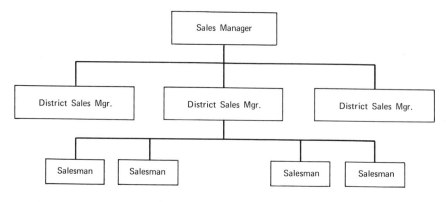

Here we find three districts with a number of salesmen reporting to each district sales manager. The work done by the salesmen and by the district sales managers tends to be similar across each level. In a sales organization, direct selling is not the only activity necessary for efficient distribution. Each salesman in this district must render reports to the district sales manager concerning changes in demand and changes in customers' needs and desires. This information filters up the line and finally must be correlated at the head of the line so that the company can obtain the entire picture of its markets. It would appear feasible at the top, where this kind of activity could constitute a full-time job, to centralize market research as an activity attached to the primary chain of command. In this way reports from the field could be sent directly to the market research group and those specialists could then forecast demand conditions and changing customer wants, and they could evaluate all factors necessary to the planning of sales and manufacturing programs. Thus, economy of effort in this phase of sales work could be achieved with the line executive merely being required to give general direction to the nature of the plans. All the detail and routine work as well as much of the creative planning could be handled by the specialists.

The same kind of coordination would probably work for other special activities as the organization grew larger. For example, advertising and sales promotion work might profitably be centralized as an activity servicing the entire sales group. In this way duplication of effort for these activities could be eliminated and advertising policies and methods made consistent for each district. If advertising were handled on a district basis, as would be necessary with strictly vertical growth in organizational structure, inconsistency in policies and programs together with overlapping of effort and responsibility would easily occur. After the addition of these specialists the organization might resemble Exhibit VII.

Exhibit VII Line and Staff in the Sales Organization

Organizational problems which have been mentioned in connection with only vertical growth would not occur—or at least would not become too apparent—in the case of a small organization. It is only with increasing size and complexity in a business enterprise that such difficulties occur to the extent that they become wasteful.

In the manufacturing division of this company one sees many instances of the necessity for the addition of specialists as the work load and the size of the organization increase. Various activities, such as purchasing, production control, the design of production, the design of production processes, product development, quality control, and maintenance, which facilitate the work of the line executives actually producing the card tables, tend to be removed from the line and centralized in one place as management specialists. In this way, the line supervisors may concentrate on the actual supervision of production and are aided directly and indirectly in this work by the technical and coordinative services of the specialists. Such specialists serving the line supervisors are known as *staff* specialists.

Organization of Work within an Enterprise. Previously it was seen that the basic kinds of work performed by any organization at the major functional level fell clearly into the three categories of creation of a utility, its distribution, and finance. If this breakdown of activities is truly basic, it should apply to any part of an organization as well as to the entire organization. Consider the situation of a zone manager in the sales division of an oil company. The work that he performs seems to conform to the following pattern.

1.   *Operations.*   The basic objective is to provide a service to the customer through the creation of place and time utility with respect to various petroleum products. These utilities are created by bringing into existence and maintaining a place of operations through which the product can be channeled to the customers. Thus, the zone manager creates or has created for him a bulk plant, which is basically a place utility.

2.   *Sales.*   He must make this utility useful to customers through his direct selling activities. Thus he distributes the utility by merchandising petroleum products.

3.   *Administration.*   Finally, he must be concerned with the administration of company policies relating to finance and other factors such as credit and collections, budgets, and real estate. Such activities fall clearly into the third basic category of *finance.* That is, they are concerned with the maintenance of the financial integrity of the zone in accordance with overall company policy.

Even beyond this basic classification of work, it is usually true that at this level office work tends to be the first type of work which is split off horizontally. Organizational structure at this level within the sales division of an oil company might appear as in Exhibit VIII.

Exhibit VIII   Organization of a Sales Division of an Oil Company

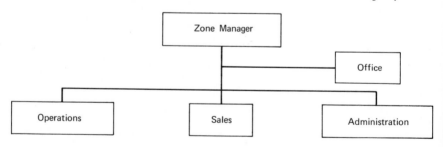

Bases for Grouping Work.   Up to this point it has been established that when a manager organizes to accomplish work, he does it first of

all on the basis of the work itself. That is, the basic activities which the company must perform in order to meet its objectives are defined on a logical basis. Then these basic activities are split off vertically as the work load grows and are used in the assignment of work to people. The people who must do the work constitute the second element in organizational structure. It has been indicated that work assignments must be equitable at each level and always constitute a full-time job. The final and equally important elements in organizational structure concerns the inanimate elements in work, the physical factors necessary for performance. The things the people work with are just as important in developing sound organizational structure as the work to be done and the people who will do it.

For example, in the production division of the card table company it was indicated that the work could be grouped according to the different methods, machines, or materials involved in different parts of the manufacturing process. A similar breakdown could be made in the sales division by dividing the work first geographically and then according to different products or different users. The important thing is that in all cases *similar work and similar physical factors necessary for the accomplishment of this work are grouped in order to determine the proper division of duties for the best organization.*

Authority-Responsibility-Accountability

The process of organizing must be accomplished in order to distribute responsibility, authority, and accountability among the people in the organization. A manager must understand the meaning of these three words and their implications in order to do a successful job of organization.

Responsibility is the obligation to secure desired results—an obligation which one assumes when he accepts any task or combination of tasks which constitute a job. Responsibility is usually specified by the assignment of a group of clearly defined duties to a person. The manner in which these duties may be derived has been described previously. But responsibility has two phases. The first is the obligation to perform to the best of one's ability those tasks which he accepts as his assignment. The second phase is his obligation to *account* to a higher authority for the degree of success achieved in the completion of those assignments. The upward phase of responsibility constitutes the main problem in allocation of tasks. The person to whom a series of tasks is assigned must be made aware that more is involved than the mere performance of those tasks. He is also going to be held accountable for the results he achieves. *Accountability* then flows upward in an organization while *responsibility* is assigned downward. Both phases must be recognized by those who accept any responsibility.

If a man is to be held responsible for the result which he achieves in the performance of his task, he must have the right to make decisions within the limits of his assigned responsibility. Without this right he can in no way be held accountable for the performance of specific tasks. This implies then that there must be a release of *authority* to cover any release of responsibility from one level of an organization to another. Authority means the power to issue valid instructions which others must follow. The right of decision is a necessary adjunct of any acceptance of responsibility. The relationship which must exist between responsibility and authority in any organization is one of co-equality. The two go hand in hand and must exist together and in equal measure if the individual is to be held accountable. *Accountability for results cannot be expected to flow upward unless commensurate authority and responsibility have first flowed downward.*

In a case where the authority released is less than the scope of the responsibility assigned, the responsibility will always tend to shrink until it is within the limits of the delegated authority. No other result can be expected. If the authority is not sufficient to enable one to carry out a given responsibility, accountability can only be expected within the limits of the authority. If the reverse were true, that is, if the authority delegated had been greater than the responsibilities assigned, the tendency would be for the responsibilities to broaden to correspond with the authority. The right of decision making will always tend to determine the extent of responsibility.

It should now be apparent that for every assignment of task and responsibility there must be ample authority accompanying such assignment if one is to be held accountable for successful performance.

Imagine that the card table company has grown so that it now looks like the organization chart in Exhibit IX.

It is clear that considerable differentiation of the three basic line activities, production, sales, and finance, has occurred as well as the development of several management specialties as evidenced by the outward growth of the organization. It can be seen that authority and responsibility flow downward from the top of the organization along the three primary chains of command. Furthermore, responsibility and authority have been delegated outward to the various specialist activities.

Exhibit IX   Organization Chart–Flow of Authority, Responsibility, and Accountability

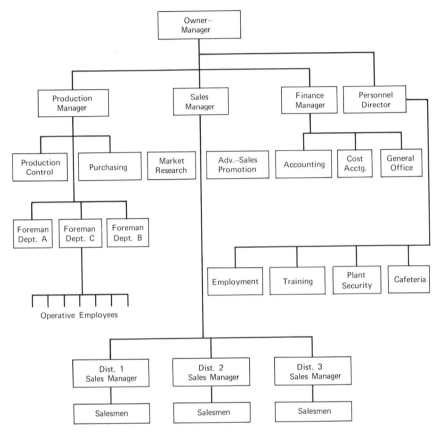

The entire structure of authority and responsibility represents the extended shadow of the man at the top.

If the organization structure only had to grow downward along the three primary chains of command, the flow of authority and responsibility would present no special problems. In that case responsibility for all activities performed could always be definitely fixed, even with increasing differentiation of the basic activities. All that would be necessary would be the proper delegation of authority commensurate with these definite responsibilities, all persons then being accountable upward for results. However, it has been seen that with increasing growth it becomes necessary to relieve these primary lines of authority and responsibility of certain special duties. Thus, an outward delegation of responsibility and authority from the basic lines becomes necessary. The management specialists must derive their authority and the assigned responsibility from the primary chains of command, but they cannot exercise authority along these lines. They can only exercise authority within their own organizational unit, not along the line to which they are attached.

These necessary definitions of the authority and responsibility of the management specialists who service the basic lines gives rise to certain special problems which must be considered. For example, the specialists who are assigned production control duties in this company are responsible for planning production within the limits of the master production program. They must determine routes over which work is to travel, schedule work, prepare materials and equipment necessary to accomplish work, and release orders and instructions to the producing department foremen. It then seems to the foreman that although his immediate line superior is the production manager, he is also receiving orders and instructions from the production control personnel. This is actually what is happening. However, the foreman does not really have two superiors nor is he accountable to two different sources. Instead, production control has received from the production manager an expressed delegation of responsibility and commensurate authority to prepare routes and schedules for the use of the foremen; production control is acting in the place of the production manager for this function. Production control is relieving the foremen of responsibilities which they would otherwise have to fulfill, and in this capacity must have the authority necessary to carry out the assigned task.

This is not to say that the production control people have acquired line authority. They can still only exercise specific authority within their own secondary chain of command. If a conflict arose and a foreman felt that the route or schedule as prepared by production control was not the best under existing conditions, he would be free to modify those orders and instructions within the scope of his authority and responsibility. The authority which is given the foreman must include this right since he is accountable for the actual results of production. The production control group is accountable for the accuracy and reliability of the records and schedules which they issue. Each, therefore, is accountable only for its own activities, and authority must be sufficient to make this accountability possible.

Consider, for example, the position of market research in the sales organization. This group takes the reports concerning demand for the product from salesmen in the various districts, correlates these data with factors known to influence demand, and produces a sales forecast to be used in planning the salesmen's activities. They release sales quotas and subsequent modifications directly to the salesmen in the various districts. They aid the salesmen in planning their selling activities to meet changing market situations. The salesmen, however, are not accountable to market research for any of their activities. They are accountable only to their district managers. Market research is responsible and therefore accountable for their estimates of demand, assignment of quotas, and revision of quotas. Just because a market research specialist may deal directly with individual salesmen does not establish an authority-responsibility relationship. The specialist acts only in an advisory capacity, relieving the sales managers of a particular responsibility. The authority of market research extends only down the secondary chain of command of their own organization.

Conflicts as to the placement of authority and responsibility do tend to arise between management specialists and the line personnel whom they serve. The above discussion should indicate the basic reasons for this kind of situation. It should also indicate that the *remedy for such conflicts lies in complete understanding of the basic flow of authority, responsibility, and accountability within the organization.*

Authority flows basically only along the three primary chains of command. Authority within the secondary chains of command is derived from these basic lines. The relationship between secondary and primary chains of command does not in any way imply a flow of authority and responsibility between the two. Rather, the authority of the secondary chain of command is only within itself. When they come in direct contact with personnel in the primary chain, they are acting under a release of authority from that same primary chain. A complete understanding of this basic relationship is essential to good organizational structure.

The Steps in Organizing

On the basis of the preceding discussion of the process of organizing, the following steps serve to summarize this process.

1. *Organization should be based on the objectives in view.* The first consideration when organizing to accomplish work is a clear statement of the objectives which the work should attain. This is necessary in order that the work to be done may be properly defined. Sound orga-

nizational structure rests basically on a logical definition of necessary work.

2. *The work to be done should be broken down into its component activities.* This second step involves the differentiation of the basic work activities into the component activities necessary for successful performance. It was seen that any business enterprise performs three basic activities concerned with the creation, distribution, and financing of some good or service. Having defined these basic work activities they must be differentiated downward. This splitting up of necessary functions should be progressive by levels until the point is reached where grouping into full-time jobs becomes possible. As this splitting up of functions occurs downward, provision must also be made for special activities common to several line functions, these being split off horizontally. This centralization of service specialties in secondary chains of command is done whenever it becomes necessary to relieve the line of some of its work activities.

3. *Build organizational structure based on work to be performed, people who must do the work, and environment.* Once all the necessary activities have been logically defined and broken down, it is possible to group the work to be done into work units which constitute jobs that can be performed by people. The activities as defined in step 2 do not bear any necessary relationship to the people who must do the work. One can only begin talking about assigning tasks to people after the tasks themselves have been defined. Thus this third step is concerned with building up practical work units which can be assigned to people. In addition to this basic consideration in grouping activities, attention must also be paid to the basis for grouping work. The manager should understand that similarity of work will constitute his first consideration in doing this, and whether or not work is complementary, his second consideration. That is, work groups should insofar as possible be made up of activities which are basically similar. But if the grouping of similar work does not result in full-time jobs, it then becomes necessary to group work which is complementary; that is, the work which precedes or follows must be included. With this attitude toward work grouping, the manager may use one or a combination of the following primary bases for organizing: physical location (geographic), product, process, physical equipment, and customer type. These five constitute the most generally useful bases for building work structure.

4. *Define clearly the authority-responsibility-accountability relationship.* The flow of authority and responsibility downward and of ac-

countability upward should be definitely established and made known to all people in the organization. Everyone in a business enterprise must be made aware of his position and of his relationship to others in the structure. A clear-cut definition of this basic relationship to others in the process is essential if cooperation and coordination of all activities is to result. Too often in business organization, people are left in the dark as to their exact status. In many cases a lack of definition of authority and responsibility leads to friction in the carrying out of the company's business. These difficulties can only be avoided if each individual understands his relative position in the company.

These basic steps in organizing have been considered primarily in relation to the work of an entire business enterprise. However, it should be easy to see that the process as described is applicable to any part of an organization as well. Managers at every level in both primary and secondary chains of command must organize to accomplish their work. In so doing they must follow this basic process. While the nature of the basic work functions may change from business to business and division to division within any one business, the process by which these functions may be organized for accomplishment remains the same. Whether a manager is organizing to accomplish personnel activities, purchasing activities, production activities, sales activities, finance activities, or any part of these, he must still consider and establish the relationship among work, people, and environment.

The Basic Principle of Organizing.   One sound and basic principle appears most important when organizing. This is called the *principle of functionalization.* It says that *any organization should be built around the work to be performed and not around individuals or group of individuals.* This may be done not only in the organization as a whole but in any part of it. If this principle is not followed, then the permanence and stability of the organization becomes dependent solely on people, and it is well known even though it may not be admitted too often that people do not last forever. You cannot upgrade men successfully if you have to train them in the image of their predecessors. No two people are exactly alike as to their skills and abilities. However, if the work has been properly and clearly defined, then people with adequate capabilities may be found and developed to do that work satisfactorily. This chapter has discussed just this thing—*rational allocation of work as the basis for organizing.*

Power and Authority

Before concluding the discussion of organization through departmentation, it is both important and appropriate that a distinction be made between the concepts of power and authority as they relate to organizations as well as discuss some of the various types and bases for authority.

Organizations rely on some type of hierarchy of authority in order to accomplish work and achieve their objectives. The assumption is that when an individual joins an organization he agrees to accept and abide by the authority structure of that organization. Within certain limits, he subordinates his own right or decision and action by agreeing to follow the decisions and directives of his superior.

Authority was earlier defined as the right to issue valid instructions which others must follow. When defined in this way, the authority to which we are referring is formal authority. It is formal because the organization has conferred it on the individual by virtue of his occupying a particular position in the hierarchical structure. Presumably, whoever occupied that same position would automatically be accorded the same degree of authority. Thus, formal authority attaches to a position rather than to an individual. Justin Longenecker has emphasized the nature of this type of authority by calling it institutionalized power.[1]

Power versus Authority.   There is a very distinct difference between power and authority. Power implies that either the organization or the individual has the ability to coerce someone into doing something that he does not want to do. This power to coerce people is illustrated most dramatically in a situation where one person can coerce another because of an advantage in sheer physical strength. In an organization the exercise of power can be attempted by manipulating rewards or applying sanctions against people. The important point is that an organization *cannot* function at a maximum level of efficiency by relying on pure power alone. At best it will result in antagonistic cooperation and minimum levels of performance. A more likely result will be subtle sabotage, open rebellion, or exodus on the part of those people who cannot be coerced.

In contrast to power, authority implies a degree of consent on the

[1]Justin G. Longenecker, *Principles of Management and Organizational Behavior* (Charles E. Merill, 1969), p. 397.

part of the person being governed. In a sense, the subordinate grants to his superior the right to make decisions which affect him. The process of a person consenting to be governed or being positively influenced by decisions which are made by others which affect him or his behavior is referred to as legitimacy. Thus, authority becomes legitimate only when those who are affected by it consent to it. By way of example, a law has our consent only if we agree that it is legitimate and that we should be governed by it. If the individual does not believe that the law is legitimate, fair, or reasonable, he is not likely to obey it or at least obey it in a consistent manner. Translated in an organizational sense, the organization can give meaningful authority to a manager only if the people he manages agree with the way in which he is selected and the basis on which he is selected. Beyond this, the manager must earn his right to manage and exercise authority over his subordinates. He does this by adopting an overall approach to leadership which his people accept and consider right. If formal authority as spelled out by the formal organization is not perceived as being legitimate, the members may subscribe to the norms of the informal group as being the proper ones. In other words, formal authority is perceived as not being legitimate while the informal rules and standards are perceived as being legitimate. An example of this would be a situation where management has established certain output standards but the informal group restricts output to a lower level.

In summary, there is a distinct difference between the concept of power and authority. Power rests on the ability to coerce people into action. The form of coercion may be strictly physical such as the "toughest kid on the block" or may take the form of manipulating various rewards such as continued employment or wage increases. In any case, in our present society the use of pure power to accomplish results is limited in its effectiveness because most people are not completely dependent on one job, with one organization, in one department of that organization for their livelihood. They have employment alternatives available and will exercise these alternatives if necessary. To the degree that some do not have alternative sources of employment available, or do not choose to exercise them, the result of reliance on pure authority is antagonistic cooperation and minimum performance.

Authority on the other hand implies a degree of legitimacy or acceptance on the part of those being governed. When authority is accepted, for whatever the reason, there is a cooperative effort between the organization and its employees or the individual manager and his immediate subordinates to achieve the desired results. Whether or not authority is perceived to be legitimate is a function of the degree to which subordinates feel the organization is living up to the many and varied expectations they bring to the job.

Basis On Which Authority Is Accepted. A pertinent question at this point would seem to be, on what basis do people accept the legitimacy of authority? Max Weber identified three bases by which authority is legitimatized.[2] Traditional authority is accepted on the basis that it has always been that way. For example, the authority of a king or monarch is accepted because the people have historically lived under this type of rule and have come to accept it as a way of life. The idea of rightful inheritance to the throne is not questioned.

A second basis for legitimacy of authority which Weber identified was a rational-legal one. This is the basis for acceptance of authority which is related to formal organizations. The authority is rational because the individual who has it is deemed to have demonstrated the necessary skill, ability, leadership, technical competence, and motivation to successfully fill his position. If subordinates do not perceive that he is adequately qualified for the position they are not likely to fully accept his authority.

Weber's final determinant of acceptance is charisma. Because of an individual's unique or magnetic personality he automatically attracts followers. Abraham Lincoln, John F. Kennedy, Dwight D. Eisenhower, and Vince Lombardi are examples of people who to one degree or another possessed a certain amount of charisma. All of us can probably think of someone who in our opinion represents a charismatic leader.

Again, it should be emphasized that the organization relies on some type of hierarchy or system or authority to accomplish its objectives. It cannot, however, afford to make an automatic assumption that this system of authority will be respected. The organization as a whole, as well as individual managers, must conduct themselves in such a way so as to earn the following and support of the members.

[2]M. Weber, *The Theory of Social and Economic Organization,* Talcott Parsons (ed.) (Free Press and Falcons Wing Press, Glencoe, Illinois, 1947).

Summary

In the process of organization three elements must be given consideration. They include the work to be done, the people who are to do the work, and the workplace. Since the purpose of organizing is to accomplish some objective, work must receive the primary emphasis, but at the same time, a balance among all three must be struck.

In addition to the elements of organizing there are three basic functions which an organization must perform to continue in existence. It must create a utility, there must be a means for distribution, and it must be financed. These are known as line functions because they are keys to continued survival. As an organization grows and develops these line functions expand downward (vertically) forming a scalar chain of command from top to bottom. This scalar chain of command or hierarchy of formal relationships specifies the lines of authority and responsibility as well as the lines of communication and decision making. As long as expansion occurs only in terms of these three basic functions it is a line organization structure.

As the organization continues to grow, however, it eventually becomes necessary to introduce into it people who have other areas of specialty such as personnel management or purchasing. These specialists are necessary for many reasons, two of which are to relieve line managers of detail and to introduce expertise. As specialists in various areas are added, the structure begins to experience horizontal organization growth and the resultant structure is one of line and staff.

The process of organization results in the distribution of responsibility, accountability, and authority among the people in the organization. Responsibility is usually specified by a group of clearly defined duties the person is expected to accomplish. Accountability, on the other hand, is the obligation on the part of the person to account to a higher authority for the degree of success achieved in performing the assigned task. Therefore accountability flows upward while responsibility is assigned downward.

Authority is the right to issue valid instructions which others must follow. Every release of responsibility must be accompanied by a release of enough authority to make decisions within the limits of the assigned responsibility. In other words, if accountability is to be expected, authority and responsibility must be equal.

It should be noted that there is a difference between power and authority. Power implies the ability to coerce someone. Authority, however, even though it is formal because it has been conveyed by the organization, implies a degree of consent. In organizations today authority is only meaningful to the degree that this consent exists.

Key Concepts

Elements In Organization.   The three key elements which must be given consideration when building the organization structure are the nature of the work, the people who are to do the work, and the workplace. Balance among the three needs to be achieved.

Functions of Organization.   There are three essential functions which every organization must perform. They include creating a utility, providing a means of distribution, and financing. These are the line functions of a business.

Line Organization Structure.   An organization which is just composed of the three basic line functions is a line structure.

Vertical Organization Growth.   This refers to growth and expansion of the line functions in a downward direction.

Scalar Chain of Command.   Refers to the hierarchy of formal relationships including superior-subordinate authority relationships, lines of decision making, and lines of communications.

Staff.   Staff refers to those activities which are necessary but serve to support the line. They are not in the primary chain of command.

Horizontal Organization Growth.   Is a result of the addition of staff to the organization structure. The organization expands sideways as opposed to just downward.

Responsibility.   Refers to the group of activities, tasks, or duties that have been assigned to a person.

Accountability.   Is the obligation to account to a higher authority for the degree of success achieved in performing certain tasks.

Authority.   Refers to the right to issue valid instructions which others are expected to follow. It is formal because it is conveyed by the organization and attaches to a position. In modern organizations it implies a degree of consent to be effective.

Power. Power implies the ability to coerce someone into doing or not doing something.

Discussion Questions

1. Following are the supervisor-subordinate relationships for ABC Co.:
    (a)   Jim supervises George and Dave.
    (b)   Jack, Ted, Bill, and John report to George.
    (c)   Mary, Jane, and Betty report to Dave.
    (d)   Nancy, Pat, and Steve report to Ted.
    (e)   Bob, Mike, and Tom report to Betty.

    Fulfill the following four requirements.
    (a)   Draw the scalar chain for the entire organization.
    (b)   What does this scalar chain represent?
    (c)   Show on your diagram what Bob would have to do if he were requested to communicate something to Steve via the scalar chain.
    (d)   What do you suppose might happen if all communication in the organization occurred in this manner?

2. Bill Hansen, the Production Superintendent for the Acme Metal Works, and Jim Doty, the Production Planning and Control Specialist, have not been on speaking terms for over a month. Bill feels that Jim keeps giving him orders and is continually "bossing him around." Jim claims that his job is to plan the production runs and schedule the necesary materials for these runs. But without the cooperation of Bill, he can not perform his job.
    Jack Smith, the Production Vice President, supervises both Bill and Jim. He did not learn of the feud between Bill and Jim because both were quite effective in keeping it away from him. However, after

speaking to Bill and Jim separately, he was able to summarize their complaints as follows.

Jim: How can I do my job when I don't have the right to schedule the production runs in the most efficient manner?

Bill: I have two bosses, Jim and you. Who do I really work for anyway? I get blamed if we do not make a deadline, yet Jim tries to schedule all the production runs.

Discuss:
  (a) What gave rise to the problem described above?
  (b) If you were the production vice president what would you do to prevent this conflict from happening in the future?
Base your discussion on the concepts of authority, responsibility, accountability, and chain of command as discussed in the chapter.

3. Assume that you have developed a patent on a new and revolutionary soap guaranteed not to pollute the water with harmful chemicals. You know that there will be a big demand for your product and have sufficient funds to start your operation through a $20,000 loan from the Small Business Administration.
Show how the organization structure of your company might grow as it went from a $20,000 company employing six people, to a $50,000 company employing 20 people, and finally, to a company with 500 employees.
In each of the three cases draw an organization chart and explain the nature of the duties of the key managers.

Selected Readings

Howard M. Carlisle, "Are Functional Organizations Becoming Obsolete?" *Management Review*, January 1969, pp. 2–9.

Ernest Dale, *Planning and Developing Company Organization Structure,* American Management Association, New York, 1965.

————, *Organization,* American Management Association, New York, 1967, pp. 61–64.

Paul M. Dauten, ed., *Current Issues and Emerging Concepts in Management,* Part II, Houghton Mifflin, Boston, 1962.

R. S. Edwards, and H. Townsend, *Business Enterprise: Its Growth and Organization,* Macmillan and Co., London, Macmillan Co. of Canada, Toronto, and St. Martin's Press, Inc., New York, 1958, pp. 32–34, 38–40, 42, 44–45, 47, 49–51, and 53–59.

William M. Evan, "Organizational Lag," *Human Organization, 25* (1), Spring 1966, pp. 51–53.

J. A. Patton, "Make and Use an Organization Chart," *Business Management,* May 1963.

Harold Stieglitz, *Corporate Organization Structures, Studies in Personnel Policy,* No. 183, National Industrial Conference Board, Inc., New York, 1961.

———, "Organization Structures—What's Been Happening," *Conference Board Record,* June 1968.

9. The Organization in Operation—A Practical Look

In Chapter 8 the growth and development of an organization through the process of departmentation was examined. The approach was a fairly straightforward one, designed to provide the student with an insight into how an organization comes into existence. Chapter 9 examines the operation of the organization on a day-to-day basis. The fact that organizations do not always operate the way books say they should, or the way the organization chart implies they do, is not new to anyone who has had practical work experience. Viewed another way, someone once said that organizations in and of themselves are fine. It is when one puts people in them that they get all "fouled up." As will be seen later in the chapter it is indeed rare, if not impossible, to find a 100 percent effective functioning organization. Things in real life just do not work that way. The remainder of this chapter discusses the role of staff in organizations, staff authority, line and staff conflict, the organization chart, control, and principles of organization.

The Role of Staff in Modern Organizations

As noted in Chapter 8 the staff enters the organization structure when it becomes necessary to relieve the various line managers of certain activities that are overburdening them. Therefore, the staff initially appears in order to handle details but this is a gross oversimplification of the role of staff in modern organizations. In organizations of today the staff plays a very important role in (1) gathering and analyzing information for top level decision making, (2) offering counsel and formulating policies which serve as a basis for the overall direction the organization is to take, and perhaps most important, (3) furnishing the expertise in such areas as personnel management, organization and management development, marketing research, and numerous other areas which in the last analysis determine how successful and competitive the organization is. Being even more specific, the staff used to be considered auxiliary in nature, or, if you will, the second-class citizens of the organization. In today's world, however, they not only are an integral part of any effectively functioning enterprise but they are a necessity.

Types of Staff Authority

Up to this point, our characterization of what is line and what is staff has been primarily in terms of the activities or type of work that the unit performs. Accordingly, we have inferred that production, marketing, and finance are the line activities in the organization and all others are staff in nature. Distinguishing between line and staff in this way was done primarily for purposes of convenience and explanation. Properly viewed, line and staff are authority relationships and do not relate to type of work performed. In fact, much of the misunderstanding surrounding them, as well as the problems encountered in everyday operation, are traceable to the failure to view them as authority relationships. More specifically, the common practice has been to call any type of staff authority advisory and this has caused much misunderstanding in organization.

Koontz and O'Donnell have set forth two broad categories of staff authority. The first is the personal staff which in turn includes the "assistant to" and the general staff. The second is the specialist staff which encompasses the advisory staff, service staff, control staff, and functional staff.

Personal Staff.   Exhibit I illustrates the position of the "assistant to" in the organization structure. As can be seen, he will typically have no major supervisory responsibilities. Instead, whoever occupies the position will have a limited set of duties designed to extend the manager's capacity for work.

Exhibit I   The Assistant To

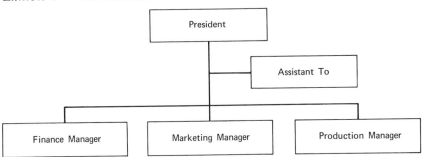

Put another way, the purpose of the position of "assistant to" is to increase the effectiveness and efficiency of the manager to whom he is attached by relieving the manager of certain more routine work that he would otherwise have to perform himself. In this connection the "assistant to" will typically do such things as collect and perhaps make preliminary evaluation of data needed for decision making, consolidate the information on various types of reports so it can more easily be assimilated and interpreted, process certain types of documents for distribution to others in the organization, act as a "stand-in" for the manager at various meetings or functions, interpret plans or budgets to others, and otherwise serve as an adjunct to the manager he serves. In some situations the manager may actually give his "assistant to" the authority to act as his agent. This, of course, means that the "assistant to" can issue instructions in his superior's name, as well as make decisions which affect the organization and other employees. The important point is that whoever occupies the position of "assistant to" should be made clearly aware of the extent of his influence and that everyone who will come in contact with him should also be appraised of his position in the everyday functioning of the enterprise.

General Staff.   Exhibit II depicts the place of the general staff in the organization structure.

Exhibit II   General Staff

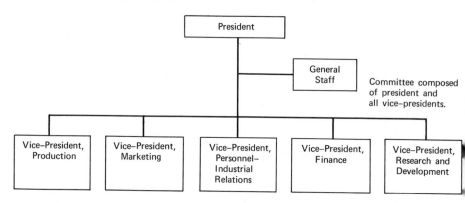

The general staff is composed of all the chief administrators in the enterprise. Its typical purpose will be to bring together into one group all the necessary expertise and input needed to make sound plans and decisions with respect to the organization. The president is still the ultimate decision maker, but he makes major decisions only after consulting with, and getting the input of his key people. The role of the general staff is perhaps best illustrated in the military. During World War II, General Eisenhower was ultimately responsible for the conduct of the war in his sphere of operation but major tactical decisions were made only after each of the key officers under him had the opportunity to contribute their particular knowledge and insight. In business the general staff would typically be involved in decisions dealing with such things as capital expenditures, plant location, introduction of new products, profit planning, and organizational development. The theory behind general staff is essentially one of a coordinated group acting to insure maximum results.

Specialist Staff.   As indicated earlier there are four basic types of specialist staff. The advisory staff, as the name implies, counsels line managers. By request or on their own initiative, they will study problems, offer advice, and prepare plans. The work and thinking of the staff man who is acting in an advisory capacity may be accepted, rejected, or modified by other managers in the organization. An example will perhaps best illustrate this advisory function. Assume there is a vacancy in one of the production departments of the organization. The personnel department will normally recruit applicants for the job and screen out two or three people who seem qualified to fill it. These two or three seemingly qualified people then are sent to the departmental manager so he can interview them and indicate which he prefers. Before making his decision the manager would probably ask the personnel officer which one he thought was the best. At this point all the personnel man can do is to offer his suggestion and give the reasons for it. In short, advise as to which one candidate he felt was best qualified. The manager, however, is free to choose one of the others if he so desires. He is not bound to follow advisory staff opinion.

In a sense this means that when the staff is acting in an advisory capacity they are to a degree on the defensive. They must do an effective job of selling. The better they are at selling their ideas and backing up their opinion with logical thought, the more likely it is that they will be listened to and their advice followed.

Service Staff.   The service staff performs activities which previously were decentralized and performed in each individual department. The need for a service staff arises when, because of duplication of effort at several points in the organization, certain inefficiencies are being encountered. Conversely, service staff departments are encouraged when concentration of facilities permits more economical performance and better control. Once the activities in question have been removed from the line they are compelled to use the service staff to prevent duplication of effort. Thus, the service staff is not on a take it or leave it basis. If the job is going to get done, the line must rely on the staff to do it.

A maintenance department in a production enterprise is a good example. When the organization was small, it is probable that each production department has its own one or two men who did the maintenance work in that department. In other words, they were under the direct supervision of the departmental supervisor. However, as expansion takes place, it becomes difficult to find enough people who have the total overall knowledge needed to handle all phases of maintenance, the number of people needed for maintenance increases rapidly, and a considerable dollar investment in special tools and equipment is required. In addition to this supervisors get overburdened as they attempt to oversee both production and maintenance. At this time the decision is made to establish a service staff (central maintenance department) which will serve the total production operation.

Control Staff. The control staff has direct or indirect control over other units in the organization. In the case of direct control they may be serving as an agent of the line manager. For example, the quality control department is in a line relationship to the production manager but not to the various production departments such as fabricating and assembly. The production manager may, however, give them direct authority to shut down the assembly line if a quality problem occurs. The case of indirect control is illustrated when the staff can require procedural compliance, submission of certain reports, or must be consulted on policy interpretation. For example, departmental foremen may be required to contact the industrial relations department before formally answering any grievance. Implied in this requirement is the idea that they will be given the answer to the grievance and transmit this to the employee as being the company's official position. In these and other ways, the manager is restricted in some phase of the operation of his department.

Functional Staff. Finally, functional staff authority exists when one manager has direct authority over a certain phase of another manager's operation and also exercises this authority along lines other than those established by the formal organization structure. More precisely, the staff manager is given limited line authority. To illustrate, assume an employee in a department is responsible for submitting a daily or weekly cost report on the department's activities. Although technically the formal structure dictates that the individual in question is responsible to his or her departmental supervisor only, someone from the cost accounting department may be given functional authority to see that the report is filled out and filled out properly. If a problem arises the cost expert may go directly to the responsible person, bypassing the immediate supervisor in the process. Obviously this type of staff authority should be restricted to exceptional situations; if carried too far, and if too extensive, it could completely destroy the line manager's effectiveness.

Line and Staff Conflict

It was suggested earlier in the chapter that organizations do not always operate exactly as they are theoretically supposed to. One of the areas where we very often find a difference between what appears to be a rather clear-cut situation as far as the organization chart is concerned but in practice causes considerable problem, is the area of line-staff relationships.

The story of line and staff is similar to the mountain feuds between the Hatfields and McCoys. It has always been there and will never end; it often seems senseless because there is really no reason for it; it originally began and continues to exist because:

1. Frequently neither side understands nor appreciates the reason for, role, and function of the other.

2. Departmental or functional area lines of responsibility, accountability, and authority are not clearly established.

3. They by nature oppose each other anyway.

In a more specific sense, line managers often claim that the staff in the organization lacks responsibility because they are not on the "firing line." In addition, it is often claimed that staff managers tend to try to overstep the amount of authority given them, that their advice, assistance, and programs they administer do not help the line manager overcome his problems and achieve output goals, and that the staff tries to take advantage of the line because of their closer ties with top management. The lines' complaints about staff can perhaps best be summed up by saying that they (the line) feel that "We are the ones who make the organization go and keep it going. We cannot do this with a lot of outside interference from staff people who do not appreciate our problems and who furthermore do not give the quality of assistance and support they are supposed to."

On the other hand, staff managers also have some complaints. They often claim that the line people resist staff assistance, that they should be given more authority in their various areas of expertise, and that the real problem lies in how the line managers implement and follow through on various programs and procedures which the staff designs and administers.

The above discussion is not meant to imply or remotely suggest that line and staff managers are always at odds with one another, that they are continually in a state of warfare, and that there is never any cooperation and integration of effort between them. Rather, the point being made is, that since it is people who fill the various positions in an organization, there is always the possibility that a certain degree of conflict may at times arise. Not only is this true of line-staff relationships, but it is possible in any situation where two or more people must interact to accomplish results. More specifically, the same type of interpersonal problems cited above could be encountered between two line managers who were to a degree dependent on each other to accomplish results in their individual departments. The line-staff example was chosen simply because perhaps a greater probability of misunderstanding occurs when the people involved are performing different functions. Whenever the organization is not functioning as smoothly as it might, the key factor in triggering improvement is communication between the areas and people involved. Organizations operate most efficiently and people integrate their efforts best when the following conditions are present.

1.   When everyone is aware of the overall goals and objectives which are being sought.

2.   When they have played an active role in determining what the objectives are, or at a minimum, in planning how they can best be achieved.

3.   When each individual is thoroughly briefed on the role and function of other members of the team and has a clear understanding of the purpose or rationale behind the various functions.

4.   When the machinery is built into the organization structure for people to come together and interact in a climate which is conducive to open communication and problem solving as opposed to defensive behavior.

5.   When lines of responsibility, accountability, and authority have been clearly established and are understood by all the people.

6.   When an atmosphere of "team effort" prevails and each member of the team is committed to the task at hand, as well as to understanding and appreciating others.

What Is Not on the Organization Chart[1]

"Organization charts come in various sizes, colors and even textures. Most are black and white and printed on paper. Some are affixed to office walls and made of materials that are easily changed. Some charts are highly detailed; some are very sketchy. Some are stamped

[1]This section draws heavily from Harold Stielglitz, *The Conference Board Record,* November 1964.

confidential and locked in the desks of a chosen few; others are broadly distributed and easily available. Despite these and other variations that might be noted, all organization charts have at least one thing in common: they don't always show how the organization works. Or, as some people say, they don't show the *real* organization."[2]

Even the most current chart is to a degree somewhat inadequate as a diagram of the organization and as an explanation of how the organization works.

What the Chart Does Show. The organization charts of most companies shows two things.

1. Division of work into components. These components may be divisions or departments or they may be individuals. Boxes on the conventional chart represent these units of work.

2. Who is (supposed to be) whose superior. The solid lines on the chart show this superior-subordinate relationship with its implied flow of delegated responsibility, authority, and attendant accountability.

Implicit in these two points are several other things that the chart is designed to show.

1. Nature of the work performed by the component. Depending on the descriptive title placed in the box, what this shows may be specific (facilities engineering), speculative (planning), or spurious (special projects).

2. Grouping of components on a functional, regional, or product basis. This is also conveyed to some extent by the labels in the boxes.

3. Levels of management in terms of successive layers of superiors and subordinates. All persons or units that report to the same person are on one level. The fact that they may be charted on different horizontal planes does not, of course, change the level.

Beyond these things it becomes difficult to pinpoint anything specific about the organization. Therefore, what the chart does not show is very often more interesting than what it does show.[3]

[2]Ibid.
[3]Ibid.

What the Chart Does Not Show.   The first thing the chart does not show is the degree of authority and responsibility of the various people. As noted previously, it is true that the chart does depict superior-subordinate relationships and the attendant process of delegation of authority, but it does not give any indication of differences in authority and influence between two people who appear on the same plane of the chart. For example a given chart may show the manufacturing manager and the personnel manager both reporting to the president; this would imply that both (with respect to their functional areas) have equal authority and influence within the organization. In actual practice, however, the personnel manager may have only very minimal influence. He may only rarely be consulted for decision-making purposes, may not be given much insight concerning day-to-day operations, and his responsibilities may pretty much be limited to the paperwork aspects of employee relations. Taken a step further, it may be that there are people at the second level of management in the production phase of the operation who have more influence and authority than the personnel manager. These phenomena are of course not apparent from viewing the chart.

Suppose, however, that all of a sudden the firm is faced with a concentrated unionization drive. The firm would probably turn to the personnel manager for help and his stature in the organization is substantially enhanced as his role takes on increased significance. If the union is defeated in its attempt at organizing the work force, the personnel manager's new-found stature may be permanent. This is because of the respect he has gained due to his successful efforts. Even if the union succeeds, his role in day-to-day operations may take on increased significance because of the need to negotiate a labor contract, train production supervisors in dealing with union stewards, administer the contract on a day-to-day basis, settle grievances, and the many facets of operating with a union as opposed to without one. In any case, the above example serves to illustrate that the chart itself does not show the degree of authority, responsibility, and influence of people within the organization.

A second thing that the organization chart does not show is the true distinction between what is line and what is staff. As stated earlier, line and staff are authority relationships and staff authority may range all the way from being advisory and counseling in nature to being functional. Since the organization chart does not typically indicate what type of authority the staff has with respect to various areas, the viewer of the chart is left in the dark as to how the organization really operates. Based on a knowledge of organizations in general, we can surmise or offer predictions on what might be the case but these suppositions may not always be true.

Third, the chart does not show all the lines of communication. It does indicate a few of the major channels of contact but if the organization sticks to only these, nothing will get done. It is a truism of organization that no one unit or individual operates in isolation from all the others. All are linked by an intricate network of communication. Proper organization performance relies on this network and on each unit and individual becoming a party to it. To chart the total communications network is practically impossible. To attempt to chart it and thus introduce certain rigidities into it might easily frustrate its workings.

The final thing that the chart of the formal organization structure does not show is the informal organization. The latter encompasses all of the informal relationships, communication channels, and influences or power centers that develop over time as people interact with one another. The informal organization is an extension of the formal and arises to facilitate the accomplishment of the task. According to some, the informal organization gets work done in spite of the formal structure. The manager who knows the informal structure and how to use it has a distinct advantage in that he can many times cut through the "red tape" and thereby get much faster results.

The essential value of the chart then seems to lie in the fact that it does strip the organization to the skeletal framework. In so doing, it serves a useful purpose both as a tool of organizational analysis and a means of communication. As a complete picture of the organization, however, it is recognized as being somewhat inadequate, but it is necessary for a basic understanding.

Span of Control

Span of control refers to the number of subordinates which a given manager supervises. The significance of span of control lies in the effect which it has on the total organization structure, the level of morale and motivation of the people, and communication and decision making within the organization. A narrow or small span of control means that the manager has a limited number of people who report to him. A broad or large span of control implies that each manager has numerous subordinates whom he directly supervises. Exhibit III depicts these concepts.

Exhibit III   Span of Control

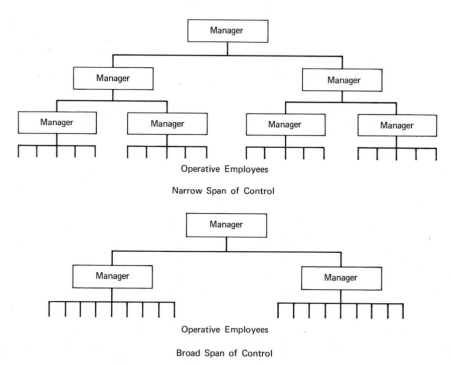

Narrow Span of Control

Broad Span of Control

As can be seen from Exhibit III, a narrow span of control leads to a tall organization structure, that is, a structure which has numerous layers of supervision and management associated with it. The chief implication of this tall structure is that it contains a considerable amount of administrative overhead in the form of salaries which must be paid to the managers at the various levels. As long as the organization is operating in a climate where the availability of profits or budget money presents no particular problem, everything can go along smoothly. (In any case, it should be noted that there is a fixed drain on the financial resources of the organization.) If, however, the organization is faced with a profit or budget squeeze, problems set in. More specifically, it may be found that it is either impossible to support this extensive administrative structure or that it can be supported but only at the expense of sacrificing other very strategic areas. Generally speaking, then, the span of control of managers should not be so narrow as to impose financial problems on the organization, particularly during times of financial stress. Viewed another way, unless there are some good reasons, the span of control should not be unduly limited.

Effect of Span of Control on Morale and Motivation. When a manager's span of control is limited the chances are greater that he will become more involved in the small details of the operation of the unit he supervises. More specifically, a limited span leads to close and detailed supervision of subordinates, restricting their range freedom in performing work, and generally a situation develops in which the manager is so heavily involved that his people find themselves performing ad hoc activities without really having a meaningful "piece of the action." These situations do not necessarily have to be true but to the extent that they are, they will tend to have a bad effect on the morale and overall level of motivation.

In contrast, by expanding a manager's span of control he is forced to supervise people less closely and must allow his people more freedom in action. In addition, he must, by necessity, delegate authority and responsibility. It is generally accepted that these factors can all be instrumental in creating a motivational climate.

Effect of Span of Control on Communication and Decision Making. As noted previously, a broad span of control reduces the number of layers in the organization. This in turn facilitates both upward and downward communications since messages are traveling through fewer layers and are therefore more direct. Another aspect of communications in an organization with fewer layers is that they are more likely to be face to face as opposed to written in nature. The opportunity to gain understanding with the former is much greater.

As far as decision making is concerned, where span of control is large it is more likely that decision making will be delegated further down the line. This is true because the manager finds himself in a situation where he cannot handle everything himself without being overburdened or letting many things go undone. The significance of this delegation of decision making lies in the effect that it can have on the motivation of subordinates.

Factors Affecting the Size of Span of Control. Up to this point it has been implied that a broad span of control is always desirable. In fact, however, the decision as to size of span of control must be made not only on the basis of the issues discussed above, but also on the basis of some very practical considerations. First, the nature of the work should have an influence in determining the size of the span. Generally speaking, the more routine, repetitive, and less specialized the work being performed, the greater can be the number of subordinates for which the manager is responsible. The reason for this is that there is less need for the manager to work and interact directly with his subordinates to get the job done. Assuming the people have been adequately trained they can perform the simplified work with a minimum of supervision. In contrast to this, if the work is more technical and less structured in nature, there will be a need for considerably more interaction and interplay not only between the manager and his people as individuals, but between members of the work group as a whole. Because of this need for more human interaction and overall teamwork to get the job done the span of control must be smaller. If it is enlarged too much the job will not get done because coordination of effort will not be possible. Thus, the nature of work being performed must receive consideration when determining the size of a manager's span of control.

Second, the size of the span of control of a particular manager must be determined in light of the training and experience of subordinates. As might be expected, the more qualified subordinates are to perform their jobs, the less need there is for supervision. Assuming they know what is expected, receive periodic feedback on their performance, and have the necessary help and support, they can, in a sense, control their own performance and function independently. Rather than exercising direct supervision over the work itself, the managers' job centers more on coordinating the efforts of individuals to insure a total team effort, and the overall planning of departmental activity. When these conditions exist span of control can be enlarged.

On the other hand, because of limited training and experience on the part of subordinates or because the work is such that closer supervision is required, the manager's span of control must necessarily be limited. If it is not, the job will simply not get done because the manager's effort will be spread too thin and he will find himself spending considerable time meeting crises that develop.

A third determinant of the size of the span concerns the manager himself. Like people in general, managers differ in their individual capabilities, energy level, and capacity for work. Also they differ in that some may pour all their effort solely into the job while others may have outside interests which occupy some of their concern. In a given set of circumstances, what may be the proper span of control for one manager may be inappropriate for another. Some consideration must be given to the individual who occupies the job in question. This is not to suggest, however, that the organization can go overboard in making adjustments in the span of control to fit every individual.

Principles of Organization

A principle is a statement formulated as a guide to action. Principles are not designed to be irrevocable laws but rather to serve as rules of thumb to be applied in light of a particular situation. While no two organizations are exactly alike there are certain fundamental characteristics common to all and therefore some basic guidelines which, when adhered to, can help insure total organizational effectiveness. The following listing of principles of organization is not complete, but it does represent some of the more important factors which must be given consideration when structuring the organization.

Principle of Objective. Prerequisite to the starting of any organization or to carrying on any activity is a clear and complete statement of the objectives in view. Only after this can the organization be built and molded to foster the attainment of those objectives with the least amount of effort and cost. As noted in Chapter 4, objectives also serve to give the organization a sense of direction and purpose on a continuing basis. Conversely, without objectives there is a greater possibility that the organization will drift and not respond adequately to its environment.

Principle of Nonconflicting Objectives. The previous chapter showed us that an organization is a complex of departments and units. If the overall objectives as discussed previously are to be achieved, then not only must each department have its own set of objectives but they must complement, supplement, support, and otherwise blend with one another. Also, departmental objectives should be derived from the overall organizational objectives. In this sense the process of objective setting is analogous to a pyramid. It starts at the top and moves down through the entire structure.

Principle of Coordination. The principle of coordination states that the organization framework must provide for the integration and blending of both human and technical resources to accomplish the task at hand. Coordination results when the systems and procedures which are established in fact facilitate the accomplishment of results and when each unit in the organization thoroughly understands the role and function of every other unit. Another aspect of coordination concerns the establishment of effective lines of communication as well as the creation of a total team climate. All of these issues will be discussed in succeeding chapters.

Principle of Parity of Authority, Responsibility, and Accountability. When an individual is held responsible for something, he must also be given the authority necessary to perform. If the assigned responsibility is greater than the authority which is granted, then responsibility will tend to shrink within the limits of the authority. If the opposite is true, that is, more authority is granted than is needed to meet a given responsibility, then there will be a tendency for responsibility to expand. In any case, accountability can only be expected within the limits of the authority extended.

Unity of Command.   The unity of command concept refers to the idea that each subordinate should be accountable and answerable to only one superior. The saying "no man can serve two masters" illustrates this. If the subordinate is receiving directions from more than one superior there is a strong possibility that confusion will arise. This is particularly true when what he is being told is not the same. He will find himself stuck in the middle, not knowing which way to turn. The result is usually either one of halfway action or no action at all.

Principle of Delegation.   As cited previously the need for organization arises when one man cannot do a job alone. Thus, other people are employed and some type of organizational structure appears. If, however, the people who are brought in are to make a meaningful contribution and be productive, then true managerial delegation, as discussed in Chapter 11, must take place. As will be noted, delegation is the process by which a manager assigns responsibility, grants authority, and creates accountability. Without delegation the manager will defeat his purpose of bringing others into the organization. He will end up doing everything himself.

In our earlier discussion of span of control it was emphasized that there is no absolute rule for determining exactly how big a given manager's span of control should be. Many variables must be taken into consideration when making such a decision. Similarly, it was noted that the organization chart does not represent an exact replica of the real organization. It does, however, serve a useful purpose as a road map and a tool for organizational analysis. To suggest that organization charts be eliminated because they are not perfect descriptions of the organizations they purport to represent would be most inappropriate.

So it is with the principles of management cited above. They are not presented in terms of their being hard and fast rules which always reflect the reality of organizational life. They do, however, present the manager with some fundamental guidelines which are of value when both designing the organization structure and when analyzing how effectively it is functioning on a day-to-day basis. By way of example, the principle of unity of command was discussed. In reality, there are many situations where a man may have more than one superior; this in itself is not necessarily bad. The important thing is that he should not be put in the position of receiving conflicting instructions from the two superiors. The principle of parity of authority, responsibility, and accountability was also cited. In practice, however, managers are many times held accountable for things over which they do not have complete control. To do otherwise would result in many serious gaps as far as total performance is concerned. Numerous other examples of discrepancies between theory and reality could be cited. The important point is, however, that classical principles of management do act as valuable guidelines and to this extent should not be glossed over.

Summary

In Chapter 8 staff was distinguished on the basis of the types of work they did. Properly viewed however, line and staff are authority relationships. There are two major types of staff authority. The first is the personal staff which includes the "assistant to" and the general staff. The "assistant to" will typically have no supervisory responsibilities. Rather, his set of duties is designed to expand a particular manager's capacity for work. He increases the manager's effectiveness and efficiency by relieving him of things he would otherwise have to do himself.

The general staff is composed of the chief administrators in the enterprise. Its typical purpose is to bring together into one group all the necessary expertise which is necessary to make key decisions and plans.

The second major type of staff is the specialist staff. There are four classifications of this type of staff. The advisory staff is, as the name implies, strictly advisory in nature. His advice can be accepted, rejected, or modified. The service staff consists of activities which were previously decentralized and performed in each individual department but are now centralized in a separate unit. To receive the service, the line manager must use the staff. The control staff has direct or indirect control over other units in the organization. They may exercise this control by requiring compliance to certain procedures, requiring submission of reports, or requiring that they be consulted for policy interpretation. Functional staff exists when one manager has direct authority over some phase of another manager's operation.

The normal view one gets of an organization is through the organization chart. Although there are many things the chart does show, such as how the work is divided into components, there are many things it does not show. From a viewing of the typical organization chart it is difficult if not impossible to determine the degree of authority and responsibility which various people have, exactly what is line and what is staff, or what the informal organization is. The two primary values of the chart lie in its use as a tool for organizational analysis and as a means for communication.

Span of control refers to the number of subordinates which a given manager has reporting to him. There is no set formula for determining exactly how large or how small a manager's span should be. It depends on the nature of work, the competency of subordinates, and other factors. The importance of the size of span of control lies in the effect which it has on the organization structure, the morale and motivation of people, communication, and decision making.

Key Concepts

Principle of Objectives.   Prerequisite to starting any organization or carrying on any activity is a clear statement of the objectives in view.

Principle of Nonconflicting Objectives.   The objectives of various units in the organization must complement, supplement, support, and otherwise blend with one another.

Principle of Coordination. The organizational framework must provide for the integration of both human and technical resources to accomplish the task at hand.

Parity of Authority and Responsibility. Authority and responsibility must be equal if people are to be held accountable for results.

Unity of Command. Each subordinate should report to one and only one superior.

Principle of Delegation. Delegation is the process by which a manager assigns responsibility, grants authority, and creates accountability. Delegation must occur if people are to make a meaningful contribution.

Span of Control. Refers to the number of subordinates reporting to a given manager.

Discussion Questions

1. Briefly describe the type of activity performed by each of the following staff positions, and give at least two examples of each type: control, functional, general, specialist, and service.

2. Jim could easily supervise eight subordinates, but his job position allows him only four. Discuss the effects of Jim's span of control on his subordinates at present. What changes would Jim have to make in the closeness of supervision if his span of control increased to eight? What would be the effect on the organization structure of other supervisors in Jim's organization had their span of control increased?

3. On the following organizational chart attempt to:

    (a)   Identify the line and staff positions.

(*b*) Determine the amount of authority in each position.

(*c*) Determine the degree of importance of each position.

At this point, you should be able to see the limitations of the organizational chart. What is the importance of adequate written information which should accompany an organizational chart? What is the main usefulness of an organizational chart?

PRESIDENT

VICE PRESIDENT   VICE PRESIDENT   VICE PRESIDENT

4. Bill Hansen, the Production Superintendent for the Acme Metal Works and Jim Doty, the Production Planning and Control Specialist, have not been on speaking terms for over a month. Bill feels that Jim keeps giving him orders and is continually "bossing him around." Jim claims that his job is to plan the production runs and schedule the necessary materials for these runs. But without the cooperation of Bill, he can not perform his job.

Jack Smith, the Production Vice President, supervises both Bill and Jim. He did not learn of the feud between Bill and Jim because both were quite effective in keeping it away from him. However, after speaking to Bill and Jim separately, he was able to summarize their complaints as follows:

Jim: How can I do my job when I don't have the right to schedule the production runs in the most efficient manner?

Bill: I have two bosses, Jim and you. Who do I really work for anyway? I get blamed if we do not make a deadline, yet Jim tries to schedule all the production runs.

Using what you learned in this chapter about line-staff relationships, conflicts, and types of staff authority, how would you resolve the problem?

Selected Readings

Louis Allan, "The Line-Staff Relationships," *Management Record, XVII* (9), September 1955, pp. 346–349.

John K. Baker, and Robert H. Schaffer, "Making Staff Consulting More Effective," *Harvard Business Review*, January–February 1969.

Ernest Dale, and Lyndall F. Urwick, *Staff in Organization*, McGraw-Hill, New York, 1960.

Melville Dalton, "Conflicts Between Staff and Line Managerial Officers," *American Sociological Review, XV* (3), June 1950, pp. 342–350.

C. A. Efferson, "In Defense of the Line-Staff Concept," *Personnel, 43* (4), July–August 1966, pp. 67–69.

G. G. Fisch, "Line-Staff is Obsolete," *Harvard Business Review*, September–October 1961.

Wendell French, and Dale Henning, "The Authority—Influence Role of the Functional Specialist in Management," *Academy of Management Journal, 9* (3), September 1966, pp. 187–203.

Gary R. Gemmill, "How Managers Use Staff Advice," *Personnel*, September–October 1968.

Hall H. Logan, "Line and Staff: An Obsolete Concept," *Personnel, 43* (1), January–February 1966, pp. 26–33.

Robert E. Thompson, "Span of Control: Conceptions and Misconceptions," *Business Horizons*, Summer 1964.

Toussaint, Maynard N., "Line-Staff Conflict: Its Causes and Cure," *Personnel, 39* (3), May–June 1962, pp. 8–20.

Lyndall F. Urwick, "The Managers' Span of Control," *Harvard Business Review, 34* (3), May–June 1956, pp. 39–47.

10.   Decentralization

As organizations have become more complex, there has been a continuing search for approaches to management which would increase the flexibility of the organization and at the same time maximize the contributions of individuals at all levels of the structure. One of the approaches that has been developed is decentralization. This chapter provides a general understanding of the philosophy of decentralization and the closely related profit center concept.

Over the years a great deal of time and effort has been devoted to the study of decentralization. However, since this chapter is to serve only as a broad introduction to the philosophy and is not intended to present steadfast rules governing decentralization, the works and opinions of many authors will be surveyed. Therefore, the material contained herein is what many authorities believe to be the most important factors involved in studying decentralization. Specifically, the following areas will be discussed.

1. Decentralization and the profit center concept defined.
2. Conditions which promote decentralization.
3. Principles and guidelines to decentralization.
4. Advantages and disadvantages of decentralization.
5. Status of decentralization today.

Decentralization in Perspective

The term decentralization has been used in many ways. A firm which has several manufacturing plants located throughout the country would be described as having a decentralized manufacturing system. Similarly, a firm with warehousing facilities located in all their key marketing centers would have a decentralized distribution system. Both of these are examples of physical decentralization. That is, they illustrate the dispersion of physical facilities to accomplish some objective such as reduced cost or better customer service. When we refer to decentralization in this chapter, however, we will be referring to the degree to which the decision-making function is decentralized or dispersed throughout the organization. The following two definitions illustrate this:

The term decentralization means "the delegation of business decisions by the owners to their immediate representatives (the board of directors and the chief executive), and then to others further down in the management hierarchy."[1]

"Decentralization is an increasing by the superior of the subordinate's authority to make decisions at any given level in the organization."[2]

Although the two definitions are closely related to delegation of authority, decentralization is much more. Decentralization implies both selective spreading and concentration of authority at the same time. As companies become more decentralized, certain other decisions must by necessity remain at the top. Because of the difficulty in deciding which decisions to delegate, decentralization is far from being an exact science.[3]

In discussing decentralization at Massey-Ferguson Limited, John G. Staiger observes the following:

"The principle upon which decentralization is carried out is most often stated thus: Authority to take initiative or initiate action should

[1]Ernest Dale, "Centralization versus Decentralization," *Advanced Management*, XX (June 1955), p. 11.

[2]Albert K. Wickesberg, *Management Organization* (New York: Appleton-Century-Crofts, 1966), p. 60.

[3]Harold Koontz and Cyril O'Donnell, *Principles of Management* (New York: McGraw-Hill, 1968), p. 318.

be delegated as close to the scene of action as possible. But, decentralization is not merely a matter of delegation on paper. In our own organization manual we state:

"Delegation of authority must be real. It includes not only what a superior says to his subordinate, but also the way in which he acts. An important ingredient in delegation is the willingness to permit the subordinate to make a reasonable number of mistakes. The question in delegation is: When does delegation and permission to make mistakes become softness? Within the broader content of company management, decentralization poses the question: When does top management give up effective control of the business."[4]

Mr. Staiger goes on to point out "three practical considerations that determines the extent to which decentralization of decision making is possible and desirable. These include (1) The competence to make decisions on the part of the person to whom authority is delegated. A derivation of this must be his superior's confidence in the subordinate's competence. (2) Adequate and reliable information pertinent to the decision is required by the person making the decision. Decision-making authority, therefore, cannot be pushed below the point at which all information bearing on the decision is available. (3) The scope of the impact of the decision: If a decision affects more than one unit of the enterprise, the authority to make the decision must rest with the manager accountable for the several units affected by the decision."[5] Therefore, if decentralization is to be effective, management must give adequate attention to the impact of the authority they are delegating. There are certain types of decisions, which if decentralized, can have major short- and long-range negative repercussions on the organization. On the other hand, if all decision making is centralized, it is doubtful that efficiency will be achieved.

The Profit Center Concept

The profit center concept is an approach which has developed as an outgrowth of decentralization. Ever since World War II, the idea of the

[4]John G. Staiger, "What Cannot Be Decentralized," *Management Record*, 25 (1) (January 1963), pp. 19–21, as reprinted in *Management, A Book of Readings*, Koontz and O'Donnell, McGraw-Hill, 1964, pp. 209–211.

[5]Ibid., p. 209.

profit center as the most efficient form of corporate organization has spread throughout the United States. The basic idea behind the profit center concept is simple enough to understand. The organization is broken down into manageable units called profit centers. Each profit center is treated as an independent organization and is operated by a management team whose responsibility is that of earning a satisfactory return on the investment at their disposal. The management of each profit center is given considerable latitude in making operating decisions; because they are held responsible for the effect of their decisions on profits, they are presumably motivated to make decisions that will result in maximum profits.

As might be expected, the creation of separate profit centers is usually characteristic of large-scale enterprises with multiple product lines. Based on similarity of products and customers who purchase these products, a number of different divisions are established. Each of these divisions then functions as a profit center unit as described previously.

Reasons Behind Decisions to Decentralize

Decentralization and the profit center concept can perhaps be better understood by examining some of the reasons for their development. The post World War II experiences of the General Electric Company serve to illustrate some of these reasons. In 1939, the company's sales volume was $342 million a year. By 1943, under the pressure of war production, sales had risen over fourfold to a level of $1370 billion. Furthermore, forecasts indicated that postwar growth would be even more phenomenal. It was obvious to management that a company with such growth potential would require a different management approach than that which was used in the past. Ralph J. Cordiner, Chief Executive Officer and Chairman of the Board of General Electric, summarized the company's position as follows.

"Unless we could put the responsibility and authority for decision-making close in each case to the scene of the problem, where complete understanding and prompt action are possible, the company would not be able to compete with the hundreds of nimble competitors who were, as they say, able to turn on a dime."[6]

[6]From "Decentralization at General Electric," *New Frontiers For Professional Managers,* by Ralph J. Cordiner. Copyright 1956, McGraw-Hill, pp. 40–79 as reprinted in *Management, A Book of Readings,* Koontz and O'Donnell (McGraw-Hill). Used with permission of McGraw-Hill Book Company.

More specifically the company perceived the following needs.

"1.   Better planning.

"2.   Greater flexibility.

"3.   Faster and more informed decisions.

"4.   The development of capable leaders.

"5.   More friendly and cooperative relationships between managers and other employees.

"6.   The need to stay ahead of competition in serving customers.

"7.   The need to make the work of managers at all echelons of the organization more manageable."[7]

It was believed that these needs could not be met within the framework of the centralized structure which existed at the time. Decentralization provides the ultimate solution. It should be noted that the decision to decentralize did not mean breaking up the company into smaller pieces. "This would be self defeating because it would lose to the public and to the company those advantages that are the distinctive contribution of large enterprises: the ability to serve as a source of major innovations in the nation's economic life, creating new products, new industries, new employment, and new outlets for small businesses; the ability to energize the flow of mass production and mass distribution; and the ability to provide a broad range of advanced technical capacity in order to produce the more complex products and systems of our times."[8]

In order to have a philosophy of decentralization, there should be principles to serve as guides. While no list could be complete, one of the most comprehensive lists is provided by Ralph J. Cordiner. The following principles make up General Electric's concept of decentralization.[9]

"1.   Decentralization places authority to make decisions at points as near as possible to where actions take place.

"2.   Decentralization is likely to get best over-all results by getting greatest and most directly applicable knowledge and most timely understanding actually into play on the greatest number of decisions.

---

[7]Ibid., p. 40–79.

[8]Ibid.

[9]Ibid.

"3.   Decentralization will work if real authority is delegated, and not if details then have to be reported, or worse yet, if they have to be 'checked' first.

"4.   Decentralization requires confidence that associates in decentralized positions will have the capacity to make sound decisions in the majority of cases, and such confidence starts at the executive level. The officers must set an example in the art of full delegation.

"5.   Decentralization requires understanding that the main role of staff or services is the rendering of assistance and advice to line operators through a relatively few experienced people, so that those making decisions can themselves make them correctly.

"6.   Decentralization requires realization that the natural aggregate of many individually sound decisions will be better for the business and for the public than centrally planned and controlled decisions.

"7.   Decentralization rests on the need to have general business objectives, organization structure, relationships, policies, and measurements known, understood, and followed, but realizing that definition of policies does not necessarily mean uniformity of methods of executing such policies in decentralized operations.

"8.   Decentralization can be achieved only when higher executives realize that authority genuinely delegated to lower echelons cannot, in fact, also be retained by them.

"9.   Decentralization will work only if responsibility commensurate with decision-making authority is truly accepted and exercised at all levels.

"10.   Decentralization requires personnel policies based on measured performance, enforced standards, rewards for good performance, and removal for incapacity of poor performance."

Factors Which Encourage Decentralization

Now that a foundation has been laid for the study of decentralization and the profit center concept, the factors which encourage decentralization will be introduced and discussed. This section will explore five factors which have encouraged the growth of decentralization: (1) growth by merger, (2) geographic dispersion, (3) diverse activities, (4) training grounds for younger executives, and (5) effects on employee motivation.

Whether authority will be decentralized frequently depends on the way the business has been built. Those businesses which expand from within show a marked tendency to keep authority centralized, as do those that expand under the direction of the owner-founder. On the other hand, companies which grow by merger tend to stay decentralized.[10]

Before a merger, officers in each company make all their own decisions and even though they give up some power when their company merges with another one, they still tend to keep a great deal of power. Quite often the officials of the merged company stay on as executives in their former company, now a division of a larger organization. These men are accustomed to making their own decisions; therefore, they resist attempts to cut down on their power. Since they do not want to give up power, and if the merged company prospers under their direction, decentralization will result.

Another factor which encourages decentralization is geographic dispersion, which is a result of the growth in size of the organization. As the number of customers grows and spreads throughout a region or nation, facilities must often be expanded to serve these customers more satisfactorily. This dispersion makes the tasks of communication and response to local needs and conditions more difficult. Increased authority is therefore often given to the local managers so that they may better cope with the local situation. Thus, geographical dispersion forces at least some decentralization of power, even if centralization of power is desired. Local managers of distant plants or branch offices are more independent simply because of the distance from headquarters.

Diverse activities is the third factor which encourages decentralization. The larger the organization becomes, the more likely it is that more diverse activities may be undertaken. As the corporation begins to handle widely different product lines and undertake different production technologies associated with these different lines, more autonomy will probably be granted. The sheer lack of overall knowledge and know-how throughout the company means that decentralization results.

The desire and need to provide a training ground for younger executives is also a factor which encourages decentralization. Broadening and perfecting the younger executive's decision-making ability can come only through the opportunity to exercise this skill. Many larger firms whose size makes decentralization a necessity continue to push

[10]Harold Koontz and Cyril O'Donnell, *Principles of Management* (New York: McGraw-Hill, 1968), p. 321.

decision making down into the organization for the purpose of developing managerial manpower. Following this philosophy, many firms have adopted this means for building a sufficient quantity of executives capable of filling higher administrative posts.[11]

A fifth factor which encourages decentralization is the effect which it has on employee motivation. A great deal has been written relating to this subject. Professor Douglas McGregor is one of the chief representatives of the effect that an increasing amount of freedom may have on employee motivation. Professor McGregor believes:

"They will accept organizational goals more readily and in doing so will exercise self-direction and self-control in seeking such goals. Employee creativity, ingenuity, and energy will be released to the advantage of the company rather than being stifled under a heavy cloud of harsh authority exercised from above."[12]

Advantages of Decentralization

The philosophy of decentralization has resulted in many advantages. A consensus of these advantages can be combined into six areas: (1) a reduced burden on top management, (2) brings decision making closer to the action, (3) helps fix accountability, (4) stimulates the individual, (5) economics, and (6) advantages of profit centers. The advantages are discussed in sequence in the following paragraphs.

One advantage of decentralization is that it greatly reduces the burden on top management. Since divisions are judged largely on their profit and loss statements, it is not necessary for top management to supervise the divisions closely. This freedom from direct day-to-day supervision enables top management to concentrate its attention on the organization's overall objectives and future planning.

Second, decentralization brings the decision-making process closer to the scene of the action. Decisions can be made more quickly because communication problems are minimized. Also, the decisions will often be more effective, because the men who make them are closer to the problem. Location of the decision-making process closer to the point of operations is believed not only to increase flexibility, reduce

[11]Albert K. Wickesberg, *Management Organization* (New York: Appleton-Century-Crofts, 1966), p. 61.

[12]Albert K. Wickesberg, *Management Organization* (New York: Appleton-Century-Crofts, 1966), p. 62.

reaction time to environmental changes, and provide a greater stimulus and incentive to managerial employees, but it is also the hope that the end result will be a reduction in costs or an increase in sales or both over the situation if decentralization did not take place.[13]

The third advantage which decentralization provides is that it helps in fixing accountability and encourages competition. Profit reporting by divisions provides a yardstick to compare the performance of one management or manager against another. Because the manager is being measured by the amount of profit growth he can produce, his efforts are in line with the primary corporate objective.[14] Top management can easily review the various profit and loss statements submitted by the division managers and judge which divisions are prospering and which are suffering.

Fourth, through decentralization, the corporation is able to instill a positive motivating force.[15] In a very large corporation, long chains of command result in an impersonal organization structure. Decentralization of decision-making provides a local motivation and encourages a feeling of individuality. Decentralization provides a feeling of freedom to the management team, as well as the individual. It is generally accepted that this freedom encourages individual creativity and gives the manager one less reason for leaving and starting out on his own.[16] The individuals can see the results of their own actions and decisions more readily and therefore take a greater interest in and greater responsibility for results.[17]

The fifth advantage of decentralization is that of the favorable economies which may result. The assignment of a management decision should depend on the "additional revenue to be gained as compared to the additional cost."[18] In light of the previous statement, decentralization offers three favorable economic factors. First, under decentralization, the resources of a large firm can be combined with the quick

[13]Albert K. Wickesberg, *Management Organization* (New York: Appleton-Century-Crofts, 1966), p. 60.

[14]Donald O. Harper, "Project Management as a Control and Planning Tool in the Decentralized Company," *Management Accounting*, L (November 1968), p. 29.

[15]Theodore Haimann and William Scott, *Management in the Modern Organization* (Dallas: Houghton Mifflin, 1970), p. 266.

[16]Donald O. Harper, "Project Management as a Control and Planning Tool in the Decentralized Company." *Management Accounting*, L (November 1968), p. 29.

[17]Raymond A. Ehrle, "Management Decentralization: Antidote to Bureaucratic Ills," *Personnel Journal*, LXI (May 1970), p. 397.

[18]Ernest Dale, "Centralization versus Decentralization," *Advanced Management*, XX (June 1955), p. 11.

222 ORGANIZATION

response of the small firm, therefore providing operational flexibility.[19] Other economies may be achieved through better utilization of lower and middle management, greater incentive, more and improved training opportunities, and the assurance that some products will not be pushed at the expense of others.[20]

A final advantage of decentralized management relates to the profit center principle. The division manager is uniquely familiar with his own division's operations, products, and markets. In theory, the company gets the best of both worlds. When divided into relatively small operational units, a large organization gains all the advantages of being small: flexibility, close control, and ability to make quick decisions. At the same time, central staff control of the individual profit center allows the company to retain the many obvious advantages of size.

The advantages of decentralization can be summarized by the results of a study of General Motors conducted by Peter F. Drucker. Drucker interviewed a number of the company's executives and summarized their views as to the advantages of decentralization as follows.[21]

"1.   Speed and lack of confusion in decision-making.

"2.   Absence of conflict between top management and the divisions.

"3.   A sense of fairness in dealing with executives, confidence that a job well done would be appreciated, and a lack of politics in the organization.

"4.   Informality and democracy in management.

"5.   Absence of a gap between the few top managers and the many subordinate managers in the organization.

"6.   The availability of a large reservoir of promotable managerial manpower.

"7.   Ready visibility of weak managements through results of semi-independent and often competitive divisions.

"8.   An absence of 'edict management' and the presence of thorough information and consideration of central management decisions."

---

[19]Donald O. Harper, "Project Management as a Control and Planning Tool in the Decentralized Company," *Management Accounting*, L (November 1968), p. 29.

[20]Ernest Dale, "Centralization Versus Decentralization," *Advanced Management*, XX (June 1955), p. 11.

[21]Harold Koontz and Cyril O'Donnell, *Principles of Management* (New York: McGraw-Hill, 1968), p. 330.

Disadvantages of Decentralization

In the last section, some of the principle advantages of decentralization were discussed. There are also a number of disadvantages which *may* result from decentralization. The disadvantages can be grouped into five areas: (1) divisions become too independent and competition results, (2) effects on innovations, (3) economics, (4) effects on the individual, and (5) the disadvantages of profit centers. These points are presented in detail in the following material.

Divisions can become so independent that they may actually begin to work against the best interests of the organization as a whole. This occurs when the managers become more "division or department" conscious and less "company" conscious. While it is good for managers to want to run their divisions or departments well, what is good for the particular unit may not be good for the organization as a whole. This conflict of interest sometimes results because the profits of a division receive so much emphasis. The managers in one division do not always care to advance suggestions that would make another division look good. Also, the division managers may be primarily concerned with making the most money they can in their own division. This results in increased politicking and bargaining which affects rational decision making.[22] Only if organization identification is quite strong, can this conflict between divisions be avoided, or at least be kept under control.[23]

Another possible disadvantage is cited in a paper entitled, "A Theory of Innovation in Large-Scale Organization," by Harvard professor James Q. Wilson. From this paper dealing with the conflict of the independent division and the overall company, Professor Wilson predicts.[24]

"1. The more decentralized the organization, the more innovations that are conceived.

"2. The more decentralized the organization, the more innovations that are proposed.

---

[22]Franklin G. Moore, *Management* (Evanston: Harper & Row, 1964), p. 350.

[23]Mayer N. Zald, "Decentralization—Myth vs. Reality," *Personnel, XLI* (July 1964), p. 26.

[24]Mayer N. Zald, "Decentralization—Myth vs. Reality," *Personnel, XLI* (July 1964), p. 24.

"3.   The more decentralized the organization, the fewer innovations that are adopted."

As a result of the decentralized organization, since power is so diffused, decisions that require a majority vote are more often than not compromise decisions. Because of this conflict, decisions are reached slowly and quite often too late to help the position of the organization.[25]

The third disadvantage is that of economics. The advantages of decentralization on profits must be weighed against the cost. One of the costs which is easily measurable is the permanent extra cost that results from the necessity of larger staffs. Since many of the staff functions at headquarters of the corporation have to be duplicated in the divisions, the result is an increase in cost. Another cost is the expenses of introducing the changes of management which may come about because of a merger or consolidation.[26]

The effect on the individual is the fourth disadvantage. This potential disadvantage is also related to economics, but in a more intangible manner. The change of the organization may have many negative effects on morale. Many critics believe that most people do not want decision-making responsibility.[27] Many of the employees are not at all committed to the company, but only interested in drawing a paycheck. It cannot be very beneficial to force these people into the position of decision making.[28]

Decentralization may also lead to some hidden costs. One of these may be "disguised unemployment" which means high-priced men who are not being fully utilized. Another hidden cost is the relinquishing of tight control by top management. In order to make decentralization work, the division manager must be given full responsibility for the operation of their businesses, and top management must adjust its attitude to face up to the dilemma that division managers must also be permitted to make mistakes.[29]

The disadvantages previously mentioned can also occur when the profit center principle is followed. In profit centers, disaster often strikes

[25]Ibid.

[26]Ibid.

[27]Ibid., p. 23.

[28]Franklin G. Moore, *Management* (Evanston: Harper & Row, 1964), p. 570.

[29]Albert K. Wickesberg, *Management Organization* (New York: Appleton-Century-Crofts, 1966), p. 66.

because of haste and lack of planning. Top management decides that profit centers are the "ideal" system, and an entirely new type of corporate system is quickly imposed on everyone from the president down to the manager of each profit center. Lower level men suddenly discover they have new responsibilities without clearly understanding the profit center concept.[30]

Harvard's John Dearden points out another disadvantage of the profit center: "When a division manager runs into trouble, he wants to keep top management out of his division unit, hopefully, he can clean up the situation. And the more serious the situation, the stronger will be the motivation to soft-pedal it."

Perhaps the greatest danger of all in the profit-centered organization is the sacrifice of overall organization objectives in the pursuit of short-range profitability. With constant pressure from top management to increase profits year after year, the division head must continually prove himself; this leaves him little time to devote to anything except his immediate performance. With only a year to maneuver in, division heads are forced to move fast to produce the results that have been targeted. Naturally, the managers protect themselves as best they can.

Business Trends Affecting Decentralization

In the 1950s the trend in industry in general was toward decentralization. More recently, however, there seems to be some movement toward recentralization. This trend toward recentralization is not inclusive of all organizations, but there seem to be four principal reasons why some organizations are recentralizing: many organizations have gone too far, rapid changes in technology, communication and transportation, and too much loss of control. This section will be devoted to a discussion of why recentralization may be taking place.

One of the current business trends which may have led to recentralization is the realization that decentralization may have gone too far. Profits may not have shown the expected increase. Subordinates may not have been ready for or inclined to accept the greater responsibility which came with decentralization. Anticipated motivation and incentive benefits from greater freedom may not have materialized.

A second trend which has caused recentralization has been the rapid and sweeping changes in technology, communication, and transportation. As automatic equipment takes over a larger and larger portion of the production activities, the need for operating personnel declines and the number of supervisors required is also reduced. Because of this reduction in supervisors, senior executives take over many of the activities and decisions which had previously been the job of lower and middle managers.

The introduction of electronic data processing equipment has also had a shrinking effect on the organization. Through the use of computers, the executives get a far better picture of the firm's activities. Top management can get a wealth of information summarizing the conditions of the firm at any given moment, and this information is supplied to the top level almost as quickly as it is generated at the point of the operation. The executive's ability to study and understand the many facets of the firm has been greatly aided by the use of computers. The top managers are once again placed in contact with the actual operation as they were when the firm was smaller.

Another technological factor which may lead to recentralization is the significant change occurring in communications. Distant plants can be tied to the home office in such fashion that summary data may be fed directly into the home office computer for consolidation with other reports within a matter of a few hours after the original events have taken place. A variety of telephones and closed circuit television devices make possible person-to-person contact over great geographical distances with a minimum of effort, cost, and time.

Transportation improvements have also cut the time distance between widely dispersed activities. The jet airplane makes commuting from coast to coast possible in a matter of a few hours. The home office executive no longer need rely entirely on written reports and infrequent trips. Now, when trouble occurs, the executive can be at a site in a matter of hours, ready to take personal command of the situation.

Given such technological changes as those mentioned, it is understandable that the top executive may become more and more reluctant to authorize maximum freedom to the local manager, regardless of the arguments raised in favor of executive development and motivation of junior executives.

The third factor which has affected decentralization is that of economy. This factor is particularly important during recessions or times of profit squeeze. Companies are likely to begin to worry about the expense of duplicating staff functions at headquarters and again in the division. When troubles or emergencies occur, most top executives

[30]G. J. McManus, "Search to Ease 'Splendid Misery' Facing Corporate Presidents," *Iron Age, CCIV* (September 4, 1969), p. 57.

tend to move right in, straighten things out, and run the division themselves. The top executives think that they have lost control and they want to reestablish it. The executive takes back, at least temporarily, a good deal of the decision-making power.[31] This means that an organization is likely to recentralize in bad times.

Another business trend affecting decentralization is that top management may find that decentralization entailed too much loss of control. The corporate trend of the past decade which exemplifies this loss of control is the formation of conglomerates. Conglomerates were introduced in the 1960s with highly decentralized organization structures. Their growth and expansion were enormous. However, in the later 1960s, such conglomerates as Litton and Ling-Temco-Vought have had terrible results. The tremendous losses incurred by these companies can be largely attributed to the loss of control.[32]

In addition to the above, an experiment conducted by two management professors at Pennsylvania State University may explain the reasons for this trend toward recentralization. The two professors, Dr. Rocco Carzo, Jr. and Dr. John N. Yanouzas, stated, "It is generally believed that operating under a decentralized organizational structure produces better decisions and more effective performance. This was not borne out in our experiments."[33]

The experiment was designed to compare the relative merits and demerits of a centralized management structure with many levels of supervision between top executives and operating managers against the decentralized management structure with just a few middle managers between lower management levels and the top.

At Penn State, two groups of 15 individuals each were organized into centralized and decentralized business structures and presented with identical management problems.

The centralized structure had eight field men, each two reporting to one of four managers. Each two managers then report to one of two vice presidents with the vice presidents reporting to the president.

The decentralized structure had 14 field men assigned to the seven marketing areas in the problem, two to each area, with each having direct access to the president.

Both organizations had the same product to sell in the same marketing areas. Each group was asked to determine market demand based

[31]Franklin G. Moore, *Management* (Evanston: Harper & Row, 1964), p. 345.

[32]"Moving Decisions Down to Where the Action Is," *Business Week* (December 6, 1969), p. 138.

[33]"Decentralizing Shows Sign of Age," *Iron Age, CCIII* (May 29, 1969), p. 27.

on past history and the economic variables of the future. Profits and rate of return on investment measured the accuracy of the forecasts.

In the results, the centralized structure consistently outperformed the decentralized organization by significant margins. Both professors agreed that their laboratory results should now be studied in the field for a more practical test. But, based on what they discovered, the professors felt "the superior performance of the centralized structure may be explained by the fact its decisions were subject to more analysis than the decisions of the decentralized group."[34]

"The centralized structure, with a greater number of intermediate supervisory levels . . . provided the means for repeated evaluation of decisions and the output was of much better quality than the output of groups in the decentralized group."[35]

The advantages of decentralization and the profit center concept which have been presented in this chapter are obvious. By delegating authority, top level management is relieved from time-consuming detail work. Subordinates are closer to the action and are in a position to make decisions without waiting for approval from a superior. This increases flexibility and permits prompt action in cases where time may be essential. To top management, decentralization serves as a method of fixing accountability and encouraging competition in the organization. To the lower level executives, decentralization increases morale, interest, and enthusiasm for work. It also provides a good training ground for junior executives because they can make decisions and learn by doing.

The advantages of decentralization become even more important as the organization grows in size. The need for decentralization of authority becomes more apparent and the use of the profit center concept comes into use. However, as evident by the trend toward some recentralization by many companies, decentralization may have become a fad and been applied in organizations where the size and the complexity of the organization did not warrant it.

On the disadvantage side of decentralization, as authority is decentralized the divisions begin to resemble small independent companies where the number of innovations being put into operation may be curtailed. Another disadvantage of decentralization of authority is the potential loss of control and the related problem of divisional competition. This is a situation where the independent divisions may attempt to optimize their own profitability at the expense of the organization's net

[34]Ibid.
[35]Ibid.

profits. Finally, increased decentralization may have unfavorable effects on the individual members and on the economy of operation.[36]

Even with all of the previously mentioned advantages and disadvantages, there are no clear-cut rules to follow in determining how much centralization or decentralization to incorporate. However, Ernest Dale does present the kind of criteria that can be used to determine the nature and extent of centralization and decentralization as follows.[37]

"1.   The greater the number of decisions made lower down the management hierarchy, the greater the degree of decentralization.

"2.   The more important the decisions made lower down the management hierarchy. For example, the greater the sum of capital expenditure that can be approved by the plant manager without consulting anyone else, the greater the degree of decentralization in this field.

"3.   The more functions affected by decisions made at lower levels. Thus companies which permit only operational decisions to be made at separate branch plants are less decentralized than those which also permit financial and personnel decisions at branch plants.

"4.   The less checking required on the decision. Decentralization is greatest when no check at all must be made; less when superiors have to be informed of the decision after it has been made; still less if superiors have to be consulted before the decision is made. The fewer people to be consulted, and the lower they are on the management hierarchy, the greater the degree of decntralization."

As is evident by the many advantages and disadvantages and even with the help of Professor Dale's criteria, the decision to centralize, decentralize, or recentralize is not easy or clear cut. The problem is complicated by the lack of hard and fast standards by which the executive can determine just how much authority to delegate to any one person at any one time in order to meet satisfactorily the demand of the situation. Only by trial and error can the wisdom or folly of the decision be determined.

Within limits, management has a considerable spread where more or less decentralization does not matter a great deal. The reason is that neither decentralization nor centralization is all good or all bad; whatever degree management chooses, they get some good and some bad.

[36]Ernest Dale, "Centralization versus Decentralization," *Advanced Management,* **XX** (June 1955), p. 11.

[37]Henry H. Albers, *Principles of Management* (New York: Wiley, 1969), p. 118.

Summary

Decentralization refers to the degree to which the decision-making function is dispersed throughout the organization. The amount of decentralization that is possible will by necessity depend on the competence of people to make decisions, the degree to which the relevant information needed to make decisions is available, and the scope and impact of decisions. Within these broad constraints there are several factors which have encouraged firms to decentralize. Some of the more important factors include growth by merger, geographic dispersion, diverse activities, to provide a training ground for younger managers, and the favorable effects that it has on employee motivation. Also, decentralization carries with it the advantages of reducing the burden on top management, bringing decision making closer to the point of action, and fixing accountability.

Just as there are advantages to decentralization, there are also some disadvantages. Principal among these disadvantages is the fact that divisions may become too independent and in the quest of immediate profit innovation may be curtailed. Also, divisions may become too competitive among themselves and management can experience a loss of control. These disadvantages combined with improvements in transportation and communication have led some firms to a degree of recentralization.

Key Concepts

Decentralization. The degree to which decision making is dispersed throughout the organization.

Profit Center Concept. Breaking down the organization into manageable units usually called divisions. Each division is operated by a management team which is relatively independent. Their performance is judged on the basis of profit earned.

Discussion Questions

1. In what way is decentralization related to decision making? If a firm were to decentralize, where would many of its important decisions tend to be made?

2. Distinguish between decentralization and delegation of authority.

3. According to this chapter (as stated by Mr. Staiger), what are three practical considerations that determine the extent to which decentralization is possible and desirable?

4. Briefly describe the profit center principle. How does it assist the company which is decentralizing?

5. What are the five factors which have encouraged the growth of decentralization? Briefly describe the effects of each on decentralization.

6. What are the advantages of decentralization as described by the author of this text and by Peter F. Drucker?

7. What are the five basic disadvantages which may result from decentralization?

8. What are the various business trends which are affecting the amount of decentralization?

9. If you were president of a firm, what indications would you use to determine whether your organization was too centralized? What specific steps would you take to decentralize the organization? What criteria would you use to determine whether the decentralization had been carried out far enough and perhaps too far?

Selected Readings

John F. Burlingame, "Information Technology and Decentralization," *Harvard Business Review, 39* (6), November–December 1961, pp. 121–126.

Ralph Cordiner, "Decentralization at General Electric," *New Frontiers for Professional Managers,* McGraw-Hill, New York, 1956.

Ernest Dale, "Centralization vs. Decentralization," *Advanced Management,* June 1956, pp. 11–16.

Raymond Ehrle, "Management Decentralization, Antidote to Bureaucratic Ills," *Personnel Journal, LXI,* May 1970, p. 397.

W. M. Jarman, and B. H. Willingham, "The Decentralized Organization of a Diversified Manufacturer and Retailer-Genesco," in *Organization Theory in Industrial Practice,* Mason Haire, ed., Wiley, New York, 1962.

"Moving Decisions Down to Where the Action Is," *Business Week,* December 6, 1969, p. 138.

Ralph C. Persons, "How to Diversify and Centralize," *Dun's Review and Modern Industry,* September 1955, pp. 41–42.

John G. Staiger, "What Cannot be Decentralized," *Management Record, XXI* (1), January 1963, pp. 19–21.

Mayer N. Zald, "Decentralization—Myth vs. Reality," *Personnel, 41* (4), July–August 1964, pp. 19–26.

11. Delegation—A Positive Approach to Management

It was 5:30 Friday afternoon and Vic Mackman, Manager of Engineering, had just finished packing his briefcase in preparation to go home. As he was about to leave the office, Gordon Schwenn, the Works Manager, popped his head in the door to wish Vic a pleasant weekend. Somewhat sarcastically Vic replied, "With all the work I have to do, I will be lucky if I get a chance to sleep." As the conversation continued Vic related how there just did not seem to be enough hours in the day to get everything done. He talked about the constant pressure of the job, how hard it was to find good people, and how no one seemed to want to assume any responsibility. When Gordon somewhat subtly suggested that maybe some of Vic's problems reflected a lack of adequate delegation, Vic countered with comments like "Subordinates lack experience, it takes more time to explain than to do the job myself, and experimentation and mistakes can be too costly. I can get quicker action myself, most of my people are specialists and don't have the overall knowledge many decisions require." He repeated the thought that most people are not willing to accept responsibility anyway.

Historically, delegation has been labeled as potentially one of the most effective available techniques of management. Writers have referred to delegation as a key ingredient that will get people excited about their work, grow in their jobs, assume more responsibility, manage their job better, and on a total basis, achieve maximum results through people. Yet the problem faced by Vic Mackman and his comments about delegation and people in general are not unusual. Although appropriate with respect to many management techniques, the old saying "easier said than done," applies perhaps even more to delegation.

In light of the confusion and difficulty that so often surround the subject of delegation the objectives of this chapter are:

1.   To discuss the importance of a positive management philosophy as a prerequisite to effective delegation.

2.   To examine the role of delegation in modern management in terms of its significance in getting results through others.

3.   To explore delegation as a total approach to management.

4.   To review some common misconceptions about delegation and why attempts at delegation often fail.

A Positive Management Philosophy— Key to Effective Delegation

Effective delegation begins with the manager's philosophy about people and their reaction to work.

The closer a manager is to having what might be viewed as a negative philosophy about people and their willingness to assume responsibility the less likely he is to practice true managerial delegation as outlined in this chapter. Rather, his management style will tend to reflect all of the following:

1.   Very close control over people and the work they do.

2.   Overinvolvement in day-to-day details.

3.   One-man decision making.

4.   Reliance on authority, power, pressure, and discipline to get results through people.

On the other hand, the manager whose general philosophy about people is positive will tend to adopt an approach to management which achieves the following:

1. Creating a climate where people are mentally and emotionally rather than just physically involved in their jobs.

2. Gaining the commitment of people by involving them in decision making and planning.

3. Concentrating his own managerial efforts on overall goals and objectives and how to achieve them, rather than on day-to-day details.

4. Freeing himself to help his people achieve results through effective communication rather than trying to perform the entire job by himself.

Thus, a positive philosophy toward people and their reaction to work serves as a cornerstone for a positive approach to management of which delegation is such an important part. Managers who are willing to "give a little" in terms of their attitude are much more open to using delegation as a way of motivating people, of making sure they grow and develop on the job, and of utilizing people to their maximum potential.

The Role of Delegation in Modern Management

Just as a manager's philosophy toward people will affect the degree to which he does or does not delegate, so will his appreciation for some of the more direct advantages of delegation have its effect. It is the purpose of this section to discuss four of the more important reasons for delegating and hopefully create a degree of sensitivity on the part of the student to the importance of this leadership technique.

Contributes to Subordinates Growth and Development. Two often-quoted and widely agreed on statements are that "people learn by doing" and "experience is the best teacher." Delegation is a key factor in making these statements operating principles rather than just academic clichés. Although the full meaning of delegation is explored in the next section, it should be pointed out here that when true delegation is present people have an opportunity to perform and, within broad limits, the freedom to work. They are involved in planning how to achieve certain results, have a certain latitude in the actual doing of the work, and as they learn by experience, are entrusted with greater responsibility. This increased responsibility may take the form of adding more tasks, upgrading the work in terms of degree of difficulty, giving increased authority, requiring greater accountability, or allowing independent decision making. Essentially, the manager must share responsibility with the people under him if they are to grow in ability.

The important relationship between delegation and subordinate growth and development was brought out in a study conducted by Professor Norman Allhiser.[1] When a group of over 1000 managers were questioned as to what they considered the most effective approach to develop subordinates, eight out of ten felt delegation was a prime developer of men. As Professor Allhiser so adequately summarized:

"Fundamentally, then, the managers were convinced of the importance of providing opportunities to learn by doing on the job. To accentuate the benefits of this principle, work must be deliberately designed to provide more and better opportunities to learn by doing as the individual grows on the job.

"Deliberate planned effort should be made to feed the subordinate increased responsibility as rapidly as he is able to assimilate the duties and tasks assigned to him. The challenge to the manager is to consciously plan new learning and encourage additional stretching. Considerable thinking must be exercised in determining:

1. What opportunities exist for learning by doing?
2. Which responsibilities should be shared?
3. How should the increased responsibility be implemented?
4. With whom? Which subordinate?
5. When would such added responsibility be appropriate?

"Depending upon the organization requirements and individual situations within the scope of the job, the manager must deliberately seek to provide more opportunities for planning, organizing, leading, coordinating and controlling on a graduated basis for all subordinates with demonstrated potential."

Maximum Utilization of Skills and Abilities of Subordinates. A second advantage of delegation is that it insures the maximum utilization of the skills and abilities of subordinates. In addition to not fully utilizing peoples' skill and ability, the manager who never delegates or delegates only to a small degree, never discovers the true capabilities

[1]Norman C. Allhiser, "Development of Subordinates In Purchasing Management," *Journal of Purchasing,* May 1966.

of those people when challenged. His gage of their present capability and future potential is based on subjective judgment. It is true that over a period of time some people will emerge as stronger performers than others, but it is also true that even they may not be performing anywhere close to the maximum level possible. Thus, not only does delegation furnish the means by which we make maximum use of peoples' skill and ability, but it is also the only way we have to determine the extent of that skill and ability in the first place.

There is a great deal of concern in organizations today about finding people who are qualified to do the work that must be done. Investigations have revealed, however, that in many cases there is a considerable amount of latent talent in people; that is, it is there, but not being used. To the extent that this is true, it reflects a problem of inadequate, restricted, or ineffective delegation. Thus, the people are not being sufficiently challenged. In the study cited above, the managers were asked to characterize their most ineffective boss; that is, the one who contributed the least to their growth and development. Such comments as "He made all the decisions—he controlled and watched over all details of the work—he restricted responsibility to only minor matters or performing physical tasks—he checked everything" were frequent. All such remarks in one way or another reflect a failure to delegate or delegate properly.

Delegation and Motivation. Over the past few years organizations have become increasingly aware of the impact that nonfinancial incentives can have on motivation. More specifically, we have learned that if people are to be motivated beyond a neutral point there must be a positive leadership climate present which gets people mentally and emotionally involved in their jobs. Such factors as a sense of achievement and accomplishment, a feeling of responsibility as well as job and individual importance, the opportunity for new experiences, growth in the present job, challenge, and advancement are all relevant. Although there are many facets to building an approach to leadership that creates this type of total job climate, delegation is without question one of the most strategic. The manager who delegates within the context that is discussed in the next section is taking big steps toward building a climate where there is more to a job than a paycheck and physically and routinely performing some series of activities. He is, in essence, giving his people something to work for by providing them with an opportunity to get fully involved in their work in a meaningful way. The result is invariably one of commitment and sincere desire to accomplish.

Frees the Manager to Manage.   As soon as a man moves into a position where he supervises the work of others his job changes in that his prime responsibility is to "get things done through people." In short, he is no longer a doer, but instead, is a manager. As a manager he must do whatever he can to help his people accomplish maximum results within the limits of their skill and ability. This means that he must define jobs in terms of results to be achieved, work with his people in determining how they can best be achieved, help his people identify and overcome problems that hinder accomplishment, counsel, coach, give assistance as needed, and, finally, he must give his people the opportunity to perform on the job. To the extent that the manager does not do these things he is not delegating, he is not getting things done through others, and consequently, he is not managing. There is a limit to what one man can accomplish on his own, and, without delegation, the total operation is by necessity confined to this limit. Thus, delegation is one of the main tools which a manager has to insure that he spends his time managing rather than doing.

The True Meaning of Managerial Delegation

Historically, the process of delegation has proved to be one of the most elusive concepts of management that there is. Also, it is one that has received a great deal of lip service, but considerably less actual practice. One of the problems lies in the fact that we have tried to over-simplify what delegation is all about. Considerable time and effort has been devoted to developing nice and neat one or two sentence definitions and in the process the true meaning of delegation has been lost. For this reason, any type of definition will not be attempted. Instead, note that delegation is a total philosophy or concept of how to manage people. Once the ingredients of this philosophy are fully understood, and once the manager is personally committed to developing a professional approach to managing, then and only then will true delegation be practiced.

What Delegation Really Means.   Whenever a manager delegates, he does three things; he assigns responsibility, he grants authority, and he creates accountability for results. Each of these phases of delegation will be discussed in sequence.

The assignment of responsibility is the phase of delegation which over the years has received the greatest emphasis. One would be hard pressed to find a manager who has not given his people a clear indication of the duties or tasks they are to perform. Similarly, most employees could give a quite adequate description of their job in a physical or "doing work" sense. In assigning responsibility, however, the manager must go beyond the typical job description which outlines what work the person should undertake or what activities they are to perform. This is only half of what assigning responsibility is all about. The other half—the important half—is to specify what results are expected to be present after the person has performed the work. It is in this latter area that we have been remiss over the last 50 years.

It amounts essentially to a question of what do we pay people for. Is it to work a given number of hours and during that time to perform certain tasks, or is it to achieve certain specified results as a culmination of having performed these tasks? The latter is much more logical. Accordingly, Hank Jones' job amounts to more than running a drill press or assembling component parts; instead, he is responsible for producing a given quantity of parts, for meeting certain quality requirements, for informing his supervisor if materials he needs are in low supply, and so on. Similarly, the job of the production control manager goes beyond designing and day-to-day administration of a production control program. This is just the physical part of his job. His stated responsibility should also include keeping downtime due to parts shortages manufactured in the plant to a certain minimum, establishing the most economical work flow and equipment utilization, scheduling so that manufacturing occurs in the most economic lot sizes, and the like. The assigned responsibility of the quality control manager in terms of results to be achieved might include such things as analyzing the quality of production, isolating the causes of problems, suggesting remedial action, and recommending quality specifications.

This means that the "assignment of responsibility" phase of delegation is not quite as simple and academic as it might appear on the surface, and goes beyond what has been done by many managers historically. Between a manager and each of his subordinates there must be a clear understanding and agreement as to:

1.   The activities or task he is responsible for performing.

2.   The areas of his job where he is responsible or accountable for achieving results.

3.   The specific results he is accountable for achieving in each area.

4.   How performance in each area of accountability will be measured.

Creating Authority.   The second phase of delegation, which historically has also been limited in its interpretation, is that of granting authority. It goes far beyond simply telling a person to go ahead and do whatever he thinks needs to be done. It also goes beyond telling someone to make whatever decisions must be made. A manager cannot grant authority without at the same time incurring some personal managerial and leadership obligations.

The process of granting authority can be divided into two phases: a preliminary planning phase and a continuing support phase. Assuming understanding and agreement have been reached concerning the results expected, the planning phase of granting authority involves the following:

1.   Having the subordinate present his ideas and plans as to how the desired results can best be achieved.

2.   By raising questions, suggesting possible alternatives, and open discussion, helping him to explore all aspects of the situation.

3.   Getting the subordinate to think about and helping him identify potential problems that might arise and how to overcome them if they do.

4.   Getting mutual agreement on the proposed course of action to be followed.

The continuing support phase of granting authority can be summed up as follows:

"The manager has responsibility downward to his subordinate managers. He has to make sure they know and understand what is demanded of them. Then he has to help them reach these objectives. He is responsible for their getting the tools, the staff, the information they need. He has to help them with advice and counsel. He has, if need be, to teach them to do better."[2]

Thus, the granting of authority is not a "you are on your own" situation. Neither is it a one-way situation where the manager tells what is

[2]Peter Drucker, *The Practice of Management,* Harper Brothers, 1954.

to be done, when it is to be done, how it is to be done, who is to do it, and single-handedly makes all the decisions in between. Instead, it is a blending of two factors: a subordinate's skills, abilities, knowledge and potential to contribute, and a manager's guidance, counsel, and help. The latter aspect is encompassed in the following thought:

"The manager is responsible for *helping* the assistant to discover how he can perform his own objectives more effectively and how to make the best use of his potentialities to carry out his, the subordinate's assigned responsibilities."[3]

Creating Accountability. Accountability on the part of the person receiving the delegation is the end product of delegation and without this accountability there is no true delegation. Accountability should not be a yes–no–on–off type of thing. It is not something that a subordinate can accept or reject on his own whim. Assuming the ingredients of effective delegation as discussed above are present, then the recipient of the delegated responsibility and authority must be held accountable for the results (good or bad) of his activities. George Hall suggests that the "act of delegation creates simultaneously, and without any further action or delegation, an accountability running from the individual receiving the delegation to the principal who made it. This accountability should be, by the act which creates it, of the same quality, quantity, and weight as the accompanying responsibility and authority."[4]

In theory, the subordinate's acceptance of accountability should be a semiautomatic process which logically flows from, and is part of the total delegation process. In practice, however, this acceptance is not always present. In fact, subordinates may quite actively resist being held accountable for results. When this situation is present there are two possible directions in which to turn for an explanation. First, we can assume that the people themselves are negative, as was discussed earlier. In that case the answer is to replace them, threaten punishment, withhold rewards, or exert constant pressure through close control and exercise of authority. Second, we can open the door to the possibility that something is either missing completely or only partially present in the work climate. The latter represents a much more constructive approach.

[3]Nathaniel Cantor, *The Learning Process for Managers,* Harper Brothers, 1958.

[4]George Hall, *The Management Guide* (Standard Oil of California, 1948).

In the process of describing delegation we have indirectly alluded to several things which it is not. In order to both reemphasize what has been discussed above, as well as remove some common misconceptions about delegation, it will help to briefly examine what is not part of delegation. In the process of doing this we will at the same time be pointing out many of the reasons why attempts at delegation may fail.

First of all, delegation is not *dumping.* It is not a matter of giving someone a job to do and telling him to go ahead and do it. When this approach is taken the results the manager wants or expects are seldom achieved. Also, the receiver of this type of delegation is put in the position of being second-guessed at the end of the period. He must justify why what was supposed to happen did not happen, when in effect he had no advance indication of what the target was. In a climate such as this it is just a matter of time until people will begin to avoid the attempts of a manager to delegate responsibility. As pointed out earlier, the delegation must be accompanied by a statement of results expected, and then, during the performance period the manager must provide support, coaching, and help, if needed.

Another aspect of dumping occurs when all that is delegated is the very routine or meaningless activities. To be effective the responsibilities delegated must be meaningful to the subordinate. He must know why the results are important, what his contribution means in terms of its impact, and, above all, receive feedback on successful completion.

Second, delegation is not *abdication or abandonment.* When a manager delegates he may very often set forth certain perimeters or limits within which the receiver is expected to operate. Very often these perimeters take the form of limiting the type or magnitude of decisions a subordinate can make without first clearing them. The perimeters may also take the form of operating within the limits of certain policies and procedures. It is important to point out, however, that if every decision must be cleared, there is no delegation because there is no opportunity to perform. Similarly, if the person who receives delegation must defend every decision or action he takes he will soon be trained not to do anything without first checking and getting approval.

With respect to the perimeters of policies and procedures it is important that they facilitate the accomplishment of results, not hinder them. Nothing will destroy delegation and the willingness to accept it more quickly than being hamstrung by "red tape." The manager can go a long way toward increasing the effectiveness of his attempts to delegate and his subordinate's willingness to accept that delegation by making sure that the climate in which subordinates operate is one which helps them achieve. Therefore, although the two perimeters on delegation discussed here can eliminate the abdication problem, they must not be carried to extreme.

Third, delegation does not mean that the manager loses control. Whenever a major delegation occurs it is assumed that various checkpoints will be established. When and where these checkpoints occur will be based on the manager's knowledge and experience of the situation. In any operation or project there are usually certain critical stages in terms of time. If results are on target at each of these stages we can be reasonably sure that the final results will meet the goal. By identifying these critical points and arranging for a review, the manager can maintain his control while at the same time not doing it all himself.

Finally, delegation is not the *avoiding of decisions.* The manager who delegates still makes decisions. The important point is that he can concentrate his efforts on those decisions and issues of most import and allow his subordinates to make those which are best made at the point of direct contact. In the proces of doing this he avoids day-to-day detail, takes maximum advantage of his people's talents and closer proximity to the situation, and gives greater support. Some of the types of decisions which always remain with the delegator or in which he will participate include: what results are desired, what problems may arise in achieving them, how specifically can they best be achieved, who should be delegated what, and in what time period should things be accomplished.

Why Managers Do Not Always Delegate

Earlier in the chapter it was implied that managers don't always delegate to the degree that they might or should. There are several possible reasons for this. Some of the more important are as follows:

1. It takes more time to explain than do it myself.
2. Subordinates lack the necessary experience.
3. The potential of mistakes being made is too great and costly.
4. Subordinates are specialists without the necessary overall knowledge required by many decisions.
5. I can get quicker action myself.

While on the surface these frequently given reasons for not delegating or delegating more may appear to have validity, further examination and analysis reveals some serious weaknesses in logic and also some long-range negative repercussions.

The first reason for not delegating is that "it takes more time than to do it myself." This may be true in the short run but not in the long run. Over time the manager who does not delegate tends to accumulate more and more tasks and decisions and becomes more heavily involved in day-to-day detail. Since there is an upper limit on his own time and energy he will eventually reach a point where "something has to give." When this point is reached, some things will necessarily be delayed while others will go completely undone. As the "pile up" grows larger it is more likely that the manager will continually be faced with emergencies and his efforts will be directed toward crisis situations. He will become a fire fighter, and many of the more important things which should occupy his time and attention will slip. At the same time that these things are happening his subordinates will slowly begin to lose their interest in their jobs and their enthusiasm will wane.

As far as subordinates lacking experience is concerned as a reason for not delegating, this may be true, but at the same time one does not learn how to play golf by never going on a course to hit the ball. The only way subordinates can get the necessary experience and grow and develop on their jobs is to learn by doing. Without delegation the process of learning by doing and subsequent growth and development cannot possibly take place. This, of course, leads to an underutilization of the skills and abilities that people have. From the subordinate's standpoint, if he is not given opportunities to perform via the process of delegation he may well eventually decide to leave and seek employment some place else. The only way to overcome this barrier is to provide opportunities for responsible work assignments which "stretch" the individual and at the same time provide the necessary training and guidance.

In the discussion of delegation earlier in the chapter, it was emphasized that delegation was not equivalent to abdication and it did not mean that the manager loses control. Rather, two essential features of effective delegation are that the manager interacts with his subordinates in planning how desired results can best be achieved, and various checkpoints along the way are established. To the extent and degree that these two things are done, the problem of costly and serious mistakes can be substantially if not completely eliminated. This does not mean that the subordinate will always necessarily approach an assignment exactly the way his superior does. Indeed, he may find a better way. If the manager interprets mistakes to mean that his way is the only way then he will have other more serious problems in the long run. The concern about mistakes being made is therefore a poor reason for not delegating.

As far as subordinates being specialists without the overall knowledge required, it is the manager's job to coach and develop his people on a continuous basis over time. In short, he must broaden their perspective, knowledge, insight, and overall understanding as they progress in tenure on the job. This can best be accomplished if there is a specific development program in existence with some type of timetable attached for each individual employee. In this way the manager can be assured that his people will gradually receive the exposure they need to give them background to be able to receive his delegation.

This final reason for not delegating, as those already discussed, is also subject to question. As the first, it only holds true in the short run and leads to overinvolvement on the part of the manager.

Why Subordinates Do Not Always Accept Delegation

The reasons why subordinates do not always accept delegation are primarily associated with fear. Most significant is the fear of failure, and this in turn can be caused by two things. First, subordinates may to one degree or another lack confidence in their own abilities. It does not really make much difference why they lack self confidence, the important point being that they do. When this is true the manager must present the delegation in such a way as to stimulate confidence and resultant acceptance. Specifically, he must clearly indicate his availability for help if it is needed and the supportive role which he plans to play. In addition, he may want to spend more time in working with the subordinate to plan on "how" to proceed as well as to establish more frequent formal review times for evaluating the progress of the delegation.

Fear of failure can also be a result of how mistakes have been handled in the past. To completely eliminate the possibility of all mistakes is tantamount to establishing a set of circumstances which would destroy the delegation. Thus, some mistakes are bound to occur at times. The critical issue is how mistakes are handled when they occur. More specifically the question is, does the manager use them constructively as a learning experience for his subordinates or is the emphasis on the mistake itself. If the latter is true and occurs too often, subordinates will be conditioned to resist further delegation attempts.

Another factor which can cause resistance to delegation is that if subordinates are overloaded with work and if, in addition, there is considerable confusion in the unit as a result of poor organization. When this condition exists there is generally an overall hectic atmosphere which tends to discourage anything more than minimal involvement.

Conclusion

This chapter can be expressed by three somewhat brief but very strategic points:

1.   The process of true managerial delegation does not fit any circumscribed or narrow definition. Rather, it is a total concept or way of managing people in a work environment. Said another way, it is a philosophy of management and what the job of the individual manager really is.

2.   The process of delegation begins (or ends) with the manager's philosophy about people, their reaction to work, and the role or function they play. An overall negative philosophy about people and their reaction to work will almost surely destroy the delegation process before it begins. Similarly, a viewpoint which sees people as only performers of activities or tasks rather than accomplishers of results will inhibit delegation.

3.   The reasons for delegation are many. They include delegation as the means by which subordinates grow and develop on the job, as the means by which we gain maximum utilization of skills and abilities of our people, as one of the most effective motivators of job performance, as freeing the manager to manage rather than do. Above all, delegation is the path to getting results through other people. The following quote would seem to sum it up quite succinctly:

"The gist of delegating, modern style, is making an enterprise strong by giving individual responsibilities which will develop the human resources in the enterprise. The major aspect is developing people who can be trusted to make many work decisions for themselves, so

they don't interrupt or overload their chief for his advice on, or permission for, every move they make."[5]

The best way to learn to delegate is by delegating.

Summary

The process of delegation begins with the manager's philosophy about people and their reaction to work. The manager with a positive philosophy is much more likely to practice true managerial delegation than a manager with a negative philosophy. When delegation is practiced it leads to the advantages of contributing to subordinate growth and development maximum utilization of the skills and abilities which people possess, contributing to motivation, and it frees the manager to manage.

The process of delegation has three major phases. The first is the assignment of responsibility phase. When assigning responsibility the manager must be sure to go beyond just the assignment of tasks or physical activities but must also specify the results to be achieved. The second phase of delegation is that of granting authority. This involves a preliminary planning step where the manager and subordinate jointly come to some agreement as to how to go about achieving the desired results and a continuing support step where the manager gives assistance and help if it is needed. Creating accountability is the final phase of delegation. Accountability is not something which a subordinate can accept or reject on his own whim. Every act of delegation must simultaneously be accompanied by accountability for results.

In addition to what delegation is there are also several things which it is not. Delegation is not dumping, it is not abdication or abandonment, it does not mean that a manager lose control, and that he avoids decisions. Although there are many reasons why managers do not always delegate, they usually do not, in general, have much substance to them. Conversely, the reason why subordinates do not always accept delegation are usually traceable to improper methods of delegation in the past.

[5]D.A. Laird and E.C. Laird, *The Techniques of Delegating* (New York: McGraw-Hill, 1957).

Discussion Questions

1. Discuss the relationship between the degree of delegation from a superior to a subordinate and the degree to which the supervisor loses control of the subordinate's actions. Can a supervisor delegate, and at the same time retain the same degree of control? In detail discuss some of the ways in which a manager can delegate authority and still maintain necessary control which does not give the subordinate a feeling of being watched.

2. Steven Relbin, Vice President of Purchasing, was engaged in a rather lengthy conference with Roger Gilbert, a buyer who was new to the company. Mr. Relbin's comments could be summarized as follows:

"Frankly Roger, I'm a bit disappointed in your performance since you came to the company a year ago. Sure, you somehow manage to get the job done and all that, but what bothers me are two things. First of all, you are a very indecisive supervisor. A manager is supposed to make decisions, but you have your subordinates making certain contracts, visiting with the suppliers in the field, and other things. I could go on all day describing the things you let them do. But let's take Jim Davis as an example. He worked for me before I was promoted to this position, and in those two years, I couldn't trust him to do anything by himself, and now you have him doing things which I did when I was in your position. Sure, I know he hasn't made any mistakes so far, but what's going to happen when he does? I'll tell you one thing, it's you who is going to get the blame, and not him. Finally, I notice that you put in only eight hours a day here, and sometimes even less than that when the weather is nice. Most of us here put in twelve to fourteen hours a day and often more than that. A manager is supposed to devote more time on the job than anyone else. All of us here burn the midnight oil, yet you think that you are too good to do this."

When Roger asked if he was performing his job satisfactorily, Steve replied that as far as the "technical" part was concerned, he was satisfactory. However, he did not see how anyone who let subordinates make major decisions and devoted as little time to the job as he did could ever perform his job satisfactorily.

Using the concepts in this chapter and in previous chapters, discuss Mr. Relbin's criticism of Roger. Would you want a man like Roger working for your organization? Explain why or why not.

3. Scott Ripum was visiting with Ken Harris, his subordinate.

Scott: Ken, there is a special project I would like you to do for me. It's not part of your assigned job, but I feel that the experience would do you good and I would benefit greatly from the information resulting from the project.

I realize that you will be doing some things on this project which are new to you and are beyond the scope of your present job, but I'll give you the necessary permission (authority) to do the job. What do you say Ken—want to tackle this project? Remember, you are under no obligation to do it, so don't feel I'm pushing you.

Ken: after consideration: Mr. Ripum, I don't feel at this time that I could handle this project. There appear to be a lot of angles and situations to cope with, and I don't know how well I can handle them. If I goofed, then things really might get fouled up. I just don't know—why don't we let this one pass, maybe later I can take on a job like this.

Scott: Okay, Ken, if that's the way you want it. I chose you because I felt that you were most qualified, but if you feel that it's too much for you, then I can understand your feelings.

Does Scott really understand Ken's feelings? How would you have handled the situation if you were in Scott's position? Apply the concepts from this chapter and previous chapters.

Selected Readings

Bernard M. Bass, *Organization Psychology,* Allyn and Bacon, Boston, 1965.

Davis S. Brown, "Why Delegation Works and Why It Doesn't," *Personnel, 44* (1), January–February 1967, pp. 44–52.

John S. Ewing, "Patterns of Delegation," *Harvard Business Review, 39* (4), July–August 1961, pp. 32–40.

Harold J. Leavitt, *Managerial Psychology,* University of Chicago Press, 1964.

Douglas McGregor, ed. by Warren G. Bennis and Caroline McGregor, *The Professional Manager,* McGraw-Hill, New York, 1962.

William H. Newman, "Overcoming Obstacles to Effective Delegation," *Management Review,* January 1956, pp. 36–41.

Lyman W. Porter, and Edward E. Lauler, "Properties of Organization Structure in Relation to Job Attitudes and Job Behavior," *Psychological Bulletin, 64* (1), 1965, pp. 23–51.

Edgar Schien, *Organizational Psychology,* Prentice-Hall, Englewood Cliffs, New Jersey, 1972.

John M. Stewart, "Making Project Management Work," *Business Horizons,* Indiana University, *VIII* (3), Fall 1965, pp. 54–68.

Albert K. Wickasberg, "Determining Relative Degrees in the Delegation of Executive Authority," *Journal of the Academy of Management,* April 1958, pp. 18–22.

James C. Worthy, "Organizational Structure and Employee Morale," *American Sociological Review, XV,* April 1950, pp. 169–179.

12.

Bureaucracy or Enterprise—Where Does the Organization Stand?

One usually gets the impression that for the average person, bureaucracy is a term normally associated with government organizations. For example, the head of the Treasury Department is a "bureaucrat" while the treasurer of U.S. Steel is an "administrator." However, the truth of the matter is that a bureaucracy is characteristic of all large-scale, complex organizations, both public and private.[1] This does not mean that there are no differences between government and industry bureaucratic segments. They are different in many important respects, but both do reveal bureaucratic characteristics. Some of the common characteristics are as follows:[2]

    1.   A clear-cut division of labor among the members of the organization such that a high degree of specialization is possible.

---

[1]Richard W. Scott and Peter M. Blau, *Formal Organizations* (San Francisco: Chandler Publishing Company, 1962), pp. 32.

[2]Ibid., pp. 32–33.

2. The organizational positions arranged in a hierarchial authority structure (usually a pyramid shaped organizational structure results).

3. A system of formal rules and regulations which govern all administrative decisions and actions.

4. Organizational members assume an impersonal attitude in
their contacts with clients and other officials.

5. Advancement of the organizational members is based on a
combination of their technical qualifications and seniority.

Therefore, the bureaucratic organization exhibits a highly formalized
structure and operation. Although some of the above characteristics
exist in a nonbureaucratic organization, it would be reasonable to assume that if all were prevalent to a high degree then a bureaucratic
organization exists.

There are two factors important to the development of these bureaucratic characteristics. The first factor is that of *size*. Size definitely
affects the role patterns of the organization's members. The management of a large organization is no longer able to supervise and directly
implement its policies and must depend on others with specialized
functions, whose roles have become dichotomized.[3] Also, verbal exchanges are replaced by written transmittals which result in standardized formats, routine procedures, and organizational structuring so that
individual responsibility and accountability can be precisely pinpointed.
The second factor is that of *time*. It takes the passage of time to firmly
root the characteristics of a bureaucracy so that participants can become experts in their functional specialities. It takes the passage of time
to destroy the informal behavioral patterns and substitute bureaucratic
operating procedures and also the bureaucratic orientation that will
eventually evolve in the minds of operating personnel.[4]

Advantages of a Bureaucracy

Basically, bureaucracy is simply an administrative device that can be
employed to accomplish an effective means-ends relationship. The
advantage of the administrative device is the simplification of complex
tasks. It is capable of subdividing a complex problem into simple prob-

[3]Daniel Katz and Robert L. Kahn, *The Social Psychology of Organizations* (New
York: Wiley, 1966), pp. 49–50.

[4]Ibid., p. 48.

lems through specialization. The second advantage follows from the first. Functional specialization can produce what is referred to as "technical superiority" of bureaucracy. Expert knowledge can focus on narrow segments of a total problem and respond with precision, speed, and maximum efficiency.[5] The third major advantage—theoretically, at least—is that a bureaucracy encourages an increase in objective, impersonal decision making at the subunit level.[6] Basically a bureaucracy offers stability, order, efficiency, uniformity, and symmetry that will create a balance in program. But a blind reliance on these factors results in excesses of bureaucracy. At its best, bureaucracy is science, technology, and scientific management; at its worst, it can develop into traditional management that has long since lost its reason for being.

Disadvantages of a Bureaucracy

One of the major problems of a bureaucracy is the area of administrative control. Simply stated: "How does a bureaucracy get its members to act the way it wants them to act?"

Often it is quite difficult to communicate to the individual the organization's demands and expectations through the hierarchal structure. Therefore, there is a tendency to try to eliminate individual behavior that is contrary to the responses desired by the organization.[7] This can be done by narrowing the discretionary range of alternate courses of action, although in practice this is difficult to do because the organization cannot anticipate all the possible alternatives that might occur, especially at management levels. A second way to eliminate undesirable individual behavior is to assume the subordinate will always gage his decision and actions in terms of the best interests of the organization. This can only be done if (1) the individual clearly understands what is expected of him, (2) he has a clear understanding of the resources which can be used to reward approved behavior, and (3) he is convinced that the risk of deviating outweighs any advantage that might be incurred.

A second problem for a large, complex bureaucratic structure is the

[5]Robert K. Merton, "Bureaucratic Structure and Personality," *Social Forces, 18* (University of North Carolina Press), pp. 560–562.

[6]Ibid.

[7]Warren G. Bennis, "Organizational Developments and The Fate of Bureaucracy," Invited address delivered before the Division of Industrial and Business Psychology, American Psychological Association on September 5, 1964.

difficulty of stating clear and precise organizational goals. For the most part, goals of bureaucratic organizations are quite ambiguous in content. Subunits translate the general goals to their specialized interest and situation. But, in the process of translation, the organization can lose a certain degree of control over its component subunits. Essentially, the organization is controlled by its subunits.[8]

A third major problem that exists in a bureaucratic organization is making effective decisions. In this age of advanced technical complexity, top level policy makers have to rely increasingly on the information supplied by their subordinates. Obviously this involves information abstraction as decisions are made from bottom to top as to which information represents relevant data as it is passed from one level to the next. Each administrative subordinate acts as a data filter for his immediate superior, who, in turn, also serves as a filter for his superior. By the time the process culminates at the apex, the top level policy officials are often confronted with the task of deciding which set of decisions to accept.[9] They then become policy ratifiers who often grant legitimacy to a given suggested course of action. The delegation of real decision power is inevitable in a bureaucracy, but the risks involved are generally high. Vital information viewed as trivial is lost or information is condensed to the point where its true value is distorted. How to keep the information channels open to the top of the organization is a fundamental problem facing every complex structure, and certainly must be considered as a major problem of bureaucratic organizations.

Bureaucratic specialization tends to encourage certain types of personal conflict. The specialist tends to monopolize information, resulting in some instances, in a "reverse dependency" of the superior-subordinate relationship. Specialization also creates a problem by limiting the organizational responsibility of an official. Also, specialization gives rise to an inflated concept of self-importance stemming from a strong conviction on the part of the expert that his judgments are not only logically sound but also objectively superior. The above conflicts result in an inherent tension between those of authority and those who play specialized roles. The superior may be in a "no-win" position. The superior might accept the recommendation of the specialist who, in all likelihood, views his decision as the only route to go. On the other hand, if the superior rejects the recommendation, the expert will perceive the de-

[8]S. N. Eisenstadt, "Bureaucracy, Bureaucratization, and Debureaucratization," *Administrative Science Quarterly, 4,* December 1959, pp. 303–306.

[9]Robert K. Merton, "Bureaucratic Structure and Personality," *Social Forces, 18* (University of North Carolina Press, 1940).

cision of his superior as wrong, and open conflict can result. Such conflicts are generally inevitable in a bureaucratic structure and the problem is not one of avoiding these conflicts, but rather of controlling them.

The problems of morale resulting from bureaucracy can also be serious. Work within narrow, set limits often results in executives and employees who are restless and dissatisfied both at the job and at home. Employees are conditioned by rules and regulations to stereotype their relations with the customer, and even "personal attention" follows a formal prescription.

These excesses of bureaucracy usually result from an overemphasis on impersonality, status, conformity, and routine which have been prescribed in formal rules and regulations.[10]

Bureaucracy and Enterprise

As previously discussed, the four main elements of bureaucracy—hierarchy, specialization, rules, and impersonality—are in large supply while the four main elements of enterprise—incentive, idea, person, and process—are fading and need to be restored. Bureaucracy is formal and orderly and its strength is authority through techological competence. Enterprise is personal and spontaneous and its strength lies in innovation and adaptation to change. The weaknesses of bureaucracy are self-centeredness, the possible avoidance of personal responsibility, and a quest of power. The weaknesses of enterprise are confusion, lack of completion of a project, and a disregard for a systematic approach to problem solving. Bureaucracy and enterprise can complement each other.

The conditions necessary to vitalized management are a social environment that emphasizes individual responsibility with a broad educational approach, incentives that encourage competition and self-development, and an innovative management under unified leadership accompanied by delegation of authority to foster the maximum development of administrators and employees throughout the organization.

Bureaucracy is the ordering of institutional management to secure the advantages of system. But bureaucracy in excess is logic carried to the point where executives and employees are more interested in tidiness than in people. Uncritical reverence for tradition is a constant

[10]Ibid.

invitation to rigidity and unresponsiveness in administration. So also is the large, hierarchical, specialized, impersonal organization associated with technology.

The extent to which bureaucracy is found in any organization depends on both external and internal factors. Among the principal external factors are tradition, legalism, concentrated economic and political power, and technology. The internal factors are administration that produces order and system: fixed targets, organization charts, procedure manuals, work plans, job classifications, and control mechanisms. Generally speaking, bureaucracy becomes necessary and important as direct, face-to-face relationships are superseded by remote, formal relationships; when this element of vitality is lost, another element, system and power, is gained. The desirable objective is to retain both elements of strength in the same organization.

Both bureaucracy and enterprise contain a large element of rationality because both are concerned with the achievement of a goal. They are alike also in being essentially neutral concepts, neither good nor bad in the customary or moral sense. Both are inherent in all administration and it is the balance between them that determines the vitality or the lethargy with which *all* organizations operate.

Bureaucracy and enterprise play out their respective roles in varying degrees of complexity. The key to their combination is a balance in the quality of the coordination that is provided. Undue emphasis on order encourages efficiency to the point of stagnation, and undue emphasis on flexibility sacrifices the efficiency of a smooth operation.

So, while bureaucracy needs the counterbalancing factors of enterprise to control its excesses, enterprise in turn needs the counterbalancing factors of bureaucracy to keep it from running uncontrolled.

Management within a Bureaucracy

Leadership.   The administrator who can rise above his daily tasks and see his organization with a fresh eye is the one capable of providing energy and drive and of preventing the onset of decline. Unfortunately, many administrators are limited to troubleshooting, to settling immediate and often petty crises, and to keeping their noses to the grindstone; as a result, they have no time or energy to devote to questions of morale, inspiration, and vitality. One of the better solutions to this situation is to have men in executive positions who can combine knowledge with power in their administrative relations and who can keep sufficiently fresh and alert themselves to be able to communicate these qualities to their organization. No administrator or political leader should stay so close to pressing events for so long that he loses perspective and the ability to innovate and to inspire without becoming tired and sluggish. A period of seclusion that broadens horizons and restores energies might do more in the long run to meet the needs of modern executives than all the courses on executive development that are emphasized today.

Leadership is a dynamic effort to combat forces of stagnation and must promote an honest conflict which denotes a healthy institution. Where friction is wholly lacking it is a sign that the institution is stagnating. In addition, leadership must promote effective communication in order to produce efficient results; although the point at which communication breaks down is never fixed, it is an ascertainable one that the alert administrator will look for and recognize when he sees it.

Where people are concerned, the real problem is not necessarily to get them to work harder, but to work more effectively. The problem is to try to inspire an achievement incentive within people. However, even if administrators of large-scale organizations were to recognize the force of the achievement motive and were to seek out and encourage gifted individuals, many problems of motivation, peculiar to the field of management, would remain. One of these is how to make that great body of supervisors and employees down the line in an organization experience the spur of competition and profit making that is felt at the top. Achievement is a matter of both character and environment; it is both internalized in the individual and prompted from without; it is both self-nurtured and socially nurtured. Such being the case, the challenge to administrators is to discover and to adopt measures that will give people the chance to develop these characteristics.

The highest expression of enterprise occurs in people who are self-starters and possessed of what the psychologists call the achievement motive. Such individuals seem to develop independence and high motivation early in life, especially under wise guidance and discipline from the family. A job of the administrator is to spot such people and to build his organization around them, to try to increase their number so as to set the multiplier of enterprise to work. But other incentives also are important, and management has a more direct control over these: profit and competition for example, both of which need to be nursed back to full vigor. New discoveries, both technological and social, come from imaginative, independent, creative people.

The administrator must also be constantly alert. When sales begin to fall off, when customers hesitate and then go elsewhere, when employees show signs of lethargy, department heads are intent only on their own work, and everyone seems to sense that something is wrong, then the organization is clearly headed for trouble. The problem of most managers is how to detect the onset of diminished vitality soon enough to arrest the trend and to apply specific remedies before it is too late.

A main resource of any institution that would survive, therefore, is the high quality of its leadership offered by men able to act creatively and to anticipate institutional and administrative needs.

Mobility.   Alert management must supply the spark and the wisdom that tie the administrative process together, and a test of this function is the manner in which the program responds to change. Growth means not only internal expansion but also adjustment to external influences. Hence, there must be mobility, coordination, and the ability to recognize opportunity; to alter patterns quickly, to select individuals who will be helpful on one job and groups that will be more helpful to one another. Therefore, an organization must be mobile in order to adjust and display the following implications.

1.   Capital must be mobile. When a part of an organization fails because it has not adapted to a new technology or for some other reason, funds that were once used in that undertaking should be channeled into a new one.

2.   Industry locations must be mobile. When a firm finds that effective demand, or a better source of raw materials, or improved transportation are to be found elsewhere, it must migrate or lose ground to competitors.

3.   Consumer choice must be mobile. If a line of goods is too rigid or becomes outmoded and consumers are not offered new or alternative choices, a competitor will fill the gap and the business will be lost.

4.   Prices must be mobile. If lower prices resulting from efficient operations are not passed on to consumers, a rival will take advantage of the opportunity to reduce his price or offer a desirable substitute.

5.   Labor must be mobile. If managers are offered better employment in another place, they must either move or lose the opportunity to improve salary and status, to broaden themselves, and to develop new skills having a higher market value.

Administratively, an organization should remain mobile with the following implications.

1. There must be a continual search for new products, new technologies, and new methods.

2. Organization objectives must be made clear, but top management should be prepared to modify them quickly to take advantage of new needs and opportunities.

3. Organization structure must be gradually reshaped when necessary to be in accord with newly defined objectives and policies, to keep pace with change, and to allow the best use of human talents.

4. Operating procedures should be kept constantly under review, to progressively simplify them rather than allow them to multiply to the point where they are intelligible only to the myopic expert.

5. Outside influences must be welcomed in policy and operational matters so as to encourage freshness of viewpoint and constructive criticism, but must not be allowed to weaken direct channels of leadership and responsibility.

The above implications are necessary in order to overcome some of the objectionable aspects of bureaucracy.

Scientific Management. Management comes down to the question of how to routinize and standardize the work of an institution and still make sure that individuals, as well as programs, will remain personable, spontaneous, and enterprising. Therefore, a justifiable complaint against scientific management in its original form was that it did not go far enough; that it should expand to include elements that would humanize it. Taylor knew this. He realized that cooperation is basic to efficiency, but *he also recognized that too little was known in a systematic way about human relations to make possible a valid contribution to scientific management at that time.*[11] But since then human relations has become a main emphasis in administration, and a remarkably good fusion with scientific management is already taking place in what is called management by objectives.

If it can be assumed that scientific management must be combined

[11]Harold J. Leavitt, "Unhuman Organizations," *Harvard Business Review, 40,* 1962, pp. 92–94.

with human relations to form a balance, that standardization must not be carried to the point of overlooking individual differences and discouraging initiative, and that the one best method is constantly subject to change and improvement, then scientific management is an indispensable tool of administration, not only in matters of technology and efficiency, but also in the matter of human relations. The attempt here, however, is to show that system is essential to efficiency, but is useful only when combined with complementary human factors.

Incentives.   There is a need both in industry and government for integrating proper incentives into the daily activities of organizations. People resent being ordered about for no apparent purpose, when nobody appreciates their opinions, and when their skill and experience are ignored. Hence, without weakening the unified responsibility of leadership, ways must be found to consult with subordinate officials and employees before decisions affecting their interests are made. Policies must be open to everyone's ideas. There must be no hindrance to the free flow of information. The key to cooperation is good faith and mutual respect among people who work together, and this requires honesty and fair dealing.

Management by Objectives.   A recent approach in management, which includes elements of both scientific management and human relations, is management by objectives, which develops the potential of the individual and makes him a willing partner in the undertaking.

If the objectives and policies of the organization can be made clear to the individual, he may find that his social and personal ambitions, which together add up to his personal integrity, coincide with the institutional goals of his employment. At this point higher management assigns him an area of responsibility and allows him a good deal of latitude regarding method. The assumption is that if the goal of the program is jointly agreed on, the working out of method should be left as far as possible to the recipient of delegated authority. This authority should be increased as the individual develops, and at the same time, he should be cooperatively engaged in the further definition of larger common objectives, so that eventually he will be qualified for responsibilities at a higher level.

If this plan is carried out well, then officials and employees throughout the organization will develop loyalty and energy because, to a considerable extent, they are their own bosses. Top management will be free to coordinate, to plan ahead, to look for evidence of decay, and to stimulate enterprise, none of which is very feasible when administrators are burdened with the details of direction and control.[12]

Management by objectives shuns the idea that an employee is like a key on a machine that moves when punched, and substitutes for that, a philosophy that appeals to the selfhood of the employee and development of his potentialities. It means giving him a wider scope that will counteract the narrowing influence of bureaucracy.

In a program of management by objectives there is no substitute for frequent face-to-face relationships. A few minutes of conference between senior and junior officials are worth stacks of memoranda. The way to get rid of paper work is to deal directly, and the way to coordinate is through the human touch; staff conferences, informal huddles, and a judicious use of committees that will allow full scope but will prevent the undermining of unified direction and control. It is only through personal relationships that an administrator can give all members of the organization the sense of the whole and of how the role of each is vital to the rest. And without this sense of relationship it is useless to suppose that people will develop a sense of belonging and of voluntary cooperation. For the plain truth is—and it has been proven over and over again in big business and in big government—that the overdevelopment of formal procedures in the absence of personal relationships drains the very life out of the organization, no matter how energetic it was in the beginning.

Measurability and Responsiveness.   Certain aspects of administration are measurable and others are not; to learn where this division occurs is part of the wisdom of the top executive. If an administrator tries to count things that cannot be counted and to measure things that should not be measured, he must expect that people will first chafe and then either give up or get out. If staff departments must justify their existence by producing measurable results such as detailed progress reports, they may spend more time in performing the measurable activities than in meeting nonmeasurable needs for serving line departments. Thus, the executive must have a sense of fitness, recognizing that attitudes, beliefs, morale, ambition, human sensibilities, and a host of other things are far more basic to accomplishment than physical things than can be counted, measured, and stored.

[12]Bernard M. Bass, *Organizational Psychology* (Boston: Allyn and Bacon, 1965), p. 254.

The executive must also resist the feeling of loneliness that the top man is bound to experience at one time or another. There are two alternatives he can take. He can try to bolster his self-confidence by administrative gadgetry such as inflated staff activities, the use of outside consultants, and the adoption of the latest measuring devices in the naive hope that these will prove to be substitutes for individual synthesis, teamwork, and decisiveness. Or he can relieve his loneliness by gregariousness, in which case he will deal personally with his subordinates and employees as often and as candidly as he is able. The latter course is easier on him, more acceptable to his employees, cheaper to his organization, and gives far more productive results than the first one.

In administration, the ability to respond is needed all the time: consumer preferences, the social environment, the impact of public policy, internal crisis, and the occasional need to reorganize all demand an alert eye and a ready response. The problem, therefore, is how to maintain a sense of responsibility and at the same time encourage the responsiveness on which the resiliency of the program depends. The connotations of response may be personal or impersonal. A response that is personal will show sensitivity and sympathy, but a response that is impersonal will be merely an answer, as in a lawyer's brief, and there will be no attempt to exceed the terms of reference. A third connotation, however, is response that is "an accord," which is a combination of answer plus sensitivity, and in administration encourages the vitality factor of consumer orientation.

A sense of responsibility may sometimes be carried too far. Thus, an excessive respect for authority ties the organization up in a straitjacket that confines response within very narrow limits. An administrator with a rigid respect for authority never takes action unless everything in the way of instructions and legislation is spelled out to the last detail, so that even punctuation becomes important. An enterprising administrator, on the other hand, stresses action and looks to rules and regulations as little as he can. What usually happens is that the administrator, tied up in red tape, dares not venture without the full support of authority on every point. He would not think of acting on an informal delegation of authority or on his own initiative because conventional rules forbid it; hence, all initiative must come from the apex of the hierarchy. Consequently, top officials wind up doing most of the work and their subordinates are underemployed. In time, this limit on their freedom corrodes morale and makes them unresponsive, even in emergencies.

Some other obstacles to responsiveness in internal administration are psychological in origin and seemingly are to be expected when many people work together in a large organization. Under such conditions, people may have understandable reasons for wanting to be cloistered. They may not like to act independently. The way to avoid this reaction is to substitute management by objective for regimentation by detailed order. Second, employees often feel lost in the institutionalized impersonality and look for a cove where they can enjoy privacy. This desire is taken care of by encouraging the informal groupings that exist along side the formal structure in all large organizations.

A group of 10 executives, drawn from 10 different employments, discussed methods of adapting to change and of maintaining vitality. These are the points they thought most significant:

1. Excessive secrecy has a devitalizing effect on effort, especially on that of senior executives.

2. A way to break down resistance to change is to show how to do a new thing yourself.

3. In recruiting for new positions, look for independent men and then set reasonable tasks, gradually increasing the complexity of the job as ability is shown.

4. Those who react strongest against change at the outset are often the most loyal after it has been made.

5. The effect of technical change is to question whether the individual's skill is worth as much as it was before.

6. Change is not the same as vitality; vitality requires a fresh mind, but change is a constant challenge.

7. Pinpricking lowers morale; sensitivity is highest at the lowest and at the highest levels; it is least in the middle ranges.

8. The way to keep alert is constantly to ask the question, "Where are the trouble spots likely to be?" and then concentrate on these first.

9. Policies are likely to change when a new man is brought in because he sees things that his predecessor had become used to.

Proper Blending. Management is a synthesis of many elements and can be analyzed realistically only in terms of blends, not discrete categories. As pointed out previously, both bureaucracy and enterprise contribute to institutional vitality. To rely exclusively on one or on the other, or to carry either to extremes, is to create a harmful imbalance in administration. The test of administrative effectiveness, therefore, is the skill with which the best characteristics of bureaucracy and of enterprise are brought together in a creative blend to produce a new synthesis.

Enterprise is carried to extremes when administration is disorderly, where people and programs are lost in a confusion of duplicating and overlapping jurisdictions, objectives are obscured by passing enthusiasms, and administrators are merely promoters with little ability to follow through.

Bureaucracy is carried to extremes when emphasis is on rules, regulations, specialization, professionalization, and impersonality. When bureaucracy becomes pathological, the attention of the group is turned inward on itself instead of outward toward the consumer.

The administrative strategy by which bureaucracy and enterprise may best be brought together in a proper blend is called management by objectives. According to this approach, institutional objectives are defined and redefined to give each unit in the program a clear idea of its role in the total scheme. In so far as this procedure succeeds, detailed rules and regulations and volumes of manuals may be deemphasized in favor of short directives of immediate application. The result is to free officials and employees to exercise as much scope as their abilities allow, to encourage their initiative and ingenuity, and to increase their satisfaction in their work. Some people are apparently born with achievement motivation and the ability to assume responsibility. Others have little of either quality and must be content to work as specialists or in nonadministrative posts. But most people can assume more responsibility than they now have if they are wisely and sympathetically dealt with by their superiors.

Delegation and decentralization must be accompanied, however, by an assured responsibility on the part of individuals in such matters as honesty, compliance with policy, and meeting standards of efficiency. To this end, appropriate policies and standards may be defined in basic charters and mandates, providing for accountability, protecting managerial freedom, and creating an environment in which people are stimulated to seek out wider responsibilities instead of trying to evade them.

In retrospect, the effective administrator will try to keep power widely dispersed, to encourage property ownership, to protect competition as a basic of efficiency and progressiveness, to resist the temptation to regiment and regulate people to the point where they are no longer free to be efficient, and to protect the values of mobility.

Summary

In this chapter we have provided the student with an insight into some of the key elements and characteristics which must be present if there is to be an effective functioning organization. The approach taken involves a discussion of bureaucracy and enterprise. Both bureaucracy and enterprise have their distinguishing characteristics as well as advantages and disadvantages. It was emphasized that what it takes to have effective functioning organization is a blend of the two. Either bureaucracy or enterprise carried to extremes results in some type of inefficiency. The key to preventing an inefficient organization and maintaining vitality is a management which is sensitive to how the organization is operating and is dedicated to making those adjustments which need to be made in order to prevent stagnation. Some of the areas which need constant observation include leadership, mobility, responsiveness, incentives, and the blending of the good elements of both bureaucracy and enterprise.

Discussion Questions

1. Briefly describe the characteristics of enterprise and contrast these characteristics with those of bureaucracy.

2. Assume that you have been appointed president of a large bureaucratic organization. Creatively discuss some methods which you would use to make the firm less bureaucratic.

3. One of the factors which makes an organization become more bureaucratic is the fact that the type of person a bureaucracy is seeking is someone who will abide by the rules and will not disturb the stable routines and practices of the organization. This type of person, in turn, seeks people who are like himself (or more so) to fill vacancies in his department. Thus, the vicious circle continues until the organization is filled with stereotyped employees.

Discuss with what aspects of this statement you agree or disagree.

4. The most efficient type of organization is one which does not have any external or internal conflict.

Do you agree or disagree with this statement? What role do you feel that conflict plays in making an organization more or less bureaucratic?

Selected Readings

Warren G. Bennis, "Organizational Developments and the Fate of Bureaucracy," Invited address delivered before the Division of Industrial and Business Psychology, American Psychological Association on September 5, 1964.

Michael Crozier, *The Beaucratic Phenomenon*, Phoenix Books, The University of Chicago Press, Chicago, 1967.

Raymond A. Ehrle, "Management Decentralization: Antidote To Bureaucratic Ills," *Personnel Journal*, May 1970.

S. N. Eisenstadt, "Bureaucracy, Bureaucratization, and Debureaucratization," *Administrative Science Quarterly, 4*, December 1959, pp. 303–306.

Richard H. Hall, "The Concept of Bureaucracy: An Empirical Assessment," *American Journal of Sociology, 69* (1), July 1963, pp. 32–40.

Harold J. Leavitt, "Unhuman Organizations," *Harvard Business Review, 40*, 1962, pp. 92–94.

Robert K. Merton, "Bureaucratic Structure and Personality," *Social Forces, 18*, pp. 560–562, University of North Carolina Press, 1940.

Part 4

A Behavioral Science View of the Organization

Part 4 will examine the organization from a behavioral science point of view. Chapter 13 is devoted to an examination of several alternative assumptions that the organization can have about people, the approach to management which each set of assumptions suggests, and an evaluation of the results and impact of that approach. In addition, this chapter will present a behavioral definition of an organization and discuss some of the more important implications of this definition. Finally the concept of group-centered versus individual-centered management is explored.

Chapter 14 deals with employee participation. After defining participation and discussing the advantages of a participative approach to management, two alternative theories of participation are presented and analyzed as to their effectiveness and the results they produce. The final section of the chapter is devoted to a discussion of some of the necessary conditions which must be present for effective participation to occur.

The role and function of the group in organizations is the subject matter of Chapter 15. Following an introductory discussion of how small groups are formed and their importance to the effective functioning of the formal organization, a definition of a small group is presented and discussed. The third and fourth sections of the chapter explore the various types of groups which can be found in organizations and the factors involved in group formation, respectively. The final three sections of Chapter 15 deal with dynamics of groups in operation. The three very important areas of group cohesion, conformity in groups, and group competition are explored extensively.

The final chapter in Part 3 is devoted to the subject of job design. After establishing the importance of job design as it relates to worker motivation and productivity, this chapter traces the historical approach that has been taken to designing work and discusses some of the negative effects in terms of morale, motivation, and job satisfaction. The final two sections in the chapter summarize some of the earlier attempts that were made to solve the problems and introduces the student to the concept of job enrichment.

13.   Overall Organization Climate and Philosophy

A major influence on motivation and productivity of individuals, as well as total work groups, is the overall climate, philosophy, and image which the organization presents and which serves as a guideline for dealing with people. In short, what are the formal and perhaps written, or informal and unwritten underlying assumptions about people that form the basis for dealing with them on a total basis?

This chapter explores some alternative philosophies about the nature of man and what motivates him. Also discussed are the overall approach to managing which each alternative suggests and the implications of this approach on creating a climate conducive to high levels of motivation. At the outset, however, there are three broader considerations that should be discussed. First, formal or informal, written or unwritten, an organizational philosophy does exist. If it is not written and formally subscribed to it is implied by actions on the part of individual managers. Also, of course, sometimes what is said is in variance with what actually happens and how the human element is handled in the day-to-day situation.

Every organization can derive substantial benefit from sitting down and formulating a written statement of their underlying philosophy about people, communicating and discussing this philosophy with all managers at every level, and continually analyzing themselves in light of the degree to which they are actually operating and working with people based on the philosophy and its underlying assumptions. This approach is the only sure way to guarantee uniformity and consistency in practicing what is professed.

A second important observation is that the organizational philosophy (as stated or implied by action) influences that which the individual manager formulates. This in turn affects how he manages his people. The widely quoted proposition that a manager tends to manage as he himself is managed most aptly applies. This is supported by research which has shown that managers learn their job primarily by example from above and, accordingly, the better the example the better the management down the line.

It is possible to engender a total organizational philosophy which will lay the groundwork for positive approaches to managing people. However, it requires a beginning and enthusiasm at the very top. The failure of top management to take a stand can lead to the development of haphazard or ad hoc and uncoordinated approaches to leadership.

A final point of concern is that the peoples' perception of the organization's climate and philosophy may be different from that which is intended by management. Two possible reasons can contribute to this difference in desired versus actual perception. First, it may be that enough effort has not been expended in communicating down the line what the guiding philosophy is. To implement effectively the principles and concepts of modern-day professional management requires that employees be prepared to respond to them. An organization can do a great deal toward building eventual favorable response by letting its guiding philosophy be known.

Similarly, the manager can enhance his own individual efforts by making known to subordinates how he perceives his leadership function and how he would like to interact with his people on a day-to-day basis; he must outline what he feels are the ingredients which are essential for effective integrated team effort to produce results. Assuming his concept of the leadership job is based primarily on a *positive* foundation he will have laid the groundwork for, and increased the probability of gaining understanding and commitment from his people.

A second factor contributing to differences in perception may be a discrepancy between what is said or professed and what actually occurs in practice. The individual's closest point of contact with the organization is his immediate superior and if his actions do not reflect the organizational philosophy a perception discrepancy will occur. The potential problem has been adequately summed up as follows.

"For most employees, the immediate superior is the chief ingredient in their company's climate. It is he who represents the firm's formal authority, defines its policies and objectives, and determines assignments, incomes, and opportunities. It follows then, that it is also the immediate superior whose management methods, attitudes, and 'styles' are most apt to be observed."[1]

Concepts of Man and the Approaches to Management They Suggest

Exhibit I depicts the assumptions, approaches to management they suggest, and the results achieved by three alternative ways of viewing the basic nature of man. In examining Exhibit I it will be obvious to the student that any one of the assumptions represents a restricted view of the situation and therefore eventually falls short of producing a climate conducive to achieving maximum results through people. The economic man concept fails because it relies so heavily on the wage and related economic incentives. Man does not live by bread alone and although it is true that this type of incentive can motivate performance up to a point, that point is usually far short of the maximum level possible. With money you can buy man's time and you can also buy a certain amount of physical activity from him, but you cannot buy his dedication, his commitment, his loyalty, his respect, or his desire. These things do not come with money or at least not on any permanent basis. These things must be earned by providing a fuller climate which is conducive to, or where at least the opportunity is present to satisfying all of man's needs.

The social man concept is equally ineffective in and of itself, primarily because it is too superficial. The approach to management which it suggests is based too heavily on artificial niceties rather than concrete positive human relationships. In addition, research has pointed out that a happy, contented, and satisfied employee is not necessarily a productive one.

[1]O. McGregor, *The Journal of Consulting Psychology, 8* (2), 1944, reprinted as The Massachusetts Institute of Technology's "Publications in Social Science," Series 2, No. 16.

Exhibit I Concepts of Man and the Approaches to Management They Suggest

	ECONOMIC MAN	SOCIAL MAN	SELF-FULFILLING MAN
ASSUMPTIONS ABOUT PEOPLE	Primary motivator is money and long-range economic security. Continual promise of and possibility of successfully higher wage will motivate increased effort to earn that wage. Fringe benefits will encourage long tenure, loyalty, and so forth. The wage is what makes a man willing to work. The higher that wage, the harder he will work. Working conditions also a key factor.	Positive social relations and interaction are a must. Within his work environment man seeks an affinity with fellow employees. Assuming this exists, he will respond with effort on the job. Close correlation between a happy and cohesive group and productivity. A key factor is a sense of belonging in the group and being accepted by it. Also having some influence within the group is a factor.	Man is self-fulfilling in that he seeks achievement, accomplishment, and meaning in what he does. Said another way, a feeling of significance and importance. Embodied in this is having a job which exercises his full range of talents and abilities. Also, he seeks a certain amount of freedom in his work in the sense that he controls the job rather than the job controlling him.
APPROACH TO MANAGEMENT SUGGESTED	Reliance on economic factors to attract, keep, and motivate employees. These factors are primary. Either the promise of higher wages or the threat to withhold a potential increase can lead to motivation. Beyond designing a motiva-	Creation of a climate where big, happy family atmosphere prevails. Manager goes out of his way to eliminate or forestall any type of interpersonal conflict. Heavy promotion and support for group atmosphere. Emphasis on creating	The premium here is on a flexible environment where the work climate permits the individual a certain degree of freedom. Fitting people to the right job is strategic. This means a job in which the man is interested, feels a sense of

tion-producing wage plan, management's prime responsibility is to design jobs and fit people to them so as to create a maximum level of technical efficiency—a purely mechanistic approach.	a feeling of belonging and group identification. Heavy emphasis on how people feel as opposed to emphasis on production per se. The latter will follow automatically if people are satisfied and happy.	responsibility, and can experience a challenge. Jobs in which people can exercise their full range of capabilities are so as to give them a sense of accomplishment is the keynote. The manager's role is supportive rather than authoritarian.
RESULTS	Although money is a strategic aspect of motivating job performance it only goes so far. Beyond that point there must be more to a job than a paycheck if high levels of commitment are to be achieved. Evidence suggests that the promise of economic rewards at best leads to only "average" performance and that other things being absent then pressure must be used. Also, there is a practical limit to how much can be given.	Contentedness or satisfaction and productivity do not necessarily go hand in hand. In fact, people can be so happy and contented that they do not want to do any work. Tendency to emphasize the social aspects of the job may detract from need to achieve results and people get trained to think in the wrong direction. Real issues that may hinder accomplishment are not confronted since they usually involve people problems.	Implies a peculiar kind of motivation which all people do not respond to for one reason or another, for example, they may prefer to satisfy these needs in off-the-job activities. Full success with this approach would depend on certain kinds of climate, situation, and people. Can result in people feeling that it is a one-way obligation, that is, the job and organization should bend to their desires to the degree necessary. All take with not much giving.

From a technical standpoint the principles and concepts underlying the self-fulfilling man concept are the soundest. Thus, rather than being a question of the soundness of the assumptions about man and his nature, it is a question of the degree to which it is applied as an overall generalization. Two factors are involved. First, it presupposes that the motivators being emphasized are powerful enough in all people to elicit the same response. This interpretation would, of course, represent an overgeneralization. The degree to which various factors act as motivators vary in type and intensity between people. Also, there are undoubtedly many people who would just as soon satisfy the kind of needs being appealed to in-off the job activities. They do not look to work itself as the be-all and end-all of their need satisfaction.

A second factor is the tendency to interpret self-fulfillment as meaning that everyone wants to rise to what might be termed the pinnacle of his profession, that is, to continually climb the proverbial ladder of success. According to this line of reasoning, all salesmen eventually want to become the district or regional manager, all operative employees want to become supervisors, all engineers technical administrators, and so forth. This line of reasoning is obviously unsound.

When looked at in this light, all people are not "self-fulfilling" to the same degree. This, however, does not mean that the individual is not motivated. Rather, it is simply recognizing that self-fulfillment is not necessarily successive upward movement. In this regard, in many instances organizations have created a climate where a man must continue to be willing to "move up" to avoid having a stigma attached to him.

Properly interpreted then, if self-fulfillment needs are to be used as motivators it means that a man has the opportunity to find his own niche, that is, to do that which he wants and enjoys doing in a climate which is encouraging and conducive to his growth and personal motivation.

The Total Man Concept

The total man concept is essentially a combination of all of the others. It recognizes that any attempt at generalization usually falls short of the mark and leads to a management approach which is restricted in its effectiveness for one reason or another. The situation is adequately summed up by the following.

"Not only is he complex within himself, being possessed of many needs and potentials, but he is also likely to differ from his neighbor in the patterns of his own complexity. It has always been difficult to generalize about man, and it is becoming more difficult as society and organizations within society are themselves becoming more complex and differentiated."[2]

Thus, it is impossible to develop one theory about the nature of man, fit everyone into it, and develop an organization approach to management which will insure absolute results at all times with all people. Rather, what is needed is a broad base or broad outlook about man, and from this, the building of an overall organizational approach which is conducive to creating a motivational climate in general.

Beyond the overall organizational climate there are also important implications for the individual manager. Schein has summarized this aspect as follows:

"Perhaps the most important implication is that the successful manager must be a good diagnostician and must value a spirit of inquiry. If the abilities and motives of the people under him are so variable, he must have the sensitivity and diagnostic ability to be able to sense and appreciate the differences. Second, rather than regard the existence of differences as a painful truth to be wished away, he must also learn to value difference and to value the diagnostic process which reveals differences. Finally, he must have the personal flexibility and the range of skills necessary to vary his own behavior. If the needs and motives of his subordinates are different, they must be treated differently."[3]

The premium, then, is on having a sensitivity to what motivates job performance in general, building an overall organizational climate conducive to motivation, a keen insight into the individual in particular, and to the degree possible, tailoring a personal approach to leadership and job design to which he will respond with commitment. The latter phase must be accomplished by the man's immediate superior and is reflected in the kind of man-to-man, day-to-day relationship which exists between the two.

2Edgar H. Schein, *Organizational Psychology* (Englewood Cliffs, New Jersey: Prentice-Hall, 1965), p. 60.

3Ibid., p. 61.

How Organizations Get Results Through People

In *Organizational Psychology*, Edgar H. Schein defines an organization as follows.

"An organization is the rational coordination of the activities of a number of people for the achievement of some common explicit purpose or goal through division of labor and function, and through a hierarchy of authority and responsibility."[4]

This concept of organization has several important implications. First, it implies that there is coordination of effort to reach common objectives. Modern organization structures are a complex of individual departmental units as well as functional areas such as production, sales, personnel, finance, engineering, research, etc. In actual practice coordination between departments and functional areas may be completely lacking or present only to a limited degree. Not only do individual units often fail to work together toward common goals but they develop competing or different objectives in regard to either the total organization or each other. We speak frequently of self-centered people, but departments or functional areas may be self-centered, also. Only after the individual department solves its problems does a broader perspective of the organization enter in. In short, over a period of time, the unit itself is the central and first concern and the organization comes second.

When the above situation exists in any degree it is because no one has stressed the total picture sufficiently. People have not been trained in the "team concept" and the idea that what is good for the team is good for everybody does not prevail. Also, there has been insufficient stress on how departments or functional areas interrelate with one another and how their achievements relate to the total. Problem solving has not taken on a team approach but rather may be restricted to just a few people at the top. Organizations could learn from some of our successful coaches of athletic teams in this regard. Whenever you find a winning team you usually find a commitment on the part of everyone involved on the team; individuals are secondary.

Another factor of obvious importance is the existence of organizational goals which are known by all. If goals do not exist or if they are hidden from those who must contribute to achieving them, chances of success are minimal. The days of ad hoc, nondirected, one-man

---

4Ibid.

management are, for the most part, over. Total organization, functional area, departmental, as well as individual success, depends on having specific goals which are developed and agreed upon by the people who must achieve them, and then managing toward results.

The second part of the definition refers to a hierarchy of authority and responsibility. As pointed out in Chapter 8, if authority is to be effective it must have the consent of those who are being governed by it. This consent hinges on whether or not the organization is providing the employee with a rounded climate in which he can satisfy his needs. If the organization or the individual manager fails to provide this climate and cannot, via wages, "bribe" the man, he will either leave or perform at low levels of efficiency.

Of significance also is the idea that the goals which are established should be common goals. This implies that objective setting is not a unilateral process. If the full commitment of the people who must achieve results is to be realized they must play a very active role in participating in the process. The superior's job is less of telling and insisting but rather consultative and guiding in nature. He makes sure that the total operation has overall direction, that goals are challenging yet reasonable, that they are consistent with one another, and that everyone and everything is moving together in the same direction and at the right speed. In some instances he may have to take an authoritative approach rather than a consultative one, but that is temporary and not his main style. The emphasis, then is on employee involvement and participation to the degree possible, on open communication in the work unit, on a group approach to objective setting, and on a group approach to solving problems that hinder accomplishment within the department.

In summary, then, if an organization is to achieve maximum results through people some of the basic requirements which must be met are as follows.

1.   There must be some central overall goals or objectives toward which the organization is striving. Preferably these will be fairly specific and will change and be modified as conditions warrant.

2.   These objectives must be communicated down the line with the idea of hopefully getting commitment and agreement as to their value, reasonableness and feasibility. The latter phase will only be accomplished if they are accompanied by explanations of the reasoning and rationale behind their formulation.

3.   Functional areas, departmental units, and individuals must

also have specific goals to obtain. These must be derived from the central goals and their interrelationships must be perceived.

4. The interdependency of all subunits within the organization to accomplish results must be clearly established and a framework and climate for inter-unit cooperation must exist. Similarly the strategic role and contribution of the individual must be specifically pinpointed and recognized.

5. Meaningful participation on the part of the individual should be the keynote. This means participation in the sense that the individual has a "real" part in determining what his job objectives should be and how they can best be achieved.

6. There must be freedom to work in the sense that a man has an opportunity to control and adjust his own performance with first being exposed to authority and pressure from his superior.

Group Centered versus Individual Management

It was not too many years ago that a manager could sit back and be fairly comfortable in the fact that to one degree or another he could operate his department or functional area on a somewhat independent basis. There were several reasons for this. First, the chances were rather certain that at one time or another he had himself performed, or was intimately familiar with all of the jobs which those he now supervises are performing. This meant that he not only knew the job from a technical standpoint, but was also acquainted with the various problems or difficulties inherent in their accomplishment. Therefore, when faced with a direct operational problem or problems in achieving certain results, the manager, if he was so inclined, could step in and get things back on the track through his own efforts.

The chances are very high however, that today's manager is supervising or must interact closely with people who are doing jobs which a few years ago did not even exist. It is also probable that for the most part these "new" jobs are technical and specialized in nature and require some specialized training or knowledge. Thus, the manager finds himself in a position where he cannot just "step in" whenever he feels a need because he is not all that familiar with the job or function in question.

In a situation such as this the premium is on closer interaction with people on a one-to-one basis. By getting involved with people in this way, the manager can begin to develop a familiarity with jobs and areas which heretofore were unfamiliar to him. He can also begin to get some insight into how these things can be used to augment the more traditional aspects of the operation and help him to achieve the maximum results possible.

Another phenomenon which points toward the need for group involvement rather than a strictly individual approach to management is that the problems and difficulties which hindered accomplishment in the past are not necessarily the same as those of today. If it can be agreed that a manager's prime responsibility is to get results through people, then we should also be able to agree that his job is essentially one of working *with* people to accomplish results. The emphasis here is on the word *with*. It presupposes that the manager interacts with his people in a coaching and counseling capacity. Given the right kind of overall climate and training, employees can usually make significant contributions both in terms of identifying problems that hinder accomplishment and make the job difficult as well as coming up with approaches to remove or at least temper them. The manager who does not actively involve his people as suggested above is by definition trying to "go it alone." Among other things this means that he is always in a telling position as far as the people are concerned. To the degree that they perceive that he is insensitive to the real issues and that he does not respond to their attempts to bring these issues to the forefront, indifference and frustration can eventually result. It is not unprobable that if things get too bad, the better performers who have other job alternatives available will leave.

The telling approach is also very often accompanied by the use of subtle or not so subtle pressure to get people to perform their jobs in the desired way. Most people have an upper tolerance level for always being told and pressured, however. Once this level is reached their performance will usually begin to decline and finally level off at a point which is just enough to get by. Continued efforts to achieve results by means of authority, control, and discipline will only lead to additional negative response.

Thus, the active involvement of people is an essential element of managerial leadership. From a strictly technical standpoint it insures that the real problems and difficulties that hinder accomplishment are in fact identified and investigated and that alternatives to removing them are thoroughly explored. From a motivational standpoint, involvement through participation insures that there is individual and team commitment to the accomplishment of commonly agreed upon goals or objectives.

Still another reason for a degree of managerial independence in the past was that accomplishment of results was more or less tied solely to internal and intradepartmental factors. In others words, goal achievement was partly a function of departmental efficiency in and of itself and this efficiency could be achieved reasonably well by keeping the department itself operating effectively.

More than ever before, however, the problem and difficulties that hinder accomplishment in organizations today are not localized or intradepartmental in nature. Rather, the factors that come into play in determining or influencing a department's success cut across interdepartmental lines and therefore interdepartmental cooperation and integration of effort is needed if total maximum results are to be realized. For these reasons the individual manager of today cannot try to "go it alone" even if he wants to. The environment within which he operates almost prohibits it.

Another development which points toward the demise of a one-man individualistic approach to management is that decisions of today may have a wider range of influence than just the immediate department or area where they are made. As organizations grow and develop in size, they also become more complex in terms of more staff-type departments, more specialists, and so forth. With respect to many areas of operation, there is a need for uniformity and consistency. This inevitably leads to the establishment of standard policies, procedures, and programs in an attempt to promote a total approach which will in the long run prove to be effective. Thus, the individual manager may to a degree find himself somewhat circumscribed as far as his area of freedom is concerned and by necessity may be forced to interact with others in many areas.

Closely related to the above is the fact that in most of today's organizations no one man has at his disposal all the information and insight necessary to make a decision which will in the long run prove sound. Whereas previously a manager could maintain contact with everything that was happening and thereby have at his disposal the information he needed, this is no longer true. Some of the problems he encounters in this respect may include physical separation from day-to-day operations, the changing nature of jobs themselves as mentioned previously, the broader range of responsibility he faces as he moves up the managerial ladder, increases in his span of control, and the need to interact with people and areas with which he is not so familiar as he progresses upward.

More than ever before, then, strategic decisions are being made by teams of key men representing numerous areas. Each man brings to the situation in question his particular knowledge, insight, and experience, and together, under proper leadership and coordination, they pool their resources to reach a decision which has the necessary quality. When this type of team decision does not take place, problems inevitably are encountered farther down the line.

Summary

Whether it is formal or informal, written or unwritten, every organization and every individual manager develop a philosophy for dealing with people. The philosophy which exists is important because it determines how the human assets of the organization will be managed. If top management has the necessary commitment it is possible to develop a total organizational philosophy which will serve as a base for positive approaches to management.

The philosophy that exists is primarily determined by what set of assumptions about man is adopted. The economic man concept views man as being only in pursuit of money and security. It leads to an approach to management based solely on economic factors and usually fails because people look for more in a job than just a paycheck. The social man concept sees man as primarily seeking an affinity with his fellow employees. He looks for social interaction on the job. This assumption suggests that management create a happy family atmosphere and forestall any type of interpersonal conflict. It also usually fails because contentedness and productivity do not necessarily go hand in hand. The self-fulfilling man concept sees man as seeking challenge as well as opportunities for achievement and continued advancement. This suggests creating an environment which is flexible and offers continued opportunity for new experiences and growth. The main weakness of this concept is that it implies a type of motivation which does not exist to the same degree in all people. What is needed is a total man concept which views man as being both complex and different from his neighbor. This means a management approach which adjusts to a degree to fit the individual.

In addition to the management philosophy which exists, there must exist within the organization coordination of effort to reach common objectives, organizational goals which are known by all, and a hierarchy of authority and responsibility. Of particular significance are the ideas of common goals and coordination of effort. For a number of reasons, more than ever before management is becoming group centered as opposed to being individual centered. The successful organizations of the future will be those that have good managerial teamwork.

Key Concepts

Group-Centered Management. This implies that the manager of today is not as independent and isolated as in the past. To accomplish results he must depend on others and therefore, the premium is on teamwork.

Total Man Concept. Man is very complex and cannot be categorized or pigeon holed with respect to his nature. An approach to management is needed which is somewhat flexible in that it offers the individual an opportunity to satisfy his needs whatever they may be.

Discussion Questions

1. Jim Rabe, a production superintendent, has just returned from an intensive management training course which was held at a major university. At this management course he acquired some new management techniques which he felt would definitely apply to his department. He was especially eager to apply the techniques pertaining to participative leadership because his job required him to supervise 10 foremen who worked in highly diversified production areas.

    If these foremen could work together and make decisions as a group, he reasoned, then he would be more effective as a supervisor and the department, as well as the company, would greatly benefit from this pooling of ideas. But, before he put these techniques into effect, he felt that he should first clear them with his own supervisor, Dave Jackson, the Production Vice President.

Dave: Well Jim, were they able to teach you anything at the management course?

Jim: Frankly, yes, Dave. I feel that the course was most worthwhile. If it's convenient, I'd like to discuss some of the new ideas which I hope to put into effect as soon as possible.

Dave: I certainly would like to touch base with you there. While you were gone, we had a series of meetings with the President. During these meetings, he repeatedly made it quite clear that one of the things which definitely needs improvement here is the leadership at all levels. We need supervisors who are not afraid to make decisions on their own—supervisors who will make the decision and then stand by that decision. After all, isn't that what a leader is supposed to do?

Okay, that's enough sermon for now. Tell me, what did they teach you at the management course which will point us in the direction of developing strong leaders?

(a) Describe the organizational climate and philosophy of this company.

(b) What type of success do you predict Dave will have if he tries to apply the leadership techniques he learned at the management course?

2. Briefly describe each of the assumptions behind the economic man, social man, self-fulfilling man, and total man concepts. What are the approaches to management that each of these sets of assumptions suggests, and what are the results of each of these approaches?

3. Discuss the implications of the definition of organization given on page 276. What are the six basic requirements which must be met if an organization is to achieve maximum results through people?

4. Steve Loski is a group leader for National Food Products. He supervises 10 research technologists who specialize in such areas as chemistry, food technology, engineering, microbiology, and physics. During the lunch hour, he was visiting with Ron Kunkel, a group leader in the Specialty Food Products Department.

Ron: Hey Steve, you look really ragged around the edges today. Are things getting you down, or is it just one of those days?

Steve: It's this Soufflé project we're working on. I've run across every type of problem in the book. First the bacteria counts are too high in the raw materials, then the ovens keep breaking down. Then the experimental batches don't have the right consistency. If it's not one thing, it's another!

Ron: What about your technologists? Aren't they able to come up with any ideas to solve these problems?

Steve: That's where the main problem is, I think. Dave, the microbiologist, knows a lot about bacteria, but he knows little about engineering or the problems involved in mixing the ingredients for the soufflé.

Jim, the process engineer, can tell you anything about mixing equipment, but he knows little about microbiology or chemistry. Therefore, I spend most of my time running around coordinating the efforts of my technologists. The result is that I have little time to do the other things which are required of my job such as formulating the departmental budget and writing the quarterly reports.

Ron: Have you delegated enough authority to these technologists?

Steve: I feel I have. Each of them is left pretty much on his own to work on his area of the project, and be accountable for his results. The only problem is that I can't seem to tie their results together fast enough to get this project going at the rate desired by management.

Ron: Well, if you come up with any ideas as to how to solve your problem, please let me know. I've got a project just like yours coming up next month, and I'm afraid I'm going to have the same problems that you're having right now on the soufflé project.

(a)   Which method of management, individual or group centered, is Steve currently using?

(b)   Which management method would help Steve in his coordination problems? Why? How might he go about implementing it?

Selected Readings

Bernard M. Bass, *Organizational Psychology*, Allyn and Bacon, Boston, 1965.

Rensis Likert, *The Human Organization*, McGraw-Hill, New York, 1967.

Abraham H. Maslow, *Eupsychian Management*, Richard D. Irwin and The Dorsey Press, Homewood, Illinois, 1965.

Lyman W. Porter, and Edward E. Lauler, "Properties of Organization Structure in Relation to Job Attitudes and Job Behavior," *Psychological Bulletin, 64* (1), 1965, pp. 23–51.

Edgar Schein, *Organizational Psychology*, Prentice-Hall, Englewood Cliffs, New Jersey, 1972.

John M. Stewart, "Making Project Management Work," *Business Horizons*, Indiana University, *VIII* (3), Fall 1965, pp. 54–68.

Robert A. Sutermeister, *People and Productivity*, McGraw-Hill, New York, 1969.

James C. Worthy, "Organizational Structure and Employee Morale," *American Sociological Review, XV*, April 1950, pp. 169–179.

14.   Participation in Management

An individual participates in something when he takes a part or share in that thing. Since taking a part or sharing is always involved, participation takes place in a social context. Subordinates in formal enterprises are responsible to their superiors for the performance of designated tasks. In such performance, they are participating in the production of the good or service of the enterprise. They also participate (share) through the receipt of wages or salaries. These types of participation are common to all organizations. But there is another type of participation which is much less frequently encountered, although its use as a managerial tool has, of recent years, grown rapidly in importance. This type involves participation by subordinates with their superiors in the managerial decision-making process.

"Decisions are made by managers in order to organize, direct, and control responsible subordinates to the end that all contributions be coordinated in the attainment of an enterprise purpose. Since managers are those who accomplish results *through* subordinates, the latter are always directly and intimately affected by managerial decisions and therefore have a considerable interest in them. Because of this interest subordinates may have a strong desire, particularly in a nation with deeply ingrained democratic traditions, to participate in the determination of matters affecting them. It is of importance, therefore, to consider the form which such participation might assume.

"The participation with which we are concerned may take place in two different ways. First, it may involve interaction solely between a subordinate and his manager. This would be the case where a worker originates a suggestion which he transmits to his boss. Secondly, it may involve interaction between a group of subordinates and their manager. This would be the case where a manager calls his subordinates together to discuss a common problem or to formulate a recommendation."[1]

Participation Defined

In Chapter 1 management was defined as getting things done by, with, and through other people. Participative management may be defined as getting things done through other people by creating a situation in which subordinates may develop mental and emotional involvement in a group situation which encourages them to contribute to group goals and share the responsibility in them.[2] Advocates of participative management stress the human element of this definition. Perhaps the key words in the definition are mental and emotional involvement.

Participative management involves not just worker behavior but also a situation. This point may be better illustrated by examining the type of participation being used. The type used has been described as a balance between pseudo-participation and excessive participation.[3] Pseudo-participation is that situation in which workers are allowed to believe that they are involved in some decision-making process when in actuality they are not. An example might be the situation in which a manager solicits suggestions when he has already made a decision. The act reflects the application of participative methods without an understanding of the underlying principles. The workers will soon

[1]Robert Tannenbaum and Fred Massarik. "Participation by Subordinates in the Managerial Decision-Making Process," as quoted by Robert A. Sutermeister, *People and Productivity* (New York: McGraw-Hill, 1963), p. 458.

[2]Keith Davis, "Management By Participation," *Management Review, XLVI* (February 1957), p. 69.

[3]Joel M. Rosenfield and Matthew J. Smith, "Participative Management: An Overview," *Personnel Journal, XLVI* (February 1967), p. 101.

realize the manipulation and feelings of mistrust will grow.[4] At the other extreme is excessive participation in which, in an effort to maintain understanding and good feelings among all concerned in the decision-making process, the decision is put off until all the participants are in agreement.[5] The obvious disadvantage to this situation is that it is time-consuming and may prevent concerted action.[6] The balance is one in which the participants are truly active and capable of producing results.[7]

The appropriate degree of participation is dependent not only on the interpersonal relationships existing in the organization but also upon the situation in which the organization is operating, crisis or noncrisis.[8] Pseudo-participation tends to arise in a crisis situation. The manager may ask for suggestions only because the situation forces him to ask for help in his desperation. This change from an authoritarian approach to a participative approach will more than likely cause feelings of uneasiness and produce few suggestions.[9] The give and take relationship of real participation must arise from feelings of mutual respect existing in the day-to-day relationships of superiors and subordinates. Participation cannot be ordered. It must be developed by involving the subordinates in the goal-setting decisions.[10]

"There are many advantages which *may* stem from the use of participation as a managerial device. The following are the principal ones.[11]

"1. A higher rate of output and increased quality of product (including reduced spoilage and wastage) as a result of greater personal effort and attention on the part of the subordinates.

"2. A reduction in the turnover rate, absenteeism, and tardiness.

[4]Ibid.
[5]Rosenfield, op. cit., p. 102.
[6]Ibid.
[7]Ibid.
[8]Ibid.
[9]Ibid.
[10]Ibid.
[11]Robert Tannenbaum and Fred Massarik, "Sharing Decision-Making With Subordinates," as quoted in Robert Dubin, *Human Relations in Administration* (Englewood Cliffs, New Jersey: Prentice-Hall, 1956), pp. 225–226.

"3.   A reduction in the number of grievances and more peaceful manager-subordinate and manager-union relations.

"4.   A greater readiness to accept change. When changes are arbitrarily introduced from above without explanation, subordinates tend to feel insecure and to take countermeasures aimed at a sabotage of the innovations. But when they have participated in the process leading to the decision, they have had an opportunity to be heard. They know then what to expect and why, and they may desire the change. Blind resistance tends to become intelligent adaptation as insecurity is replaced by security.

"5.   Greater ease in the management of subordinates. Fewer managers may be necessary, the need for close supervision may be reduced, and less disciplinary action may be called for. Subordinates who have participated in the process leading toward a determination of matters directly affecting them may have a greater sense of responsibility with respect to the performance of their assigned tasks and may be more willing to accept the authority of their superiors. All managers possess a given amount of formal authority delegated to them by their superiors. But formal authority is not necessarily the equivalent of effective authority. The real source of the authority possessed by an individual lies in the acceptance of its exercise by those who are subject to it. It is the subordinates of an individual who determine the authority which he may wield. Formal authority is, in effect, nominal authority. It becomes real only when it is accepted. Thus, to be effective, formal authority must coincide with authority determined by its acceptance. The latter defines the useful limits of the former. The use of participation as a managerial device may result in a widening of these limits, reducing the amount of resistance to the exercise of formal authority and increasing the positive responses of subordinates to managerial directives.

"6.   The improved quality of managerial decisions. It is seldom if ever possible for managers to have knowledge of *all* alternatives and *all* consequences related to the decisions which they must make. Because of the existence of barriers to the upward flow of information in most enterprises, much valuable information possessed by subordinates never reaches their managers. Participation tends to break down the barriers, making the information available to managers. To the extent that such information alters the decisions which managers make, the quality of their decisions may thereby be improved."[12]

12Ibid., p. 226.

Alternative Theories of Participation

One of the main problems confronting the modern manager is how he can be "democratic" in his dealings with his subordinates and at the same time maintain the necessary authority and control within the organization for which he is responsible.

In the earlier part of this century, the successful manager was usually pictured as intelligent, imaginative, ambitious, dynamic, able to make rapid decisions, and capable of inspiring subordinates. Most people thought of the world as being divided into "leaders" and "followers."

Some of these ideas were challenged as the social sciences developed the concept of "group dynamics" which had its focus on the members of the group rather than only on the leader. Many of the research efforts of social scientists underscored the importance of employee involvement and participation in decision making. The research results began to challenge the efficiency of highly directive leadership, and increasing attention was being paid to problems of motivation and human relations.

The result of these findings and the human relations training based on them was to develop a questioning of the stereotype of an effective leader. This has resulted in the modern manager frequently finding himself in an uncomfortable state of mind.

He often is unsure of how to behave. He feels torn between existing "strong" leadership and "participative" leadership. Although the new knowledge pushes him in one direction, his experience pulls him in another direction. He often feels unsure of whether a group decision is really appropriate or whether he is using staff meetings merely as a means of avoiding his own decision-making responsibility.

While participation has apparently been well merchandised and widely purchased, there seems to be a great deal of confusion about what has been sold and what has been bought. Managers do not appear to have accepted a single, logically consistent concept of participation. In fact, there is reason to believe that managers have adopted two different theories or models of participation—one for themselves and one for their subordinates.[13]

Although the suggestion that managers are accepting a two-sided

[13]Robert Tannenbaum and Warren H. Schmidt, "How to Choose A Leadership Pattern," *Harvard Business Review, 36* (2), pp. 95–101 (March–April 1958), as quoted in Robert A. Sutermeister, *People and Productivity* (New York: McGraw-Hill, 1963), pp. 428–429.

approach to participation may be disturbing, it should not be too surprising since the concept of participation has not always been dealt with in a consistent manner. An examination of the various treatments of participation reveals two significantly different models of participative management.

One of the models—the human relations model—closely resembles the concept of participation which the managers appear to accept for use with their own subordinates.

The second, and not fully developed theory—the human resources model—prescribes the sort of participative policies that managers would apparently like their superiors to follow.

"Both the human relations and the human resources models have three basic components:

"1.   A set of assumptions about people's values and capalities.

"2.   Certain prescriptions as to the amount and kind of participative policies and practices that managers should follow in keeping with their assumptions about people.

"3.   A set of expectations with respect to the effects of participation on subordinate morale and performance.

"This third component contains the model's explanation of how and why participation works—that is, the purpose of participation and how it accomplishes this purpose."[14]

Human Relations Model.   The human relations model approach is not new. Spokesmen began to challenge the classical autocratic philosophy of management as early as the 1920s. The employee was no longer pictured as merely being an appendage to a machine, seeking only economic rewards from his work. Often managers were instructed to consider him as a "whole man" rather than merely a bundle of skills and aptitudes.[15] They were urged to create a "sense of satisfaction" among their subordinates by showing interest in the employees' personal success and welfare. As Reinhard Bendix notes, the "failure to

[14]Raymond E. Miles, "Human Relations or Human Resources?", as quoted in *Creative Personnel Management,* Max S. Wortman, Jr., editor (Boston: Allyn and Bacon, 1969), pp. 441–442.

[15]Reinhard Bendix, *Work and Authority in Industry* (New York: Wiley, 1956), pp. 287–340.

treat workers as human beings came to be regarded as the cause of low morale, poor craftsmanship, unresponsiveness, and confusion."[16]

"The key element in the human relations approach is its basic objective of making organizational members *feel* a useful and important part of the overall effort. This process is viewed as the means of accomplishing the ultimate goal of building a cooperative and compliant work force. Participation, in this model, is a lubricant which oils away resistance to formal authority. By discussing problems with his subordinates and acknowledging their individual needs and desires, the manager hopes to build a cohesive work team that is willing and anxious to tangle with organizational problems.

"One further clue to the way in which participation is viewed in this approach is provided in Dubin's concept of "privilege pay." The manager "buys" cooperation by letting his subordinates in on departmental information and allowing them to discuss and state their opinions on various departmental problems. He "pays a price" for allowing his subordinates the privilege of participating in certain decisions and exercising some self-direction. In return he hopes to obtain their cooperation in carrying out these and other decisions for the accomplishment of departmental objectives.

"In sum, the human relations approach does not bring out the fact that participation may be useful for its own sake. The possibility that subordinates will, in fact, bring to light points which the manager may have overlooked, if considered at all, tends to be mentioned only in passing. This is treated as a potential side benefit which, while not normally expected, may occasionally occur. Instead, the manager is urged to adopt participative leadership policies as the least-cost method of obtaining cooperation and getting his decisions accepted.

"In many ways the human relations model represents only a slight departure from traditional autocratic models of management. The method of achieving results is different, and employees are viewed in more humanistic terms, but the basic roles of the manager and his subordinates remain essentially the same. The ultimate goal sought in both the traditional and human relations model is compliance with managerial authority."[17]

[16]Ibid., p. 294.

[17]Raymond E. Miles, "Human Relations or Human Resources?", as quoted in

Human Resources Model. The human resources model represents a dramatic departure from traditional concepts of management. Though it has not yet been fully developed, it is emerging as a new and significant contribution to management thought. The magnitude of its departure from previous models is illustrated first of all in its basic assumptions concerning people's values and abilities. The focus of attention in this respect is on all organization members as reservoirs of untapped resources. These resources include not only physical skills and energy, but also creative ability and the capacity for responsible, self-directed, self-controlled behavior. Given these assumptions about people, the manager's job cannot be viewed merely as one of giving direction and obtaining cooperation. Instead, his primary task becomes that of creating an environment in which the total resources of his department can be utilized.

The second area in which the human resources model differs dramatically from previous models is in its view on the purpose and goal of participation. In this model the manager does not share information, discuss departmental decisions, or encourage self-direction and self-control merely to improve subordinate satisfaction and morale. Rather, the purpose of these practices is to improve the decision-making process and the total performance efficiency of the organization. The human resources model suggests that many decisions may actually be made more efficiently by those directly involved in, and affected by, the decisions.

Similarly, this model implies that control is often most efficiently exercised by those directly involved in the work in process, rather than by a person or a group removed from the actual point of operation. Moreover, the human resources model does not suggest that the manager should allow participation only in routine decisions. Instead, it implies that the more important the decision, the greater his obligation to encourage ideas and suggestions from his subordinates.

Along this same vein, this model does not suggest that the manager allow his subordinates to exercise self-direction and self-control only when they are carrying out relatively unimportant assignments. In fact, it suggests that the area over which subordinates exercise self-direction and control should be continually broadened in keeping with their growing experience and ability.

The crucial point at which this model tends to differ dramatically from other models is in its explanation of the casual relationship between

Creative Personnel Management, Max S. Wortman, Jr., editor (Boston: Allyn and Bacon, 1969), pp. 442–445.

satisfaction and performance. In the human relations approach, improvement in subordinate satisfaction is viewed as the variable that is the ultimate cause of improved performance.

In the human resources model the casual relationship between satisfaction and performance is viewed as being quite different. The increased subordinate satisfaction is not pictured as the primary cause of improved performance; improvements result directly from creative contributions which subordinates make to departmental decision making, direction, and control. Subordinates' satisfaction is viewed instead as a by-product of the process—the result of their having made significant contributions to organizational success.

The human resources model does not deny a relationship between participation and morale. It suggests that subordinates' satisfaction may quite possibly increase as they play more and more meaningful roles in decision making and control. Moreover, the model recognizes that the improvements in morale may not only set the stage for expanded participation, but create an atmosphere which supports the creative problem-solving process.

Extra-Participational Conditions for Effective Participation

In addition to the factors governing the relationship between participation and possible resultant motivation, certain other conditions "outside" the individual must be considered by the managers as they decide whether or not this particular device is suitable to their application. It would be possible to distinguish a great number of such outside conditions which may determine whether or not the use of participation would be feasible in a given situation. The conditions indicated here are suggestive rather than fully definitive. All are to be viewed with this question in mind: "Granting that participation may have certain beneficial effects, is it useful in a given instance if the ends of the enterprise are to be achieved?"[18]

To answer this question affirmatively, the following list of conditions must be met:

1. Time Availability.   The final decision cannot be of a too urgent nature. If an emergency decision is needed, it is obvious that even if

[18]Robert Tannenbaum and Fred Massarik, "Sharing Decision-Making With Subordinates," as quoted in Robert Dubin, *Human Relations in Administration* (Englewood Cliffs, New Jersey: Prentice-Hall, 1956), pp. 226–227.

participative decison making may have a beneficial effect in some areas, the slowness of the decision may thwart other goals of the enterprise or even may pose a threat to the existence of the enterprise.

2.　Rational Economics.　The cost of using participation in the decision-making process must not be so great that it will outweigh any positive values that will be directly brought about by it.

3.　Intraplant Strategy.

(a)　Subordinate Security.　When you give subordinates an opportunity to participate in the decision-making process, you must not bring with it any awareness on their part of unavoidable catastrophic events. As an example, a subordinate who is made aware in the participation process that he will lose his job regardless of any decisions towards which he might contribute may experience a definite drop in his motivation.

(b)　Manager-Subordinate Stability.　When you give subordinates an opportunity to participate in the decision-making process, you must not threaten seriously to undermine the formal authority of the managers of the enterprise. As an example, in some cases managers may have good reasons to assume that the participation may lead nonmanagers to doubt the competence level of the formal leadership, or that serious crises would result were it to develop that the subordinates were right while the final management decision was in disagreement with them and was incorrect.

4.　Interplant Strategy.　Although you provide opportunities for participation, you must be careful not to open channels of communication to competing enterprises. "Leaks" of this information to a competitor from subordinates who have been participating in a given decision-making process must be avoided if the use of participation is to be applicable.

5.　Provision for Communication Channels.　For participation to be effective channels of communication must be provided through which the employee may take part in the decision-making process. These channels must be readily available continuously and their use must always be convenient and practical.

6.　Education for Participation.　For participation to be an effective means, efforts must be made to educate the subordinates regarding its function and the purpose in the overall functioning of the enterprise.[19]

19Ibid., pp. 227–228.

The bridge between the philosophy of participation and its application is communication. Participative management, before it can be
successful, must be built on a day-to-day operational relationship of
mutual trust and respect.[20] The superiors and subordinates must be
able to communicate without fear of reprisals and threats to security.
Without open communication the flow of new and critical ideas is diminished and a state of pseudo-participation arises.[21] The subordinate must
know what is expected of him and have standards by which he may
direct and control his own performance. Unless he knows the standards
and objectives and how his job relates to the attainment of those ends
he cannot be greatly committed.[22]

Summary

In Chapter 13 it was noted that management was increasingly becoming
group centered. Chapter 14 has explored in greater detail the area of
participation. Participation was defined as getting things done through
other people by creating an environment in which they develop mental
and emotional involvement in a group situation which encourages them
to contribute to goals and share responsibility for them. The type of
participative climate which is created must be meaningful to the employee. The climate should not reflect pseudo-participation nor should
it be excessive. A balance must be struck. Some of the more important
advantages of participation include better quantity and quality, less
turnover and absenteeism, acceptance of change, fewer grievances,
improved decisions, and ease of management.

There are two alternative theories of participation. The human relations model sees participation as a way of increasing job satisfaction
and hopefully, therefore, job performance. Managers who use participation in this way view it as a more acceptable way to get compliance to

[20]Paul R. Lawrence, "How To Deal With Resistance To Change," *Harvard Business
Review, XXXII* (July–August 1954), p. 51.

[21]Joel M. Rosenfield and Matthew J. Smith, "Participative Management: An Overview," *Personnel Journal, XLVI* (February 1967), p. 102.

[22]Ibid.

their authority. The human resources model sees participation as a way of improving decision making. Managers adopting this view sincerely believe that subordinates can make significant contributions if given the opportunity. Job satisfaction is a by-product.

Key Concepts

Pseudo-Participation.   Implies that the manager tries to make people think they are participating and having an influence when they really do not. It is manipulative in nature.

Excessive Participation.   Carrying participation to a point where important decisions are not made or using it where it is not appropriate.

Human Relations Model.   Views participation as a lubricant which oils away resistance to authority.

Human Resources Model.   Views participation as a means to improving the quality of decisions.

Discussion Questions

1. What are the advantages available to a manager who uses participative management?

2. What is the main flaw of the human relations model of participation?

3. How does the human resources model differ from the human relations model?

4. What are the conditions which must be met if participative management is to be successful?

Selected Readings

Robert C. Albrock, "Participative Management: Time for a Second Look," *Fortune Magazine, LXXV* (5), May 1967, pp. 166–170, 197–200.

Keith Davis, "The Case for Participative Management," *Business Horizons, VI* (3), Fall 1963, pp. 55–60.

————, "Management by Participation," *Management Review, XLVI,* February 1957.

Norman R. F. Maier, *Psychology in Industry,* 3d edition, Houghton-Mifflin, Boston, 1965, pp. 153–203.

Hene M. Newport, "Participative Management: Some Cautions," *Personnel Journal, 45* (9), October 1966, pp. 532–536.

Joel M. Rosenfield, and Matthew J. Smith, "Participative Management: An Overview," *Personnel Journal, XLVI,* February 1967.

Robert Tannenbaum, and Fred Massarik, "Participation by Subordinates in the Managerial Decision-Making Process," *Canadian Journal of Economics and Political Science,* 1950, pp. 408–418.

Robert Tannenbaum, and Warren H. Schmidt, "How to Choose a Leadership Pattern," *Harvard Business Review, 36* (2), March–April 1958.

Richard E. Walton, "Contrasting Designs for Participative Systems," *Personnel Administration, 30* (6), November–December 1967, pp. 35–41.

15. Role and Function of the Group in Organizations

Why does one study groups in organizations? One answer is that groups exist in any organization and that they are essential to an organization's actual performance. There is ample evidence that groups *do* have a major impact on their members, on other groups, and on the host organization.

An organization divides its ultimate task into subtasks which are assigned to various subunits. Division of the task and passing it down is continued until a level is reached where several people take a sub-goal and divide it among themselves as individuals, but no longer create work units. We have the basis for group formation along functional lines at this level of formal organizations. Thus, division of labor is what basically breaks an organization into groups. It becomes evident, therefore, that the organization itself generates forces toward the formation of various functional task groups within itself.[1]

If one wishes to better understand an organization and how it operates, he needs to understand groups and how they operate. He needs

---

[1] Edgar H. Schein, *Organizational Psychology* (Englewood Cliffs, New Jersey: Prentice-Hall, 1965), p. 67.

to know: When, and under what conditions do groups form? What is a group? What conditions are necessary for their growth and effective functioning? What functions do groups fulfill for the organization and for their members? How does one manage and influence groups? These are some of the questions that will be discussed.

The study of small groups is a major area of current research in sociology and social psychology.[2] The small group is an essential mechanism of socialization and a primary source of social order. Little doubt remains that a small group provides the major source of the values and attitudes people have, and provides an important source of pressures to conform to social values and attitudes. The small group serves as an important mediating function between the individual and the larger society.[3]

Small Groups Defined

It is easy to appreciate the importance of the study of small groups but it is a little more difficult to define exactly what a small group is. Although composed of people, a group is certainly more than a collection of people. On a bus or in a waiting room we are part of a cluster of people, yet we cannot claim to be part of a group. A first approximation of a definition of a small group is that it is two or more people interacting.[4] If we accept this definition without qualification, we still have many situations which have little in common with each other; a conversation between people on the telephone (two persons interacting) or the behavior of the employees of some large manufacturing plant (people interacting).

Another more conditional and more acceptable definition of a group is needed. Since we are examining behavior in organizations and because this involves psychological questions, a more appropriate definition would include psychological terms.

A psychological group is any number of people who (1) interact with

---

[2]Over 1300 articles and books have been referenced on the subject, most have been published since 1950. See A. Paul Hare, *Handbook of Small Group Research* (New York: The Free Press of Glencoe, 1962).

[3]Leonard Broom and Philip Selznick, *Sociology* (New York: Harper and Row, 1963), p. 135.

[4]Clovis R. Shepherd, *Small Groups* (San Francisco: Chandler, 1964), p. 2.

one another, (2) are psychologically aware of one another, and (3) perceive themselves to be a group.[5]

Qualifications. This definition should be further expanded to contain certain qualifications outlined by Clovis Shepherd.[6]

One qualification which can be made is that the small group is a kind of social phenomenon which is more enduring and tighter than a social relationship but is looser or less organized than a formal organization. These loose groups are illustrated by parties or bridge games, where people gather for some purpose but where those attending do not intend to meet periodically for the same purpose.

Another qualification is that small groups of two or three persons possess characteristics due to their size which are sharply modified or tend to disappear in groups of four or more.[7] As would be expected the size of a group affects the interaction among the members as well as the behavior of the group as a whole.

A third qualification is that as a small group increases in size it reaches some upper limit where the group seems to become altered so that its members establish formal rules and regulations and the group becomes more like a formal organization than a small group. For the purposes here, an adequate criterion is that a group be large enough for group characteristics to develop and become stable, but small enough so that the members feel a sense of common identity and mutual awareness according to the above definition.

The fourth qualification is that a small group possesses some general characteristics. The general characteristics or elements of groups are four in number.[8]

"1.   Group members share one or more goals or objectives. These goals or objectives may not be the same for every member but every member has an objective in being a part of the group.

"2.   Groups develop norms or informal rules and standards which mold and guide the behavior of group members.

[5]Edgar H. Schein, op. cit.

[6]Shepherd, op. cit., pp. 3–5.

[7]Robert F. Bales and Edgar F. Borgatta, "Size of a Group as a Factor in the Interaction Profile," *Small Groups, Studies in Social Interaction* (New York: Knopf, 1955), p. 396.

[8]A. Paul Hare, *Handbook of Small Group Research* (New York: The Free Press of Glencoe, 1962), p. 10.

"3.   When a group exists for an extended period of time, structure develops which has individual members more or less permanently filling different roles.

"4.   When a group exists for an extended period of time, the members develop attractions for other group members, the group itself, and the things it stands for."

Types or Kinds of Groups

Having defined groups and qualifying the definition, we now look to different types or kinds of groups.

Formal Groups.   Formal groups are created and maintained to fulfill specific needs or perform tasks which are related to the total organizational mission. Formal groups can be either permanent or temporary according to the organization's need for the group. A permanent formal group is a body such as the board of directors, accounting division of a company, or other work units in the organization. Temporary formal groups are committees or task forces used to perform a particular job or function; they are dissolved when that function or need no longer exists. A budget committee for a Christmas party is an example. However, temporary formal groups may continue over an indefinite period of time. The temporary nature of the group is dictated by the purpose which the organization assigns to the group.[9]

Informal Groups.   Schein contends that informal groups are formed because of the nature of man; that is, he will seek fulfillment of some of his needs through developing a variety of relationships with other members of the organization. If the environment permits, these informal relationships will develop into informal groups. If the organization wants to prevent the formation of these groups it can do so by the manipulation of the workers' environment.[10]

Assuming that the organization does not actively try to limit these informal groups and the work environment permits it, several types of informal groups or cliques will be formed. To label these cliques, Dalton

9Schein, op. cit., p. 68.

10Schein, op. cit., p. 69.

relies on the basis of the clique's relationship to the formal organization chart and the service they give to members. Approached in this way, cliques fall into three major categories: vertical, horizontal, and random.[11]

Vertical Cliques. Vertical cliques can be broken down into vertical symbiotic and vertical parasitic cliques. Vertical cliques usually occur in a single department. The tie is between the top officer and some of his subordinates. It is vertical in the sense that it is an up-and-down alliance between formal unequals. It could be represented by a rectangle with the altitude greater than the base, thus, vertical.

In the vertical symbiotic clique the top officer is concerned about aiding and protecting his subordinates. He does this by concealing or minimizing their errors. He humanizes the impersonal situations and the demands he must make. The subordinates advise him of threats to his position. They tell him of current work situations, confer on ways of dealing with "troublemakers" outside the clique, and discuss interdepartmental maneuvers. When urgency demands action and the leader is absent, lower members confer and make decisions with the superior's welfare in mind. This is the most common and enduring clique in large organizations. It is most effective when lower members are relatively indifferent about promotion or reasonably patient in waiting.

The vertical parasitic clique is the popular clique writers of supervisory manuals have in mind when they make such statements as, "No person may work under the direct or indirect supervision of an officer to whom he is related by blood or marriage."[12]

This is a negative approach which assumes that collusive behavior is inevitable among persons with kinship ties who are in certain job relationships. This is an incorrect approach as the clique need not be an affair of kinship at all. The term "parasitic" is used because the exchange of services between lower and higher clique members is unequal. The lower-ranked person or persons receive more than they give and may greatly damage the higher officer. This relationship is one where the subordinate owes his position to one of his superiors. Most of the harm of this type of clique to the firm stems from its interference with the operation of the vertical symbiotic clique.

Horizontal Cliques. The horizontal defensive clique is characterized by cutting across departments and includes the officers of the various

[11]Melville Dalton, *Men Who Manage* (New York: Wiley, 1959), pp. 57–65.
[12]Ibid., p. 59.

departments. It is usually brought on by what its members regard as crisis. The threat of reorganization or the introduction of new, disliked controls are conditions that bring on this crisis condition.

Usually this clique is strong for only the limited time necessary to defeat or adjust to a threat. Since nothing is served by its persisting longer, it becomes dormant until another crisis arises. It is weak because of the vertical breaks likely to occur from action by resurgent symbiotic cliques.[13]

The horizontal aggressive clique is distinguished from the defensive clique chiefly by its goals and the direction of its action. Its members are the same, and probably have ties based on past victories in getting favors or outwitting others. The action is a cross-departmental drive to effect changes rather than resist them and to redefine or possibly shift responsibility. As with the defensive clique, interdepartmental friction subsides as the clique becomes a mutual aid bloc. The goals may be to get increased operating allowances, to bring on reorganization, or to win favored consideration over other units in the organization.[14]

Random Cliques.   Random cliques are so named because its members usually cannot be classified in terms of formal rank, duties, or departmental origin, though they associate intimately enough to exchange confidences. Typically they have no consciously shared formal goal in the organization or policy they are working to change. The attraction is clearly friendship and social satisfaction. As compared with more functional cliques, this one is random in that its members come from all or any part of the personnel, managers and managed, and that they do not expect major consequences of their association.

Generally, members of the random clique are not solidly in any of the functional cliques. They are most often persons who are not sure why they are in the department; since they are there, they are given things to do, often less desirable tasks. They resent this, and therefore do not fit into the changing informal arrangements around them. They want to escape this situation and often get away from their jobs to indulge in gossip. They rarely interact with members of the other cliques; when they do, interaction is superficial. This relatively aimless association is important in organization affairs, however. As small unattached gossip groups moving freely around the organization, these cliques are both a point of leaks from the functional groups as well as a source of

13Ibid., p. 61.
14Ibid., p. 62.

information for them. Thus, the random clique often intensifies informal activities in the organization.[15]

Other Types of Groupings

The group with possibly the strongest ties is the family. Intense loyalty and satisfaction are characteristics of this group. The relationship among its members is strong, spontaneous, and often self-sacrificing.

Friendship cliques are probably the next most common type of group. These are people with whom we socialize. Friendship cliques can and do exist in a work environment within the network of formal and informal groups discussed earlier.

Task or work groups are formed by people whose jobs and environment bring them together. They usually are formed by a department or work force, and work together in both time and proximity.

All groups are not necessarily composed of peers, although many are. One of the most important groups in organizations is the command group, which consists of a superior and his immediate subordinates. This type of group was discussed earlier as a vertical clique.

Factors in Group Formation

People form groups or join already formed groups for various reasons. These reasons can be divided into two areas—social elements which are the satisfactions a person hopes to realize from group membership, and task objectives, which a person wants accomplished but are difficult or not possible to accomplish outside of team activity.[16]

A person may be attracted to a group by the social element or the personal attractiveness of the group members. When the members of a group have qualities which a person deems attractive he will lean toward membership in that group. This situation is most predominate in friendship cliques. On an organizational level, a person may prefer to work for one company over another because he has friends already there or because the people there are pleasant.

[15]Ibid., p. 64.

[16]D. Cartwright and A. Zander, *Group Dynamics* (New York: Evanston, Row, Peterson, 1953), pp. 73–91.

Another social element that affects group membership is the activity of the group. People join bridge clubs, sports teams, and church choirs because they enjoy the activity. The attractiveness of persons already in the group may or may not be a strong factor in determining group membership.

A second category of elements in group membership involves the goals or means to achieve goals.

Sometimes people join groups because the goal of the group is one which they personally would like to see achieved. Examples of groups of this nature are charitable organizations and political parties.

In the course of accomplishing the group goal the members of the group receive personal satisfaction or advancement. Sometimes the goal of the group is not important to the member but the fact that he is a part of an advancing group is important. A member of a sports team wants to be known as a member of a winning team. Likewise, a member of a rapidly advancing company enjoys the publicity that the company brings.

A person may join a group because it is a means by which he may achieve his personal goals. The group may not achieve its goal but if it provides a means for him to achieve his personal goal it is attractive to him. A student may want to be president of the Student Senate, a personal goal, but needs the group to achieve this goal.

Finally, a person may join a group for the status he will gain from it. This element is similar to the social elements but differs in that the status he obtains occurs outside the group. A freshman may join Alpha fraternity over Beta fraternity because Alpha has a higher reputation or status on the campus.

Group Cohesiveness

One of the major perplexities confronting those who want to understand groups and to work with them effectively is how to explain the great differences in "groupness" that distinguish one group from another. What do we mean intuitively when we speak of the cohesiveness of a group? A number of meanings quickly come to mind. We think, for example, of a group that has a strong feeling of "we-ness," meaning that the members are more likely to talk in terms of "we" than "I." We think, too, of a group where everyone is friendly or where loyalty to fellow members is high. A cohesive group might be characterized as one in which the members all work together for a common goal, or one where everyone is ready to take responsibility for group chores. The willingness to endure pain or frustration for the group is yet another possible indication of its cohesiveness. Finally, we may conceive of a cohesive group as one which its members will defend against external criticism or attack.

Conditions Influencing Group Cohesiveness

Dependency. The more dependent a person is on the group, the greater the attractiveness that group will have to the individual. The greater the dependence of the members of the group as a whole, the greater the cohesiveness the group will have.[17] This situation is illustrated in Exhibit I.

Exhibit I   Group Cohesiveness Influenced by Dependency

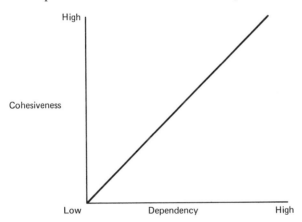

Size. Size has an inverse relationship on group cohesiveness.[18] The definition given earlier of what a group is, reinforces this point. Cohesiveness increases in part through interaction among group members. The larger a group becomes the less opportunity exists for interaction among the members. In this situation we have the large group splitting into subgroups.

17Joseph A. Litterer, *The Analysis of Organizations* (New York: Wiley, 1965), p. 92.
18Ibid., p. 93.

Homogeneity and Stable Membership.   Groups whose members have different interests and backgrounds are often less effective in promoting their interests. When, for example, people with sharp differences in rates of pay and job duties work near each other, the resulting group is seldom cohesive. The group may often be characterized by conflicting cliques, which hinder common action. Stable membership also contributes to higher cohesion. With time, the members come to know each other, they learn the values and expectations of the group, and they learn how to behave.

Communication.   To be a group, people must be able to talk with one another. Only in this way can their similarities and common interests be developed, their values and standards established, and joint action initiated. Groups in which the members can communicate easily with one another are more likely to be cohesive.

Isolation.   Physical isolation from other groups tends to build cohesiveness. Miners have demonstrated, in many lengthy strikes, that isolated workers will stick together more stubbornly than workers who are socially integrated with the rest of the community. Even simple physical boundaries on a group may be essential for cohesion. If a group cannot identify its members and clearly differentiate itself, cohesion will be low.

Outside Pressure.   Members of groups tend to herd together under stress. Continuous outside pressure from management may produce high cohesion. Personal differences are minimized when threatened by a common danger, or a tough supervisor. This closeness may remain after the threat is relieved. A tough management policy toward personnel may well encourage them to form strong informal groups as a protective and retaliatory device.

Stable Relationships.   The relationships within the groups must exist for a period of time to give the members a chance to know one another and develop common understandings of values and goals.

Competition.   Two classes of competition have a very vital effect on group cohesion: competition between members of the same group (intragroup) and competition between groups as wholes (intergroup). Competition between members of the same group is usually destructive to group cohesiveness. Studies made in this area have indicated that when competition between members of the same group occurs, hostility and bitter feelings may leave the group totally ineffective.[19] However, competition between groups usually has a positive influence on group cohesion. Success resulting from intergroup competition increases cohesion even further. However, losers in intergroup competition usually experience tensions and disruptive forces which upset internal relationships. If the group continues after defeat, a stabilization will occur and the degree of cohesion will return to near the former level.[20]

Disruptive Forces on Group Cohesion.   Factors that tend to disrupt or decrease cohesion other than competition fall into three categories.[21]

"1.   Cohesiveness declines as members or subgroups within the group tend to use different methods to accomplish the same goal. The "how" of accomplishment of the goal is the disruptive factor here. This situation often is found in competitive situations; how to win and choice of strategy are examples.

"2.   Differences regarding the goal or goals of the group can have an adverse effect on cohesiveness. Differences of this nature, however, are not as disruptive as differences about methods to achieve a single recognized goal.

"3.   If the goals of the individual members of the group are in conflict, the cohesion of the group is lessened."

Status Position of the Group and Its Effect on Cohesion.   Generally, a group's cohesiveness increases as the status of that group is recognized as being higher.[22] (See Exhibit II.)

[19]Litterer cites the research of Elton Mayo and George F. Lombard in *Teamwork and Labor Turnover in the Aircraft Industry of Southern California,* Business Research Report, No. 32 (Boston: Graduate School of Business Administration, Harvard University, 1944), p. 8.

[20]Robert R. Blake and Jane S. Mouton, "Reactions to Intergroup Competition under Win-Lose Conditions," *Management Science, VII,* July 1961, p. 420.

[21]John R. P. French, Jr., "The Disruption and Cohesion of Groups," *The Journal of Abnormal Psychology, XXXVI,* November 1941, p. 361.

[22]Joseph A. Litterer, *The Analysis of Organizations* (New York: Wiley, 1965), p. 97.

Exhibit II   Cohesiveness Increases as Status Increases

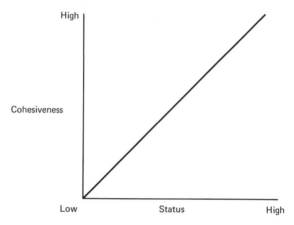

The straight line may not always hold and does not mean that all low-status groups have low cohesion or that all high-status groups have high cohesion. When low-status group members see no possibility of bettering themselves, many times they tend to "make the best of it."

Results of Group Cohesion

If group cohesion is high, the interaction between members of the group is high and the amount of agreement in group opinion is high.[23] The greater the group cohesiveness the greater will be its influence on the behavior of the members. If an individual has intentions that are incongruent with the group, the pressure is on to suppress those intentions because (1) a person does not want to be ostracized from a group which is highly attractive to him, (2) a highly cohesive group has clearer goals and the detection of any deviation is readily recognized, and (3) the opinions in a highly cohesive group are more uniformly held and a break will be a break with all group members.

All members of highly cohesive groups tend to produce at a similar level. In groups with low cohesiveness a wide deviation in production is usually present.[24] This is to say that high group cohesiveness pro-

[23]James G. March and Herbert A. Simon, *Organizations* (New York: Wiley, 1958), p. 60.

[24]Joseph A. Litterer, *The Analysis of Organizations* (New York: Wiley, 1965), p. 88.

motes high group control over the level of production of the individual members and this reduces variation among those members.

If management and labor have a similar goal there is little problem. But, for example, if management wants high production to cut costs and labor wants low production to protect jobs and group cohesion is high, then there is little possibility of any member of the group approaching management's norm. However, if there is little or no group cohesion then some members of the group will probably approach management's standard.

Behavior in Groups—Conformity

The area of behavior in groups has received a great deal of study. For our purposes, group behavior will be discussed primarily in terms of conformity.

Norms. Group members tend to form and conform to norms. "Norms are rules of behavior or proper ways of acting, which have been accepted as legitimate by members of a group."[25] The kinds of behavior that are expected of group members are specified by these norms. These rules or standards of behavior are for the most part derived from the goals which a group has set for itself. When a group has its set of goals, the norms define the kind of behavior which is necessary for, or consistent with, the realization of these goals. Norms will develop in those areas where group members find it necessary to influence one another's behavior and this condition will occur where members are particularly interdependent.[26]

Groups very often use pressure to make their members conform. There are two functions served by the uniformity in behavior resulting from such pressure. The first function is to help the group accomplish its goals. Approved procedures for movement toward an agreed on goal are often the sources of pressure toward uniformity. If the methods are seen as assuring progress toward a goal, then members view these procedures as the proper way to behave.

The second function of norms is to help the group maintain itself

---

25A. Paul Hare, *Handbook of Small Group Research* (New York: The Free Press of Glencoe, 1962), p. 24.

26Litterer, *The Analysis of Organizations* (New York: Wiley, 1965), p. 109.

as a group. Examples of this are the requirements that members regularly attend meetings or wholeheartedly support the party platform. These serve to assure the group that it will continue to exist as an entity. Also, pressures against behavior that may bring disgrace to the group or divide the group and threaten its existence or make members uncomfortable and ready to resign also serve to insure that the group survives.[27]

Determinants of Group Influence. Berelson and Steiner offer the following findings regarding group influence: (1) the more stable and cohesive the group is, and the more attached the members are to it, the more influential it is in setting standards for their behavior; (2) the deviant members of the group are more likely to change their behavior to meet the standards of the model members of the group than the other way around; (3) a single individual tends not to hold out against the weight of an otherwise unanimous group judgment, even on matters in which the group is clearly in error; (4) the group strongly influences the member's behavior by providing them with support, reinforcement, security, encouragement, and protection for their "proper behavior," and by punishing them for deviations through the use of ridicule, dislike, shame, and threat of expulsion; (5) the response of the group to deviation from the norms for behavior is, first, discussion and persuasion to bring the dissenting minority into line; second, disapproval of the dissenters; third, lowered ranking for the dissenters; and fourth, their expulsion or induced resignation from the group.[28]

Intergroup Competition

As groups become more committed to their own goals and norms, they are likely to become competitive with one another and seek to undermine their rivals' activities, thereby becoming a hindrance to the organization as a whole.

The consequences of intergroup conflict were first studied systematically by Sherif. He organized a boy's camp in such a way that two groups would form and would become competitive. He then studied the

[27]D. Cartwright and A. Zander, *Group Dynamics* (New York: Evanston, Row, Peterson, 1953), pp. 142–144.

[28]Bernard Berelson and Gary Steiner, *Human Behavior* (New York: Harcourt, Brace, and World, 1964).

effects of the competition between the groups.[29] The effects can be described in terms of the following categories:

1. What happens within each group.

(a) Each group becomes more tightly knit and elicits greater loyalty from its members; members close ranks and bury some of their internal differences.

(b) Group climate changes to work and task oriented and away from informal, casual, and playful; concern for task accomplishment increases while concern for member's psychological needs decline.

(c) Leadership patterns move toward being more autocratic; the group becomes more tolerant of autocratic leadership.

(d) Each of the groups becomes more highly organized and structured.

(e) In order to show a unified front, each group demands more loyalty and conformity from its members.[30]

2. What happens between competing groups.

(a) Each group views the other as an enemy.

(b) Each group begins to experience distortions of perception by tending to perceive only the best parts of itself while overlooking its weaknesses and perceiving only the worst parts of the other group while denying its strengths. Negative stereotypes of the other group are likely to develop.

(c) It becomes easier to maintain negative stereotypes and more difficult to correct perceptual distortions because hostility toward the other group increases while interaction and communication with the other group decreases.

(d) If groups are forced to interact they listen only for that which supports their own position and stereotype.

Thus, we see that intergroup competition can have some very favorable effects as far as the functioning of each individual group is concerned. More specifically, the introduction of competition tends to solidify each group and to make it more effective and highly motivated in task accomplishment. However, the same conditions which result in

[29]M. Sherif, O. J. Harvey, B. J. White, W. R. Hood, and Carolyn Sherif, *Intergroup Conflict and Cooperation: The Robbers Cave Experiment* (Norman, Oklahoma: University Book Exchange, 1961).

[30]Edgar H. Schein, *Organizational Psychology* (Englewood Cliffs, New Jersey: Prentice-Hall, 1965), p. 81.

bettering intragroup performance may have the opposite effect as far as intergroup cooperation is concerned. This is illustrated by examining what happens to winners and losers in a competitive situation.[31]

The consequences of winning or losing in an intergroup competition can change a group and its self-perception. The winners (1) become more cohesive; (2) release tension and may lose their fighting spirit; (3) tend toward high intragroup cooperation and concern for members' needs; (4) lower concern for work and task accomplishment; and (5) tend to be complacent and feel little need for reevaluating.

The losers (1) may not accept the loss if there are excuses available; (2) accept the loss and look for the cause; (3) tend to become more tense and work harder; (4) look for someone to take the blame; (5) tend toward lower intragroup cooperation; (6) develop low concern for members' needs and high concern for recouping by working harder; and (7) reorganize and become more cohesive and effective if the loss is accepted realistically.[32]

Although the gains of intergroup competition may under some conditions outweigh the negative consequences, the opposite is usually true and management generally looks for ways of reducing intergroup tension. The conflict of goals and the breakdown in cooperation between departments and individuals is the fundamental problem of intergroup competition. Reducing the conflict can be accomplished by finding goals upon which groups can agree and reestablishing valid communication between the groups.

An organization's strategy should include preventive measures to reduce intergroup conflict before it can start. Schein lists four steps the organizational planner should follow in creating and handling his different functional groups.[33] The first step is giving more emphasis on total organizational effectiveness and the role of departments in contributing to it. Departments should be measured and rewarded on the basis of their contribution to the total effort rather than their individual effectiveness. High interaction and frequent communication should be stimulated between groups to work on problems of intergroup coordination and help. Organizational rewards should be given partly on the basis of help which groups give to each other. This is the second step. The third step is the frequent rotation of members among groups or departments to stimulate a high degree of mutual understanding and empathy for one another's problems. Finally, win-lose situations should

---

[31]Ibid.

[32]Ibid., p. 82.

[33]Schein, Edgar H. Organizational Psycholgy, 2nd ed. Prentice-Hall, Inc., p. 102.

be avoided. This can be done by never putting groups into the position of competing for the same organizational award. Emphasis should be placed on pooling of resources to maximize organizational effectiveness and sharing of rewards equally with all the groups or the departments.

It is important to recognize that the preventive strategy does not imply absence of disagreement and artificial "sweetness and light" within or between groups. Conflict and disagreement at the level of the group or organizational task is not only desirable but essential for the achievement of the best solutions to problems. What is harmful is interpersonal or intergroup conflict in which the task is not as important as gaining advantage over the other person or group.

It can be assumed that the great interest in the study of group dynamics will continue. A democratic society derives its strength from the effective functioning of the multitude of groups which it contains. Its most valuable resources are the groups of people found in its homes, communities, schools, churches, business concerns, union halls, and various branches of government. Now, more than ever before, it is recognized that these units must perform their functions well if the larger system is to work successfully.

Summary

A group was defined as any number of people who interact with one another, who are psychologically aware of one another, and who perceive themselves as a group. Some of the key elements of a group are that they share one or more goals, they develop norms and a group structure where different members fill certain roles, and where attractions for other members or the group itself exist.

Groups may be formal or informal. A formal group is created by the organization and may be either permanent or temporary in nature. Informal groups are those that arise spontaneously. Vertical informal groups occur within a single department or unit and represent an up and down alliance between formal unequals. In a vertical symbiotic clique the manager aids and protects his subordinates and in return they protect his interests. In a vertical parasitic clique the lower level receives more than it gives.

Informal horizontal groups cut across departmental lines and include managers of different departments. A horizontal aggressive clique forms in order to effect some type of change while a defensive clique will form to prevent a change from being enacted. People join groups either because of social reasons or because it is the only way to accomplish a task.

Two important aspects of the study of groups are group cohesion and group competition. The more cohesive a group is the stronger it will be. There are many factors that affect cohesion such as size, homogeneity, stability of membership, and others. Generally speaking, intragroup competition tends to destroy cohesion while intergroup competition tends to build cohesion.

Key Concepts

Norms.   Informal rules or standards of conduct to which the group develops and members are expected to adhere.

Formal Groups.   Those created by the formal organization. They may be either permanent or temporary.

Informal Groups.   Those which arise spontaneously. They may be vertical or horizontal. Vertical groups are up and down alliances of formal unequals. Horizontal groups cut across departmental lines.

Symbiotic Clique.   The manager aids and protects his people as well as humanizes the work situation. In return they exhibit loyalty and look out after him.

Parasitic Clique.   The lower level receives more than it gives.

Aggressive Clique.   Forms to effect some wanted changes.

Defensive Clique.   Forms to prevent the introduction of unwanted changes.

Cohesiveness.   The amount of "we-ness," "groupness," or sense of mutual identification that exists in a group.

Discussion Questions

1. Briefly describe the four elements which are basic to small groups.

2. What are the four types or kinds of groups?

3. What are the two basic reasons why people form groups? Give an example of a group which is attractive to a person for the following reasons.
   (*a*) Activities of the group.
   (*b*) Personal attractiveness of the group members.
   (*c*) Means to achieve goals.
   (*d*) Achieving status.
   (*e*) Give an example of a group which would provide all of the above.

4. What are the conditions influencing group cohesiveness? Give an example of a group which is cohesive due to any three of these conditions.

5. What factors or forces will result in a decrease in group cohesiveness?

6. Which of the following is characteristic of a cohesive work group? Explain your answer.
   (*a*) Highly variable productivity.
   (*b*) Stable productivity.
   (*c*) High productivity.

7. Why does intragroup competition tend to decrease group cohesiveness? Why does intergroup competition tend to increase group cohesiveness? What factors are involved in each of the above two types of competition?

Selected Readings

Solomon E. Asch, "Opinions and Social Pressure," *Scientific American, CXCIII* (5), November 1955, pp. 31–35.

Anthony G. Athos, and Robert E. Coffey, *Behavior in Organizations,* Prentice-Hall, Englewood Cliffs, New Jersey, 1968.

J. A. C. Brown, "The Informal Organization of Industry," *The Social Psychology of Industry,* Penguin Books, Baltimore, 1954, Chapter 5, pp. 124–156.

Edgar Schien, *Organizational Psychology,* Prentice-Hall, Englewood Cliffs, New Jersey, 1965, Chapter 5.

William G. Scott, *Organization Theory,* Richard D. Irwin, Homewood, Illinois, 1967, Chapter 4.

Stanley E. Seashore, "Group Cohesiveness in the Industrial Work Group: Summary and Conclusions," *Group Cohesiveness in the Industrial Work Group,* The University of Michigan Press, Ann Arbor, 1954, Chapter 7, pp. 97–102.

Marvin E. Shaw, *Group Dynamics: The Psychology of Small Group Behavior,* McGraw-Hill, New York, 1971.

Ross Stagner, "Motivational Aspects of Industrial Morale," *Personnel Psychology, XI,* 1958, pp. 64–70.

Edwin J. Thomas, and Clinton F. Fink, "Effects of Group Size," *Psychological Bulletin, LX* (4), 1963, pp. 371–384.

16.   Job Design

The way in which jobs are designed has a significant impact on the level of motivation and productivity of people. In a later chapter dealing with motivation we learn that high levels of productivity are most often achieved when the work that people do has meaning and significance. More specifically, if employees are to be motivated, they must be able to get a sense of achievement and accomplishment out of their jobs. Also, the work must be challenging and offer opportunities for new experiences and growth. With these general thoughts in mind, Chapter 16 explores the area of job design. The following major topics will be dealt with.

1.   The issue of job design in perspective.

2.   A review of the historical approach to designing jobs.

3.   Effects of this historical approach on worker, morale, motivation, and job satisfaction.

4.   Early attempts to solve the problem.

5.   The concept of job enrichment.

The Issue of Job Design in Perspective

"In 1913 they established the assembly line at Ford's. That season the profits were something like twenty-five million dollars, but they had trouble in keeping the men on the job. Machinists didn't seem to like it at Ford's."

—JOHN DOS PASSOS, *The Big Money*

"Long regarded as the paragon of American industrial efficiency, the assembly line is coming under attack as an uneconomical and basically inhumane form of production. Needed in the future are entirely new concepts of job design based on a mixture of engineering, economics, and human psychology."[1] When we refer to the assembly line approach to designing jobs in this chapter we mean more than the application of this term to the typical factory situation. Rather, we are referring to the whole breadth and scope of routine and semiautomatic clerical jobs as well as the historical trend toward management's control of people via machine pacing, standardization, overspecialization, and control via conformance to well-defined systems and procedures. Thus, the human problems (to be discussed later in the chapter) which our traditional approach to designing jobs has created are as prevalent for the engineer, scientist, and accountant as they are for the secretary, file clerk, or assembly line worker. The question surrounding job design is essentially this: Does the job via its design and structure control the man and force him into a standard, routine, and controlled level of performance, or does the man via his own motivation control the end product of his efforts?

Historical Approach to Designing Jobs

Historically, time and motion study has been used to design jobs and to analyze the performance of workers. The two men considered pioneers in the field of time and motion studies are Frederick Taylor and Frank Gilbreth.

Frederick Taylor put the most stress on time study. He believed that by using time studies, management would gain in that the work would

---

[1] Edward E. Lawler, III, "Motivation And The Design of Jobs," *ASTME Vectors,* August 1968, p. 14.

be scientifically planned and the workers' production increased. Employees would also gain because they could substantially increase their wages by meeting the standards and participating in piecework incentive rates.

Frank Gilbreth, on the other hand, placed more stress on motion studies. He felt that motion studies would indicate how each job, operation, or process could be performed with the greatest economy of movement and hence, in the fastest possible time.

There are two important phases in time and motion studies. The first is the research phase, which involves finding the best method for performance of the task. An observation is made of a good worker, completion time is recorded, efficiency is indicated, and a time standard constructed. The time standard is in actuality the second phase, or the standardization phase. A time standard is set up to be used as a basis for a piece rate or to furnish data which will be used in estimating costs of a particular job. It is further used in connection with scheduling machine production times.

To further understand the concept of time and motion study it is essential to understand their goals. They are as follows.

1.   Redesigning a job in order to make the movements simpler and quicker.

2.   Developing more efficient patterns of movement for workers, so that they can do the job faster and with less fatigue.

3.   Setting standards for given jobs to be used as a basis for determining pay scales and criteria for the evaluation of the worker.

4.   Developing a complete job description to aid in the process of recruiting and selecting new workers, orienting and training them.[2]

In the quest for even more productivity management turned to mass production technology. The principles of mass production technology consist of five concepts, some of which are also found in time and motion studies. The principles of mass production include the following.

1.   Standardization.

2.   Interchangeability of labor.

3.   Orderly movement of the product through the plant in a series of planned operations at specific work stations.

[2]Edgar H. Schein, *Organizational Psychology* (New York: Prentice-Hall, 1965), p. 26.

4.   Mechanical delivery of parts to work stations and removal of assemblies.

5.   Breakdown of operations into simple, constituent motions.[3]

It was believed that mass production technology combined with a time and motion study approach to designing individual jobs would solve all the problems of productivity. More specifically, increased quantity, reduction in costs, and better quality of workmanship were anticipated.

Most frequently, the result was higher costs, poor quality of workmanship, more absences, grievances, turnover, and often a feeling of hostility toward management. To understand why these concepts backfired is to recognize the effect that the tightly constructed jobs had on the employees. Specifically, fatigue, boredom, frustration, and low morale led to feelings of disinterest and apathy on the part of workers. It has been found that dissatisfaction of workers toward their jobs does not arise from the circumstances usually considered important by management, such as pay, security, working conditions, fringe benefits, and supervision. The workers regard these factors as reasonably satisfactory but dislike certain special aspects of the job design. These include:

1.   The anonymity of the individual worker—a consequence of designing out of the job virtually everything that might be of personal value or meaning to the worker, specifically:

(a)   The worker has no control over his work space.

(b)   His job is highly repetitive, having been broken down into the simplest motions possible.

(c)   There is little or no need for skill because of the simple movements required.

(d)   Methods and tools are completely specified and the worker has no control over them or over any changes made in them.

(e)   Because he never works on more than a small fraction of the product, the worker does not see the final results of his work, has no identity with the product, and he cannot estimate the quality of his contribution to it.

(f)   Since the job requires only surface attention, the worker does not really become mentally involved in his work.

(g)   The geographic arrangement of the production line severely

[3]Louis E. Davis, "Job Design And Productivity: A New Approach," *Personnel, 33* (March 1957), p. 42.

limits social interaction. Men on the line work as individuals rather than as a team.

2. The depersonalization of the job—evidenced in the lack of job progression vertically. Since tasks have been simplified, skill differences between the jobs are practically eliminated.[4]

Louis Davis expresses the problem felt by the workers when he states that "the assembly line has designed out of the job virtually everything that might be of personal value or meaning to the workers."[5]

Mass production technology has forced the workers to perform a standardized, highly repetitive task that requires little knowledge and skill, and the utilization of only a few, low-order abilities within an environment that, first, offers practically no challenge, and second, forces the worker to accept the controlled, steady pace of the assembly line.

Anticipated Advantages and Actual Results of the Historical Approach to Job Design

Exhibit I summarizes the anticipated advantages and actual results of the approach to designing jobs outlined previously. As indicated by the items listed as anticipated advantages, for the most part, they were oriented toward a desire to gain maximum productivity and keep control of the total production process. It should perhaps be noted that for many years a good many organizations did, to a degree, realize these advantages. It is only in the period since the latter 1940s that the disadvantages really began to become apparent. In particular, developments during the last five years has served to focus attention on the negative effects which historical approaches to job design have created. These negative effects are manifested primarily in the areas of worker motivation and apathy.

In summary of Exhibit I, many of the economic and productivity advantages of the historical approaches to designing jobs have not been realized. The primary reason is that economic and social conditions of today are substantially different from those of the past. Of particular significance is the higher educational level of the average employee. He has learned to expect more from his job and has become increas-

[4]Ibid., p. 422.

[5]Ibid., p. 430.

Exhibit I   Anticipated Advantages and Actual Results of the Historical
Approach to Job Design

ANTICIPATED ADVANTAGES	ACTUAL RESULTS
1. Jobs can be learned quickly, thus little training is required.	1. Savings in training cost fail to materialize because of excessively high turnover.
2. Jobs can be filled with unskilled people—presumably an inexpensive, readily available commodity.	2. High rates of absenteeism require that extra workers must be available on a standby basis. This increases labor costs.
3. Because of low skill required and ease of training, workers are interchangeable.	3. Because assembly line work is so dissatisfying in nature, a high wage must be paid just to get people to accept jobs on the line.
4. Because of mechanization, workers do not become physically tired.	4. Substantial quality problems occur because of a lack of commitment on the part of workers.
5. Standardization permits ease of quality control. Also, the chance of mistakes is minimized.	5. Because of turnover, costs of recruiting and selection of workers are also increased.
6. Mechanization makes production predictable.	6. Problems of supervision develop as the gap between labor and management broadens.
7. Management has control over workers and to a degree can supervise by observation.	

ingly vocal about deficiencies in the work climate. Also, the fact that people are generally more mobile and have more employment alternatives available is a factor.

Early Attempts at Solving the Job Design Problem

Having become aware of some of the above-mentioned problems, many organizations in recent years have taken an active interest in the question of job design. Although some of the impetus for this concern has come from the continued desire of organizations to meet their objectives in such areas as cost, quality, and quantity of output, there is ample evidence to support the contention that they also have the worker's welfare in mind. In addition, all evidence seems to indicate that job design will receive more and more attention in future years.

In the remainder of this section of the chapter we will turn our attention to some of the earlier attempts to solve the human problems associated with work. The final section will deal with the "state of the art" at this point in time, that is, the concept of job enrichment.

Lawler has divided the solutions to job design into two groups. The first group he calls first-aid approaches to redesigning jobs. In this group he includes such things as more time off the job, job rotation, and some forms of horizontal job enlargement.[6] Herzberg delineates four alternative forms of job enlargement. They include challenging the employee, assigning the worker more tasks, rotating assignments, and removing more difficult parts of the job.[7] Each of the above will be briefly discussed in the remainder of this section. The second solution of job design is designated by Lawler as being the major surgery approach. This involves the concept of job enrichment, to be discussed in the concluding part of this chapter.

Time Off the Job. "Unions have been the strongest proponents of the more time off solution. Their proposals in this regard range from sabbaticals to more and longer coffee breaks."[8] According to Lawler, this would seem to be a defeatist approach since it assumes that a

---

[6]Lawler, op. cit., p. 18.

[7]Frederick Herzberg, "One More Time: How Do You Motivate Employees?" *Harvard Business Review,* January–February 1968.

[8]Lawler, op. cit., p. 18.

tight job structure must exist and that work is inherently unpleasant. He also states that the result of this approach is destined to produce a subculture of alienated workers who must necessarily look to off the job activities for all of their satisfactions. Commenting on the same area, Herzberg states the following.

"This represents a marvelous way of motivating people to work— getting them off the job! We have reduced (formally or informally) the time spent on the job over the last 50 or 60 years until we are finally on the way to the 6½ day weekend. Any interesting variant of this approach is the development of off-hour recreation programs. The philosophy here seems to be that those who play together, work together. The fact is that motivated people seek more hours of work, not fewer."[9]

Job Enlargement.   Job enlargement represents a horizontal approach to job design. It involves making a job structurally bigger by any one of the methods mentioned earlier.

1.   Challenging the Employee.   This represents one of earlier, more superficial, and as usually applied, naive attempts at job enlargement. According to this approach, if the secretary types 50 letters a day— challenge her to see if she can do 75. If the worker assembles 20 sub-assemblies a day, challenge him to see if he can do 26. The very logical response of the worker to this situation is the question, "Why should I?" This type of response should be easy to understand since all the challenge really amounts to is asking the individual to do more of something he does not like to do in the first place.

2.   Removing More Difficult Parts of the Job.   The theory here is that if we take away the more difficult parts of the job the employee can accomplish more of what is left. The thinking represented here is obviously backward, since removing the more difficult task amounts to nothing more than simplifying and making a job even more meaningless than it was in the first place. As Herzberg has stated; "this traditional industrial engineering approach amounts to subtraction in the hope of accomplishing addition."[10]

9Herzberg, op. cit., p. 55.

10Ibid., p. 59.

3. Assigning More Tasks. Under this approach, instead of doing just one thing over and over again, the employee is given several tasks to accomplish. Although this can relieve some of the monotony, the problem lies in the fact that the new tasks which are assigned are usually no more meaningful than the old. Thus, it is unlikely that any long-lasting positive gains of any great significance can be achieved.

4. Job Rotation. This attempt at horizontal job improvement involves moving the employee from job to job. This movement may occur every few hours or two or three times a day. Research has shown that job rotation is somewhat effective in offsetting monotony and boredom, and workers generally prefer it as opposed to performing one and only one assignment. It is still an incomplete solution to the problem, however. The fact remains that usually the jobs are still paced, simplified ones that give the individual no control over what he does or how he does it.

Job Enrichment

The concept of job enrichment which encompasses vertical job loading holds the key to creating more meaningful work for employees. By meaningful work we mean work which is structured to provide the person performing it with a sense of satisfaction and accomplishment. Work designed in this way has built into it all the ingredients which will contribute to releasing the motivational potential within the individual. Thus, not only does proper job design enable the organization to accomplish its objectives, but also the welfare of the individual is taken into account in the sense that he has the opportunity to satisfy his full range of needs on the job.

The difference between job enlargement and job enrichment as well as horizontal versus vertical job loading is illustrated by Exhibit II, which summarizes some principles of vertical job loading and the motivators involved with each principle.

The key feature of the points listed in Exhibit II is that instead of giving the worker just some more of the same medicine with a different label, his job is truly enriched by upgrading it. Viewed another way, when a job is enriched as opposed to being simply enlarged, it allows the individual performing it to exercise to a fuller range his skills and abilities. The job is upgraded in the sense that the talents which the individual has are fully utilized as opposed to being underutilized,

Exhibit II[11]   Principles of Vertical Job Loading

PRINCIPLE	MOTIVATORS INVOLVED
1. Removing some controls while retaining accountability.	1. Responsibility and personal achievement.
2. Increasing the accountability of individuals for own work.	2. Responsibility and recognition.
3. Giving a person a complete natural unit of work (module, division, area, and so on).	3. Responsibility, achievement, and recognition.
4. Granting additional authority to an employee in his activity; job freedom.	4. Responsibility, achievement, and recognition.
5. Making periodic reports directly available to the worker himself rather than to the supervisor.	5. Internal recognition.
6. Introducing new and more difficult tasks not previously handled.	6. Growth and learning.
7. Assigning individuals specific or specialized tasks, enabling them to become experts.	7. Responsibility, growth, and advancement.

which is many times the case. As will be noted in Chapter 17, there is ample evidence that the initiative, ingenuity, creativity, and skills and abilities of people are in many cases being only partially utilized in organizations today.

An Experiment in Job Enrichment.   The distinction between horizontal and vertical job loading is illustrated by an experiment conducted by Frederick Herzberg among a group of stockholder correspondents employed by a very large corporation.[12] With respect to the job being performed and the employees involved, Herzberg noted the following:

"Seemingly, the task required of these carefully selected and highly

[11]Ibid., p. 59.

[12]Ibid., p. 59.

trained correspondents was quite complex and challenging. But almost all indexes of performance and job attitudes were low and exit interviewing confirmed that the challenge of the job existed merely as words."[13]

Exhibit III summarizes the types of change which were made in the job. The changes listed on the left represent horizontal or job enlargement suggestions which were eventually rejected. The ones on the right are vertical or job enrichment suggestions which were the changes actually introduced over a period of months. The numbers to the right of the vertical suggestions represent the corresponding motivators involved as listed in Exhibit II.

Without going into all the details of the format of the experiment, the following represent some of the results and findings.

1. At the end of six months the groups where the new job design changes had been introduced were outperforming their counterparts by a considerable amount.

2. Marked increases in liking for their jobs were exhibited.

3. Absenteeism was lower among those whose jobs had been enriched.

4. There were improvements in quality of letters, accuracy of information, and speed of response to stockholder's inquiries.

5. Sharp increases in positive job attitudes were noted.

An Additional Experiment in Job Enrichment. Lawler cites an additional experiment in job enrichment involving an electronics firm that manufactured measuring instruments by assembly line techniques.[15] Some of the problems being experienced included those of poor production flexibility, low quality, and high labor turnover. A change in job design was introduced whereby a worker had responsibility for the assembly of an entire instrument instead of just a small part of that instrument. In addition, upon completion of the job the employee tested the instrument, certified its accuracy, packed it, and sent it to the customer. In case the instrument was returned to the company the employee was assigned the responsibility for correction.

[13]Ibid., p. 59.

[14]Ibid., p. 61.

[15]Lawler, op. cit., p. 19.

Exhibit III Enlargement versus Enrichment of Correspondents' Tasks[14]

HORIZONTAL LOADING SUGGESTIONS (REJECTED)	VERTICAL LOADING SUGGESTIONS (ADOPTED)	PRINCIPLE
Firm quotas could be set for letters to be answered each day, using a rate which would be hard to reach.	Subject matter experts were appointed within each unit for other members of the unit to consult with before seeking supervisory help. (The supervisor had been answering all specialized and difficult questions.)	7
The women could type the letters themselves, as well as compose them, or take on any other clerical functions.	Correspondents signed their own names on letters. (The supervisor had been signing all letters.)	2
All difficult or complex inquiries could be channeled to a few women so that the remainder could achieve high rates of output. These jobs could be exchanged from time to time.	The work of the more experienced correspondents was proofread less frequently by supervisors and was done at the correspondents' desks, dropping verification from 100 percent to 10 percent. (Previously, all correspondents' letters had been checked by the supervisor.)	1
The women could be rotated through units handling different customers, and could then be sent back to their own units.	Production was discussed, but only in terms such as "a full day's work is expected." As time went on, this was no longer mentioned. (Before, the group had been constantly reminded of the number of letters that needed to be answered.)	4

Outgoing mail went directly to the mailroom without going over supervisors' desks. (The letters had always been routed through the supervisors.)	1
Correspondents were encouraged to answer letters in a more personalized way. (Reliance on the form-letter approach had been standard practice.)	3
Each correspondent was held personally responsible for the quality and accuracy of letters. (This responsibility had been the province of the supervisor and the verifier.)	2, 5

What was the result of this experiment? Lawler notes the following.

"1.   Initially the gain in production was nil, for it required approximately six months for the employees to acquire the necessary skills involved in producing the complete unit.

"2.   After six months production increased but only slightly. The increase could be due to chance.

"3.   Quality improved greatly.

"4.   Quality improved to the extent that the quality control department was being disbanded.

"5.   Lower absenteeism was experienced.

"6.   Production flexibility was increased.

"7.   Higher job satisfaction among employees was experienced."

Lawler concludes by observing that his review of the literature indicates 10 instances where changes of this type have produced comparable results.

The Automation Continuum

Perhaps one of the greatest contributions to conceptualizing the problem and issues involved in job design is the concept of the automation continuum as developed by Lawler. Lawler's automation continuum is depicted in Exhibit IV.

With respect to this continuum Lawler writes the following:

"At one end of the continuum is unit production performed by individual craftsmen. At the other end is the completely automated production facility, where the worker controls vast amounts of automated equipment. By virtue of its position in the continuum, the assembly line is neither fish nor fowl—neither highly automated nor highly individualized. Research suggests that unit production is quite satisfying, involving, and motivating to the worker. It provides him with responsibility for production of an entire product—it enables him to take justifiable pride in his work.

"Research also suggests that jobs in automated plants can be

Exhibit IV   The Automation Continuum[16]

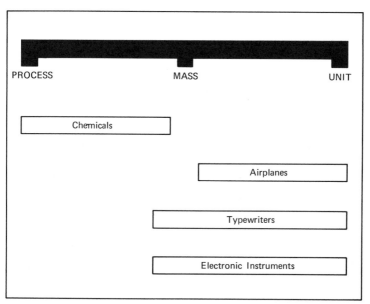

satisfying and involving because high skill levels are required. More-over, the workers—even at the lower skill levels—feel that they are controlling the production process. In contrast, assembly line work-ers feel that the production process controls them. Thus, despite their basic differences, jobs at both ends of the automation con-tinuum fit the needs of the workers in that they provide opportunities for the satisfaction.

"The graphic portrayal of the automation continuum presents a rec-ommendation for a change in strategy. Essentially, it suggests that jobs be moved away from the center of the continuum toward either end, a process that would often involve reversal of the historic move-ment from unit production toward mass production. The kinds of changes that any organization could make would, of course, be dictated by its products. In the case of automobile manufacture, a move toward greater automation is suggested. In the manufacture of electronic instruments, however, it would make good sense in many instances to move from mass production to unit production."[17]

16Ibid., p. 18.

17Ibid., p. 19.

As stated in the introductory portion of this chapter, the way in which work is structured has a significant impact on employee motivation and subsequently also on the level of productivity which is achieved. We have tried to show how, through proper job design, the welfare of the worker is taken into account and at the same time the objectives of the organization can be met.

Summary

In Chapter 8 it was pointed out that one of the elements of organization was the people who do the work. The way in which jobs are designed and work is structured has a significant effect on the level of motivation and productivity of employees. The historical approach which has been taken to designing jobs has been primarily mechanistic, based mostly on principles and concepts of industrial engineering. The result has been that jobs, in many cases, have been reduced to their least common denominator, in that they are highly specialized and require only a minimum degree of skill. It should be emphasized that this highly structured approach to designing work is true not only of manufacturing jobs but also of clerical, semiprofessional, and professional work.

Because of social and economic changes over the past 40 years, as well as increased expectations on the part of employees, several disadvantages have resulted from this historical approach to job design. These disadvantages can be summed up by the words boredom, apathy, turnover, absenteeism, low quality, low quantity, and many similar terms.

To solve these and similar problems organizations have undertaken several approaches to redesigning jobs. Some have been successful while others have not. When they have not been successful it has been due to the fact that either the approach itself was unsound or the way it was implemented left something to be desired. Some of the early approaches which were tried included time off the job, challenging employees, removing the more difficult parts of the job, assigning more tasks, and job rotation.

More recently the concept of job enrichment has come into focus. Job enrichment represents a vertical approach to job design. It is vertical in that it involves expanding the scope of the job in any one of several ways. These may include removing some controls, increasing accountability, expanding the scope of the job, granting additional authority, introducing new and more difficult tasks, and others.

Key Concepts

Job Enlargement. Job enlargement represents a horizontal approach to job design. It can be accomplished in any one of four ways, including challenging the employee, removing the more difficult parts of the job, assigning more tasks, or job rotation. Unless properly implemented, job enlargement techniques generally fail.

Job Enrichment. Job enrichment represents a vertical approach to job design. It implies that the job is enriched by making fuller use of the skills, abilities, and potentialities of the job incumbent.

Discussion Questions

1. What are the five basic principles of mass production? What negative effects often result from mass production? Why did these concepts often backfire on management?

2. What are the primary reasons given in Chapter 16 as to why the anticipated advantages of the historical approach to job design differed from the actual results?

3. Why have the concepts of time off the job and job enlargement failed to be effective in job design?

4. What is meant by the term "meaningful work" as defined in this chapter?

5. What is the basic difference between job enlargement and job enrichment?

6. Which of the following types of production methods will generally be more satisfying to the worker: process, mass, or unit? Why?

Selected Readings

Eaton H. Conant, and Maurice D. Kilbridge, "An Interdisciplinary Analysis of Job Enlargement: Technology, Costs, and Behavioral Implications," *Industrial and Labor Relations Review, 18* (3), April 1965, pp. 377–395.

Louis E. Davis, "Job Design and Productivity: A New Approach," *Personnel, XXXIII*, 1957, pp. 418–430.

Fred K. Foulkes, *Creating More Meaningful Work*, American Management Association, 1964.

Frederick Herzberg, "One More Time: How Do You Motivate Employees?" *Harvard Business Review*, January–February 1968.

Charles L. Hulin, and Milton R. Blood, "Job Enlargement, Individual Differences, and Worker Responses," *Psychological Bulletin, 69* (1), 1968, pp. 41–58.

Edgar F. Huse, and Michael Beer, "Eclectic Approach to Organizational Development," *Harvard Business Review, 49* (5), September–October 1971.

Edward E. Lawler, III, "Motivation and the Design of Jobs," *ASTME Vectors*, August 1968.

Norman R. F. Maier, "The Design of Jobs," *Psychology in Industry*, 3rd ed., Houghton-Mifflin, Boston, 1965, pp. 339–370.

Scott M. Myers, "Every Employee a Manager," *California Management Review, 10* (3), Spring 1968, pp. 9–20.

Raymond F. Pelissier, "Successful Experience With Job Design," *Personnel Administration, 28* (2), March–April 1965, pp. 377–395.

Charles R. Walker, and Robert H. Guest, "The Man on the Assembly Line," *Harvard Business Review, XXX* (3), May–June 1952, pp. 71–83.

Part 5

Managerial Direction and Leadership

Part 5 discusses the all important function of managerial direction and leadership. Chapter 17 is devoted to a discussion of modern motivational theory. After presenting and discussing a definition of motivation, the question of what motivates people is examined. Also, the dynamics of the process of motivation on a day-to-day basis will be explored as well as some of the more significant theories of motivation.

Chapter 18 lays the groundwork for a rather comprehensive examination of the leadership function. In the initial section of this chapter, some general observations about leadership are made. This is followed by a presentation of two alternative sets of assumptions about people and their reaction to work and the implications of these assumptions on the manager and his leadership style.

Chapter 19 will provide the reader with a comprehensive insight into managerial leadership. The theories of leadership of four prominent scholars are summarized and discussed in considerable detail.

Organizational and interpersonal communications comprises the subject matter of Chapter 20. The chapter opens with a discussion of the problem of communications and the role of top management in establishing an effective communications climate. The latter portion of the chapter concentrates on the communications environment of the individual manager. Communications is defined and the implications of the definition are discussed, two-way communications are explored, some of the human and technical barriers are cited, and finally, the problems in establishing effective communications are presented.

The final chapter of Part 5 deals with coaching and developing subordinates. The elements of a complete and comprehensive coaching program are pinpointed, reasons for poor performance are examined, some problems and difficulties with coaching and appraisal programs are explored, and the fundamentals of a sound system are outlined. The final sections in the chapter emphasize a results approach to performance review.

17. The Mainsprings of Human Motivation

Perhaps the best definition of motivation ever given is that which Dwight D. Eisenhower gave of leadership. He said that leadership was the ability to get a man to do what you want him to do, when you want it done, in a way you want it done, *because he wants to do it.* It is on the final part of this definition that we will be concentrating our attention. Why should employees want to cooperate and work toward a goal of productivity?

In answer to this question, psychologists tell us that people behave in certain ways and pursue particular courses of action in order to satisfy needs which they have. Behavior is goal-directed toward need satisfaction. Thus, what people want out of a job is of strategic importance if they are to be motivated. In terms of a motivation equation the process appears as follows:

$$\begin{matrix} \text{NEED} \\ \text{WANT} \\ \text{DRIVE} \end{matrix} \quad + \quad \text{INCENTIVE} = \text{ACTION}$$

On the left side of the equation are those things that people want or need. These are the drives that cause and explain behavior. Added to this is the incentive. If the proper incentives are provided, that is, incentives which hold the potential for satisfaction of needs, we get the type of action we are looking for. Viewed another way, if the organization can build a total work climate, the ingredients of which are conducive to offering employees an opportunity to satisfy their needs, a positive motivational response will be elicited. What appears to be a rather simple process on paper, however, is not quite so simple when applied to a real situation. Two initial considerations are of importance.

First, with respect to needs, the big challenge for a manager is to know and understand his people as individuals. We can talk about needs in a general sense, but it is necessary for the manager to relate this information to the individual. Motivation is a personal thing. It occurs within the man himself. The incentives which appeal to and work with one man may be less than fully successful with another. It becomes necessary to know something about needs in a general sense but more important to know each employee in terms of those things that he personally wants most. Only when we have this type of insight are we in a position to motivate people as individuals.

The incentive side of the motivation process holds most significance for the organization and individual manager. The needs of people— what each wants as an individual—are pretty well fixed. They are part of an individual's personal frame of reference and his personality. Therefore, there is not much that can be done to change what people want. As stated above, the big job in this area is to understand.

On the other hand, much can be done to contribute significantly to the incentive side of the equation. If, via an overall favorable organizational climate, job design, or individual approach to leadership, the proper incentives are built in, that is, those incentives which offer people an opportunity to satisfy their needs, we are more apt to get high-level performance from people. In other words, they will be motivated on the job.

The Need Hierarchy

The psychologist usually talks about needs in terms of some type of hierarchy or priority. Although the number of steps or levels in the hierarchy, as well as the descriptive terminology, may vary among authors, the following framework developed by Abraham Maslow is representative.[1]

[1]The five-step hierarchy outlined here follows that which was developed by Maslow

• Physiological Needs–These are the needs of the body: shelter, hunger, and thirst. Man, like other animals, has a strong drive toward self preservation.

• Security Needs–Two types of security are of significance: physical and economic. The latter is perhaps of more significance to the manager. Once a man reaches a given economic level he wants the assurance he will stay there. He doesn't want to worry about loss of income due to old age, loss of job, accident, or other reasons. Also, of course, he wants to reach what to him is a reasonable economic level or standard of living in the first place.

• Social Needs–In addition to being an economic creature, man also has a social side. Most important here, he wants to feel he belongs, that he is an accepted member of the group, and an integral part of the operation.

• Psychological Needs–The psychological needs represent man's ego in operation. He wants such things as status, recognition, prestige, and a high estimate of himself.

• Self Fulfillment–The final step in the need hierarchy is the need for self-fulfillment. What a man can be he must be. He has a need for feeling that he is making progress toward reaching his full potential; that he is doing what he is fitted for in terms of his skill and ability as related to the type and level of job he has. Such things as a feeling of job importance, accomplishment, individual importance and achievement, responsibility, advancement, new experiences, challenging work, and growth opportunity are included here.

Significance of the Need Hierarchy

With respect to this need hierarchy, several very important points must be stressed. First and most basic, the most strategic motivators of on-the-job behavior are the physiological and security needs. (It is convenient to lump these together into a category called "economic needs" and recognize that basically they can be satisfied through wages.)

Not until these economic needs become reasonably well satisfied do any of the higher level needs take on a great deal of significance as motivators. To illustrate, if a man's general wage level is so low that he is having trouble satisfying the basic physiological and security needs,

in his work concerning a theory of motivation. A. H. Maslow, "A Theory of Human Motivation," *Psychological Review, 50.*

it is not likely that he will respond very much to incentives designed to satisfy the social, psychological, or self-fulfillment needs. Thus, the needs in the hierarchy as described above operate in a descending order of importance. We must first reasonably satisfy the economic needs through an adequate and relatively secure wage before efforts in other directions will bear fruit.

A second important point is that once a need is fairly well satisfied it starts to decrease in importance as a strong motivator of behavior relative to other needs. Fairly well satisfied does not, of course, mean 100 percent satisfied. A need is seldom completely satisfied nor does it ever cease completely to be a motivator. However, once a man feels that the wage he is receiving is consistent with the type of work he is doing, that the wage is at a reasonable level, and that he is secure in feeling that he will continue to receive it, continued attempts to motivate him to high levels of performance on the basis of wages alone will meet with something less than full success. What is happening is that the economic needs, having been satisfied at least for the present, are decreasing in importance to him while other needs are becoming more important. He is more apt to respond to incentives which offer him the opportunity to satisfy his social, psychological, and self-fulfillment needs.

Very closely tied to the above two points is the fact that people tend to attach most importance to those things they do not have. This merely reemphasizes that a man is continually attempting to satisfy those needs which as yet have not been taken care of, and at the same time places less stress on those which have been satisfied to an acceptable degree.

No two people are alike; therefore, needs vary in type and intensity from individual to individual. For one man the economic and social needs may be satisfied rather readily, but he has an almost insatiable need for recognition, prestige, and status. For another, the overwhelming driving force, at least for the present, may be the economic needs and consequently the desire for more money. In the third case the need to belong and be an accepted and important part of the group may prevail. The very difficult task which the manager faces is to translate what he knows about needs in general to discovering what specific needs individual workers have. In essence, he must ask himself where each individual stands on the need hierarchy and, in light of this, what incentives can be provided which will offer the employee the opportunity to satisfy these needs.

It should also be recognized that usually the social, psychological, and in some cases, the self-fulfillment needs are not outwardly expressed, at least in a direct sense. It is not quite socially acceptable to ask for a feeling of belonging and sense of importance. Instead, the typical answer to a question, "What motivates you?" is money. The manager, however, must be sensitive to when his people are seeking, in indirect ways, other satisfactions. He must be able to sense whether or not they feel that their work has purpose, meaning, and direction, whether they are properly challenged, when new experiences are desired, when accomplishment and recognition are sought, and when growth and advancement are important.

For example, a tremendously strong on-the-job motivator for one person may be the desire to receive recognition, particularly from his superior. In fact, this need may be so strong that he either actually asks for recognition or noticeably goes out of his way to call attention to achievements which he thinks will result in getting recognition. In such a case the desire for recognition plus the reinforcement that occurs when he gets it can lead to continued positive performance. Similarly, the failure to receive recognition can result in frustration, and eventually either apathy toward the job or negative behavior with the hope that this will get the attention he needs and wants.

Contrast this with the person who, like most of us, wants his share of recognition, but of more importance and meaning to him is a sense of "belonging" to the group; that is, to feel he is an accepted and important part of the group, that he has influence within it, and that his contribution is a valued one. Thus, the kind of recognition that is important to him is not so much praise from his superior for his work but rather acceptance by his peers.

As noted later in the chapter, both factors in these two examples are aspects of creating a motivational climate on the job, but clearly they are of varying degrees of importance. This is true because of differences in orientation and individual personalities.

A fifth factor which complicates the process of motivation is that what constitutes the strongest motivators today may not be the same as those of a year ago. Similarly, those of today may not retain their same degree of potency tomorrow. In short, motivational needs change over time and the manager must be sensitive to these changes. A young man may be interviewed for a job and express considerable interest and concern with respect to what that job pays. This should not be too surprising to the organization or the manager since the young man is married, has two small children, lives in an apartment, and would very much like to be able to build a small nest egg to get established in his first home. It is natural, in this position, to ask first about the pay. Clearly then, money for this young man is a strong (but not the only) motivator. If we expect to keep the man on the job and motivate him to his full level of ability we must pay attention to the wage issue. We must make sure he is adequately rewarded for performance and that he is given the chance to develop new skills so he can move up to higher levels of work. Assuming that he is a fairly competent employee with average or above average potential, for his first few years on the job the manager can undoubtedly do a relatively effective job of motivation by stressing and providing growth opportunities, by giving the man an opportunity to perform and, above all, by rewarding his performance in financial terms.

Now assume that three or four years have passed. The young man in our example has bought his house, the children are in school, and, to a degree, he is established. Does money still motivate him? Yes, it does, but now some other things are important, also. When he talks about his job he thinks more in terms of achievement and accomplishment. He is concerned about the challenge involved, and whether or not he is getting a chance to exercise his full range of capabilities. He thinks in terms of the degree of responsibility attached to his work. Receiving recognition, beyond just wage increases, is significant. His relationships with co-workers and the extent and degree of their esteem become a point of concern. In short, he has reached a point in time and personal development where there must be more to the job than just a paycheck and physically and routinely performing a series of activities. Wages alone will not continue to elicit the same level of motivational response as in the past, and the manager must be sensitive to the changes that have taken place.

A final factor which complicates the motivation process revolves around the fact that people may behave in different ways to satisfy a given need. We mentioned earlier that all of us want recognition and a certain amount of individual attention. One man (probably above average ability) gets this recognition and attention through positive behavior. In other words, he produces top quality and quantity work, has positive attitudes toward the job, and is always willing to put forth a little extra effort in an emergency. Hopefully, of course, he gets recognition for this type of performance.

Doing essentially the same job and perhaps in the same department is another person who seeks recognition and attention. This time, however, quality is marginal and the quantity schedule is just met, but invariably there is last minute pressure to meet it. The individual in question is always (in a very broad sense of the word) in a discipline situation. The big question—does this employee get recognition and attention? The answer—yes, he does. In fact, very often he gets more attention than the first man does. If you doubt this, look at our school system where in many cases the delinquents (again, this word is used in a very broad sense) get more attention than do the good students.

Of critical importance in understanding the second man is the realization that in 10, 15, or 20 years of working, he has become convinced that to do everything right means lack of attention. Here is a man who has as a very strong part of his personality the desire for attention and recognition. Here is a man who, for whatever reason, is dependent to a degree on getting this recognition on the job. Over the years he has literally been trained to get his attention and recognition through negative behavior. This is the way that has proved to be successful for him. The manager may disagree, but the employee can cite case after case where, when you do everything right, "they" ignore you. Therefore, in a very real sense, he is getting a recognition need satisfied in the best way he knows. The problem for the manager is, of course, to retrain the man—to show him by example and through personal experience that he can get more and better recognition through positive behavior.

Motivation-Hygiene Concept

Maslow's development of this need hierarchy was indeed a significant step but it still remained for this material to be applied more directly to the work setting. For the most part, organizations, as well as individual managers, were preoccupied with the idea that the only incentive that could be provided to motivate people was money. The first significant breakthrough in dispelling not only this philosophy but the very serious ramifications which it holds was made by Herzberg.[2] Summarized below are some of the more important concepts as they were developed in the Herzberg studies.

1. There are two distinct dimensions to the motivational problem. On one end of the continuum are those factors which, if not present, can cause dissatisfaction. Herzberg calls these "hygiene factors." On the other end of the continuum are those factors which, if present, can actually lead to positive attitudes and motivation and which, if not present, result in no positive attitudes. These are the motivational factors.

[2]Fredrick Herzberg, "The Motivation-Hygiene Concept and Problems of Manpower," *Personnel Administration*, January–February 1964, pp. 3–7.

2. The hygiene factors (those that can either cause or prevent dissatisfaction) include such things as wages, fringe benefits, physical working conditions, and overall company policy and administration. When these things are adequately taken care of dissatisfaction will disappear, but more important, *no positive attitudes and motivation result.* Thus, the hygiene factors are preventive. They can prevent dissatisfaction but do not act as personal incentives which motivate people to high levels of productivity. As Herzberg points out, people can only be brought to a neutral point on the basis of hygiene factors.

3. The motivational factors (those which actually lead to the development of positive attitudes, motivation, and act as individual incentives) include such things as recognition, feelings of accomplishment and achievement, opportunity for advancement and potential for personal growth, responsibility, a sense of job and individual importance, new experiences, and challenging work. As Herzberg notes, these are things which surround the job. While the hygiene factors satisfy the physiological and security needs the motivational factors are concerned with the social, psychological, and self-fulfillment needs.

The insight into the motivational process which was gained via the Herzberg research ties in very well with two points made earlier. First, that once the economic needs are fairly well satisfied they start to decrease in importance as motivators of behavior relative to other needs; also, we attach most significance to those things we do not have. In addition, of course, the fact that wages and related items can only bring a person up to a neutral point and not really motivate him to high levels of achievement is of great importance. Herzberg effectively summarized the situation.

". . . Because the factors on the left serve primarily as preventives, that is to prevent job dissatisfaction, and because they also deal with the environment, I have named these factors 'the hygiene' factors in a poor analogy with the way the term is used in preventive medicine. The factors on the right I call the 'motivators' because other results indicate that they are necessary for improvement in performance beyond that pseudo improvement which in substance amounts to coming up to a fair day's work . . ."[3]

The motivation scale (Figure I) adequately depicts the situation. On the left side of the scale is a minus sign representing employee dis-

[3]Ibid., p. 5.

satisfaction. On the right is a plus sign representing a maximum level of motivation. In the middle of the scale is the typical employee performing at about 66⅔ percent of efficiency (a fairly representative and accepted figure for the typical level of performance of an average employee).

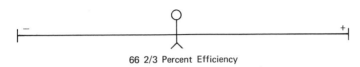

66 2/3 Percent Efficiency

Figure 1   Motivation Scale

As suggested earlier, the organization or individual manager who has traditionally approached the subject of motivation from a solely "hygiene" angle has been seriously handicapping himself in several ways. First, assuming he has correctly applied the hygiene factors, all he has succeeded in doing in most cases is preventing dissatisfaction. Second, no positive motivation has resulted beyond perhaps that neutral level depicted on the scale. Third, it should be recognized that to some degree every manager is limited in his control over wages (one of the most important of all the hygiene factors). Generally speaking, the lower the wage level, the less the control. In any case, there are organization policies concerning salary review dates, wage and salary structures, and a limit of some sort with respect to the general level of wages paid. Therefore, not only is the effectiveness of money as a motivator in question but also the extent to which any individual manager has control over it. The manager cannot motivate people with something over which he has no control. Fourth, Maslow has estimated that for the average person the physiological needs are 85 percent satisfied, the security needs 70 percent satisfied, the social needs 50 percent satisfied, the psychological needs 40 percent satisfied, and the self-fulfillment needs only 10 percent satisfied.[4] If we assume that these

[4]An extension of Herzberg's work was undertaken by Myers at Texas Instruments Company. His study included salaried as well as hourly employees, and managers as well as nonmanagers. Using essentially the Herzberg research approach, he came to the same general conclusions with regard to specific motivational factors as they relate to various classifications of employees. In addition, Myers stated his belief that managers on all levels have two responsibilities: (1) to provide for satisfaction of the economic needs or potential dissatisfiers and (2) to provide conditions for motivation. M. Scott Myers, "Who Are Your Motivated Workers?" *Harvard Business Review,* January–February 1964, pp. 73–88.

estimates concerning the degree to which the various needs are satisfied for the average person are somewhere near representative, the greatest potential for motivation quite obviously lies in providing incentives which satisfy the social, psychological, and self-fulfillment needs.

All that has been said above is not intended to imply that the economic needs and the hygiene factors are not important. They are indeed very important and if not given adequate attention any effort in the direction of the social, psychological, and self-fulfillment needs and the motivational factors will necessarily meet with less than full success. The key point once again is that lack of hygiene factors can cause dissatisfaction but they do not get at the root of job satisfaction and motivation as far as the individual is concerned. The latter is a separate dimension and depends on a totally different set of needs and factors. The relationship can best be set forth in the following manner:

	Hygiene Factors	Motivational Factors
If Not Present	JOB DISSATISFACTION	NO JOB SATISFACTION
If Present	NO JOB DISSATISFACTION	JOB SATISFACTION

Also of importance is the fact that to a certain degree some weaknesses on the hygiene side can be offset by positive factors on the motivational side. The opposite, however, does not hold true. Many organizations which pride themselves on their wage and fringe benefit programs as well as general working conditions have found that these things alone have not furnished the answer to maximum cooperation and productivity from employees. It is true that they may help to attract good people in the first place but after a few months they are pretty much taken for granted and only a neutral point of 66⅔ percent efficiency is reached. Motivation beyond a neutral point requires that attention be given to social, psychological, and self-fulfillment needs.

Theory of Expectancy and Path Goal Relationships

A final concept which will contribute to the development of an initial understanding of the motivation process is the expectancy theory of behavior and path goal relationships. According to this theory the extent and degree of motivation is a function of two things—the value of the particular incentive to the individual in question and his perception of whether or not a given pattern of behavior will lead to satisfaction of the need the incentive is designed to satisfy. Thus, the incentive being offered must be somethings of importance to the individual and he must perceive that he can achieve or attain it through positive behavior. Stated conversely, if the incentive itself is not valued or is valued only to a small degree and if the individual does not believe positive response on his part will achieve it, he will not be motivated. The important point is that both of the above-specified conditions must exist at the same point in time.

The phrase "his perceptions of" is a key one. Both the incentive being offered and the path or kind of behavior needed to achieve it *must* be viewed from the employee's frame of reference. By way of example, if the organization holds forth the potential of a wage increase based on the achievement of a given level of performance it will only act as a motivator if from the employee's point of view the following conditions are present.

1.   That superior performance does in fact result in some type of "extraordinary" financial reward. The fact that the organization advertises that this relationship exists is of no consequence. If rightly or wrongly over a period of time employees have come to feel that there is no relationship or that it is only a small one they will not be motivated to perform.

2.   The size of the potential increase must be perceived as being worth the extra effort required to earn it. If employees have been accustomed to receiving a four or five percent increase more or less as a matter of course and only a six to eight percent increase is held out as an incentive the desired motivation may not take place.

3.   The employee must value the potential of money in the first place.

By way of another example assume that what a given employee seeks is recognition or attention, or, in short, to be noticed. This, in a sense, is his goal. One would expect that the normal path to follow to achieve this goal would be positive job performance. Perhaps, however, the individual in question has had a series of superiors whose philosophy was that people are paid to do things right and they will hear something only when things go wrong. The employee soon becomes conditioned to the fact that the path to being noticed is not positive performance but rather something less than what is expected. Consciously or unconsciously he periodically builds into his performance pattern some of those "little things" that will call attention to his presence. Assuming he does not err too often or too seriously he finds that this approach has the advantage of at least preventing total obscurity. To change his behavior will require a manager who is achievement oriented and makes a point of recognizing positive performance in tangible ways.

Thus, the issue of what the individual employee's goals are in the first place and his perception of what path will lead to achieving them is strategic. He must value the incentive as a satisfier of a particular need and he must believe that the path of behavior which is advocated to achieve the incentive will in fact be successful. Also, as indicated above he may adopt a path which is contrary to one which the organization wishes he would adopt. If it is successful over time he becomes conditioned to a wrong response. The latter is akin to the child who wants attention and does not get it when he is good so he reverts to being bad and then does get attention.

Summary

The behavior of people is goal directed in the sense that it is conditioned by an attempt to satisfy certain needs or to prevent need dissatisfaction. Abraham Maslow arranged needs in a five-step hierarchy ranging from physiological needs to the self-fulfillment needs. According to Maslow's theory, man first attempts to satisfy his lower level needs and not until they are reasonably well taken care of does he direct his behavior toward satisfying the higher level needs. In their attempts to motivate employees, organizations have traditionally centered their efforts on appealing primarily to the physiological and security needs. To the extent that this has been true these efforts have fallen short of their goal because they neglect everything else that people look for. If the opportunity to satisfy other than economic needs is not present on the job a good share of the employee's effort, ingenuity, and creativity will be directed toward off the job activities to satisfy his remaining needs.

Building on Maslow's original theory Herzberg formulated a motivation-hygiene theory. According to this theory the factors that lead to job satisfaction and motivation are distinctly different from those that cause dissatisfaction. Herzberg labeled the factors associated with dissatisfaction as hygiene factors. They included such things as pay, fringe benefits, working conditions, and company policy. He maintained that the absence of the factors would lead to dissatisfaction but their presence would only serve to bring an individual to a neutral point. In order to motivate people, Herzberg maintained that the job climate must offer the employee an opportunity to satisfy his higher level social, psychological, and self-fulfillment needs.

A final concept about motivation which was discussed is the theory of expectancy and path goal relationships. According to this theory, if an employee is going to be motivated he must first value or want the incentive being offered and second he must believe that good performance will in fact result in his achieving that incentive. If either of these conditions is not present no motivation will result.

Key Concepts

Need Hierarchy. The needs, wants, or drives which motivate people's behavior are arranged in a hierarchy, or order of priority. Not until the needs at one level are fairly well satisfied do the needs at successively higher levels come into play as motivators.

Motivation-Hygiene Theory. This theory states that the factors which cause job dissatisfaction and those which result in motivation beyond some neutral point are completely different. The motivators are represented by man's higher level needs.

Theory of Expectancy. In order to motivate an individual, two conditions must be present. First, he must value the incentive being offered and second, he must perceive that through good performance he can achieve that incentive.

Discussion Questions

1. Compare Maslow's and Herzberg's theory of motivation. Which of Maslow's needs correspond to Herzberg's hygiene factors? Which of Maslow's needs correspond to Herzberg's motivators? Are Herzberg's and Maslow's theories consistent with each other? Explain why or why not.

2. After Jim requested a transfer, his supervisor replied:

> "Jim, I can't understand why you want to transfer to the Research and Development Department. They don't pay their draftsmen as well as they do here in the Engineering Department. You'll spend a lot of your time working alone and won't have the close guidance on the projects which we give you here.
>
> "Oh well, I guess you're one of those people who like to work long hours and don't mind low pay."

Apply both Herzberg's and Maslow's concepts of motivation to explain what has happened in the above situation.

3. After Frank requested a transfer, his supervisor replied:

> "Frank, I can't understand why you want to transfer back to the manufacturing plant. It's a routine job which anyone could perform and there is no chance to apply any creativity or initiative. The job you now have in the office allows you to really use your head and apply your initiative. There are no routine aspects to your job here, and you can really see what's happening around here.
>
> "I'm really disappointed in your decision, Frank. Sure, I know the pay in the production department is significantly better than what we pay you in the office, but the challenging type of work should more than make up for it.
>
> "Oh well, I guess you're one of those many people who is interested only in the money."

Apply both Herzberg's and Maslow's concepts of motivation to explain what has happened in the above situation.

4. Cite some specific examples (perhaps from your own experiences) where the pay, supervision, and job environment might be good,

but yet the job posed few motivators. Could people who work in these types of jobs ever be satisfied on the job? Could they be kept from being dissatisfied? Are there many jobs which have few motivators? What are your suggestions for (1) putting motivators in these job situations and (2) eliminating these types of jobs if motivators cannot be put in them?

5. Jim received a pay raise of 10 percent of his hourly rate. What conditions must be necessary in order for this pay increase to have a positive effect on his motivation to work?

Selected Readings

Orlando Behling, George Labovitz, and Richard Kosnue, "The Herzberg Controversy: A Critical Reappraisal," *Academy of Management Journal*, March 1968, pp. 99–108.

Frederick Herzberg, "The Motivation-Hygiene Concept and Problems of Manpower," *Personnel Administration*, January–February 1964, pp. 3–7.

Frederick Herzberg, Bernard Mauser, and Barbara Block Snyderman, *Motivation Versus Hygiene, The Motivation to Work*, New York: Wiley, 1959, Chapter 12, pp. 113–119.

Robert J. House, and Lawrence A. Wigdor, "Herzberg's Dual-Factor Theory of Job Satisfaction and Motivation: A Review of the Evidence and a Criticism," *Personnel Psychology, 20,* 1967, pp. 369–389.

Charles L. Hulin, and Milton R. Blood, "Job Enlargement, Individual Differences, and Worker Responses," *Psychological Bulletin, 69* (1), 1968, pp. 41–55.

Rensis Likert, "Motivation: The Core of Management," American Management Association, *Personnel Series*, New York, No. 155, 1953, pp. 3–21.

A. H. Maslow, "A Theory of Human Motivation," *Psychological Review, 50*, pp. 370–396, 1943.

356 *MANAGERIAL DIRECTION AND LEADERSHIP*

David C. McClelland, "That Urge to Achieve," *Think Magazine, 32* (6), November–December 1966, pp. 19–23.

M. Scott Myers, "Who Are Your Motivated Workers?" *Harvard Business Review*, January–February 1964, pp. 73–88.

Harold F. Rotle, "Does Higher Pay Bring Higher Productivity?" *Personnel, 37*, July–August 1960, pp. 20–27.

18. Developing a Management Philosophy

To come up with a single word that describes all the goals that a manager might have for his department is perhaps a little presumptuous, but the word "Productivity" comes fairly close to being all-encompassing. If productivity can be accomplished, the manager will at the same time be accomplishing all those other goals that might come to mind. As with any other result, however, productivity in an organization does not occur by chance. Instead, it is a culmination of the effective blending of several key elements.

First, there are the technical factors. These include the tools and equipment which are available to do the work, as well as the raw materials at the manager's disposal. A second influencing factor has to do with systems and procedures which are in operation. These systems and procedures are designed to insure that there is uniformity, consistency, and smoothness in day-to-day operations. The third and most important element of a productive operation is people. In the last analysis it is the human factor which makes the difference as far as the level of productivity is concerned. Although a manager's job involves many things, and can be described in many ways, his central responsibility is the management of people to obtain maximum results.

Put another way, the results he gets will depend a great deal on how effectively he can manage people.

In managing people to obtain maximum productivity, there are three general objectives which are of significance. These can be summarized as follows.

1.   To improve the performance of people on their present job in terms of results accomplished.

2.   To prepare individuals to accept increasing responsibility in present jobs.

3.   To help individuals grow and develop in terms of higher level jobs.

The key ingredient to having any of these things happen is *initiative and desire* as far as the man himself is concerned. He must be motivated to want to grow and develop both in his present job and the longer range future.

Thus, the key to productivity in total is individual job performance on the part of the people concerned, and the key to job performance is motivation. This, then, is the challenge which faces each manager—to motivate his people toward maximum levels of productivity. The situation can be diagrammed as below:

THE CHALLENGE OF MANAGEMENT
Maximum Productivity—depends on—Individual Job Performance—
depends on—Individual Motivation

The idea that motivation is a personal thing and that it must be generated within the man himself is not new. In a strictly technical sense, a manager cannot motivate anybody. What he can do, however, is to create a climate which will trigger and point in the right direction the motivation potential that is already there.

There are two aspects to creating the proper motivation climate. First is the manager's personal approach to leadership as it reflects in his day-to-day contacts with subordinates; second is the general structure of the job climate he creates.

This chapter will set the stage for the succeeding chapters on direction and leadership by first making some general observations about leadership and second, by exploring some alternative management philosophies and how they influence the leadership process.

Some General Observations Concerning Leadership

The first general observation that might be made concerning leadership is that by and large, *people are already motivated.* The important questions are: (1) How strong is the motivation? and (2) In what direction is it working? If a man is consistently performing below standard or just at standard when he is capable of a higher level, it is clear that the strength of his motivation is insufficient; for some reason, he is not getting what he wants from the job and this dampens his initiative. The challenge to the manager is to build into the job climate and his own approach to leadership those incentives which will trigger the latent potential.

In terms of the direction of motivation, it may be working either for the manager, against him, or it may be neutral. Again, the challenge is to adopt an approach to leadership that will insure maximum commitment to departmental and organizational objectives on the part of each individual.

Effective Leadership Is Not an Easy Job. Too often managers read a book or an article concerning some technique of leadership and expect that implementing it will solve all their problems. This simply is not true. *There are no magic words or formulas which, when applied, serve as a cure-all!* Rather, effective leadership is one of the most challenging and difficult tasks which a manager faces. It is the result of a comprehensive approach which emphasizes the total climate and recognizes individual differences. Also, it is a task which demands continuous effort and conscientious application.

Effective Leadership Should Foster Commitment and Involvement on the Part of the People. The fact that a man is performing various tasks in the course of his job means that is he physically involved in that job, but this does not necessarily mean that he is totally involved. To achieve this, he must become *mentally and emotionally involved.* The key factor in producing this type of involvement and the resulting commitment which it creates is an opportunity to participate in the total job climate. This requires mutual agreement between the boss and the man concerning work itself, why it is important, the results or objectives to be accomplished, how performance will be measured, and how he is doing on the job.

The Manager Sets the Pace.   In any operation it is the *manager who sets the pace* as far as ultimate accomplishment of results is concerned. The level of accomplishment he gets from his people will, to a large degree, be a reflection of what he expects and what he demands. If he expects the worst, the chances are good he will get exactly that. If he is satisfied with a medium level of performance, the chances are equally good that this is what most of his people will give him. Research and practical experience have demonstrated that the manager who has consistently high expectations of subordinates usually secures the highest level of performance.

Of particular importance is the idea that standards of performance can be set by default if the manager is not careful. Not letting subordinates know what his expectations are and keeping them in the dark on where they stand signify approval of the results he is getting.

Leadership Must Be Genuine.   There is a difference between leading people and trying to manipulate them. People will be able to see through insincere or artificial application of various leadership techniques. They may be fooled for a while but very soon they are able to sense the phoniness and develop a feeling that someone is trying "to take them for a ride." Effective leadership stems from a *sincere desire to accomplish results through and with people.* Various leadership techniques are a means to an end and not an end in themselves.

Enthusiasm Is a Must.   Sometimes we wonder why people are apathetic and seem to be disinterested in their job. When this is true to any appreciable degree among a total work group a good question for any manager to ask himself is, "How much enthusiasm am I generating toward the department in general, the work that we are doing, what is being accomplished, and what particular individuals are accomplishing?"

Enthusiasm in an organization is very contagious. Once it catches, it is difficult to stop. The individual manager can do much toward building a favorable climate for maximum results by establishing a good "mental set" himself. If he is excited and interested, the chances are good that his people will be the same way.

The Key to Better Performance from Subordinates Is Better Leadership from the Manager. Some time ago, the Champion Paper Company produced a film entitled "1104 Sutton Road," which contains the following two statements.

1. "To get more of what you want, you must produce more of what the other people want."

2. "We can't control what comes to us, but only what goes from us."

These statements are apropos to both individual job performance and managerial leadership. A manager cannot dictate the level of job performance he wants and then simply apply pressure and use authority to get it. This approach inevitably fails to produce the desired results. When it has been used and fails, the natural tendency is to blame the people, to say they don't want to work, that they are not motivated, and that they are "slacking off." Although these observations may be true in some cases, the reason is usually *not that the people are this way inherently, but rather that they are reflecting the fact that there is nothing in the job that they want other than a pay check!* In other words, they have nothing else to work for.

The answer to higher levels of individual job performance (more of what the manager wants) is to produce more of what his people want via providing a better leadership climate, that is, a climate where there is more to a job than just physical activity and a paycheck. The ability of the manager to control what comes to him is limited. The only long-range way of effectively controlling what comes to him in terms of his people's job performance is to control what goes from him to them in terms of making sure they can get what they want out of a job; or, the objectives of the organization must be integrated and blended with the needs of the individual. Every manager has within his individual control the means to bring about this integration. If what goes from him in terms of his personal leadership pattern is good, what comes to him in terms of performance will also be good.

Developing a Management Philosophy—Theories X and Y

A manager's philosophy toward people and their normal reaction to work will, to a great extent, consciously or unconsciously determine his overall approach to management. With this in mind, it is appropriate to begin our study of direction and leadership by examining some alternative philosophies. In his book, *The Human Side of Enterprise*, Douglas McGregor sets forth two alternative sets of assumptions which a manager may have about people.[1] These two sets of assumptions are summarized in Exhibit I.[2] As the reader will note, the assumptions underlying what McGregor has labeled Theory X represent extremely negative viewpoints while those underlying Theory Y are positive in nature.

McGregor's thesis was that much of management practice in the past has been based on a set of assumptions about people which are substantially open to question if used as generalizations. More specifically, to the extent that a Theory X philosophy has prevailed, the direction of people has proceeded in a fashion which is not conducive to motivating people, but has actually caused antagonism. On the other hand, McGregor advocates that the assumptions underlying Theory Y represent a much closer approximation to the real situation and are therefore a much sounder base on which to structure a management approach to leadership. Exhibit II[3] summarizes the implications of Theories X and Y as far as a management approach is concerned.

Exhibit I Assumptions

Theory X

1. The average person has an inherent dislike for work and will avoid it if he can.

2. Because of this dislike for work, most people must be coerced, controlled, directed, threatened, and punished to get them to put forth adequate effort toward the achievement of organizational objectives; even promise of reward is not enough. Will accept and demand more. Only threat will do the trick.

3. Average person prefers to be directed, wishes to avoid responsibility, little ambition, wants security above all—mediocrity of the masses.

Theory Y

1. Expenditure of physical and mental effort in work is as natural as play or rest; depending on controllable conditions, work may be either a source of satisfaction or dissatisfaction.

[1]From *The Human Side of Enterprise* by Douglas McGregor. Copyright 1960 by McGraw-Hill. Used with permission of McGraw-Hill Book Company.

[2]Ibid.

[3]Ibid.

2. External control and the threat of punishment are not the only means for bringing about effort toward objectives. Man will exercise self-direction and self-control in the service of objectives to which he is committed.

3. Commitment is a function of the rewards associated with their achievement.

4. Under proper conditions people will not only accept but seek responsibility. Avoidance of responsibility, lack of ambition, emphasis on security, not human characteristics.

5. Capacity to exercise imagination, ingenuity, creativity is widely, not narrowly distributed.

6. Intellectual potential of average persons are being only partially utilized.

Exhibit II Implications

Theory X

1. Central principle of organization derived from Theory X is that of direction and control through exercise of authority.

2. Organizational requirements take precedent over needs of members. In return for rewards offered, the individual will accept external direction and control.

3. We do not recognize the existence of potential in people and therefore there is no reason to devote time, effort, and money to discovering how to realize full potential.

Theory Y

1. Central principle derived from Theory Y is integration: the creation of conditions such that members of the organization can achieve their own goals best by directing their efforts toward the success of the enterprise.

2. The organization will be more effective in achieving its objectives if adjustments are made to the needs and goals of its members.

3. We are challenged to innovate, to discover new ways of organizing and directing human effort.

The assumptions of Theory Y are dynamic rather than static. They indicate the possibility of human growth and development. They stress the necessity for selective adaptation rather than absolute control. They are framed in terms of a resource which has substantial potential.

Above all, the assumptions of Theory Y point to the fact that the limits on human collaboration in the organizational setting are not limits of human nature, but limits of management's ingenuity in discovering how to realize the potential represented by its human resources. Theory X offers management an easy rationalization for ineffective organizational performance: it is due to the nature of the human resources with which it must work. Theory Y, on the other hand, places the problem squarely in the lap of management. If employees are lazy, indifferent, unwilling to take responsibility, and uncooperative, Theory Y implies that the causes lie in management's methods of organization and control.

Theory Y assumes that people will exercise self-direction and self-control in the achievement of organization objectives to the degree that they are committed to those objectives. Managerial policies and practices materially affect this degree of commitment.

Implications of Theory X and Y on the Individual Manager

In formulating Theories X and Y, Douglas McGregor opened up new vistas for other writers to reflect on and for management development people to emphasize in their training sessions. Admittedly, they represent the two extreme ends of the management philosophy continuum and, in a given case, a manager usually falls somewhere between the two extremes.

The point of departure for this discussion, however, is not so much with the assumptions underlying the two theories as it is with their implications as far as the manager is concerned.

Our Philosophy Determines How We Manage.   The first important ramification of McGregor's work is that every manager does have a philosophy of some kind and that this philosophy determines how he manages people. If he starts with a negative feeling about people and their reaction to work, the chances are good that he will build into his approach to leadership certain negative aspects. He will be more likely to adopt approaches to supervision which reflect an autocratic style. This, of course, means a great deal of reliance on authority, power, and discipline. That this style or approach to leadership has important long-range negative implications and that it leads to something less than maximum results has been well established. Only when people are fully and completely dependent on one job, with one organization, in one department can the ingredients for the management of people suggested by Theory X be at all effective. Generally speaking, this extreme degree of dependence on the part of most workers simply does not exist. Even in cases where a high degree of dependency is present, and the manager tries to capitalize on this by using authoritarian management techniques, he usually encounters subtle techniques on the part of workers to sabotage accomplishment.

On the other hand, a positive philosophy toward people and their normal reaction to work (suggested by Theory Y) will serve as a cornerstone for building a positive approach to management. Managers who are willing to "give a little" to Theory Y principles are much more open to exploring and implementing the techniques of modern management which are studied and successfully implemented by so many managers today. These techniques are embodied within the framework of results management, motivation, and coaching and developing subordinates in a results-oriented climate.

It is clear, then, that every manager does have a philosophy toward people and consciously or unconsciously his philosophy will influence his management approach. The important thing is that on an individual basis managers crystalize and become consciously aware of their own attitude; this is not with the idea of defending it in a given case, but rather that he can then better understand his approach to supervision and why it does or does not yield maximum results.

To illustrate this, a line supervisor of unionized production people may feel differently than a manager of other managers or a manager of technical people. Clearly his situation is different and because it is different he might well rely on a different approach to leadership in an overall sense. Yet, it is possible that certain principles of leadership would be effective in both cases if they were properly used. Whether or not they are even tried, however, will depend on the attitude of the individual manager.

Every manager must place himself somewhere along a philosophy scale where Theory X represents one extreme and Theory Y another. In the process of classifying himself he must also ask why he feels this way and if this feeling is a true representation of the real situation. Assuming that it is, he can then begin to evaluate whether or not he is building into his approach to leadership everything possible to create a motivational climate for his people in light of the situation he faces. The process presupposes, of course, an objective analytical approach as well as a sensitivity to the elements of motivational leadership as discussed in Chapter 19.

People Are Trained in Theory X Responses.   The second very important implication as far as the individual manager is concerned is that people are trained to react in a Theory X way rather than being that way inherently. A great deal of research has been done which supports the idea that the organizational climate which exists will greatly influence the response from employees. For example, Etzioni[4] in his research identified three organizational types and the employee responses they tended to create. The three types were coercive, utilitarian, and normative. The first type relies heavily on authority, power, force, and discipline, and tends to produce an alienative response from employees. They will fight the system and wherever possible try to sabotage results. They will do what they are told to do but no more. In other words, they will perform at an absolute minimum level, or just enough to get by. The words "antagonistic cooperation" summarize the response from people under coercive management.

The utilitarian approach relies on the wage and contingent benefit bargain to get results and produces what Etzioni calls "calculative behavior." The employees as individuals or the total work group together calculate the worth of what is offered and produce accordingly. In other words, so much work for so much pay. In this type of organization, the higher performer who can get a better deal someplace else often leaves. Those who remain are average performers either because they possess less potential or are lulled into being that way.

The normative organization emphasizes involvement of people, participation, and an opportunity to satisfy self-fulfillment needs as outlined in the chapter on motivation. It tends to produce a moral reaction among employees which can be characterized by such words as commitment, motivation, initiative, desire, and dedication.

Just as the overall climate within the total organization can trigger a given response, so can an individual manager's personal approach to leadership determine a response. The latter is particularly strategic since the manager can, to a degree, offset or augment the organizational climate. University of Michigan research, for example, has pointed out that the strictly production-centered manager tends to have lower department productivity than does the people-centered manager. Simi-

[4]A. Etzioni, *A Comparative Analysis of Complex Organizations* (Glencoe, Illinois: The Free Press, 1961).

larly, the manager who integrates his people's needs with his department's objectives will get better results.

In summary, when we say people are trained to react a given way, we are trying to point out that there is a reason for this reaction. In an organization, they are reacting to the climate in which they work and the way they perceive that climate. It is too easy to blame lack of initiative and unwillingness to assume responsibility on people. It might well be that the organization is expecting more in response from employees than it is giving in terms of opportunity for need satisfaction.

Better Management for Better Results. All this leads to a third and perhaps the most important implication of McGregor's work, which is that the key to better performance is better management. As stated by McGregor, "Theory X offers management an easy rationalization for ineffective organizational performance; it is due to the nature of the resources with which it must work. Theory Y, on the other hand, places the problem squarely in the lap of management. If employees are lazy, indifferent, unwilling to take responsibility, uncooperative, Theory Y implies that the causes lie in management's methods of organization and control."[5] To a degree, a manager gets the type and level of performance he deserves because it is a reflection of the way in which he manages. In the case of lower than desired levels of performance in total or on an individual employee basis, the manager should first consider whether there is anything which could be done better in a leadership sense. More specifically, what is the reason for the poor performance? Some possibilities a manager should examine are:

1. Have I made it clear what is expected in terms of results?

2. Have I let him know where he stands?

3. Does he know how to do the work?

4. Have I done a good job of training and development?

5. Have I ever discussed candidly with him the situations which he faces in his job that make accomplishment difficult?

6. Do I give him all the support I could?

7. What have I done or not done to cultivate a positive personal relationship?

[5]McGregor, op. cit.

8.   Does he know why the job is important, where it fits, and the ramifications of poor performance?

9.   Have we discussed and agreed on what is expected, how reasonable these expectations are, and where he stands?

10.   Is he kept informed of what is going on in the department and company? (Not just those things he needs to know, but also things he would like to know.)

11.   Does he have adequate freedom to work, rather than being overcontrolled?

12.   Is he put in a defensive position regarding his performance?

13.   What have I done to get him mentally and emotionally involved in his job rather than just physically involved?

14.   Has he been allowed to participate in setting goals and how to achieve them?

15.   Has the good in his performance received adequate and periodic recognition?

16.   Do I accentuate the positive rather than the negative?

17.   Have I shown adequate concern for him as an individual as well as for his personal goals?

18.   Am I flexible in terms of encouraging and listening and giving him a chance to implement ideas and suggestions?

19.   Have I ever consciously assessed his strengths and weaknesses with the idea of structuring the work to capitalize on these strengths?

20.   Is he adequately and reasonably challenged?

This list of questions reflects some (certainly not all) of the ingredients of effective management of people. Each manager should answer them for himself if he really wants to be objective and honest. In doing so he should also keep in mind how he would be ranked by his subordinates if they were asked the same questions about their manager!

Other Factors Affecting Motivation and Productivity.   The foregoing discussion might imply that a manager's approach to leadership is the only factor that affects motivation and productivity. This, of course, is not true and represents an oversimplification of the problem. In addition to the manager's approach to supervision and his skill in planning, the following factors play a part in determining the type of response we get from employees.

1. The attitudes and philosophies which the employee himself brings to the job in the first place.

2. The total organizational climate with respect to policies, procedures, rules, regulations, and other factors that affect the individual in performance of his job.

3. Specific environmental factors, other than physical conditions, such as the system of giving awards, promotions, and opportunities for growth.

It is within this more structured organizational framework that the individual manager performs his leadership function. To the extent and degree that he must overcome sources of pressure and perhaps dissatisfaction on the part of employees with these factors, his leadership job is made more difficult. This is especially true when he has no control or influence in changing the factors. Generally speaking, the lower a manager is on the managerial ladder, the less control he has over these broader aspects of job climate and, paradoxically, the more subject he is to bearing such pressures if they exist. This puts a premium on higher management to continually analyze, evaluate, and, if necessary, change the overall structure. It is perhaps also worth noting that the people who are most sensitive to specific problems are usually those farther down the management line. In other words, a manager exercises leadership within a total climate and framework, and his effectiveness is to some degree influenced by elements beyond his control.

Differences in Perception. A final point of concern is the possible difference in perception concerning the job, the organizational climate, and the leadership climate that the manager has, as opposed to those he supervises. It is possible, for example, to ask a manager if he delegates and get an affirmative response. When his subordinates are asked the same question, they disagree, or else feel that his delegation is very limited and closely controlled. Similarly, many managers believe that communications within the department or organization are good, but when asked the same question, employees consider them to be only fair. This same type of problem is illustrated by the following instance cited in McGregor's book, *The Professional Manager.*

"During a study of management development practice in some twenty-five blue-chip companies a few years ago, I queried representatives of middle and lower management concerning the extent to which they perceived salary increases to be related to successful effort in developing subordinates. By far the most common response was a cynical smile! In only two or three companies did there seem to be a genuine perception that the relationships between these factors amounted to more than 'talk.' "[6]

The crucial point is that the way an employee perceives and understands his total climate is an important determinant of his response. Whether or not his perception and understanding are reasonable is a separate issue. In any case, the manager must be sensitive to these feelings and, where necessary, either change them or, through communication, create better understanding on the employee's part. This is a prerequisite to successfully implementing otherwise effective methods of management.

Summary

In Chapter 18 it has been emphasized that there is a very close relationship between the level of employee motivation and the quality of leadership. In fact, effective leadership is one of the most difficult and challenging tasks which a manager faces. A manager's approach to leadership is conditioned by his assumptions about people and their reaction to work. Theory X represents a negative set of assumptions about people and usually results in a negative approach to leadership. Theory Y represents a positive set of assumptions about people and usually leads to positive leadership techniques. Thus, there is a direct relationship between the type of leadership and the level of motivation; the type of leadership is influenced by a manager's assumptions about people, and positive approaches to leadership tend to elicit positive employee response.

[6]From *The Professional Manager* by Douglas McGregor, edited by Warren G. Bennis and Caroline McGregor, p. 143. Copyright 1967 by McGraw-Hill. Used with permission of McGraw-Hll Book Company.

Key Concepts

Theory X. Theory X represents a negative set of assumptions about people and their reaction to work. It results in approaches to leadership not conducive to creating a motivational climate.

Theory Y. Theory Y represents a positive set of assumptions about people and results in positive approaches to leadership which tend to generate a strong motivational climate.

Discussion Questions

1. Control must exist in any work situation involving people:
   (a) Where does the *source* of control tend to be in a situation involving a Theory X manager?
   (b) Where does the *source* of control tend to be in a situation involving a Theory Y manager?

2. If a manager held the Theory X assumptions, how would you expect him to manage? What type of reactions do you think he would receive from his subordinates?

3. If a manager held the Theory Y assumptions, how would you expect him to manage? What type of reactions do you think he would receive from his subordinates?

4. Is it possible that a gentle, mild-mannered, soft-spoken person who seldom uses a demanding tone of voice could, in reality, be a Theory X type of leader? Describe how a person with this type of outward personality might manage while holding the Theory X type of assumptions.

5. Is it possible that a rather gruff, short-tempered person who speaks in a loud, demanding tone of voice and is generally quite assertive could actually be a Theory Y type of leader? Describe how a person with this type of outward personality might manage while holding the Theory Y assumptions.

6. Would a Theory Y supervisor be less successful than a Theory X

supervisor if both were supervising a group of unskilled workers performing a routine task on a production line? If you feel that he would, then go back to the Theory X and Theory Y implications (Exhibit II). If you think he would not, explain why.

Selected Readings

D. E. Berlyne, "A Decade of Motivation Theory," *American Scientist, 52,* 1964, pp. 447–451.

A. Etzioni, *A Comparative Analysis of Complex Organizations*, The Free Press, Glencoe, Illinois, 1961.

Douglas M. McGregor, "The Human Side of Enterprise," *The Management Review*, November 1957, pp. 22–28, 88–92.

Douglas M. McGregor, *The Human Side of Enterprise*, McGraw-Hill, New York, 1960.

Douglas M. McGregor, *The Professional Manager*, edited by Warren G. Bennis, and Caroline McGregor, McGraw-Hill, New York, 1967, p. 143.

Donald C. Pelz, "Influence: A Key to Effective Leadership in the First-Line Supervisor," *Personnel, 29,* 1952, pp. 209–217.

Burt K. Scanlan, "Your Philosophy Determines Your Approach," *Personnel Journal,* July–August 1968.

Ross Stanger, *Perception: Applied Aspects, the Psychology of Industrial Conflict*, Wiley, New York, 1956, pp. 53–88.

19.   Managerial Leadership

When leadership contributes to producing results it is usually because an atmosphere has been created which the employees regard as compatible with satisfying some of their own needs. As a result, they are likely to involve themselves more wholeheartedly in their work. The employee is seldom aware of precisely why he feels free to give so fully of himself to his job; usually he can point to the fact that his manager is a nice enough fellow, as are his fellow workers, and that the work itself is rather enjoyable.

To sum this up, McGregor formulated a functional relationship; performance (P) of an individual at work in an organization is a function of certain characteristics of the individual (I), such as his knowledge, skills, motivation, attitudes, and of certain aspects of the environmental situation (E), for example, the nature of his job, the rewards associated with his performance, and the leadership provided him.

$$P = f(^I a,b,c,d. . .^E m,n,o,p. . .)^1$$

One can therefore conclude that leadership is directly related to performance and by varying leadership styles in an organization, the

[1]D. McGregor, op. cit., p. 5.

degree of effectiveness and productivity of that organization will also vary.

This chapter concentrates on various theories of leadership. The views of four different authors will be discussed and compared. They will provide the reader with a comprehensive insight into the leadership function.

Blake and Mouton—The Managerial Grid[2]

Blake and Mouton developed a framework for describing managerial styles which they call the "managerial grid." (See Exhibit I.) The purpose of the grid is to compare management styles in terms of how each deals with (1) organizational needs for production and profit and (2) human needs for mature and healthy relationships. The horizontal axis of the grid represents the manager's concern for production while the vertical axis represents his concern for people. Each axis is on a one-to-nine scale indicating that a manager may have all the way from a one, or minimal degree of concern for either production or people, up to a nine, or a maximum degree of concern.

On the grid are five basic styles located at each of the corner positions and at the midpoint. Each style is labeled with a name, which gives some clue as to its nature, and a numeral. The first number in the numeral always denotes the manager's concern for production, while the second one indicates his concern for people. It should be noted at the outset that the grid has three principle values.

1.   It can help a manager identify what his style is.

2.   It can help him understand why he gets the reaction that he does from subordinates.

3.   In total or for a given situation it can suggest some alternative styles that may be available.

Task Manager (9.1).   The task manager has nine degrees of concern for production and only one degree of concern for people. In

[2]The Managerial Grid figure from "The Developing Revolution in Management Practices," by Robert R. Blake and Jane Srygley Mouton. *Journal of the American Society of Training Directors,* 1962, *16*(7), 29–52. Reproduced with permission.

Exhibit I The Managerial Grid[3]

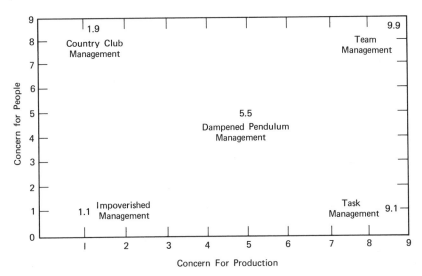

other words, the manager who has a 9.1 style is primarily concerned with output and sees his central responsibility as that of achieving production objectives. Similar to machines, people are seen as tools of production. They are paid to do what they are told, when they are told, and how they are told and not to ask too many questions in between. To question their superior is equal to insubordination. When interpersonal conflict arises, the way to handle it is through disciplinary action. Under the task management theory, if people do not comply after a certain amount of control has been applied, they should be replaced. With respect to certain selected areas the task manager feels as follows.

· Decision Making–Inner directed. Depends on own skills and beliefs in approaching problems and making decisions.

· Conflict with Subordinates–Suppresses by the use of authority.

· Creativity–Ideas the responsibility of the few. Negative creativity often appears. Creative ideas serve personal goals to succeed.

· Promotion of Creative Effort–Competition among employees to develop new ideas by use of rewards and promotions.

[3]Ibid.

• Conflicts with Superiors and Peers–Takes a win-loss approach and fights to win his own points as long as possible.

Country Club Manager (1.9). In contrast to the task manager, the country club manager has only one degree of concern for production but nine degrees of concern for people. Under this style the assumption is that if people are kept happy and harmony is maintained, a reasonable amount of productivity will be achieved. In short, people are pretty much like cows and if you keep them contented they will produce. If human problems and conflicts arise they are glossed over or ignored with the idea that this will take care of them. If the country club manager is asked the question, "What is your primary responsibility?", he would most likely answer "To keep people happy." When employed to its extreme, the people who work for the 1.9 manager will usually sense a phony quality in human relations because they are not related to the conditions of work and production. Thus, long-run, meaningful human relations gains are not achieved in the organization. The following observations summarize the approach of the 1.9 country club manager.

• Decision Making–Outer directed. Anxious to find solutions which reflect opinions of others so the solutions will be accepted.

• Conflict with Subordinates–Smoothes over conflict and tries to release tension by appeals to "the goodness of man."

• Creativity–Innovations usually are to make jobs easier and the workers more comfortable. Ideas usually further group morale rather than production goals.

• Promotion of Creative Effort–Encourage innovations by accepting any and all ideas uncritically. Ideas which will generate conflicts are sidestepped.

• Conflict with Superiors and Peers–Avoids conflict by conforming to the thinking of the boss or his peers. He seeks knowledge of the boss's position so that expression of this position will put him "in."

Impoverished Management (1.1). The manager at this position deemphasizes concern for production with just enough being done to get by. He also disregards the importance of human relationships. More directly, the impoverished manager is going nowhere and trying to take everybody with him. For all practical purposes he has retired although he may be around for several more years. An impoverished management orientation can be found in circumstances where a person has been repeatedly passed over for promotion or feels he has otherwise been unjustly treated. Rather than looking elsewhere, he adjusts to the work setting by giving minimal performance. Obviously if the organization had too many 1.1 managers it would disappear.

• Decision Making–Problems are avoided or deferred to others for solutions.

• Conflict with Subordinates–Just does not get involved. Usually able to avoid completely issues which might give rise to conflict by not discussing them with subordinates.

• Creativity–Good ideas will sometimes "pop up" but ideas are usually not related to company goals or morale. Often connected with outside hobbies and the like.

• Promotion of Creative Effort–Supervisory actions will not affect creativity. Ideas are not discussed on the job so conflicts are not likely.

• Conflict with Superiors and Peers–Keeps his mouth shut and does not express any dissent.

Dampened Pendulum Management (5.5). Push enough to get acceptable production but yield to the degree necessary to develop morale is the theory behind dampened pendulum or middle-of-the-road management. The 5.5 manager constantly shifts between his emphasis and concern for production and people. It represents a live and let live approach under which the real issue is muted. Most dampened pendulum managers are basically task managers at heart, but they read a book or went to a training seminar and learned that you cannot ride roughshod over people, so they have adopted a compromise approach. The point is, however, that they have missed the real issue.

All the approaches described so far see the matter of people and production as being in conflict with one another. In other words, they assume that you can have one but not the other, or you can have a little of one and a little of another, but you cannot have both together.

Team Management (9.9). The team manager believes that people and production can be integrated. Put another way, he believes that a situation can be created whereby people can best satisfy their needs and objectives by working toward the objectives of the organization. He seeks to integrate people around production. When a problem arises, the manager will meet with his group, present the situation, encourage discussion, and get ideas and commitment. He will delegate results and give his people some freedom to operate. When problems of feelings and emotions arise in working relationships, the team manager will confront them directly and work through the differences.

•   Decision Making–Solutions are developed with aid of those who have relevant facts and knowledge to contribute.

•   Conflict with Subordinates–Confronts conflict directly. Feelings and facts are communicated so that there is a basis for understanding and working through the conflict.

•   Creativity–High degree of interplay of ideas and cross stimulation. Experimentation is rule rather than exception. Innovations further shared goals and solve important problems.

•   Promotion of Creative Effort–Feedback used as a basis for further development and thinking. Innovation encouraged by defining and communicating problems that are in need of solutions.

•   Conflict with Superiors and Peers–Confronts conflict directly and works it through at the time it arises. Those involved are brought together to work through differences.

Significant Observations about the Managerial Grid

1.   Although the four corners and the midpoint of the grid are emphasized, these extreme positions are rarely found in their pure form in the working situation. In other words, a manager would more likely have a style of 8.3 or 4.6 or some such thing.

2.   In their research on the grid, Blake and Mouton have found that managers tend to have one dominant style which they use more often than any other. In addition, they have a backup style which is adopted if the dominant style does not work in a particular situation. For example, a manager with a 9.1 orientation who finds that subordinates will not submit to his authority may have a 5.5 backup style. Similarly, a 1.9 manager attempts to keep people happy and forestall interpersonal conflict; however, if this does not work, he may retreat and move in a 1.1 direction.

3.   Another research finding is that the style that an individual manager chooses as being best descriptive of himself (is his dominant style) is very often not the way he really is. Rather, it reflects how he

would like to be or how he would like to think his subordinates see him. His second choice usually gives a better reflection of how he really manages.

4. The ingredients of each managerial style are found to some degree in every manager.

5. What a manager's style is will be influenced by any number of factors, including his superior, the kind of people he supervises, the situation in which he finds himself, and his own personality. Although it is obvious that it is being suggested that the closer a manager can come to a 9.9 style the better it is, *it should also be noted that it has been found that there is no one style that works best in all situations and with all people.*

The Managerial Grid In Third Dimension. In 1967 Blake and Mouton added a third dimension to their managerial grid. The third dimension represents the thickness or depth of a given style. It also ranges from one to nine. This third dimension deals with how long a managerial style is maintained in any given situation of interaction, particularly when the manager is under pressure from tension, frustration, or conflict. If, when confronted by conflict which is threatening, the manager changes his style very readily, he has a thin style. However, if regardless of the circumstances he tends to maintain his style, it is a thick one. For example, if a manager's style is a 9.9 style but he tends to turn away fom it at the slightest hint of pressure, he would be a 9.9.1. *If another 9.9 manager under the same pressure continues to resist changing his style, he would be a 9.9.9.* Exhibit II depicts this third-dimensional aspect of the grid.

W. J. Reddin—The Tridimensional Grid[4]

Reddin conceptualized a three-dimensional grid, borrowing some of the ideas from the management grid. (See Exhibit III.)

A central part of the three-dimensional theory is an eight-style model of management behavior. These eight styles result from the eight

[4]This discussion of the tridimensional grid is based on material contained in the following sources: *Managerial Effectiveness* by W. J. Reddin. Copyright 1970 McGraw-Hill Series in Management. Used with permission of McGraw-Hill Book Company. W. J. Reddin, "The 3-D Management Style Theory," *Training and Development Journal,* April 1967.

Exhibit II　The Managerial Grid in Third Dimension

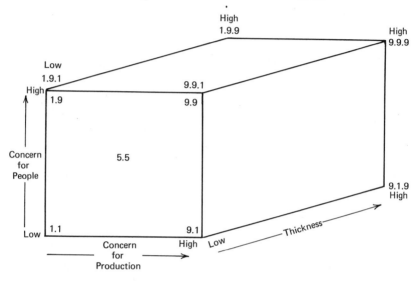

Exhibit III　The Tridimensional Grid[5]

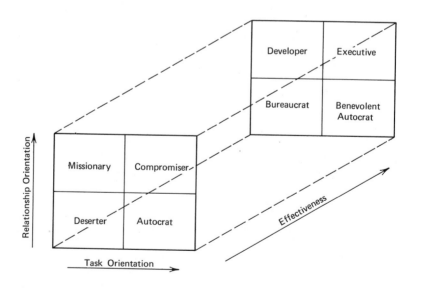

[5]Ibid.

possible combinations of task orientation, relationship orientation, and effectiveness. The main purpose of this concept is an attempt to show leaders that they can move from a plane of less effectiveness to one of more effectiveness by changing their management styles.

Three-Dimensional Axes. Task orientation is defined as the extent to which a manager directs his subordinates' efforts toward goal attainment. It is characterized by planning, organizing, and controlling.

Relationship orientation is defined as the extent to which a manager has personal job relationships. It is characterized by mutual trust, respect for subordinates' ideas, and consideration for employee feelings.

Effectiveness is defined as the extent to which a manager achieves the output requirements of his position.

Either a degree of task orientation (TO), relationship orientation (RO), or a combination of both are used by leaders in managing. Reddin says managers sometimes emphasize one element and sometimes the other, since these two elements of behavior can be used in large or small amounts. As shown in Exhibit IV, when both TO and RO behaviors are high, Reddin calls the resulting style integrated. When TO is high and RO is low, the style is dedicated. When RO is high and TO is low, the style is related, and the use of each element to a small degree is the separated style.

These four styles represent four basic types of behavior. Any of the styles could be effective in some situations and not in others. Each one

Exhibit IV Task and Relationship Orientations[6]

	Related	Integrated
RO		
	Separated	Dedicated

TO →

[6]From *Managerial Effectiveness* by William J. Reddin. Copyright 1970 McGraw-Hill, p. 12. Used with permission of McGraw-Hill Book Company.

of the four basic styles has a less effective equivalent and a more effective equivalent. (See Exhibit V.) When one of the basic styles (for example, integrated) is used inappropriately, a less effective style (compromise) results. When it is used appropriately, a more effective style (executive) results.

Exhibit V More and Less Effective Styles[7]

Basic Style	Less Effective Managerial Style	More Effective Managerial Style
Integrated	Compromiser	Executive
Dedicated	Autocrat	Benevolent Autocrat
Related	Missionary	Developer
Separated	Deserter	Bureaucrat

Arranging the more and less effective leadership styles around the four basic styles, Reddin brings the third dimension of effectiveness into play. The manager's effectiveness cannot be measured just by the extent he achieves production requirements. He must be flexible in selecting styles and must strive for the most effective styles and therefore higher output. His flexibility is not used to keep the peace or to lower pressure, but to maintain an appropriate style under stressful situations.

The Four Basic Styles. The four basic styles with their more and less effective equivalents are: (1) separated (bureaucrat, deserter), (2) related (developer, missionary), (3) dedicated (benevolent autocrat, autocrat), and (4) integrated (executive, compromiser).

Separated Manager. The separated manager is concerned with correcting deviations. He writes rules and policies and strictly enforces them. Other than routine work is avoided, and his employees do not feel he recognizes their achievements sufficiently. The more effective style (bureaucrat) is characterized by belief in rules for their own sake. The less effective style (deserter) is uninvolved and passive.

Related Manager. The related manager accepts others as he finds

[7]Ibid., p. 13.

them, knows employees, does not worry about time, sees the organization as a social system, likes to work with others, and obtains cooperation of others by setting the example. Stressful situations tend to make him dependent and depressed. Subordinates characteristically suffer from lack of direction. The more effective style (developer) tends to display implicit trust in people. The less effective style (missionary) shows only interest in harmony.

Dedicated Manager. This manager is domineering, interested only in production, and does not identify with subordinates. He cannot work without power. He does not communicate to subordinates any more than is absolutely necessary for production, and uses punishment to correct deviations. The most effective style (benevolent autocrat) results in a directive manager who knows what he wants and can often get it without creating resentment. The less effective autocrat is concerned with only the immediate job and has no concern for others.

Integrated Manager. The integrated manager gets himself and his people involved with the organization. There is free two-way communication with others and strong identification and emphasis on teamwork. The more effective style (executive) has a high task and high relationship orientation in a situation where such behavior is appropriate. He is a good motivator who sets high standards, treats people as individuals, and prefers team management. The less effective style in this plane (compromiser) uses a high task and relationship orientation in a situation that may not require a high concentration in either. He is a poor decision maker and allows various pressures in the situation to influence him too much.

Style Flex Concepts. The three-dimensional theory recognizes that a manager may use more than one style. A manager who can use a variety of more effective styles is said to have style flexibility. A manager who maintains a single style has style resistance. Some managers change styles to lower pressure on themselves rather than to increase effectiveness in the situation. This is called style drift. Managers who maintain an inappropriate, less effective style are demonstrating style rigidity.

The styles of three-dimensional theory are designed to give a clear and comprehensive picture of the managerial world. It is assumed that all the styles have an equal chance of occurring and, thus, if a sufficiently large number of managers in a sufficiently diverse number of organizations were tested, an equal number of each style would be obtained.

R. Likert—Four Systems of Management

After a long series of research studies on leadership styles, Likert developed what he called the "four systems of management" to describe four general management styles.

System 1:   Exploitive–Authoritative[8]

1.   Managers have no confidence and trust in subordinates.

2.   Subordinates do not feel free to discuss things about the job with their superior.

3.   Managers seldom get ideas and opinions from subordinates in solving job problems.

4.   Motivation is through fear, threat, punishment, and occasional reward.

5.   The amount of responsibility felt by lower levels is very little. Some even welcome the opportunity to behave in ways that defeat the organization's goals.

6.   There is very little communication, the direction of the flow of information is downward, and is viewed with great suspicion.

7.   Upward communication tends to be inaccurate.

8.   Managers have no knowledge or understanding of the problems of subordinates.

9.   There is little interaction between supervisor and subordinates and subordinates always feel a faint distrust.

10.   There is no cooperative teamwork.

11.   The bulk of the decisions are made at the top.

12.   Subordinates are not involved in decision making.

13.   Company goals are overtly accepted but are covertly strongly resisted.

14.   Control is concentrated in top management.

[8]From *The Human Organization* by R. Likert. Copyright 1967 McGraw-Hill. Used with permission of McGraw-Hill Book Company.

15. Informal organization is present and opposes the goals of the formal organization.

System 2: Benevolent Authoritative[9]

1. Managers have condescending confidence and trust in their subordinates in the same manner as a master has in a servant.

2. Subordinates do not feel free to discuss things about the job with their superior.

3. Managers sometimes obtain ideas and opinions in solving job problems.

4. Motivation is through rewards and some actual or potential punishment.

5. Lower levels feel some responsibility for achieving organizational goals.

6. Communication is mostly downward and may or may not be viewed with suspicion.

7. Upward communication deals only with what the boss wants to hear.

8. Managers have some knowledge and understanding of the subordinates' problems.

9. There is little interaction between superior and subordinates and when interaction does take place fear and caution are exercised by subordinates.

10. There is relatively little cooperative teamwork.

11. Policy making is at the top, with some decisions within a prescribed framework made at lower levels.

12. Subordinates are never involved in decisions; they are only occasionally consulted.

13. Goals are overtly accepted but are often covertly resisted, at least to a moderate degree.

14. Control is relatively highly concentrated, with some delegated control to middle and lower levels.

15. Informal organization is usually present with partially resisting goals.

[9]Ibid.

System 3:   Consultative[10]

1.   Managers have substantial but not complete confidence and trust in subordinates; they still wish to keep control of decisions.

2.   Subordinates feel rather free to discuss things about the job with their superior.

3.   Managers usually get ideas and opinions from subordinates and try to make constructive use of them.

4.   Motivation is through rewards, occasional punishment, and some involvement.

5.   A substantial proportion of personnel feel responsibility and generally behave in ways to achieve the organization's goals.

6.   There is quite a bit of communication, both downward and upward.

7.   Downward communication is often accepted but at times is viewed with suspicion.

8.   Upward communication is usually information that the superior wants to hear. Other information may be limited or cautiously given.

9.   Management knows and understands the problems of subordinates quite well.

10.   There is moderate interaction, often with a fair amount of confidence and trust.

11.   There is a moderate amount of cooperative teamwork.

12.   Broad policy and general decisions are made by top management. More specific decisions are made at lower levels.

13.   Subordinates are usually consulted but ordinarily are not involved in decision making.

14.   Moderate downward delegation of review and control process exists; lower as well as higher levels feel responsible.

15.   Informal organization may be present and may either support or partially resist goals of formal organization.

System 4:   Participation[11]

1.   Superiors have complete confidence and trust in their subordinates.

[10]Ibid.

[11]Ibid.

2. Subordinates feel completely free to discuss things about the job with their superior.

3. Managers always try to get ideas and opinions from subordinates and try to make constructive use of them.

4. Motivation is through economic rewards based on compensation system developed through participation.

5. Personnel at all levels feel a real responsibility for the organization's goals and behave in ways to implement them.

6. Much communication, upward, downward, and horizontal.

7. The extent of downward communication is generally accepted, but, if not, it will be openly questioned.

8. Managers know and understand the problems of subordinates very well.

9. There is extensive, friendly interaction with a high degree of confidence and trust.

10. Very substantial amounts of teamwork exist throughout the organization.

11. Decision making is widely done throughout the organization although well integrated through a linking process provided by overlapping groups.

12. Subordinates are involved fully in all decisions related to their work.

13. Except in emergencies, goals are usually established by means of group participation.

14. Goals are fully accepted both overtly and covertly.

15. There exists quite a widespread responsibility for review and control, with lower units at times imposing more rigorous reviews and tighter controls than top management.

16. Informal and formal organization are the same, hence all social forces support efforts to achieve the organization's goals.

Likert also isolated three variables which were representative of his total concept of System 4, or participative management. These include (1) the use by the manager of supportive relationships, (2) the use of group decision making and group methods of supervision, and (3) his high performance goals. The first variable is exemplified by such factors as (1) the degree to which the superior exhibits confidence and trust, (2) his interest in the subordinate's future, (3) understanding of, and desire to help overcome problems, (4) training and helping the subordinate to find better ways of doing the work, (5) giving help in solving problems as opposed to always giving the answer, (6) giving support by making available the required physical resources, (7) communication of both information that the subordinate must know to do his job and also those things he would like to know to be able to identify more closely with the operation, (8) degree to which the superior seeks out and attempts to use ideas and opinions, (9) his approachableness, and (10) the extent to which he uses credit and recognition for accomplishments.

The second variable (use of group decision making and supervision) is somewhat self-explanatory but should not be interpreted literally. It does not mean that the group necessarily makes all decisions or that a nonaction committee-type approach is used. Rather, the emphasis is on the involvement of people in the decision-making process to the extent that their perception of what the problems are that hinder accomplishment are sought, their ideas on alternative solutions to problems are cultivated, and their thoughts on the "how to" of implementing decisions which have already been made are solicited. It should be remembered that the participative process can be applied on an individual as well as a group basis and that participation is not synonymous with abdication.

The final variable (high performance goals) implies that the superior is maximum-result oriented. This also must be interpreted with some caution. It does not mean that people take a back seat to production and that the latter is achieved at all cost without regard to the people involved. By definition, participative management involves the integration of people around production. There must be a climate where psychological satisfaction is a potential reward and the achievement of this satisfaction is tied directly to accomplishment on the job. In short, building a job climate where there is more than just a paycheck and physical activity involved.

Having defined these three key variables, Likert proceeded to measure their relationship to productivity. Without going into the details of his research, there was strong evidence to suggest that the manager or organizations which exhibited a high degree of supportive relationship, which utilized the principles of group decision making and supervision, and where there were high performance aspirations also had much higher levels of achievement with respect to both individuals and in total in the long run.

Causal, Intervening, And End Result Variables.   Likert also makes a distinction between what he calls causal, intervening, and end result variables. The causal variables refer to the characteristics of the four different management systems as discussed above.

The end result variables refer to such tangible items as volume of sales and production, lower costs, higher quality, and so forth. Of key importance are the intervening variables. These include such things as loyalty, performance goals of subordinates, degree of conflict versus cooperation, willingness to assist and help peers, feelings of pressure, attitude toward the company, his job, and his superior, and finally, his level of motivation.

As Likert points out, an authoritative approach may initially achieve improvements in the end result variables, but at the same time, the intervening variables will begin to disintegrate. Eventually turnover, absenteeism, and a progressive deterioration in the end result variables themselves will occur. On the other hand a participative group approach will lead to a gradual upgrading of the intervening variables and long-run permanent gains in the end result variables. The critical factor is, of course, time.

In summary then, participation is one of the very important ingredients in gaining employee commitment on an overall basis. This commitment in turn can lead to less need for the use of formal authority, power, discipline, threat, and pressure as a means of getting job performance. Therefore, participation and its resultant commitment become a substitute for pure authority. Commitment may be much harder to achieve initially, but in the long run will usually prove much more effective.

Leadership Behavior

Tannenbaum and Schmidt state that the problem of the modern manager is being democratic in his relationships with subordinates and at the same time maintaining the necessary authority and control in the organization for which he is responsible.

At the turn of the century, people tended to think of the world as being divided into "leaders" and "followers." However, social scientists have now developed the concept of "group dynamics" which focuses on members of the group rather than solely on the leader.

Many managers emerged from training laboratories not quite sure how to behave. There are times when a manager is torn between exerting "strong" leadership and "permissive" leadership. He is uncertain as to when a group decision is really appropriate or when holding a staff meeting will merely serve as a device for avoiding his own decision-making responsibility. Exhibit VI is a framework which managers may find useful in grappling with this dilemma.

Exhibit VI   Possible Leadership Behavior[12]

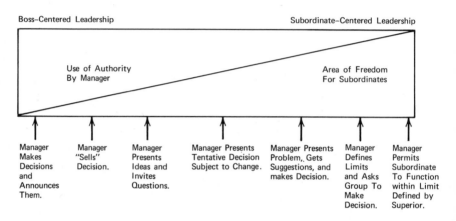

Boss–Centered Leadership   Subordinate–Centered Leadership

Use of Authority
By Manager   Area of Freedom
                                                        For Subordinates

| Manager Makes Decisions and Announces Them. | Manager "Sells" Decision. | Manager Presents Ideas and Invites Questions. | Manager Presents Tentative Decision Subject to Change. | Manager Presents Problem,. Gets Suggestions, and makes Decision. | Manager Defines Limits and Asks Group To Make Decision. | Manager Permits Subordinate To Function within Limit Defined by Superior. |

1.   *The manager makes the decision and announces it.*   The superior identifies a problem, chooses a solution, and then tells his subordinates. He may or may not give consideration to what he believes his subordinates will think. No opportunity is provided for subordinates to participate directly in the decision-making process. Coercion may or may not be used or implied.

2.   *The manager "sells" his decision.*   After making his decision, the manager takes the additional step of persuading his subordinates to accept it. In so doing, he recognizes the possibility of some resistance among some subordinates and tries to reduce this resistance by selling the decision on the basis of what the employees have to gain if the decision is carried out.

3.   *The manager presents his ideas and invites questions.*   After presenting his ideas, the superior invites questions so that his associates can better understand what he is trying to accomplish. This "give and take" also enables the manager and the subordinates to explore more fully the implications of the decision.

[12]Robert Tannebaum and Warren H. Schmidt, "How to Choose A Leadership Pattern," *Harvard Business Review, 36* (2), March–April 1958.

4. *The manager presents a tentative decision, subject to change.* The manager makes a tentative decision. Before finalizing it, he presents his proposed solution for the reaction of those who will be affected by it. The final decision still rests with the manager.

5. *The manager presents the problem, gets suggestions, and then makes his decision.* The manager's initial role involves identifying the problem. From an expanded list of alternatives developed by the manager and his subordinates, a solution is chosen that the manager regards as most promising.

6. *The manager defines the limits and requests the group to make the decision.* The manager passes to the group the right to make decisions. Before doing so, however, he defines the problem to be solved and the boundaries within which the decision must be made. The subordinates can do what they want so long as it does not exceed the limiting boundaries which have been set.

7. *The manager permits the group to make decisions within prescribed limits.* This represents an extreme degree of group freedom only occasionally encountered in formal organizations. Here the team of managers or employees undertakes the identification and diagnosis of the problem, develops alternative solutions, and decides on one. The only limits directly imposed on the group by the organization are those specified by the superior of the team's superior. If the superior participates in the decision-making process he attempts to do so with no more authority than any other member of the group. He commits himself in advance to assisting in implementation of whatever decision the group makes.

Practical Leadership Behavior. The manager's style depends on three forces: (1) forces in the manager, (2) forces in the subordinates, and (3) forces in the situation.

1. *Forces in the manager.* The manager's behavior in any given instance will be influenced greatly by the many forces operating within his own personality. Some of these forces include the following.
   (a) His value system: How strongly does he feel that individuals should have a share in making the decisions which affect them? His behavior will also be influenced by the relative importance that he attaches to organizational efficiency, personal growth of subordinates, and company profits.
   (b) His confidence in his subordinates: This depends on the

amount of trust he has in people generally and his feelings about his subordinates' knowledge and competence with respect to the problem.

(c)   His own leadership inclinations: Some managers seem to function more comfortably and naturally as highly directive leaders. Others seem to operate more comfortably in a team role where they are continually sharing many of their functions with their subordinates.

(d)   His feelings of security in an uncertain situation: The manager who releases control over the decision-making process thereby reduces the predictability of the outcome. Some managers have a greater need than others for predictability and stability in their environment. This "tolerance for ambiguity" is increasingly being viewed by psychologists as a key variable in a person's manner of dealing with problems.

2.   *Forces in the subordinate.*   Each employee, like the manager, is influenced by many personality variables. In addition, each subordinate has a set of expectations about how his superior should act in relation to him. Generally speaking, the manager can permit his subordinates greater freedom if the following essential conditions exist.

(a)   The subordinates have a relatively high need for independence.

(b)   The subordinates possess a readiness to assume responsibility for decision making.

(c)   They have a relatively high tolerance for ambiguity. (Some prefer to have clear-cut directives, others prefer a wider area of freedom.)

(d)   They are interested in the problem and feel that it is important.

(e)   They understand and identify with the goals of the organization.

(f)   They have the necessary knowledge and experience to deal with the problem.

(g)   They have learned to expect to share in decision making. Persons who have come to expect strong leadership and are then suddenly confronted with the request to share more fully in decision making are often upset by this new experience. On the other hand, persons who have enjoyed considerable amounts of freedom resent the superior who begins to make all the decisions himself.

3.   *Forces in the situation.*   There are certain characteristics of the general situation which will also affect the manager's behavior.

Among the more critical environmental pressures that surround him are those which stem from the organization, the work group, the nature of the problem, and the pressures of time.

(a) Type of organization: Like individuals, organizations have values and traditions which inevitably influence the behavior of the people who work within them. These values and traditions are communicated through job descriptions, policy pronouncements, and public statements by top executives. For example, some organizations want their executives to be dynamic, imaginative, decisive, and persuasive. Others put more emphasis upon the executive's ability to work effectively with people. The fact that his superiors have a defined concept of what the good executive should be will very likely push the manager toward one end or the other of the behavior range.

In addition, the amount of employee participation is influenced by such variables as the size of the working units, their geographical distribution, and the degree of inter- and intraorganizational security required to attain company goals. For example, the wide geographical dispersion of an organization may preclude a parochial system of participative decision making. Similarly, the size of the working units or the need for keeping plans confidential may make it necessary for the superior to exercise more control than would otherwise be the case. Factors like these may limit considerably the manager's ability to function flexibly on the continuum.

(b) Group effectiveness: This is perhaps the most clearly felt pressure on the manager. The more he feels the need for an immediate decision, the more difficult it is to involve other people. In organizations which are in a constant state of "crisis" and "crash programming," one is likely to find managers using a high degree of authority with relatively little delegation to subordinates. When the time pressure is less intense, however, it becomes much more possible to involve subordinates in the decision-making process.

Therefore, the successful manager of men can be primarily characterized neither as a strong leader nor as a permissive one. Instead, he is one who maintains a high "batting average" in accurately assessing the forces that determine what his most appropriate behavior at any given time should be and in actually being able to behave accordingly. Possessing both insight and flexibility, he is less likely to see the problems of leadership as a dilemma.

Summary

This chapter has been devoted to the discussion of four alternative theories of leadership. Blake and Mouton's managerial grid is based on the fact that in any particular situation a manager has two basic concerns: a concern for production and a concern for people. The grid depicts the former on the horizontal axis and the latter on the vertical axis. Each axis is labeled one to nine. They then proceed to identify several different management styles based on where the manager places his greatest emphasis. The grid suggests that a 9.9 style which emphasizes maximum concern for both people and production should be the ultimate goal for the leader to achieve.

Reddin's tridimensional grid depicts a manager's task orientation, relationship orientation, and his effectiveness. The grid then identifies eight styles of management behavior. Four are labeled as less effective styles and four as more effective styles. The eight styles result from eight possible combinations of task orientation, relationship orientation, and effectiveness. Each of the less effective styles has a complement of a more effective style. The purpose of the grid is to show a manager how he can move from a plane of less effectiveness to one of more effectiveness.

Likert developed four systems of management to describe various management styles. The four systems which he identified were the explorative authoritative, benevolent authoritative, consultative, and group participative. Each of these systems is characterized by distinct conditions which exist in the management climate. Of the four systems, the group participative holds the most long-run potential for the long-range development of the human assets of the organization. The three distinguishing characteristics of the group participative manager is that he exhibits supportive relationships, uses group decision-making techniques, and has high performance standards.

Tannenbaum and Schmidt classified leadership as being either superior or subordinate centered, depending on the degree to which the manager used his authority or allowed an area of freedom. Along a continuum they then identified and defined seven alternative positions. They then pointed out that a manager's style depends on three forces: forces in the manager, forces in subordinates, and forces in the situation. The manager must assess each of these forces to determine his most appropriate behavior at any given time.

Discussion Questions

1. What are the three forces which determine a manager's leadership style?

2. What are the advantages available to a supervisor who uses participative management?

3. The following quotation is from a supervisor who is describing his leadership style. He supervises 15 computer programmers in a fast-growing data processing company. The average age of these computer programmers is 21.

"If a leader is going to be successful, he has to be respected by his subordinates. I've observed supervisors who are weak and are afraid to make decisions. Before they knew it, they soon discovered that there are enough 'empire builders' around to quickly grab all the power they can. During the 10 years I've been here, I've seen more than one supervisor squeezed out of his job either by another manager who reached into his area of authority or by subordinates who start out as 'do gooders' and then get permission from the 'higher up' to maintain the authority which the supervisor once had.

"Another thing a supervisor should keep in mind is consistency. Changing your leadership style, I think, is really bad. Subordinates would rather have a supervisor be tough all the time, rather than one who is lenient one minute and hard nosed two minutes later.

"Finally, there is the delicate matter of control. A supervisor who is not able to maintain tight controls in the work situation simply cannot do his job effectively. Tight controls assume proper discipline of the subordinate. Without these controls, you would soon have chaos. Also, keep in mind that, in spite of what they may say, subordinates really want you to provide discipline. They simply will not respect you unless you give them discipline and the best way to do that is close control."

(a) Locate this manager with respect to the (1) Blake-Mouton managerial grid, the (2) tridimensional grid, the (3) leadership chart given on page 390, and (4) Likert's four systems of management.
(b) What factors influence the leadership style which a manager develops?

4. Two supervisors were visiting during coffee break. Both were production foremen supervising approximately 50 workers who perform routine activities on an automobile assembly line.

Dale: "You know, Jim, it's interesting to see these guys working on the line. Some of them remind me of combines as they go through the motions like robots. I actually saw Bob Jamer tighten the five jimson bolts on the center chassis with his eyes closed. I guess he just wanted to see if it could be done."

Jim: "Yeah, the ones in my section are always doing stuff like that. It's tough to cut down on the horseplay, and I really don't care as long as it doesn't slow up the line. You need to let them know that they have to maintain production. If they slow up the line as much as five minutes, then they better knock off the clowning. After all, they're here to do a job. They can clown around *after* work."

Dale: "I'm probably going to sound idealistic but wouldn't it be great if somehow we could set up the line so that they could clown around or at least talk to each other, but still maintain the high production rate? I mean, as long as production is still high, why don't we see if we can set things up to relieve the monotony of this work. For instance, if we placed the turent lathe by the . . . ."

Jim: "Hey! You really are idealistic, aren't you? You've only been here six months, and one thing you'll have to learn is that you can't keep these guys happy, satisfied, or however you want to say it, and at the same time expect them to be productive. I don't care who or what type of person you are supervising. It's like mixing day and night and expecting a sunrise. I ought to know, I tried to do just what you are suggesting, but now I know it can never be done."

Dale: "Well, I don't know if I totally agree with your philosophy, although I sometimes think that it might apply around here in some cases. Anyway, I won't be satisfied until these guys are more productive and at the same time happier with their jobs."

Jim: (Laughingly) "Well, when that happens the sun will rise over your head, and at that time I'll bow down and say "Swami." As long as the men maintain the company's production standards, which, by the way I think are too high, and don't slow the line down, then I *know* I'm doing my job properly. You're going to be frustrated forever with your outlook on supervision. Oh well, you'll change your mind, everyone else here has."

(a) Applying the managerial grid, how would you classify (1) Jim and (2) Dale?

(b) What basic assumptions or beliefs separate these two supervisors?

(c) If Dale were to maintain this type of supervisory job for a long period of time, is it likely that he might move to a different position on the grid. If so, where?

(d) Who do you think might be more successful supervising a group of managers, Dale or Jim? Explain why.

Selected Readings

Chris Argyris, "Leadership Pattern in the Plant," *Harvard Business Review, XXXII* (1), January–February 1954, pp. 64–75.

Robert R. Blake, and Jane S. Mouton, *The Managerial Grid,* Gulf Publishing Co., Houston, 1964.

Rensis Likert, *The Human Organization: Its Management and Value,* McGraw-Hill, New York, 1967.

David C. McClelland, "Achievement Motivation Can be Developed,

Harvard Business Review, 43 (6), November–December 1965, pp. 6–24.

Norman R. F. Maier, "Comparison of Behavior Traits Revealed Under Two Different Types of Leadership," *Principles of Human Relations, Applications to Management,* Wiley, New York, 1952, p. 149.

George V. Moser, "Consultative Management," *Management Record, XVII* (1), National Industrial Conference Board, November 1955, pp. 438–439.

Scott M. Myers, "Conditions for Manager Motivation," *Harvard Business Review, 44* (1), January–February 1966.

W. J. Reddin, *Managerial Effectiveness,* McGraw-Hill, New York, 1970.

Stephen M. Sales, "Supervisory Style and Productivity: Review and Theory," *Personnel Psychology, 19* (3), Autumn 1966, pp. 275–286.

Robert Tannenbaum, and Warren H. Schmidt, "How to Choose a Leadership Pattern," *Harvard Business Review, 36* (2), March–April 1968.

Aurin Uriv, "How Good a Leader Are You?" *Factory Management and Maintenance,* McGraw-Hill, New York, July–August and October 1951.

20. Organizational and Interpersonal Communications

Communications play a major role in determining how effectively people work together and coordinate their efforts to achieve objectives. Put even more succinctly, there is a direct relationship between communications and productivity. Employees work more effectively and with greater satisfaction when they understand not only their own job objectives but also those of their work group and the total organization. To the extent that communications are lacking, the effectiveness of the organization will be undermined. Management's awareness of the importance of communications is evidenced by the fact that since the mid 1950s American business and industry has been spending over $1 billion annually on efforts to communicate with employees.[1] With this great expenditure it would seem that all of the communications problems that exist would have been solved long ago. However, most managers agree that communications continues to be a major problem. With these observations about the importance of effective communication as a background, the remainder of this chapter will be devoted to a discussion of both the organizational and interpersonal aspects of communication.

[1]C.J. Dover, "Management Communication on Controversial Issues" (Washington, D.C.: BNA, Inc., 1965), p. 1.

The Communications Problem in Perspective[2]

When communications are neglected or overlooked, the organization is depriving itself of some very important benefits that could be derived from a progressive, forward-looking communications program. Regardless of the size of the organization, it is composed of individuals, each of whom is charged with certain duties and responsibilities. In order to accomplish objectives there must be communications between the members of the organization. When communications, whether overlooked or neglected, are kept to a minimum, an environment for potential misunderstanding is created. Inadequate communications fall mainly into two types. The first type results from poor or inadequate instructions from the manager to the subordinate concerning the work which he is expected to perform. Failure to communicate properly job requirements and task assignments can result in misunderstandings and lead to the job being performed incorrectly or incompletely with a resultant monetary loss to the organization. The importance of giving clear and precise instructions cannot be overemphasized.

The second inadequacy comes from the failure to communicate to employees information that may bear no direct relationship to the actual work which they perform. Nevertheless, failure to communicate this information may result in the damaging and lowering of morale, not only of just a few individuals but also of the entire organization. Therefore, it becomes important for an organization to be aware of the benefits that can be derived from communicating information that the employees wish to know but do not necessarily have to know to do their jobs.

Management should realize that employees must not only be well informed concerning their interest in the affairs of the organization, but, since they do have a stake in the success of the organization, they also want to be well informed about matters which affect them on their jobs. This imposes some specific responsibilities on management to communicate on subjects affecting the organization and job security of employees. This type of information is being constantly generated and if properly communicated, enables the employees to feel that they are a part of the organization, that is, that they are working *with* it, not just *for* it.

[2]The material in this section draws heavily from the following source: Lynn Townsend, "A Corporate President's View of the Internal Communications Function," *Journal of Communication,* December 1965. In 1965, Lynn A. Townsend, President of Chrysler Corporation, was awarded the "Communicator of the Year" award for his

Information To Communicate. Experience in the subjects about which employees have expressed an interest can serve as a foundation for supplying the desired information. Employees like to know something about the history of the organization and about how it began and developed. Knowledge of what the organization has done, what it is currently doing, and how its products are used by its customers develops a sense of pride in belonging to the organization. Closely allied to a company's history is its basic objective or reason for existence. Not only is this good communications but it is good policy for the organization to restate its objectives occasionally. Employees also like to be informed as to what the prospects for the future are. Since management is always planning for the future, employees should be informed as often as possible what the organization is faced with in the way of competition, business trends that may affect the firm's operations, and future plans for improvement of facilities or changes in methods. It becomes very important that employees be informed of changes that will affect them directly, since any changes which are effected without prior notice tend to arouse suspicion and distrust.

Greater job satisfaction is derived when employees feel they have a thorough knowledge of what is going on in the organization. The firm's financial operations should be passed on to the employees since the success of the firm determines the employment prospects for the workers. If changes for the future are adverse, such as the prospect of layoffs, more may be lost than gained by suppression of this information. News of this type usually has a way of leaking out and it is far better to announce such changes as soon as possible to allow employees to make their plans accordingly. Not much can be gained by withholding such information, as sudden and unexpected layoffs are bound to cause suspicion and insecurity among the remaining workers. It is usually far better for management to communicate as early as possible the complete details and be completely honest.

In summary, management must recognize that internal communication is an essential tool of good management and that through its influence on employees' attitudes, it is a better way to achieve organizational objectives. Effective communication should be viewed as an important motivating force and management must recognize that employee attitudes and resulting performance are improved when they are well informed about the affairs of their organization and how such matters affect them as individuals.

firm's program. C. J. Dover headed the team which developed the communications program at Chrysler.

Importance of Top Level Commitment.   The initiative for effective communications must come from the top and therefore it becomes necessary for top management to establish a good communication climate. Most frequently communication is man-made in that the communication patterns in a given department, group, or unit reflect the communications behavior of the man in charge. If the superior in charge is silent and uncommunicative, his subordinates are likely to be the same. If he takes a negative attitude toward the communications program, then those who are under him will likely reflect the same attitude. Therefore the communications behavior which is present at the top level will likely be reflected throughout the organization. So it is the top man in the organization who must establish the right communications climate by initiating and taking an active part in the communications program. He must make sure that the communications effort is a continuous process. In short, the top man must himself set the example and give his full support to the communications effort. Although necessary, it is not sufficient that only the top executive support the effort. Individual managers must also actively support it. Due to the complexity of most organizational structures it is a mistake to assume that oral communications from top or bottom will filter through the many layers in its original form. Managers must not view information that is passed to them as their own possession to be passed on as they see fit. They must cooperate with the total communications effort and be aware of their responsibility in the flow of information by giving their active individual effort. The guide for individual managers is that they must be denied the privilege of deciding whether communication is desirable or not, and recognize that it is part of their duties to communicate regularly with superiors and subordinates.

Perhaps the greatest difficulty and most common deficiency in communication is in the area of the upward flow of information. Employee suggestions and opinions should be regarded as an important organizational asset which can contribute to increased production and organizational efficiency. The opportunity for employees to communicate upward can be widened if supervisors will only take the time to go around the work environment and listen to their people. One of the things that organizations frequently do not realize is the extent to which employees have a desire to help the organization operate better. Hence, many managers have a tendency to underestimate the willingness of employees to help the organization and also to underrate the power of good communications to turn this latent desire into constructive action.

Summing up this discussion, the following factors will provide a solid foundation for building a results-producing communications program within the organization.

1.   Internal communications must be recognized as an essential tool of good management.

2.   Employees must be well informed concerning their mutual interest in organizational success.

3.   Individual managers must actively support the organization's communications effort.

4.   Substantial emphasis must be placed on communications planning and measurement.

5.   Top management must establish a good communications climate.

6.   A long-term investment in professional talent and communication programming must be made.

7.   Management must recognize the responsibility to listen as well as to speak.

8.   Managers must recognize the desire of employees to help their company and the power of communications to tap this great potential.[3]

Communication and the Individual Manager

As suggested earlier in the chapter, communications or, perhaps more appropriately, the lack of effective communications, has very often been identified as the number one problem facing management. Also, research has pointed out that lack of communications is often the number one complaint which subordinates have about their boss. With these two general observations in mind, the purpose of this section is to explore the key elements of the communications process as it affects and is influenced by the individual manager. The overall objective is to develop an awareness of the need to communicate and an appreciation of why managers do not always communicate effectively. More specifically, the following topics will be discussed.

1.   Communications defined and an overview of what effective communication entails.

[3]Ibid.

2. The communications environment in which the manager lives.
3. The information side of the communications process.
4. Barriers to creating understanding and how to overcome them.
5. Keys to building a positive communications climate.

Communications Defined and an Overview of What Effective Communication Entails

Communications can be simply defined as the process of passing information and understanding from one person to another.[4] There are two important ramifications of this rather simple definition, however.

First, there must be a receiver if communication is going to occur. The receiver side is too often either forgotten completely or else taken for granted. As communicators, we sometimes assume that having sent our message, the process has been consummated. This is seldom true. The sender of a communication must consider the receiver both when structuring his message from a technical standpoint as well as in delivering it, or halfway effort and halfway results are produced. When the receiver is not considered, one of two things happens: there is either no response or there is a wrong response.

Second, this definition stresses the importance of the creation of understanding. Communication is not an end in itself. Its purpose is to elicit a positive action or response on the part of the receiver, and this requires understanding. Therefore, communications is the means by which a manager interacts with his people in a leadership capacity. To the extent and degree that he can effectively communicate with them, he can also motivate them. Understanding involves more than just using words the receiver can comprehend. It involves an attitude of wanting to respond positively. There is both the technical and human side of communication.

Communications Environment of the Manager

Every manager lives in what can be described as two-way, tridimensional communications environment. It is tridimensional in the sense that regardless of where he stands in the management hierarchy, he be-

---

[4]Keith Davis, *Human Relations at Work* (New Jersey: McGraw-Hill), p. 344.

comes involved in communications with respect to his superior, the people he directly supervises, and also other departments with which he must interrelate in order to accomplish results. These other departments include both line and staff. It is a two-way process in that the manager must be concerned with both the downward and the upward, flow of information. These relationships are depicted in Exhibit I.

Exhibit 1   Communication as a Two-Way Tridimensional Process

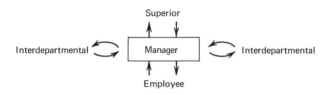

There is often a tendency for the manager to sit back and look everywhere but to himself when identifying communications problems. In other words, it is always the other fellow who falls down in his communication responsibilities. Even if this is true, most of the time there is a great deal that the individual can do to improve the situation. The Exhibit I very effectively illustrates the idea that it is managers as individuals who stand at the crossroads of effective communication. It is the individual who must take the initiative if communication is going to occur. If it is information from his own superior he would like to get and is not getting, he can take the initiative by asking for it. If feedback from his employees is not forthcoming, there are positive things he can do to initiate it. If communications on an interdepartmental basis are something less than perfect, perhaps he can foster improvement. Only when each manager approaches the process and problem of effective communication in this way and with this attitude can improvement be made.

Information Side of the Communications Process

Exhibit II summarizes the information side of the communication process as it relates superiors and subordinates.

Exhibit III summarizes some of the things each manager should be communicating to other departments and they in turn should communicate to him. It should be emphasized that these lists are only guides.

Exhibit II   Information Side of Communication Process

Types of information the manager should communicate to employees and that he wants his superior to communicate to him: downward communication

1. Key areas where he is accountable for results and what specific results he should be achieving in each area.
2. Periodic feedback on his performance in a quantitative sense.
3. Information relating to overall departmental performance and achievements.
4. Where the department fits into the total operation and where his job fits and why it is important.
5. Information concerning both short-term and long-term changes and developments as they relate to, and affect the employer presently and in the future.

Types of information the manager should communicate to his superior and that he wants his people to communicate to him: upward communication

1. Problems and difficulties as they relate to accomplishing results in his job.
2. His feelings and attitudes toward the company in general, the department, and his own supervision.
3. Ideas and suggestions to improve the overall operation or a particular job or process.
4. Advance information concerning his progress on the job as it relates to a schedule or specific standards.

Exhibit III   Interdepartmental Communications

Types of information managers want communicated to them and they should communicate to others:

1. Areas of difficulty which, as they see it, are hindering interdepartmental cooperation and effectiveness.
2. Specific data on the status of production in their department which might later affect other departments.

3. Ideas and suggestions on how we might work together to solve common problems.

4. Advance notice of a potential development which will have later repercussions in other areas.

In examining Exhibit II in total, it willl be noted that there is a definite overlap in the various lists. This phenomenon brings out two important ideas as they relate to the process of communication.

First, effective communications is an interdependent process. A manager cannot fully meet his communications responsibility unless someone else meets theirs. For example, one type or classification of information he should be communicating to his subordinates is what the department is achieving in certain key areas of accountability such as quality and quantity. Unless his superior gives him this information, he obviously cannot pass it down to his people. Therefore, the interdependent nature of communication creates a situation where everyone in the organization must be conscious of the need to communicate and have a clear understanding of what it is they should be communicating. Similarly, the manager cannot give his superior feedback in areas in which he is interested unless he gets the same feedback from his people.

The second important idea that Exhibit II illustrates is that effective communication is a continuous chain and that any break in the chain can have far-reaching repercussions. It takes an overall, concerted effort and dedication on the part of everyone involved to insure that the process is completed and effective.

Two-Way Communications

When a manager enters into two-way communications with a con-scious—or more likely unconscious—objective of persuading or selling the receiver his point of view, he does not achieve understanding. Rather, it is what might be called a coercive communication. No matter what the sender thinks he is doing, it is in fact a one-way communication. In a superior-subordinate situation, the superior will inevitably win. Over a period of time, the subordinate will learn that communication is really one-way.

Two-way communication requires listening to understand, rather than just listening to reply. It requires a willingness to change or to be changed. In short, an openness not only to hear what others have to say but also giving their ideas a chance to become operative is needed.

In any situation, the manager will do well if he first determines what this communication objective is and then proceeds on that basis. If the objective is, in fact, to persuade someone, to win them over, then the communication climate should recognize this. Explain the situation, explain why, get reaction, resell, but do not try to disguise it and make it something that it is not. One hundred percent agreement is not always present, but, handled properly, a high degree of commitment usually is. *Again, however, an important point is that sometimes when two-way communication is supposedly taking place, it really is not.*

Barriers to Creating Understanding and How To Overcome Them

The barriers to creating understanding and thereby getting cooperation and enthusiasm from people can be classified into two categories. First are what might be termed the technical barriers. These relate to the organizational framework in which communication occurs. Second are those barriers which are human in nature.

Technical Barriers.   The first of the technical barriers is that of bypassing or omitting someone from the communication chain. Whether these two things occur singularly or in conjunction with one another, they have the effect of undermining the person involved, thereby creating a problem of morale, hard feelings, and, eventually, an uncooperative "I don't care" attitude.

The second barrier is incomplete communication. Because the person who sends the communication knows what he means, it is easy to oversimplify and not be specific. The receiver is left on his own to assume what is wanted. When he assumes wrong and the results the communicator had in mind are not achieved, the tendency is to blame the receiver, particularly if he is in a subordinate role. The overall result is a breach between two people who must cooperate to get results.

A third potential problem revolves around poor personal relationships and going outside the chain. Two people who are fully versed in all the principles and concepts of effective communication still may not communicate if they do not get along with each other or lack respect for each other. Many companies have spent considerable sums of money on communications training for all their people and find they still have a higher than normal degree of problems. The missing link is often traceable to conflict between people or departments.

The final barrier is "spur of the moment" communication, incomplete communication, and someone being left out. With respect to "spur of the moment" communication, communication is most effective when it precedes action or events. Late communication is usually accompanied by, and occurs in conjunction with someone applying pressure to achieve some results. Full cooperation is seldom gained in these situations.

The communication can be incomplete in the sense that the reason "why" is left out. Most people will cooperate and go out of their way to help if they know why something is important or why a particular action is needed. Communicating the "why" shows respect for the individual and indicates that his help is valued and appreciated. This applies to all situations.

The matter of leaving someone out of the communication chain occurs when an inadequate job of planning is done. The manager who is seeking a given result becomes so preoccupied with the details of the initial phases of the project that he forgets to think about and follow through on the overall total.

Human Barriers. The first important human barrier to effective communication is *failure to see the need.* Poor communication is very often not so much a problem of someone not wanting to communicate or not knowing how as it is of realizing why certain information is important to another individual or department. The first step toward overcoming this barrier is a realization and crystallization of what information we should be communicating. The second step to overcoming the failure to see the need is developing empathy, the ability to put ourselves in the other man's shoes. Once the manager develops a sensitivity as to how he feels when someone does not communicate with him, he is more likely to do a better job of communicating with others.

A second barrier is embodied within the concept of *semantics*, the meaning of words. This barrier can become operative in a number of different ways, for example, using specific words with which the receiver is not familiar, using words which have a variety of meanings and assuming they are interpreted the way they were meant, talking over the head of the receiver in general, or making a message unduly complicated and long. For example, the industrial engineer who talks to the line supervisor about therbligs or economic lot sizes may meet with no response. Similarly, the line supervisor who tries to train a new worker using unfamiliar terminology or "shop jargon" may find that he "can not get through." Talking over peoples' heads usually results in creating a negative impression and, consequently, getting negative results.

A third human barrier involves the *failure to listen*. When a sender does not listen, he has no way of getting feedback to see if his message is being understood. He will build a wall between himself and his receiver. The latter is true, because all of us are, to one degree or another, self- or ego-centered. We respond most favorably to people who respond to us, and listening is tangible evidence of response. When listening on the part of a communicator is absent, either consciously or unconsciously, an "I don't care about what you have to say" attitude develops in the receiver. Listening is also complicated by the fact that our capacity to listen in terms of words per minute is far greater than the average speaking rate. This gap leaves a lot of time available for "woolgathering" or planning a reply rather than listening to understand.

Related to listening is the barrier of *self-interest or preoccupation with one's own situation*. Very often when people try to communicate, we are in a different world, thinking about different things. We hear, but nothing really registers. We hear, but push what we hear to the backs of our minds. To communicate effectively, therefore, requires the sender to be sensitive to the state of mind of his receiver, to be able to sense whether or not he is tuned in.

A final human barrier is inadequate planning in terms of the what, when, how, who, and why of communications. Before every communication commences, these questions should be asked.

1. What is the specific idea or message I want to get across? Simply stated.

2. When is the best time to do it? Timing is important.

3. How can it best be accomplished? Media is strategic. Verbally, in writing, a meeting versus individually.

4. To whom should it be communicated?

5. Why is it necessary?

Good communication does not occur by accident. Like anything else, it requires some advance planning, and the time spent in planning is usually more than compensated for in long-run results. Similarly, most communication failures can be traced to one or more failures in the planning stages.

Problems in Establishing Effective Communication

A number of barriers to effective communication were mentioned in the previous section. The purpose here is to touch very briefly on some additional barriers and potential problems. They arise as a result of the organizational structure as well as in the makeup of the people in the organization.

Problem Created by the Organization Structure. Individuals viewing the formal structure of an organization in chart form get an impression of the relative power of various positions. This impression carries over into their functioning in the organization. As a result, we find communication barriers presented by the following perceptions of organization structure and the individual's role or place in that structure.

1. *Positional and Authority Difference Barriers:* Persons in higher positions may fear a loss of power or status if they engage in open communication with subordinates. Viewed another way, communications is the thing that binds people together, that brings them closer. If the manager feels that this closeness will threaten him in the sense that he will not command the same degree of respect from his people, he will naturally be hesitant to communicate too much. On the other hand, subordinates sometimes hesitate to send any but the most favorable communications upward because of a fear of consequences of making the superior unhappy.

2. *Interdepartmental Competition:* This category includes such situations as "line-staff" relationship problems and secrecy between departments striving for high output recognition. The persons involved in both these cases fail to communicate because they fear that to do so will give advantage to the other department and lessen their own standing in the eyes of superiors. This is a great barrier to horizontal communication in the organization.

3. *Hiding Behind the Organization Chart:* In this case the individual draws a wall around his block on the chart and makes a conscious effort not to get outside it. The reasons may be a fear of incompetence or of having others infringe upon his area of responsibility. He refuses to entertain ideas about topics not spelled out in his position description. He will not let others cross into his "territory."

4. *Physical Layout of the Organization Facilities:* The problem

412   MANAGERIAL DIRECTION AND LEADERSHIP

created here is related to the status problem mentioned earlier. There seems to be some tendency in organizations that requires that people on the same level be located or housed in the same type of facilities in close proximity. The result is that many times the manager finds himself physically isolated from those with whom he should be communicating most. He ends up conducting most of his daily business with subordinates who are as much as a half mile away. Thus, face-to-face relationships are replaced by telephones and written memos and the result is inadequate communication.

People Problems in Communication. The communication problems presented by people in organizations result both from their perception of the role expected of them by the organization and their own individual attitudes. Probably one of the greatest barriers to effective organizational communication is the individual who communicates more effectively toward his own ends than anyone elses. This paradox in communication effectiveness is the "empire builder." He utilizes interpersonal communication and persuasion to enhance his own image. He is a manipulator of communication.

On the other end of the spectrum we find the person who is reluctant to communicate at all. The main reason is that no one has let him know that the organization depends on his communicative efforts.

In between these two extremes lie various degrees of communication problems. The thing to remember in establishing a communication program is to take these things into account and make a definite effort to eliminate the problems.

Summary

In this chapter we have tried to point out the importance of both organizational and interpersonal communications. From the organizational standpoint, a totally comprehensive and effective communications program must exist if the objective of employee loyalty and identification is to be achieved. An absolute essential for a successful program is commitment at the top management levels.

Communications was defined as passing information and understanding from one person to another. This definition stresses the importance of the fact that more is involved in communications than just a sender dispensing information. There must also be a receiver and understanding. Every manager lives in a two-day, tridimensional communications environment. It is two way in the sense that there are certain key types of information that he must communicate to his people that he in turn wants them to communicate to him. It is tridimensional in the sense that he must communicate with his own superior, his subordinates, and managers of other departments.

The barriers to effective communications can be classified as technical barriers such as bypassing, or incomplete communications, as human barriers such as semantics or failure to see the need, or as organizational barriers such as positional and authority differences. A complete awareness and understanding of the barriers to communications is a necessary first step to overcoming them.

Key Concepts

Tridimensional Communications.   Refers to the fact that the manager must communicate with his own superior, his subordinates, and managers in other departments.

Two-Way Communications.   Stresses the idea that if understanding is to be achieved there must be both an up and down flow of information.

Discussion Questions

1. Dave Jameson, Sales Manager for Adleson Manufacturing Company, was visiting with Ted, a salesman who had been with the company for two years.

Dave: "Ted, sales have dropped in your territory by over 15 percent. Do you have any idea as to why this has happened?"

Ted: "Well, the sales have dropped in most of the territories. Jim

Davis, who handles the usually active Chicago north side told me that his sales have dropped over 20 percent. Everyone seems to think that our regular customers are switching to Brownsen Company products because their prices are lower and also their quality is . . . ."

Dave: "Listen Ted, you know as well as I do that the reason for the low sales volume is because you're not getting around to our present customers as well as trying to make new contacts. When I first started here 15 years ago I used to see at least 20 people in one day."

Ted: "But I have been contacting more customers and potential customers than I have in any previous months, but still . . . ."

Dave: "Look Ted, I really don't want to hear any more of your excuses. That's all you guys seem to be able to do well these days. Just get with it and get to those customers. I expect to see a big improvement in sales next month. Do you think you can do it?"

Ted: "Yes, sir."

Discuss the type of communication which has taken place here. What barriers to communication are applicable here?

2. Before any communication takes place, what are the five basic questions a person should ask himself before he does any sending?

3. From each of the statements below, identify the barriers to communication which are created by the organizational structure.

   (a) The enemy was in the process of overrunning the base camp. The base commander radioed the General and in a confident voice announced that his troops were now going through the final stages of a "tactical withdrawal."

   (b) During World War II, a British Torpedo plane was searching for the German battleship Bismarck. Through the dense cloud cover he spotted a huge hulk below, went into a steep dive, and released two torpedoes. As he pulled out of the dive, he noticed that it was not the Bismarck—it was a British battleship. Fortunately, both torpedoes missed, and the plane was in the clouds before the British crew knew what had happened. When the anxious admiral of the fleet radioed the pilot and asked the pilot if the torpedoes had hit the Bismarck, the pilot sheepishly radioed back "no hits."

   (c) The production department head was discussing a new project for planning the rate of future production runs with the head of the production planning and control department. The production department head agreed with everything the production planning and control department head said, even though he knew that unless they were drastically modified, many of the ideas that the production planning and control man presented would not work. The production planning and control man smirked to himself because he knew that they would not work either. He was trying to take some readings on the production department head to see how he would react to ideas which were poor. The production department head, however, knew that the production planning and control man was playing this game but went along with it to show the production planning and control man that he had no desire to cooperate with him.

4. John, a young research engineer, asked his group leader, Ed, if the recent cutbacks in expenditures for the department would affect the status of the current projects he was developing.

Ed, who was an older, fatherly person, put his arm consolingly on John's shoulder and replied:

"You let me worry about that; you have enough to worry about. The main thing you should be concerned about is in showing a greater interest in your work. As soon as you show me that you are able to do this, then I'll let you in on a few of the 'details' around here."

Using concepts from this chapter, describe Ed's communications problem. How would you suggest that this vicious circle described above be broken? What concepts relating to barriers to communication apply here?

Selected Readings

Gerald Albaum, "Horizontal Information Flow: An Exploratory Study," *Academy of Management Journal, 7* (1), March 1964, pp. 21–33.

John Anderson, "What's Blocking Upward Communication?" *Personnel Administration, 31* (1), January–February 1968.

Alex Bavelas, and Dermot Barret, "An Experimental Approach to Organizational Communication," *Personnel, 27* (5), pp. 366–371.

Keith Davis, "Communication Within Management," *Personnel, 28* (3), November 1954, pp. 212–217.

Margaret Fenn, and George Head, "Upward Communication: The Subordinates Viewpoint," *California Management Review, 7* (4), Summer 1965, pp. 75–80.

T. M. Higham, "Basic Psychological Factors in Communication," *Occupational Psychology, 31*, 1957, pp. 1–10.

Schuyler Dean Hoslett, "Barriers to Communication," *Personnel, 28* (2), September 1951, pp. 108–114.

Harold S. Leavitt, "Communication: Getting Information From A into B," *Managerial Psychology*, The University of Chicago Press, Chicago, 1958, Chapter 9, pp. 118–128.

Ralph G. Nichols, "Listening is Good Business," *Management of Personnel Quarterly, 1* (2), Winter 1962, pp. 2–9.

Carl R. Rogers, and F. S. Roethlisberger, "Barriers and Gateways to Communication," *Harvard Business Review, 30* (4), July–August 1952, pp. 46–52.

Richard L. Simpson, "Vertical and Horizontal Communication in Formal Organizations," *Administrations Science Quarterly, 4* (2), September 1959, pp. 188–196.

Lynn Townsend, "A Corporate President's View of the Internal Communications Function," *Journal of Communications*, December 1965.

21. Coaching and Developing Subordinates[1]

In earlier chapters the idea was stressed that a manager's central and prime responsibility is to get things done through people. This concept is widely accepted and should not require defending, but if it does, it can be justified on two grounds. First, from an overall departmental standpoint, the efficiency of the department is the sum total of the efficiency of each of its members. To the extent and degree that one or a number of people are not performing their job at a 100 percent level, the general level of efficiency will be lower than it might otherwise be. Similarly, if each individual's performance level can be raised by just a small amount, the total departmental level of efficiency will increase significantly.

Second, someone once made the observation that a man is judged by the company he keeps. Paralleling this, a manager's own performance is a reflection of the performance of his people. The one sure way for a manager to improve his image is to do everything possible to

[1]Grateful acknowledgment is given to Professor Norman Allhiser for his help and guidance in formulating the basic outline for this chapter as well as for specific ideas and material which he contributed.

ensure that his people are performing at their maximum level of capability.

With these two thoughts in mind, the purposes of an effective coaching and developing program for subordinates are:

1. To close a performance gap which exists now.

2. To promote growth in the present job in terms of preparing them for greater responsibilities as well as independence.

3. To promote growth in terms of possible future advancement

These three purposes are necessarily listed in order of priority. The first concern should be to close any gaps which might presently exist between the actual versus the desired level of performance as it relates to the key areas of responsibility and accountability. Only after this has been accomplished should attention be given to the latter two areas.

The remainder of this chapter will be devoted to exploring the essential elements of a results-oriented coaching and development plan. Specific attention will be focused on the following areas.

1. Performance analysis.

2. Providing a positive basic climate.

3. Some possible reasons for poor performance and difficulties with typical systems.

4. A step-by-step coaching plan.

5. Qualifications and rules for a good coach.

Setting the Stage for Effective Coaching

The achievement of maximum levels of performance on the part of subordinates does not happen by accident. Instead, it is first the result of a personal commitment on the part of the manager to help each one of his people perform to their maximum level of capability. Beyond this, a great deal of analysis, planning, and conscientious effort on the part of the manager is required. Setting the stage for an effective coaching atmosphere involves first, a performance analysis, and second, agreement on what the job encompasses.

Analysis of Performance

Performance analysis begins with the manager listing the names of all the people over whom he has direct supervision. After this listing is complete, he must crystallize in his own mind what constitutes a 100 percent level of efficiency. If, with respect to the job in question, the man is performing at a 100 percent level, what would he be accomplishing? This crystallization will be made easy or difficult depending on whether or not the manager has ever given previous consideration to various jobs in this way and also to the extent that measurable standards already exist as they pertain to major areas of accountability. In either case, some judgment as to what constitutes 100 percent efficiency must be made.

The third step in performance analysis is to rate each subordinate in terms of the 100 percent standard. Essentially what is being done is to ask, "How well is the man doing?" Typically, ratings will range all the way from a few in the upper nineties to a few in the sixties or seventies. It should be emphasized that the point of concern is not how well the man is doing in terms of what the manager thinks his potential might be, but rather how well he is doing in terms of what the job requires.

After this judgment of performance level has been made, the question of *why* this particular rating must be asked with respect to each man. It must be remembered that the purpose of coaching and developing is to improve performance; therefore, the rating is not an end in itself but rather a means to an end. By asking the question of why this level of rating for this man, the manager is beginning to define what he feels are the major areas of performance which need improvement as well as those areas where strength is being exhibited.

Exhibit I provides a convenient and systematic approach for carrying out a performance analysis. Column one contains a listing of the names of subordinates and column two is used for the rating of present efficiency in terms of the 100 percent standard. In column three, space is provided for specifying the key factors that account for that particular rating. It is divided into two parts: one part for listing particular strengths and assets and one part for areas where improvement is needed.

At the bottom of the name column it is suggested that the manager add his own name, make a similar estimate of his own level of efficiency, and explain this estimate. The efficiency figures in column two are then totaled to arrive at a gross level of departmental efficiency. This total is divided by the number of people involved to determine the average level of departmental efficiency. Essentially what has been done is to recognize in a practical way the principle which was stated earlier in the chapter; namely, that overall department efficiency is the sum total of the efficiency of each of its members.

The fifth step in the performance analysis is to set specific improvement objectives for each individual and for the department as a whole. Here the manager is recognizing that if the performance level for each man can be improved, even by just a small amount, the total departmental efficiency will increase significantly. Taking into consideration each man's present efficiency level, his strengths, and areas where improvement is needed, an individual improvement objective is set. This objective is set forth in column four. By totaling the percentage improvement goals for each man, adding this total to the previously determined gross level of departmental efficiency figure, and again dividing by the number of people involved, a departmental improvement goal is determined.

At this point, a few general observations concerning setting improvement goals are perhaps in order. First, it must be remembered that performance improvement takes time and dynamic sweeping changes cannot be accomplished overnight. This means that the individual improvement objectives which are set must, by necessity, bear some relationship to the present level of performance as well as to the type of work involved. To set a performance goal of 95 percent to be achieved within three months for a man who is presently at a 75 percent level and has been on the job only six months is a little ambitious. This would be especially true if the job involved developing somewhat complex technical skills. In short, the goals which are set must be reasonable and realistic.

On the other hand, performance improvement goals must present a challenge to the individual. They must give him something to work for by stretching him and requiring some special effort. Goals which are too low will tend to result in apathy and disinterest on the job; the man could become accustomed to putting forth halfway effort and achieving halfway results. A third factor of significance is the need for everyone in the operation to have improvement goals. There is sometimes a tendency to neglect the above-average performers and concentrate only on those who are at average- or below-average levels. This situation can have serious repercussions, especially for the above-average performers. They can very easily begin to lose interest in the job because they feel that the work is routine and repetitive in nature. Also, a relatively high rating may suggest that the man is ready to

Exhibit 1 Performance Analysis Chart

Name	Present Efficiency Level in Terms of 100 Percent	Reasons for Rating		Specific Improvement Objectives (Area and Degree of Improvement Sought)
		Strengths	Areas for Improvement	

Manager's Name

Gross Level of D
Department Efficiency
(sum of efficiency
levels)

Average Department
Efficiency Level (gross
level divided by num-
ber of people)

undertake, where possible, some new and more demanding job assignments.

Gaining Mutual Agreement

The first step in setting the stage for effective coaching has been accomplished by specifying what the manager wants from the man in terms of job performance. As noted in the chapter on motivation, however, there are also some things that the subordinate looks for in a job, and these two things must be integrated to get desired results. He wants such things as recognition, job importance, achievement, new experiences, freedom to work, growth opportunities, and dollars. The key to integrating what the manager wants and what the subordinate wants is mutual agreement in the areas of:

1.   The work that the man does or major activities for which he is responsible.

2.   The factors upon which his performance will be judged, such as quality, quantity, cost, innovation, estimating accuracy, self-development, and service to other people or departments.

3.   How performance will be measured.

4.   Specific minimum results or standards of performance which should be met in each of the above areas of accountability as they apply to his job.

It is necessary for the manager and the man to meet, discuss, and agree on what the job involves in a physical sense (what work the man should be doing), and why that particular phase of activity is important. This first area of mutual agreement is akin to the typical job description. The problem with job descriptions is that too often they have been written without the man himself being involved and consequently their use and value are limited. After a man is on the job for a short period of time he thinks of the formal description as the viewpoint of an outsider who really does not know the true situation. He becomes engrossed in meeting crises on a constant basis with the main purpose of getting the work out. Although in a technical sense he may be doing much of what the formal description says he should be doing, the emphasis and concern is mainly with output. This is the day-to-day source of pressure. In this type of climate it is not long before one or two factors dominate at the expense of everything else and balance is lost. The fact that the manager of the department, and others, eventually become concerned about, and at least verbally emphasize other phases of the work generally does not alter the situation. Limited emphasis continues to exist until perhaps a major crisis is reached.

In any job the reaching of fairly high levels of efficiency on a consistent basis requires somewhat uniform attention to anywhere from four to seven major areas of activity. If the manager and subordinate can agree as to these areas, as well as why each is important to total success, it is more likely that balance will be maintained in actual practice and on a continuing basis. This is true because the subordinate looks at his job with a broader perspective.

Once agreement has been reached with the individual or between the manager and a number of people performing essentially the same job, it is, of course, the manager's responsibility to make sure that each man gives adequate attention to all phases of activity. This first area of agreement then, is concerned with *what* work the man does.

The second area where mutual agreement is necessary concerns the factors on which performance will be judged. As stated previously, agreement in the first area centers around the question of what work the man does. Agreement in the second area is concerned with the question of *how well* he does it. In other words, what factors will be used to judge how well you do what you do? What is recognized here is the idea that people are paid not just for performing certain activities, but more important, how well they are performed. Some typical factors which are used to judge how well people do their jobs are quantity, quality, cost control, cost savings, estimating cost, estimating times, innovation, service to other departments or people, schedules met, training and developing people, income generated, and many others.

Depending on the situation in question, the most difficult areas in which to get mutual agreement are very often the manner in which performance will be measured and what the minimum standards should be. The degree of difficulty experienced will, to a large degree, be a function of the relationship between the manager and his subordinates and the climate which now exists. Where rather obvious, clear-cut, and quantifiable measures are available for measuring performance, the prime difficulty may be getting agreement on what the standards should be. Employees may be accustomed to working in a climate where, traditionally, demands have been excessive and unrealistic, where they must always be on the defensive with respect to actual levels of performance, and where identifying weaknesses rather than constructive analysis and seeking improvement has been emphasized. It is obvious, then, that they will either resist the setting of minimum standards completely, or claim that there are too many variables and unforeseen circumstances involved to set any meaningful minimum.

Where the jobs involved are those which traditionally have been considered unmeasurable, difficulty may be encountered in both areas. It was emphasized in the chapter on objective setting that ways of measuring performance with respect to various aspects of *all* jobs could be established. Although no one measure by itself may be perfect, collectively they are infinitely better than nothing at all. Generally speaking, the average or below-average performers will offer more resistance than the better performers since, in spite of how much they complain about inequities, they are more comfortable and much safer with subjective judgments. Also, the biggest problem is sometimes the manager himself. The people would welcome exploring and experimenting with a system of more quantitatively measuring performance but the manager provides the greater resistance.

The key point to remember is that there must be mutual agreement in all four areas because this agreement is what fosters commitment on the part of the man. If he is not committed in terms of the importance of performing certain activities as they relate to his job, in terms of agreement on factors for performance judgment, performance measurement in each area, and what minimum standards are to be met, it is very likely he will pour considerably more energy and effort into resisting the manager than in working with and for him. The way to get the needed mutual agreement is *not* through a telling and persuading approach, but rather one of mutual interchange and involvement in setting up the criteria.

Reasons for Poor Performance

Research has uncovered several important reasons for poor performance on the part of subordinates. Some of these are:

1. He does not know what is expected.

2. He does not know how he is doing.

3. He cannot do the job because he does not know how.

4. He lacks organizational support and help and assistance from the superior.

5. He has a poor relationship with the superior.

Most of these reasons for poor performance are fairly self-explanatory. The interesting thing is the fact that they all reflect something very basic which is missing in the leadership climate. The convenient approach, of course, is to dismiss any or all of these as possible explanations for performance weaknesses in a given case. The challenging approach is to look at each case of performance weakness with a critical eye toward identifying if one of the above, or some other factor, is missing in the leadership climate. It should be cautioned that sometimes it is easy for the manager to assume that he has taken care of some item, but from the subordinate's standpoint, it has not had its effect. When the desired result of a performance improvement effort is not evident, backtracking and reexamination may be necessary.

Some Possible Problems and Difficulties
with Coaching and Appraisal Systems

In addition to the reasons for poor performance cited above, there are some closely related factors which very often contribute to a less than fully effective coaching and development program. Some of these factors, with a brief comment concerning them, are discussed in the following material.

No Clearly Defined Standards of Performance in Certain Important Areas of Job Accountability. When no standards have been established and agreed on it is difficult to discuss performance with a man. Without a definite agreement with respect to desired accomplishments on all phases of the job, a standoff can be the result. The manager is very often in a position of saying that the actual level is not high enough, while the subordinate claims it is about all that can be expected under the circumstances. Therefore, the man justifies his actual level of performance and the manager defends his judgment. Also, without specific standards, the subordinate lacks something to work for and his efforts have no meaning.

No Goals or Objectives Against Which to Measure Improvement.
Very often a manager will undertake a performance analysis and discuss the results with the man, but no improvement objectives and plans

for implementing them are established. The results of this approach are twofold. First, remembering that the purpose of coaching is to improve performance, there is no definitive way to identify how much improvement has taken place. Second, research conducted by General Electric has demonstrated that performance improves most when specific improvement goals are established, and also plans for achieving them.[2]

Second-Guessing as to What Should Have Been Done. When both the previous points are present, there is very often a lot of second-guessing on the part of people as to what should have been accomplished but was not. At the end of a given period the manager may decide that the subordinate has not reached the level he should have achieved. On the other side of the coin, the subordinate did not know precisely where he should be heading in the first place. The result is one of strained relations between the parties. Instead of being in a supportive role the manager finds himself in a judging role.

Wage and Salary Emphasis at the Expense of Other Valuable Objectives.[3] Intentionally or not, many appraisal systems end up centering on the wage and salary action which will be taken rather than on improving performance in a subsequent period. Certainly, rewarding people on the basis of performance is important and should not be underemphasized. As soon as the wage and salary issue comes into play, however, planning for improvement takes a backseat. This would suggest that reviews for improving performance should be separate from those whose purpose is to communicate wage decisions. Not only is separation desirable, but the review for improving performance should be held first. This has the important advantages of insuring that definite plans for improvement will be made, laying the groundwork for the wage decision itself, and communicating that decision to the man.

Mistake-Centered Rather Than Improvement-Centered. As recognized earlier, one of the main purposes of a coaching and appraisal

[2]Herbert H. Meyer, Emanual Kay, J.R.P. French, Jr.: "Split Roles In Performance Appraisal," *Harvard Business Review, 43,* No. 1 1965.

[3]The fourth through the seventh items are derived from the findings of the General Electric study cited in footnote 2. These same ideas have also been referred to by many other writers. For a complete summary, the reader is urged to see the original article.

system should be to lay the groundwork for, and stimulate the desire to improve in subsequent periods. The chances are good that this objective will not be accomplished if the appraisal dwells too heavily on the negative. People have a maximum tolerance level for the amount of criticism they can accept, whether it be levied at several areas of performance or just one or two areas. Once this level is reached, the effect of further criticism is one of producing defensiveness and justification on the part of the employee. Also, he begins to reject the criticism.

The manager undertaking a performance review must guard against the tendency to overemphasize the negative aspects of present performance in a particular area where he would like to see improvement. Instead, once the area in question has been established and agreed on as being important, the major emphasis and majority of time should center on developing plans for improvement. A second caution concerns the need to avoid trying to accomplish too much too soon. If there are several areas of concern, the one or two most important areas should receive attention first and the rest left for another time. A final caution is that the negative effects which overcriticism produces cannot be offset by sandwiching in a few complimentary remarks here and there.

Too Infrequent and After-the-Fact.   Effective coaching is a day-to-day, not a once-a-year activity. The more time that a manager spends in a supportive role with his subordinates, rather than doing the work or telling them how to do it, he will get better results. His function should be one of discussing problems, getting agreement on objectives, and being of whatever assistance he can in terms of facilitating accomplishment of results by his people. Therefore, the process of coaching is a continuous and informal one which takes place as the need arises. This is not to suggest that a once-a-year formal review is not desirable. Indeed, this type of review has its advantages. Too often, however, it becomes a substitute for the day-to-day interaction between the manager and his men.

Subordinate Plays a Passive Rather Than Active Role.   A final weakness in many systems is that the subordinate's role is a passive, listening one rather than an active and participative one. As noted in the chapter on objective setting, successful implementation requires involvement and commitment on the part of the individual. The same principle holds true in coaching. Participation in performance analysis and improvement planning will tend to produce more favorable results than simply a telling approach.

Fundamental Principles of a Good Coaching and Development System

Based on this discussion of the reasons for poor performance and the weaknesses and difficulties of many systems, five basic principles of a good coaching and development system can be emphasized as discussed in the following sections.

Knowledge of What Is Expected.   Most employees can fairly adequately describe their job in a physical sense, that is, in terms of the various activities they perform. Effective delegation, however, requires that jobs also be defined in terms of results expected. The man should have a clear understanding of what the major areas of accountability are for his job and, specifically, what results he should be accomplishing in each area. In other words, he knows the criteria for successful performance of the various activities of his job. Delegation simply by activities is not enough. To be effective a statement of delegation must include the results to be achieved as a culmination of undertaking certain activities. It is fundamentally a difference between the questions of what to achieve and how to achieve it. In too many cases too much attention is placed on the latter at the expense of the former. The result is a superior who spends his time doing instead of managing.

Opportunity To Perform.   A second criterion of effective delegation is the granting of authority, or allowing a subordinate the freedom to work. If there is too much overcontrol in terms of detailing exactly how and when everything is to be done, the results actually achieved do not fully reflect the efforts of the individual. Within broad limits he should be able to exercise his own initiative and ingenuity in determining how to achieve certain objectives. The manager should not get bogged down in the detail of "how" but rather should concentrate on control in a broader sense. The confidence and trust he exhibits will usually be rewarded by successful performance. When mistakes do occur, they should be used to contribute to future growth and development. Emphasis should not be on the mistake itself, but rather why it happened, what can be done to avoid it in the future, and what can be learned.

Know How He Is Doing. On a continual and periodic basis the man must receive feedback on his performance in all key areas of accountability. This enables him to gage his own progress and make adjustments where needed. It also frees the manager from the distasteful role of a "policeman" who watches performance, notes deviations, and "issues tickets" when necessary. He truly begins to operate in a supportive capacity.

Receive Assistance and Support. Accomplishment of results is very seldom a "single-handed" proposition. People will require assistance and support from any number of sources, including the immediate superiors. The manager should do all that he can to coordinate the efforts of his people with those of other departments and to remove whatever difficulties may be hindering or making accomplishment of their goals difficult. In short, he should be a liaison between his staff and others. Also, of course, he should be open for direct consultation. Many managers show only minimal concern for the problems their people face which hinder accomplishment. They are either completely insensitive to these problems, or else they brush them off when they are brought up. The result is frustration for the subordinate and, eventually, an "I don't care, either" attitude. Particularly, when problems that hinder accomplishment are interdepartmental in nature, assistance and support from the superior are needed.

Be Rewarded on the Basis of Results Achieved. A final basic ingredient is a good system of rewards (financial as well as nonfinancial) on the basis of results achieved. Nothing can destroy a results-oriented system more quickly than an inequitable distribution of rewards. If its reason for being is to encourage accomplishment and improvement then it logically follows that the reward system should reflect these same purposes.

*A Coaching Plan To Help Subordinates
Improve Job Performance*

With these five basic principles in mind, Exhibit II presents a step-by-step outline for an effective coaching plan.

Exhibit II   Outline for an Effective Coaching Plan

   I. Let Subordinate Know What Is Expected of Him.
     A. Clearly define job duties and responsibilities.
     B. Let him know the standards you expect him to achieve.

  II. Let Subordinate Know How He Is Doing.
     A. Make an accurate appraisal of performance.
     B. Discuss with the subordinate—get agreement.

 III. Develop a Plan for Improvement.
     A. Orient it to one job weakness.
     B. Have subordinate assist in developing plan.
     C. Get agreement on plan.

 IV. Help Subordinate Implement the Plan.
     A. Observe performance and improvement.
     B. Praise improvement—encourage new efforts.
     C. Constructively correct failures.
     D. Teach by example.
     E. Periodically review progress.

  V. Reward on Results Achieved.
     Give or withhold rewards on the basis of improvement and results.
     A. Praise and recognition.
     B. Salary increase.
     C. Increased responsibilities.
     D. Promotion.
     E. Other rewards—financial and nonfinancial.

Exhibit III outlines the essential elements of the coaching interview. Emphasis throughout the interview process should be on gaining mutual understanding and agreement through candid and open discussion. Both parties should have an opportunity to express feelings, opinions, and ideas in a receptive climate. The objective is not to dwell on the past but to outline plans for the future. Once subordinates have had an opportunity to experience this type of positive climate they will generally respond to performance and coaching reviews in a positive way. This assumes that the elements of effective coaching discussed previously have been followed.

Exhibit III   Essential Elements of the Coaching Interview

STEP I	—*Get off to a good start.*
	—Gear your approach to the man.
Tell	—Pin down the performance problem.
	—Tell him where he stands.
STEP II	—*Present one performance objective at a time.*
	—State and clarify objective.
Listen	—Locate areas of agreement.
	—Spot areas of difference.
STEP III	—*Secure agreement and action.*
	—Sum up areas of agreement and conflict.
Discuss	—Clarify by whom follow-up action is to be taken.
	—Restate results required.
	—End talk on positive reassurance.
STEP IV	—*Follow-up actions.*
	—Observe, correct, and encourage.
Check	—Coach as needed for more improvement.
	—Set the *example.*

Performance Review—A Critical Issue[4]

When one sorts through the tremendous variety of practices and purposes associated with the process of appraisal, performance review, work planning, personnel evaluation, counseling, or superior talking with subordinate, the primary objectives emerging from this process are improved performance on the present job and a plan of development for future growth. Underlying the successful achievement of these objectives is a clear sense of the desired results and some means of measurement of the actual results obtained.

There has been a growing interest in the measurement of performance (as contrasted with the appraisal of performance, which may or may not include measurement) over the past decade. A cursory review of management literature since Peter Drucker's, *The Practice of Management,*[5] will attest to the almost explosive growth of books and arti-

[4]This section was written by Dr. David Schreiber, Assistant Professor of Commerce, Management Institute, University of Wisconsin. It was previously published in article form in *Personnel Administration.*

[5]Peter Drucker, *The Practice of Management,* McGraw-Hill, 1957.

cles on why and how to measure management activities. The parallel growth of management science, with its emphasis on quantitative decision making, has aided in spreading the concept of measurement of results throughout the total spectrum of management functions. It is therefore logical that the area of individual performance is being included in this "results" climate.

Why Review Performance?

A number of reasons can be given which support the concept of performance review, but none of them hold any significance for an organization or department if the system does not "pay-off" in long-term profitability or improved performance. There seem to be three beneficiaries of an effective review system: the company, the employee, and the manager conducting the review. Some of these benefits include:

1. For the organization
   (a) A consistent, standardized basis for developing, maintaining, and updating the manpower inventory.
   (b) A history of employee performance for salary and promotional purposes.
   (c) An effective means of communicating management goals and objectives.

2. For the employee
   (a) The knowledge of "how am I doing" on my job.
   (b) An opportunity for motivation based on measurable achievement and recognition, plus the opportunity to participate in setting future goals.

3. For the manager
   (a) An opportunity to practice a critical executive task; the ability to develop subordinates may well become recognized as the key executive skill.
   (b) A means for building rapport with subordinates.
   (c) An opportunity to improve group productivity by focusing on the developmental needs of each employee.
   (d) An opportunity to develop one's replacement.

What Should Be Reviewed?

In analyzing the current documents used to support the process of performance review, topics such as these are covered:

attitude	attendance/absenteeism
loyalty	accuracy of work
dependability	quantity of work
cooperation	timeliness of work
initiative	promptness/tardiness
tact	job objectives of employee

Examine the two lists and ask yourself, "How are the two lists different? Which list would you prefer to review with a subordinate?"

An attempt to answer these questions reveals several points. The left list contains items which are subjective, individual-related, and very difficult to measure. The items in the right list are objective, job-related, and capable of being measured. Not only is the right column preferable, but the right column contains the only kind of subject matter which is really pertinent. While the personal characteristics listed in the left column are important, they are important only as they affect the items in the right column. For example, loyalty is a valuable personal characteristic, but no organization is paying for loyalty except as loyalty is translated into some job-related, quantifiable result or goal sought by the organization.

In recent discussions with management groups concerning this approach, a number of managers correctly have pointed out that the list of objective and subjective factors will vary from organization to organization and group to group. Some items may fall into either list. For example, "apperance" in most organizations is a highly subjective, nonquantifiable item. On the other hand, in those organizations where a uniform is required and where appearance is akin to the quality of the service being offered, appearance may be a measurable, job-related factor rather than a matter of individual discretion. However, even when appearance can be measured, it may not prove to be a valuable developmental item. Thus, the manager must concern himself with a review system which emphasizes meaningful job results and development for future results.

Managers have limited resources (time, money, and personnel) with which to accomplish particular objectives. Much more effective time and energy utilization is another benefit which can be obtained from objective, job-oriented factors. Agreement is much more likely when discussing an objective "fact" than when discussing subjective, unmeasurable judgment (opinion). Facts also have a much lower emotional content than opinions. Further, in building for the future, the use of objective data makes it much easier to:

1. Get agreement as to where (what level) the individual is performing now.

2. Define the state which will exist when a meaningful goal has been reached.

This approach suggests the possibility of spending less time per subject discussed and at the same time operating in a much safer emotional climate.

Implementing a Results Approach

Perhaps one of the major reasons for the recent popularity of this "results" approach to management is the growing awareness that the mechanistic, economic model of man is antiquated. According to the economic model of man, employees are motivated primarily by direct and indirect financial compensation. However, it has been demonstrated in actual practice and in experimental laboratories that social and psychological rewards may be much more important than material incentives.

In implementing a "results" approach to performance review, it is important to recall that the two objectives of this review process are improved performance on the job and a plan of development aimed toward long-range opportunities and growth. Exhibit IV incorporates some of the previously discussed material and cites research findings which have a bearing on this particular approach.

Subject Matter of Review.   The real difference between the traditional and results approach lies with the results of the review process. In other words, even if some general character improvement can be achieved as a result of an emphasis on personality characteristics, this has nothing to do directly with performance or skills development. On the other hand, setting specific job goals is directly related to performance and skills development and, not surprisingly, ties directly into

Exhibit IV   Results Approach to Performance Review

	TRADITIONAL APPROACH	RESULTS APPROACH
1. Subject matter	Emphasis on personality	Emphasis on goal setting
2. Review process	Emphasis on shortcomings	Problem solving, limited criticism
3. Source of direction	Boss determines how and why	Mutual goal setting
4. Frequency of review	Comprehensive annual review	Day-to-day coaching

the research findings on key sources of motivation to work as discussed in Chapter 17. Further, research results covered earlier in this chapter suggest very strongly that improved performance is highly related to the establishment of realistic, measurable goals rather than general character improvement. Therefore, wisdom would seem to dictate a direct approach which avoids the pitfalls of personality discussion, and recognizes that the emphasis should be on the job performance, not the personal characteristics of the individual.

The Review Process.   Closely associated with subject matter is the technique used to accomplish the objectives of the review session. The traditional approach again has been premised on the importance of general character improvement and the value of overcoming individual shortcomings. Research done by Meyer, Kay, and French affirms the serious limitations of criticism as a means of overcoming individual shortcomings.[6] In their study, these researchers discovered the low tolerance of most individuals for criticism and the actual negative effect on performance of too much criticism in the period following the review session. In fact, praise in this appraisal environment did not prove to be effective, inasmuch as it was viewed merely as a "sandwich" effect —a means of masking the preceding ensuing criticism.

In contrast, the results approach places the emphasis on problem solving as the vehicle by which to discuss past performance and on

[6]Meyer, Kay, and French, op. cit.

which to plan for future goals and development. Unfortunately, the ability to make the transition from concentration on individual short-comings to problem solving may require extensive training and practice; it certainly requires more than mere intellectual assent to the concept.

One helpful approach is to provide a completely new form with which to conduct review sessions, a form which eliminates all reference to individual traits and instead uses a column for goals, a second column for comments on the effectiveness of goal accomplishment (timeliness, accuracy, cost, and completeness), and a third column for comments, problems encountered, and suggestions for future goals and development needs.

Source of Direction for Goal Determination. Again using the work of Meyer, Kay, and French as a point of departure, their research has shown that the traditional ways of goal determination are far inferior in terms of end results than are the more participative means of goal determination. Unilateral determination by the superior of the objectives and the methods (means) by which these objectives are to be accomplished produced much poorer performance than when the objectives are the outcome of mutual interaction and than when the methods (means) are left to the individual responsible for the achievement of these objectives. Again, these research results corroborate the results of the motivational studies of Herzberg and Meyers in explaining the likelihood of obtaining greater commitment and, therefore, better performance from participative techniques as contrasted to nonparticipative means of goal setting.[7] As has been previously stated, goal setting in itself is an important element in achieving meaningful results. Add to this the opportunity to participate in setting one's own objectives, and the motivation to attain these goals is increased. A number of organizations are trying participative management and, in the process, have encouraged subordinates to bring their own objectives to their review sessions. However, recent research evidence has indicated that the source of the objectives is less significant to the achievement of these objectives than is the opportunity for a mutual discussion of, and agreement on the specific details of these goals. Real mutuality in goal setting would therefore seem to be the key to making the participative approach more than just a passing fad.

[7]Herzberg, op. cit.

Frequency of Review. The final and least definitive phase of the review format is the frequency of review. There seems to be no question that the traditional comprehensive annual review, with its "laundry list" of pros and cons stored up for a year, has had remarkably little positive effect on the recipient and was a distasteful task for the manager conducting the review. The alternative is not as clear. Job objectives may or may not need much more than an annual review, so are we just trying to make a "big deal" out of progress reports? Inasmuch as the intent of these reviews is to provide the manager with an opportunity for downward and upward communication as well as to provide occasions for meaningful coaching where the situation warrants, the frequency of the reviews should be dictated by the efficiency of other communication means and by the work cycles of those being supervised, but not by the necessity of making a salary decision or by the arrival of an anniversary date.

The basic nature of the traditional approach is an historical review. Its primary focus looks backward rather than to the future; it is not oriented toward performance and growth but rather toward a report card approach to satisfy the salary administration process. On the other hand, the results approach, properly done, provides the manager with a review system which:

1. Operates on an adult level—a problem-solving session between relative equals rather than a superior passing judgment on a subordinate.

2. Incorporates current knowledge concerning motivation, provides meaningful participation—therefore, encourages mutuality in goal setting.

3. Puts an emphasis on a forward look—what is going to happen is more important than what has happened!

A Good Coach in Perspective

1. Qualifications of a Good Coach
   (a) A sincere and unselfish interest in helping his subordinates to improve.
   (b) Thorough knowledge of position requirements.
   (c) Complete understanding of individual with whom he is working.

(d)   Awareness of the extent to which positive and progressive work will be approved and applauded by superiors.

2.   Rules for the Coach

(a)   Operates from the sidelines. (Cannot coach and play at the same time.)

(b)   Recognizes individual differences. (Does not make all members of team act alike or as he does.)

(c)   Knows men learn best by doing.

(d)   Earns and maintains team respect.

(e)   Satisfied with success in one phase at a time, with gradual progress.

(f)   Gears work to average man.

(g)   Has clearly definable standards of performance.

Summary

In Chapter 1, management was defined as getting things done by, with, and through people. This definition emphasizes the idea that a big part of a manager's job is coaching and developing his people. A manager who is sincerely interested in helping his people perform at their maximum level of capability will not take these aspects of his job lightly. The process of effective coaching involves making a performance analysis, gaining mutual agreement as to what the job involves, recognizing the reasons for poor performance, and performance appraisal and counseling. A good coaching plan will insure that the subordinate knows what is expected and how he is doing, that a plan for improvement is developed, that the subordinate has the help and support of his superior, and that he is rewarded on the basis of results.

Of critical importance to effective coaching is the matter of performance appraisal and review. Too often reviews have focused on personality-related and intangible factors as opposed to quantifiable job-related factors. To this extent the objectives of removing a performance gap and insuring continued growth and development have not been met.

Key Concepts

Mutual Agreement. Between a superior and subordinate there must be mutual agreement with respect to the tasks to be performed, the results expected, how performance will be measured, and where the subordinate stands.

Results-Oriented Appraisal. Results-oriented appraisals focus on job-related factors which are measurable as opposed to personality factors and those which are intangible.

Discussion Questions

1. In your own words, describe each of the steps for employee appraisal.

2. In this chapter, two essential areas of mutual agreement between subordinates and superior are necessary in an effective performance appraisal. Briefly describe each of these areas. Which of these is usually the most difficult for subordinate and superior to agree on? Why is this area so difficult?

3. Seven possible problems and difficulties with coaching and appraisal systems have been given in this chapter. Describe each of these difficulties and relate each of these to your own experiences in which:

   (a) Your supervisor did not experience these difficulties.
   (b) Your supervisor did experience these difficulties.

   Comment on how effectively you were able to perform the job in each case.

4. Briefly describe each of the five basic principles of a good coaching and development system.

5. What are the two basic objectives of the "results" approach to performance review?

6. Compare the traditional methods of subordinate appraisal and goal determination with the methods presented in this chapter. Which method would you prefer to work under if you were the subordinate? Which method would your prefer as a supervisor? Explain why in each case.

Selected Readings

Ralph L. Cullen, and Herbert Hubben, "Motivating the Boss: The Key to Executive Development," *Business Horizons, 3* (3), Indiana University, Fall 1960, pp. 49–54.

Peter Drucker, *The Practice of Management,* McGraw-Hill, 1957.

Robert M. Guion, "Criterion Measurement and Personnel Judgments," *Personnel Psychology, 14,* 1961, pp. 141–149.

Robert J. House, "A Commitment Approach to Management Development," *California Management Review, 7* (3), Spring 1965, pp. 15–26.

Edgar F. Huse, "Putting in a Management Development Program That Works," *California Management Review, 9* (2), Winter 1966, pp. 73–80.

Douglas McGregor, "An Uneasy Look at Performance Appraisal," *Harvard Business Review*, May–June 1957.

Herbert H. Meyer, Emanual Kay, and J. R. P. French, Jr., "Split Roles in Performance Appraisal," *Harvard Business Review, 43,* No. 1 1965, pp. 123–129.

Arch Patton, "How to Appraise Executive Performance," *Harvard Business Review, 38* (1), January–February 1960, pp. 63–70.

Robert C. Sampson, "Train Executives While They Work," *Harvard Business Review, 31* (6), pp. 42–54.

Edgar H. Schein, "Management Development as a Process of Influence," *Industrial Management Review,* May 1961, pp. 59–76.

Walter S. Wikstrom, "Developing Managers: Underlying Principles," *Management Record, 29* (11), November 1962, pp. 14–18.

Part 6

Control

Part 6 examines the control function in management. Chapter 22 will serve as a general introduction to Part 6. In it control is defined in terms of its purpose; it also examines some possible weaknesses that may be associated with control systems. This is followed by a discussion of the areas where management must exercise control, the essential elements of a control system, and some fundamental principles of a good system. In the final portion of Chapter 22, attention is centered on the human aspects of managerial control. Some historical assumptions underlying control are explored along with an examination of some of the possible unintended consequences of control, the reasons behind these unintended consequences, and some guidelines of effective control administration.

Chapter 23 investigates three aspects of control as they relate to the production function in business as well as the area of sales control. The three areas of production control to be discussed include quality control, production planning and control, and inventory control. Since each of these areas could in itself comprise several chapters of a book or a book in itself, our objective will be limited to developing an appreciation for, and a general understanding of what is involved.

Chapter 24 concentrates on the control function as it relates to the areas of finance and accounting. Following some brief introductory material and a discussion of internal controls, attention is centered on the area of budgetary control; the nature of budgets as well as the concepts of flexible budgets, responsibility accounting, and standard costs are discussed. Numerous examples are used to illustrate the practical application of the principles and concepts being dealt with. The final portion of Chapter 24 centers on a discussion of profit analysis and ratio analysis.

22.   Managerial Control

Although the function of control usually appears last on the list of managerial functions, it nevertheless is one of a manager's prime responsibilities. In many respects, control can be considered the essence of management. It is the function which gives meaning and depth to all the functions previously examined. The importance of control lies in the fact that a manager's job is to get things done or, put more specifically, to achieve results in certain key areas of accountability. Although most of the work will be done by other people, it is the individual manager who remains ultimately responsible for the results achieved. To insure the desired level of achievement, he must develop and use a control system which will let him know at all times and on a continuous basis whether the work being done is on target. With these preliminary observations in mind, the remainder of this chapter will be devoted to the following subject areas.

1.   Definition and purpose of control.
2.   Areas where management exercises control.
3.   Essential elements of control.
4.   Principles and fundamentals of a good control system.
5.   Human aspects of control.

The purpose of control is to *insure that events conform to plans.* By necessity this implies that control is concerned with the *present.* Viewed another way it involves a regulation of what is happening *now.* Control involves the *location of operational weaknesses and where and when appropriate, taking the necessary corrective action* to insure desired results. The emphasis on control, therefore, is not on what has happened in the past but rather on what is happening in the present.

The essence of control can perhaps best be brought out by briefly mentioning some of the *common weaknesses* that are sometimes associated with control systems. First, some control systems place *too much emphasis on the past* and are therefore *"after the fact"* in nature. To *the extent that this condition exists the purpose of control as cited above is defeated.* As an example, it does little good to discover at the end of the year that the organization or department has exceeded its budget. If properly used as a control device, expenditures should be compared to budget figures on a periodic basis to insure that the end results will be satisfactory. Similarly, to discover a major quality defect after hundreds or thousands of dollars worth of parts have been produced is equivalent to locking the gate after the horse is out of the corral. A good quality control system would identify the problem when it initially happens so that corrective action could be taken. This first problem area reflects a fault in the way the control system is structured.

A second and closely related potential problem area is that the control system may be *mistake centered rather than cause and correction centered.* This means that the way in which the system is administered places too much emphasis on finding out who made a particular mistake rather than identifying a problem area and then taking constructive action to remedy the problem. The weakness of a control system is potentially most serious when it occurs in combination with problems being identified after the fact. Another aspect of a mistake-centered control system is that it tends to produce adverse and defensive reactions on the part of those people who are negatively affected. The human aspects of control will be discussed in more detail later in this chapter.

A third factor that can inhibit the effective functioning of a control system is that it may *become too involved* and *not specific enough.* Many control systems are designed and administered by staff departments. Certain units within the organization are given the task of monitoring various aspects of the operation and functioning of other units on a continuous basis. When this situation occurs, as it must, it is only natural that points of friction develop. As this friction occurs and continues over time there is a danger that the control system becomes an end in itself rather than a means to an end. The department administering the system may get carried away with the system itself and forget about what it is supposed to accomplish in terms of aiding in the achievement of results. The departments subject to being controlled attack the system as being inadequate, and this sets the stage for conflict and defensive reactions on the part of everyone involved. In this climate the whole purpose of control soon becomes obscured.

A final potential weakness of control systems is that they *may not be based on key factors* that affect results. In any operation the list of factors which can be subject to control of one kind or another is endless. If an attempt is made to control everything the manager will very soon be so overwhelmed with detail and reports that he will not have time to manage. There are always certain key factors and points at which, if proper control is exercised, there is a high degree of certainty that results will be achieved. A good control system will therefore focus on these key areas only and thereby be a practical aid to management.

In summary, the whole thrust of the control function is to help the organization and the individual manager achieve desired results. It is extremely important that this philosophy be the guideline whenever control systems are being designed and administered. It is also advantageous for the organization to periodically review the systems it has to ensure that they are making a positive contribution.

Areas Where Control Is Necessary

As with the managerial function of planning, control is of concern to both the total organization as well as the individual manager in his particular department. It is therefore possible to talk about areas of control in a broad general sense as well as in a very specific sense as it relates to such functions as personnel management, marketing, research and development, production, finance and accounting, or any other functional speciality. With respect to viewing control in the latter terms, it would be necessary to have a separate chapter (or major portion of a chapter) to cover each particular area. Also, to be really meaningful would require that the reader be thoroughly familiar with that particular functional speciality. For these reasons it is not our purpose to treat control in such detail. Instead, it is our concern to develop a more general overall insight into some areas where control is exercised.

Exhibit I sets forth eight general areas where the organization becomes involved in the control function. In studying Exhibit I it can be seen that the concern and need for control cuts across the whole spectrum of organizational activities.

Exhibit II is somewhat more specific in that it sets forth some areas where control is necessary as it relates to four of the more common functional specialties. It should be noted that this Exhibit is not designed to be all encompassing but rather to simply provide the reader with some insight into typical things which would be of concern to management.

Essential Elements of Control

As suggested by the purpose of control (insuring that events conform to plans) and by the fact that it involves the location of operational weaknesses and taking corrective action, control assumes the existence of some type of *target or objective.* Therefore, the first essential element of control is some predetermined standard or objective. Maximum productivity requires that the manager be results oriented; this means he must have something against which to measure results. Some standards will be set for the manager as part of the total organizational plan, while he will develop others himself. In any case, there should be objectives set in all key areas of accountability.

The second essential element of a control is a system of reporting what is going on. The reporting system may give the manager feedback on a day-to-day basis or over longer periods of time. The key point is that the information which is generated must be practical and usable as well as timely. With respect to the former, the information which the manager receives should enable him to pinpoint quickly where deviations are occurring so that he can do something about them. A major problem with some reporting systems is that they are so complex and detailed that they are of little practical use to managers who must try to interpret them. With respect to timeliness, if control is to aid in the accomplishment of results, the manager must receive the necessary feedback soon enough to make adjustments if and when they are needed. The particular situation will dictate how frequently feedback should be given.

The third element of control involves interpretation and evaluation of

Exhibit I Types of Control Systems[1]

1. Controls used to standardize performance in order to increase efficiency and to lower costs. Included might be time and motion studies, inspections, written procedures, or production schedules.

2. Controls used to safeguard company assets from theft, wastage, or misuse. Such controls typically would emphasize division of responsibilities, separation of operational, custodial, and accounting activities, and an adequate system of authorization and record keeping.

3. Controls used to standardize quality in order to meet the specifications of either customers or company engineers. Blueprints, inspection, and statistical quality controls would typify the measures employed to preserve the integrity of the product (or service) marketed by the company.

4. Controls designed to set limits within which delegated authority can be exercised without further top management approval. Organization and procedure manuals, policy directives, and internal audits would help to spell out the limits within which subordinates have a free hand.

5. Controls used to measure on-the-job performance. Typical of such controls would be special reports, output per hour or per employee, internal audits, and perhaps budgets or standard costs.

6. Controls used for planning and programming operations. Such controls would include sales and production forecasts, budgets, various cost standards, and standards of work measurement.

7. Controls necessary to allow top management to keep the firm's various plans and programs in balance. Typical of such controls would be a master budget, policy manuals, organization manuals, and such organization techniques as committees and the use of outside consultants. The overriding need for such controls would be to provide the necessary capital for current and long-run operations and to maximize profits.

8. Controls designed to motivate individuals within a firm to contribute their best efforts. Such controls necessarily would involve ways of recognizing achievement through such things as promotions, awards for suggestions, or some form of profit sharing.

---

[1] William Travers Jerome, III, *Executive Control—The Catalyst* (New York: Wiley, 1961), pp. 32–33.

Exhibit II   Areas of Control

Production
1. Quality.
2. Quantity.
3. Cost.
4. Machine output.
5. Individual job performance.

Personnel Management
1. Labor relations.
2. Labor turnover.
3. Absenteeism.
4. Wage and salary administration (labor costs).
5. Safety.

Finance and Accounting
1. Capital expenditures.
2. Flow of capital.
3. Liquidity.
4. Inventories.
5. Costs.

Marketing
1. Sales volume.
2. Sales expenses.
3. Credit.
4. Advertising costs.
5. Individual salesman's performance.

---

the information generated by the feedback system. This is a key step, as it becomes the basis for taking corrective action when needed. The quality of evaluation of information by individual managers can be assured to the degree that the feedback given them about their operation is easily and readily assimilated.

The final element of control is that of taking corrective action. It is this step which links control so closely to the planning function and enables the manager to accomplish the purpose of control. It should also be noted that in order to take corrective action the manager must be a good decision maker. More specifically, he must be able to identify the real problems hindering accomplishment and causing deviations, he must develop, analyze, and choose between alternative approaches to overcoming the problems, and he must then plan for the implementation of the decisions he makes. The process of decision making was discussed in detail in Chapters 6 and 7.

Fundamental Principles of a Good Control System

Using the discussion of the managerial control function up to this point as a base, it is possible to delineate several fundamental elements that must be present if a particular control system is to function effectively and accomplish its basic purpose. The following principles are particularly important.

1.   The control system must be current.
2.   The control system must develop records on all objectives.
3.   The control system should focus on deviations from objectives.
4.   The system should report deviations to the man himself.
5.   The system must reflect individually responsibilities as well as overall results.

The first principle requiring that the control system be current reflects a concern for the basic purpose of control. As stated earlier, in the chapter, control is concerned with the present, with what is happening now to insure that plans will, in fact, be achieved. If this purpose is to be achieved then the system must be current.

The second principle recognizes that the achievement of the total organization's overall goals and objectives is possible only if individual departments and functional areas accomplish their objectives. Therefore, to insure success the control system must develop records on all objectives for all units of the organization. Assuming that corrective action is taken wherever and whenever it is needed, there will then be a coordinated thrust throughout the entire organization.

The job of a manager is not only a very responsible one but one which demands a great deal of time and concentrated effort. It might also be noted that the manager is almost constantly faced with varying degrees of pressure of one kind or another. A system of control which is properly designed and administered can go a long way toward simplifying the manager's task. As the third principle suggests, the control system should focus on deviations from objectives so that problem areas can be quickly spotted. The idea behind focusing on deviations is not, of course, to chastize the manager, but rather to help him to be able to quickly pinpoint where some type of corrective action needs to be taken. If the control system does not specifically pinpoint deviations, the manager must spend a considerable amount of time analyzing and trying to interpret the reports with which he is being furnished. Also, there is the danger that some potential problem areas will be overlooked.

The fourth principle states that deviations should be reported to the man himself. This is not to say that a man's superior should not also receive feedback on the status of the operation, but it recognizes that if an individual is to direct and control his own performance he must know where he stands on a periodic basis. By making progress reports available to those who are actually doing the work, a climate is created where they can adjust their own performance as opposed to being told to do so. Also, there is less need for the manager to be acting in a "policing" capacity. Rather, he can function as a coach. The only time he needs to "step in" is when adjustments are not being made or if the performance gap is such that he wants to make sure that it has been spotted and something is being done. This represents a more positive approach to control.

The final principle acknowledges that overall results are the sum total of those which are accomplished by individuals. Therefore, the control system must be complete in that it produces records for individuals as well as the total. If the system does not deal with individual responsibilities, there is not only the danger that overall results will not be achieved but also the danger that attention will focus on identifying after the fact who made a mistake. This, of course, is not congruent with the purpose of control.

Human Aspects of Managerial Control[2]

Someone once made the observation that there is nothing wrong with most organizations, it is only when you put people in then that they get all fouled up. In a slightly different way this observation most assuredly applies to managerial control. As pointed out previously, control

---

[2]This section of the chapter draws very heavily from the following source: Douglas McGregor, *The Professional Manager* (New York: McGraw-Hill, 1967), Chapter 8.

is not only an important but a necessary function for the individual manager and the organization as a whole. It is important to note, however, that it is people and their performance who becomes the subjects of control, and when this human element is introduced problems invariably result. The problems are a reflection of the emotional response of those being controlled to the control system. It is the purpose of this portion of the chapter to examine some of the unintended consequences of control systems, the reasons for these unintended consequences, how management can induce perceived threat as a result of control, and finally, to present some guidelines which will lead to a positive reaction to attempts at control.

Historical Assumptions Underlying Control. Historically, management's approach to installing control systems has many times been based on a Theory X set of assumptions about people. More specifically, we overgeneralize about people based on some people who are not motivated, who try to get by with as little as possible, and who try, or attempt to try, to take all the shortcuts. As a result many control systems have, been for the most part, either structured or administered in a negative sense. That is, consciously or unconsciously they have been used to exert pressure as a basis for disciplining people and as a measure to force compliance with externally imposed standards.

Unintended Consequences of Control. To the extent and degree that the above situations have and do exist, several unintended consequences of control have developed. Douglas McGregor has delineated these unintended consequences as follows.[3]

"1. Widespread antagonism to the controls and to those who administer them.

"2. Successful resistance and noncompliance. This occurs not with respect to a few people but with respect to many. It occurs not alone at the bottom of the organization, but at all levels up to the top.

"3. Unreliable performance information because of 1 and 2 above.

"4. The necessity for close surveillance. This results in a dilu-

3Ibid., p. 117.

tion of delegation that is expensive of managerial time as well as having other consequences.

"5.   High administrative cost."

McGregor further notes that these consequences are readily observable inside any large organization, and to different degrees are characteristic of all management control systems. This should not be interpreted to mean, however, that these negative consequences are the inevitable result of all attempts at exercising the control function. This is far from the truth, and in a given situation quite the opposite conditions may exist. The key to a successful system lies in how it is administered. Some fundamental principles of effective administration of control systems will be pointed out and discussed later in the chapter but first the reasons why these consequences sometimes develop must be considered.

Reasons for These Unintended Consequences of Control.   The reason for the sometimes present negative reaction to control systems is explained by how people react to perceived threat. More specifically, if people feel, for whatever the reason, that the system represents a threat to their overall security, they will adopt a pattern of behavior which in their estimation will, to a degree, defeat the system and thereby eliminate or at least temper the threat.

McGregor lists these primary conditions under which threat is likely to be perceived.

"1.   Where punishment as opposed to support and help in meeting standards and objectives is emphasized.

"2.   Where trust is lacking in the relationships involved.

"3.   Where feedback negatively affects the individual in terms of his employment relationship and career expectations."[4]

With respect to McGregor's first point, research conducted by Rensis Likert and others has indicated that the manager who attempts to achieve results through people by exerting pressure and having a "perform or suffer the consequences" attitude, tends to achieve lower levels of productivity within his unit. Conversely, as noted in Chapter 19, the

[4]Ibid., p. 119.

highest levels of productivity tend to occur in situations where the manager exhibits supportive relations as far as his people are concerned.

Any number of conditions can lead to lack of trust. It may be that the subordinate does not know what is expected of him or where he stands. As a result he is constantly being called upon to account for, or defend his past performance when in fact he was for all practical purposes left completely on his own with little or no direction. Another condition leading to a lack of trust occurs when the superior is not consistent in the ways in which he exercises the leadership function on a day-to-day basis. One day he "runs hot" and the next "cold." Subordinates must constantly try to figure out what will be next.

The final condition leading to perceived threat reflects a violation of the purpose of control and also of the job of a manager as a coach whose responsibility is to help people achieve maximum results within the limits of their skill and ability. As mentioned several times previously, the information feedback which is generated by the control system should be used to pinpoint deviations as a basis for taking corrective action. The emphasis should not be on individuals per se but rather on the eventual objectives to be achieved.

Fundamental Guidelines of Effective Control Administration

If a control system is to accomplish its purpose it must not only be structurally sound from a technical standpoint, but it must be properly administered. The objective of effective administration is to prevent or minimize the human problems which might otherwise arise. There are four important guidelines to effective control administration.

First, the manager must communicate, discuss, and gain the highest possible degree of commitment among his people to the goals and objectives of the unit or department and their individual jobs. The greater the extent to which people are committed to a particular objective the higher their level of job performance tends to be. Also, people who are committed to goals are more likely to self-direct and control their own performance. It therefore behooves the manager to do everything within his power to gain this commitment. This should be his first and prime concern.

Second, enough emphasis cannot be placed on educating subordinates with respect to the purpose of control. The first point of concern relates to the purpose of control in terms of helping to accomplish overall departmental goals. The second point of concern relates to the purpose of control as it affects the individual. In the latter case it must be made clear that the control procedure does not exist for the purpose of finding out who made mistakes and who should be disciplined and subject to various types of pressure. It should instead be clearly communicated that the control system is a tool to help the individual perform at his full level of capability.

Third, in his day-to-day dealings with subordinates, and in particular those dealings involving aspects of control, the manager must establish a climate of help and support. He must create a climate where his people are convinced that he is truly concerned about helping them to do the best job possible. No amount of talking can create this type of feeling among subordinates. Their perception is a result of actions, not words.

Fourth, in order to gain commitment and to reinforce the true purpose of control and keep people results oriented, the manager should continually review with the individual and the total work group the status of achievement and progress toward objectives. This includes getting their ideas as to the problems and difficulties being encountered, alternative courses of action that might be followed to overcome these problems, and jointly developing plans for action.

In summary, successful performance of the control function goes far beyond the designing of a control system which is just technically sound. Like all other aspects of management, the human element must receive consideration if the expected results are to be forthcoming.

Summary

Control is the function of management which is designed to insure that events conform to plans. To be effective the control system must focus on the present; it must be correction centered as opposed to being mistake centered, and it must be specific in the sense that it concentrates on key factors that affect results. The control function must be universal in that it covers all phases of the organization's operations. The four essential elements of a control system include the presence of standards or objectives, a system of reporting, interpretation and evaluation of information, and corrective action.

In many cases control systems have resulted in creating some unintended negative human responses. When this occurs the reasons most often lie in the way the system is administered. For example, if a climate of punishment rather than a climate of help and support exist, people will react negatively. Similarly if people perceive threat they will work to defeat the system. To prevent negative reactions to control systems requires that people know what the objectives are, that they understand the purpose of the controls, that they work in a climate of help and support, and that they receive continual feedback.

Key Concepts

Purpose of Control. To insure that events conform to plans, control must concern itself with the present, with what is happening now.

Elements of Control. The essential elements of control included the presence of standards, a system of reporting, interpretation and evaluation of information, and corrective action.

Discussion Questions

1. Describe the four factors which can inhibit the effective functioning of a control system.

2. Name five types of control systems.

3. Briefly describe the four essential elements of a control system.

4. Dave Williams is quality control inspector for the Davis Lightbulb Company. His job is to take a sample of lightbulbs from the production line and run various tests on these bulbs to determine whether they have met the buyers' specifications. The final test involves a "severity test" in which the bulb must burn for at least 12 hours under an overloading of electricity. If a significant number of lightbulbs do not meet the buyer specifications, then Dave notifies the superintendent of the problem. The production line is then imme-

diately shut down and is not started up again until the condition producing the faulty lightbulbs has been corrected.

At the end of each day, Dave prepares a summary of his day's activities and submits them to his supervisor, the president of the corporation. Dave's daily reporting stemmed from some complaints by a few buyers that their lightbulbs were not meeting specifications. The president felt that more inspections of the product would reduce these complaints, but he wanted to be certain that these inspections actually took place. The daily summaries submitted by Dave included the name of the buyer for whom the product was being produced and the lot number in the warehouse. If the buyer complaints continued, then the president felt that another inspector would be needed to make an even closer inspection of the production process.

Identify each of the elements of the *two* control systems described in the above case.

5. Describe each of the six fundamental principles of a control system.

6. What basic attitudes do you feel a Theory X manager holds regarding control systems in his department? How do these attitudes differ from a Theory Y manager with respect to control?

7. What are the unintended consequences of control? Under what conditions are these unintended consequences most likely to come about?

8. What are the five guidelines for effective control administration?

Selected Readings

Chris Argyris, "Human Problems With Budgets," *Harvard Business Review, XXXI* (1), pp. 97–110.

Kenneth J. Arrow, "Control in Large Organizations," *Management Science, 10* (3), April 1964, pp. 397–408.

Charles C. Gibbons, "Management by Exception," *Advanced Management Journal, 29* (1), January 1964, pp. 12–16.

John Leslie Livingston, "Management Controls and Organizational Performance," *Personnel Administration, 28* (1), January–February 1965, pp. 37–43.

Douglas McGregor, ed. by Warren Bennis and Caroline McGregor, *The Professional Manager,* McGraw-Hill, New York, 1967, Chapter 8.

Raymond E. Miles, and Roger C. Vergin, "Behavioral Properties of Variance Controls," *California Management Review, VIII* (3), Spring 1966.

Douglas S. Sherwin, "The Meaning of Control," *Dun's Review and Modern Industry,* January 1956, pp. 45, 46, and 83.

Raymond Villens, "Control and Freedom in a Decentralized Company," *Harvard Business Review, XXXII* (2), pp. 89–96.

E. Kirby Warren, "Measurement and Control: Developing a Better Approach," *Long Range Planning: The Executive View Point,* Prentice-Hall, 1966.

23.   Control of the Production and Marketing Functions

It was mentioned previously that all aspects of an organization's operation are subject to the managerial function of control. Chapter 23 discusses control as it relates to the production and marketing functions. With respect to the former, three major topical areas will be discussed.

1. Quality control and inspection.
2. Inventory control.
3. Production planning and control.

The discussion of control in marketing in this Chapter will center on sales management.

Quality Control and Inspection

The quality of a product is defined by a set of specifications governing the functional performance, composition, strength, shape, dimensions, workmanship, color, and finish of that product. Quality is meaningful only in relation to the purpose and end use of the product. Good quality is attained when a product or a service fully satisfies the purpose for which it is designed. The fact that even better quality might be achieved is immaterial as long as the product or service meets the objectives of the consumer who uses it; this is the key point of concern. Viewed another way, the better the quality, the greater the cost of production. There will always be some upper quality limit which, when surpassed, would require the consumer to pay a price for something which in his judgment he does not need.

Quality control refers to the recognition and removal of identifiable causes of defects and variations from set standards. Various techniques can be used for the systematic observation of quality and interpretation of the causes of variability. These techniques may run the gamut from very simple visual observations to those which are highly statistical in nature. Once quality control has pinpointed the why of defects, corrective action can be taken. It is important to note, therefore, that the objective of quality control goes beyond the identification of defects only. The reasons for these defects must be pinpointed.

Inspection is the application of test and measuring devices to compare products and performance with specified standards. Inspection determines whether a given item falls within specified limits of variability and, therefore, is acceptable. Inspection, per se, cannot inspect good quality into the product but can aid in identifying the causes of defective work. Some of the tangible benefits of quality control and inspection include a higher degree of customer satisfaction, uniform quality necessary for interchangeable parts, and prevention of waste of labor and machine time.

Establishing Standards and Specifications.   Standards and specifications are usually determined by engineers in cooperation with the sales, manufacturing, inspection, and purchasing departments. Standards define the measurable characteristics of products, including such things as performance, weight, and composition. Since absolute uniformity is not economically attainable in most production situations, standards usually take into account permissible variations. These variations are called tolerances. The tolerances should allow for chance variations with anything beyond those assumed to be assignable to a specific removable cause. A good set of standards and their accompanying tolerances must be definite, reasonable, understandable, and achievable.

Determination of Points of Inspection. Where and when to inspect can be determined by analyzing the stages in the manufacturing of the product. Generally, lower-priced products will require fewer points of inspection than will higher-priced products. The reason for this is economic in nature. By way of example, if a fountain pen, upon completion, is found to be defective, it can be scrapped with a very minimum loss in labor and material costs. In contrast, if a television is carried through to completion and then found to be defective, the loss would be considerable. In determining points of inspection it is therefore necessary to weigh the cost of inspection against the potential savings in terms of scrap reduction and reduced labor costs. Defective items should be rejected at points which will result in the lowest production costs. As far as work in process in concerned, inspection may be required at any of the following points.

1. Before or after key operations where there is a high probability of defects that is, at each major machine.

2. Before costly operations where checking the accuracy of fabricated parts will prevent trouble and delay in assembly.

3. Where succeeding operations could conceal defects.

4. At the last step of any logically grouped series of operations.

5. After each setup of a job on a machine.

6. Anywhere along a single assembly line where inspectors may sample work.

7. At the close of departmental responsibilities.

Layout of Inspection Activities. Inspection may take place either on the floor as production is in process, or products may be transferred to some centralized location for inspection. In the former case, quality is checked at the machine or where the operation is being performed. In the latter case, goods are moved to the central inspection point after they are complete. The advantages of floor inspection include (1) quick discovery and correction of defects, (2) handling of materials is reduced, and (3) line layout of machinery need not be disrupted. The principal disadvantages of floor inspection are that (1) costs are higher because of the need for skilled inspectors and tools and (2) the inspectors are frequently under pressure to accept work in order to avoid delays and interruptions of production.

The advantages of centralized inspection include that (1) there is no pressure on inspectors, (2) the flow of the production process is not interrupted, and (3) larger quantities of work can be checked. The principal disadvantage of central inspection is that defects are not detected until considerable labor and material costs have been incurred. If defects in the product are found, they may require a large amount of rework to correct defects and, also, the spoilage of material is larger.

Closely related to the decision of whether floor or central inspection is most appropriate is the decision as to whether each piece is to be inspected or if there is to be inspection by samples. Sample inspection means that at certain intervals only a small percentage of the total product being produced is subject to inspection. Through the use of various statistical techniques it is possible to establish the degree of probability that all products meet the quality requirements if the items selected for inspection do. In any case, the method of inspection should be selected on the basis of the importance of maintaining quality at each selected point or stage of manufacture. In general, the more expensive the end product and the greater the number of steps or stages involved in its production, the more need there is to guarantee that standards are met all along the way. Conversely, the less expensive the end product and the fewer the number of stages in its production, the less is the premium on maintaining absolute quality throughout the manufacturing process.

Production Planning and Control

The purpose of a production planning and control system (PPC), is to integrate and coordinate the use of manpower, machines, and materials for efficient output of goods to meet sales requirements. The production planning and control department is usually organized separately from the manufacturing function to relieve supervisors from certain non-operating responsibilities.

Production planning and control is comprised of a series of related activities, each predetermined and timed to coordinate the total manufacturing program. It guides production by preparing and issuing manufacturing orders which direct the use of facilities, materials, and labor to the output of the required quantity of goods. In short, it regulates the how, when, and where work is to be done.

Benefits of the Production Planning and Control System.   Every organization needs some type of system to plan and control production. How elaborate and detailed the system is will depend on the nature and size of the operation. In any case, however, there are certain basic benefits which accrue to the organization with an effective PPC system. Some of the more important benefits are summarized below.

1. Promotes steady production at high output levels. This is accomplished by insuring rapid processing, by minimizing the need for overtime and rush orders and by reducing interruptions and idleness of men and machines due to nonavailability of materials and parts.

2. Promotes efficiency by eliminating confusion.

3. Achieves low investment in inventory by keeping work in process at a minimum and maintaining rapid stock turnover.

4. Promotes sales through the maintenance of finished goods inventories adequate to meet the demand for standard products and through accurate determination of delivery dates and cost of products.

Factors Influencing the Design of the Production Planning and Control System. The design of the PPC system will be influenced by both the type of manufacturing process and the type of work produced. There are two basic types of manufacturing processes. In the continuous production process, there is an uninterrupted cycle of work from raw material to finished product. Oil would be an example. Continuous production makes use of highly integrated facilities that are largely automatically controlled. The second type of manufacturing process is assembly. In assembly production, component parts are fabricated separately and brought together for erection of the finished product. It should also be noted that the manufacturing process may be a combination of both continuous and assembly production.

The type of work being produced may be either repetitive or a job order operation. In repetitive production, the same product and production sequence is repeated over and over again. In a job order situation, each order which is received will have variations of one kind or another; the product being manufactured is tailored to the customer's particular specifications. The closer the manufacturing process is to being a repetitive and continuous one, the simpler the PPC system will be. This is because the same thing is being done over and over again. The biggest problem presented to production planning and control in this situation is to insure an uninterrupted supply of raw materials in order to provide for a continuous production cycle.

In a job order situation, PPC becomes much more involved and a more sophisticated system is needed. Some of the reasons for this are that the operations that need to be performed will vary, the sequence in which of these operations need to be completed may change, product specifications are different, and there is likely to be more variability in terms of the kinds of raw materials needed. In an assembly situation, particularly one in which a large number of different component parts are involved, the problem of PPC also looms larger. The primary reason for this is explained by the need for coordination. The more different manufacturing departments involved and the greater the number of component parts, the more chance there is that shortages of raw materials and subassemblies can occur. When this happens, there are repercussions throughout the entire operation because of the interdependence of departments. One can perhaps better appreciate the problem of coordination and the importance of PPC if we think in terms of what it takes to manufacture an automobile or to prepare a manned space flight.

Tasks of Production Planning and Control.   There are four primary tasks which every production planning and control system must accomplish. These include routing, scheduling, dispatching, and follow-up. Routing refers to the designation of the processing method and the sequence of operations for the manufacture of each part, assembly, or product. Routing is therefore concerned with the sequential flow of the product through the total manufacturing process. An analogy would be an individual who planned to travel by car from New York to Los Angeles. Before commencing the trip, he would probably procure a highway map of the entire country and then proceed to "red pencil" the path he proposed to take.

Scheduling is concerned with establishing the rate of output and the beginning and end dates for the various phases of production. Scheduling, therefore, deals with the time element. Obviously, any deviation from schedule will throw the entire manufacturing process off balance and can prove costly to the extent that some departments or work stations may have to shut down because of unavailability of parts or subassemblies. Using the travel analogy cited previously, once the route to be followed was determined it would then be necessary to block out the trip in terms of time segments. Usually this would take the form of specifying the number of hours to be driven each day and the number of miles to be covered.

Dispatching represents the paperwork aspects of production planning and control. It involves the preparation of manufacturing orders and the clerical control of work in the plant. Depending on the nature of the operation, these manufacturing orders may be very involved, as they set forth which machines are to be used for which jobs, contain detailed engineering data, information for machine setups, and other technical data. At a minimum, the manufacturing order will contain all pertinent data with respect to routing and scheduling. Continuing our analogy of the traveler, dispatching would correspond to the making of motel reservations at the beginning of each day for that evening, compiling gasoline and mileage records, and·keeping track of expenses for lodging, food, and miscellaneous items.

The final task of PPC is follow-up, which is designed to assure the achievement of output goals. Follow-up will require that the PPC department receives constant feedback on the status of production throughout the entire operation. What is actually happening must be monitored on a continuous basis and if deviations from plans exist, they must be pinpointed and corrective action taken. In a large plant, this will necessitate a very elaborate reporting system.

Inventory Control

Controlling inventories means deciding at what levels inventories can be economically maintained and then holding them at these levels. This applies to raw materials, purchased parts, goods in process, and finished products. Inventories must be controlled because with every unit of inventory there are certain cost advantages and disadvantages. There will always be some level of inventory which will yield a lower total cost than that generated by any other level. What the firm must do is determine what the most economic level of inventory is.

Functions of Inventories. If inventories cost money to maintain, why carry them? The answer to this is that there are several functions or advantages which the firm derives as a result of having a certain level of inventory on hand. First, inventories serve to offset errors in forecasting. Whether it be raw material, purchased parts, or manufactured parts, it is virtually impossible for the firm to always predict exactly what its needs will be. Rather than face the possibility of incurring the tremendous costs which would be involved in shutting down the operation because of a lack of necessary production parts, it is more feasible to carry a given-size inventory as a form of insurance. Similarly, the firm cannot predict exactly what customer demand for its own product will be. To avoid a potential loss in sales due to shortages, it becomes necessary to carry inventories.

A second function of inventories is to permit more economical utilization of equipment, buildings, and manpower when the nature of business is such that fluctuations in demand exist. The demand for many types of products is seasonal in nature. This means that perhaps as much as 70 or 80 percent of sales may occur within a period of only two or three months. Rather than producing enough to meet the projected demand all at once and then completely suspending operations for a period of time, it is more economical for the firm to even out its production over the entire year. To realize the cost advantages of a stable production schedule requires the building up of inventories.

Third, inventories enable the company to purchase or manufacture in economic lot sizes. Every time a particular item is purchased or manufactured, certain fixed costs are incurred. For example, in the case of manufacturing something, the machine(s) must be set up or prepared, and this costs money in the form of labor. The setup cost is the same whether 10 items or 100 items are produced. If, within every two-week period, 20 of the items are needed, it does not make sense to keep incurring the same setup cost over and over again every two weeks. It becomes much more economical to produce a three-month supply and thereby spread the fixed cost over more items. The surplus would be carried in inventory and drawn on as needed. This is what is meant by purchasing or manufacturing in economic lot sizes. It is the quantity of goods which balance the fixed costs of purchasing or manufacturing something against the cost of carrying the inventory.

Finally, inventories serve to minimize the adverse effects of ahead of schedule or behind schedule production. If production is ahead of schedule and an inventory of needed parts is available it can continue without interruption. If production is behind schedule, then inventories can be drawn on to meet requirements.

Having inventories available to perform these functions involves a price, however. The price is the cost of maintaining inventories. The goal of inventory control is to establish levels of inventory which will serve to minimize the company's cost and maximize its revenues. Although the relevant costs will vary, there are some more likely to be relevant in most situations.[1]

___

[1]This discussion of the functions of inventories is based on Raymond R. Mayer, *Production Management* (New York: McGraw-Hill Inc., 1962), pp. 316–317.

Relevant Costs Involved in Inventory Control. The relevant costs associated with inventories can be divided into three major categories: (1) those concerned with the lot sizes a firm should produce or purchase, (2) those suggesting an inventory buildup, and (3) those which discourage an inventory buildup. Each of these categories will be discussed separately.

Relevant Costs Relating to Lot Sizes. Quantity discounts are the first of the relevant costs associated with lot sizes. Lower unit purchase prices are usually available if items are purchased in larger lots. However, a decision to increase lot sizes in order to take advantage of available quantity discounts is also a decision to increase the average amount of inventory on hand. Therefore, quantity discounts tend to encourage purchase of larger lot sizes and hence larger inventories.

Direct material costs are a second factor in determining the proper lot size. There are cases where a relatively fixed number of units are scrapped every time a piece of equipment is set up for production purposes. If three units are scrapped before the correct adjustments can be made and then three good units produced, there is an average of two units of raw material used per unit of output. If, however, 10 units are produced, the average raw material used is only 1.3 units. This yields a lower average direct material cost, and therefore encourages larger lot sizes and inventories.

As discussed previously, setup costs are fixed and are incurred every time a production run is inaugurated. Larger lot sizes mean few production runs per year and consequently, lower setup costs. Again, however, as lot sizes increase the average inventory also increases. This element encourages larger inventories.

Another relevant cost is that of direct labor. Labor efficiency will usually increase after a warmup period leading to a higher average efficiency as lot sizes increase. This tends to promote larger lot sizes and inventories.

Finally, procurement costs are also a factor. The cost of preparing an order is usually independent of the size of the order or else increases but at a relatively lower rate. As lot sizes increase, fewer orders will be processed and average annual procurement costs will decrease. As with quantity discounts, therefore, procurement costs tend to encourage the purchase of larger lot sizes and hence also larger inventories.

Costs Suggesting an Inventory Buildup. If a company is caught short in terms of being able to meet the demand for a particular product, they will be forced to work overtime or add additional shifts. Both overtime and additional shifts require that some premium be added to the regular wage. The alternative to this possibility is to carry inventories. Hiring, training, and layoff costs are also factors of importance. If the firm is unable to supply current market demand, more people may have to be added to the payroll and this will necessitate additional expenses. After the firm catches up with demand, layoffs will occur, and this also entails such costs as unemployment compensation. The alternative is inventories to meet possible emergencies.

Depreciation costs also enter the picture. Plant and equipment represent fixed costs, and if they are standing idle in slack periods, there will be increased depreciation expense per unit of output. Building inventories allow for less equipment and full utilization of that equipment at all times.

A final factor which encourages inventory buildup is the possibility of lost orders and production delays. Inventories enable the firm to meet delivery dates and eliminate delays due to shortages of materials.

Costs Which Discourage Inventory Buildup.   The following are costs which tend to discourage the building up of inventories.[2]

1.   Deterioration.
2.   Obsolescence.
3.   Taxes.
4.   Interest.
5.   Storage costs.

The Problem of Inventory Control in Perspective.   From the previous information, it is obvious that carrying an inventory of any given size can have both positive and negative cost aspects. In almost all cases, some minimum level of inventory is desirable in order to gain the advantages of inventories cited earlier in the chapter. Given this minimum inventory, as the reorder quantity or the lot size increases, the average inventory increases. As a result, we can expect an increase in lot size to be accompanied by a rise in such costs as storage, interest, deterioration, and taxes per time period. On the other hand, as the reorder quantity or size of lot being manufactured increases, fewer orders must be placed or fewer lots manufactured per time period. Thus, we can expect a drop in such costs as per unit setup, material, labor, purchase price, materials handling, and procurement.

2Ibid. The relevant costs discussed in this section were based on pp. 317–326.

In summary, there are two forces at work, one encouraging and one discouraging the purchase and production in larger lot sizes. What the firm must do is find the lot size or reorder quantity which results in the minimum cost. A number of techniques are available for making the necessary cost comparisons. Those which are of real practical value are rather detailed in nature and therefore are beyond the scope of this text. Our objective has been to acquaint the reader with the problem and significance of inventory control.

Control in the Marketing Function—Sales Analysis[3]

In almost all companies, sales are analyzed on a regular and routine basis, as sales analysis is generally indispensable in (1) overall management of the concern, (2) formulation of marketing strategy and plans, (3) control of the sales effort, and (4) administration of a number of nonmarketing functions, such as production planning, inventory control, cash management, and facilities planning.

The Ingredients of Sales Information. The initial steps in sales analysis involve deciding:

How Sales Should Be Defined for the Purpose of Analysis. Businesses attach several meanings to the word "sales": orders or bookings (expressed in product units or dollars), shipments (in units or dollars), cash receipts, dollar billings, and consumer purchases. However sales are defined, sales analysis in many companies encompasses the appraisal and evaluation of selling expenses and sales activities, such as the number of customer calls, and number of orders.

How Sales Figures Should Be Grouped. It is common for information about individual transactions or items to be grouped in one or more of the following ways: sales by product, sales by geographic territory, sales by market, sales by individual customers, and sales by sales unit.

What Forms of Information Are Most Appropriate to the Company's Needs. Sales information is commonly presented in the form of physi-

[3]Material for this section of the chapter was derived from "Sales Analysis," A Research Report from the Conference Board. (New York: National Industrial Conference Board, Inc. 1965), Library of Congress catalog card No. 65—20774.

cal units, revenues, profitability, selling and distribution expenses, market share, and various measures of selling activity.

What Comparisons Are Most Relevant for Sound Interpretation of Sales Figures.   Sales analysis almost always entails a comparison of the sales of each selling unit or item for the period under study against sales of the same unit or item in a previous period, sales of other units or items during the period under study, or a norm or standard such as a budget or quota.

Establishing and Meeting Sales Information Needs.   In many companies the reporting of sales data has evolved on an uncoordinated basis. In recent years, however, quite a number of firms have made thorough reviews of what they have to know about sales and how these data can be most efficiently furnished. As a rule, the impetus for taking this step has come from one or more of the following factors.

1.   Failure to give adequate sales information to lower levels of management.

2.   Shortcomings in the procedures for collecting raw sales data and for preparing sales reports.

3.   A rapid proliferation of sales information needs.

4.   Availability of machine-tabulating equipment and computers.

A broad reappraisal of a sales information program generally involves three distinct tasks.

1.   Defining the output—the information about sales routinely needed by the organization.

2.   Furnishing the input—the information that will efficiently produce this output.

3.   Planning how to convert input data into output data.

Once these tasks have been accomplished, the attendant cost has to be estimated. It is then up to management to evaluate how important the information will be and whether the company's financial resources justify this particular expenditure in light of the many other claims on the company's resources. If the cost is considered excessive, the output of information may be selectively reduced and the means of furnishing it adjusted as required.

In undertaking a reassessment of its sales information program, experienced executives suggest that a company would do well to observe the following ground rules: (1) members of marketing management should participate in all planning that involves the possible revision of sales reports; (2) enough time and money should be provided to do the job properly; (3) procedures for preparing sales reports should be flexible; and (4) alterations in the sales information program should be compatible with other company information programs.

Effective Presentation of Sales Data.   Many companies take pains to see that the figures appearing in sales reports are arranged and presented in such a way that their significance can be easily and quickly comprehended by the reader. Among the techniques used to accomplish this are:

- Including comparative data.
- Including summary statements of purpose and definitions.
- Standardizing the format of sales reports.
- Highlighting key results (by exception reports and other means).
- Using symbols and codes.
- Using narrative summaries and charts.

Ensuring Effective Use of Sales Reports.   How to ensure effective use of sales reports, particularly by members of the field sales force, is a problem encountered by a number of companies. Because salesmen and field sales managers are as a rule action and customer oriented, they often have a distaste for studying reports of any kind. Sometimes, too, discrepancies between figures in sales reports and the salesmen's own records produce a distrust of sales reports. Also, several companies have discovered that delays in getting sales reports to the field have vitiated the reports' helpfulness.

The most common solution to the problem of ensuring effective use of sales reports is to have marketing management direct inquiries to the field sales organization about the facts and figures in the reports. In some companies, salesmen and their supervisors routinely submit written comments on the results shown in sales reports. Another practice is to schedule meetings of the field sales force, marketing management, and report-preparing units for the purposes of reviewing the content and rationale of the company's sales reports and making sure that the reports are filling the recipients' needs.

Manuals, books, bulletins, and newsletters are also relied on to inform recipients how and why they should use sales reports to maximum advantage.

The Uses of Sales Analysis.   Sales analysis involves the gathering, classifying, comparing, and studying of company sales data. It is a universal and indispensable tool in the conduct of business. Such analysis may simply involve the comparison of total company sales in two different time periods, or it may entail subjecting thousands of component sales (or sales-related) figures to a variety of comparisons—among themselves, with external data, and with like figures for earlier periods of time.

Whatever its breadth and depth, sales analysis contributes to the:

1.   Overall management of the company.
2.   Formulation of marketing strategy and plans.
3.   Control of the sales effort.
4.   Administration of a number of nonmarketing functions.

Overall Company Management.   Top management relies on sales analysis both in the setting of policy and the control of operations. By bringing to light information about the organization's performance in the marketplace, sales analysis affects decisions about the company's orientation, expansion, diversification, competitive effort, and the like. It also provides objective standards for evaluating and controlling the volume and profitability of company sales and the managerial competence of the marketing and sales units.

Marketing Strategy and Plans.   Sales analysis is a vital ingredient in the development of long-range marketing strategy and short-term sales plans. It facilitates the accomplishment of the first of these two tasks by revealing past demand for each of the company's products or services; the relative importance of given customers or classes of customers to the company; strength and weaknesses in specific market areas; and the relative success of the company in exploiting its markets as compared with that of its competitors.

Sales analysis contributes at every stage to the development of the company's annual sales plan, which details assignments of the sales organization in the years ahead. For example, it offers realistic historical benchmarks for the purposes of forecasting the coming year's sales,[4] establishing sales goals for units and individuals in the sales organization, and setting guiding norms of activity or efficiency (such as for salesmen's frequency of calls on customers or prospects, allocation of salesmen's time, and size of orders). The analysis of sales is also invaluable to sales management in pointing out the need for changes in the design of sales territories, the size and dispersion of the field sales force, salesmen's compensation, and sales training methods. Other important applications in the area of sales planning are policy determination (for example, setting minimum order size), and preparation of sales expense budgets.

Control of the Sales Effort.   The most obvious as well as the most common use of sales analysis is in the control of the company's sales effort—both guiding it during the period covered by the sales plan and auditing its effectiveness afterward. Such control typically requires appraisal of:

1.   The performance of individual units of the field sales organizations relative to one another and to quotas.

2.   Actual versus planned sales of major product lines or individual products.

3.   Actual versus planned sales by market, class of trade, or even by individual customer.

Such comparisons help sales management in three principal ways. First, having been apprised of the most significant discrepancies between planned and actual performance, it can seek out causes for these discrepancies and take appropriate counteraction, such as improving the servicing or coverage of accounts, having the sales force give more emphasis to some products and less to others, or counseling members of the field sales force whose performance is unsatisfactory. (See Exhibits I and II.)

Second, if despite counteraction, it seems likely that sales results are not going to reach target levels, sales management can make appropriate adjustments in the sales plan and supporting tactics. Finally, facts and figures about sales results carry considerable weight in decisions

---

[4] For a review and appraisal of sales forecasting techniques used in business, see The Conference Board's "Sales Forecasting," *Studies in Business Policy,* No. 106, 1963.

Exhibit I   Sales Analysis Work at the National Gypsum Company

---

At the National Gypsum Company, sales analysis is performed by members of the marketing research department. This work includes:

1. Assisting management in the allocation of overall company sales quotas among sales divisions and districts.

2. Reviewing and commenting on actual sales performance as compared with company objectives and industry performance (industry data are provided by trade associations and the federal government).

3. Providing sales management with market data relevant to the realignment of existing sales territories, districts, and divisions, or the establishment of new ones.

4. Providing various other divisions of the company with special sales analyses.

---

about salary increases, bonuses, and promotion for sales department personnel.

Members of the field sales force also find sales analysis helpful in carrying out their responsibilities. For example, periodic reviews of their sales to and calls on individual accounts often suggest how they can improve their selling efforts.

Administration of Nonmarketing Functions.   The findings of sales analysis are, of course, also useful in the administration of a number of nonmarketing functions of the business, such as:

1. Production planning; for example, when and at what plant to produce each product.

2. Inventory management and control; for example, how great a stock of each product to have on hand and where to maintain it.

3. Purchasing; for example, when and in what quantities to obtain raw material.

4. Cash management; for example, how much money to provide, and when, for financing finished product inventories.

5. Research and development; for example, what kinds of product refinements, new applications of products, or new products to concentrate on in the laboratory and testing ground.

Exhibit II   Applications of Sales Analysis and the Reports Used in These Applications

---

An industrial equipment company selling through eight company-operated and 34 franchised dealers in the United States and Canada uses sales analysis in the following areas of management decision making.

1. Sales forecasting.
2. Product and dealer appraisal.
3. Setting production schedules.
4. Planning plant and manpower requirements.
5. Determining cash requirements.
6. Directing sales promotion.
7. Planning new designs for its products.

The reports underlying the company's sales analysis program include the following facts.

1. Factory shipments to dealers (daily).
2. Factory orders received from dealers (daily).
3. Factory orders received from dealers (weekly, with comparable data for each of the preceding five weeks).
4. Dealer inventory (bimonthly).
5. Dealer sales in units and by class of trade (bimonthly).
6. Annual report of sales by dealer and market.

---

6. Traffic management; for example, how many rail cars, trucks, barges, and so forth, to obtain to get the product to market.

7. Facilities planning; for example, what additions to plant and equipment to make.

Summary

Three key areas of control related to the production function include quality control and inspection, inventory control, and production planning and control. Quality control and inspection involves establishing of standards and specifications, determining the points of inspection, and the layout of inspection activities. Production planning and control is concerned with establishing through the plant a smooth flow of work which will enable the organization to meet its product commitments. It includes the task of routing, scheduling, dispatching, and follow-up. Inventory control is concerned with balancing the costs of carrying inventories with the costs of running out of product. The objective is to determine that level of inventory which will yield the lowest total cost.

Key Concepts

Quality.   Quality is defined by a set of specifications governing the performance, composition, or workmanship of a product.

Quality Control.   Refers to the recognition and removal of identifiable causes of defects and variations from standards.

Inspection.   Application of testing and measuring devices to compare products and performance with standards.

Routing.   Refers to the sequence of operations to be performed in manufacturing of a product.

Scheduling.   Determining the rate of output and beginning and end dates for various phases of production.

Dispatching.   Represents the paper-work aspects of production planning and control. It includes issuing manufacturing orders and clerical control of the work in process.

Inventory Control.   The objective of inventory control is to determine the least-cost level of inventories to carry. It balances the costs of carrying inventories with the cost of running out of product.

Discussion Questions

1. Describe the factors involved in determining whether a product should be inspected by floor inspection or centralized inspection. What *general* factor is involved?

2. Of the following products, which should be inspected by floor inspection and which by centralized inspection? Explain your answer in each case.
   (a) Automobiles.
   (b) Typewriters.
   (c) Light bulbs.
   (d) Dynamite.
   (e) Sweaters.
   (f) Phonograph records.

3. What are some of the benefits of a production planning and control system?

4. Describe each of the four primary tasks of production planning and control.

5. What is the main advantage of having a large inventory?

6. What is the main advantage of having a small inventory?

7. What should a company do in order to minimize its inventory costs, but still maintain the advantages of having an inventory on hand?

8. "The main objective of a quality control system is to assume the highest possible quality." Do you agree with this statement? Explain why or why not.

9. Describe the ground rules which a company should follow in establishing or reappraising its sales information program.

10. Briefly describe what is involved in making a sales analysis.

11. Discuss how sales analysis contributes to:
    (a) Overall management of the company.
    (b) Formulation of marketing strategy and plans.
    (c) Control of the sales effort.
    (d) Administration of nonmarketing functions.

12. Name and briefly describe seven nonmarketing functions which can benefit from the findings of sales analysis.

Selected Readings

Vernon E. Buck, "Too Much Control, Too Little Quality," *Business Horizons, 8* (3), Fall 1965, pp. 34–44.

Elwood S. Buffa, "Modern Production Management," Wiley, New York, 1969.

Marvin Flaks, "Total Cost Approach To Physical Distribution," *Business Management*, April 1967, pp. 51–61.

Bola Gold, and Ralph M. Kraus, "Integrating Physical with Financial Measures for Managerial Controls," *Academy of Management Journal, VII* (2), June 1964 pp. 109–127.

William K. Halstein, "Production Planning and Control Integrated," *Harvard Business Review, 46* (3), May–June 1968, pp. 121–140.

James I. Morgan, "Questions For Solving The Inventory Problem," *Harvard Business Review, 41* (4), July–August 1963, pp. 95–110.

Edward B. Roberts, "Industrial Dynamics and the Design of Management Control Systems," *Management Technology, III* (2), December 1963, pp. 110–118.

24. Accounting and Financial Controls

The primary function of accounting is to convey useful financial information to those who need such data. Financial data are used to evaluate performance of individuals, departments, and the firm as a whole. The conventional financial statements, which normally include an income statement, a funds flow statement, and a balance sheet, are prepared for distribution to the firm's shareholders. The purpose of these conventional financial statements is to convey to owners, creditors, and other external parties information as to the firm's financial position on a given date and the results of the firm's operations for a specific period of time. These statements must conform to "generally accepted accounting principles." The use of generally accepted accounting principles still leaves room for selection among various alternatives for implementing such principles. For example, declining balance depreciation or straight-line depreciation may be selected as a method for depreciating a firm's assets.

Conventional financial statements are to be prepared on a basis consistent with that of preceding years. This is one of the "generally accepted accounting principles." When statements for a number of years have been prepared on a consistent basis, analysis can be prepared as to a firm's progress over a time period without being distorted by varying accounting methodology. Comparison of a firm's balance sheets from one period to another can show a change in the composition of the firm's assets, possibly from current assets to plant, property, and equipment or from current liabilities to long-term debt. Comparing a firm's income statements for different periods might indicate a greater or smaller percent of gross margin on sales from one period to the next or a greater or smaller percentage of selling expenses from one period to the next. These variations, which are discussed in more detail later in this chapter, may indicate areas which require management attention.

Another conventional financial statement which is frequently produced for distribution to external users of financial data is the funds flow statement. This statement is designed to show either the inflows and outflows of a company's working capital, or a company's inflows and outflows of cash. The statement has been described as a "where-got, where-went" statement. The statement is often used to show why a firm's cash or working capital position changes by more than the amount of the firm's current period profits. The various sources of funds which a firm may have include operations, sale of noncurrent assets, owner's investments, and issuance of long-term debt. A firm may apply funds to operations, purchase of noncurrent assets, distributions to owners, and reduction of long-term debt.

The statement shows where the company obtained its working capital and where it used its working capital. The reasons for change in a firm's working capital are thereby indicated and if action is needed to correct the flow of funds such action can be directed to the area requiring correction. Management's need for financial data about the firm is different from the needs of owners, potential owners, creditors, or other outsiders, and therefore, different information is available to management. Conventional financial statements may indicate that the cost of sales is increasing, but additional financial data may be needed by management to determine what corrective action should be taken.

Care should be taken to insure that the appropriate data is available for the decision to be made.

Although financial data is quite useful to management in measuring and evaluating performance, one must always keep in mind that accounting figures are approximations. No one knows what the exact amount of depreciation for a given year is. However, an approximation available today is often more useful to management than a more accurate figure determined six months from now. Before embarking on a study of financial controls, one final point should be made. "People, not figures, get things done." Figures can assist management in controlling a firm's activities, but figures as such do nothing. Figures may indicate a weakness in operating performance but figures will not take corrective action. People (management) must take the action indicated by the figures.

Some of the tools available to management to control a company's activities are presented in the remainder of this chapter.

Internal Control

The controls employed by management to safeguard company assets from theft, wastage, or misuse are known as internal controls. Internal control has been defined by the American Institute of Certified Public Accountants as ". . . the plan of organization and all of the co-ordinate methods and measures adopted within a business to safeguard its assets, check the accuracy and reliability of its accounting data, promote operational efficiency, and encourage adherence to prescribed managerial policies."[1] This definition includes both accounting and administrative controls, which the American Institute of Certified Public Accountants defines as:

"Accounting controls comprise the plan of organization and all methods and procedures that are concerned mainly with, and related directly to, safeguarding of assets and the reliability of the financial records. They generally include such controls as the systems of authorization and approval, separation of duties concerned with record keeping and accounting reports from those concerned with operations or asset custody, physical controls over assets, and internal auditing.

"Administrative controls comprise the plan of organization and all methods and procedures that are concerned mainly with operational efficiency and adherence to managerial policies and usually relate only indirectly to the financial records. They generally include such controls as statistical analysis, time and motion studies, performance reports, employee training programs, and quality controls."[2]

---

[1]Committee on Auditing Procedure of the American Institute of Certified Public Accountants, *Auditing Standards and Procedures* (Statement on Auditing Procedure Number 33, 1963), p. 27.

[2]Ibid., p. 28.

An internal control system is designed to detect intentional or accidental errors in the accounting process. Through a system of authorizations and approvals and by separation of duties, errors can be detected. The work performed by one person should act as a check but not a duplication of the work performed by another person. For example, one person may authorize the sale of some company asset such as an unneeded machine. Another person will actually contract for the sale of the machine and still another person will collect the funds received from the sale.

In the area of accounting controls, the division of duties is of utmost importance. The person performing a particular function should not be the person responsible for recording the activity. One person should collect cash receipts; another person should record cash receipts. One person should authorize an invoice for payment, but a different person should actually pay the amount due.

In a small firm, the division of duties is more difficult to accomplish because of the fewer number of people. Even in very small businesses, however, some division of duties can be obtained which will help safeguard the firm's assets. The more people there are in an organization the easier it is to obtain the desirable degree of separation of duties.

A good internal control system starts with a well-designed organizational plan with clearly defined responsibilities. The procedure to be followed from the performance of an activity to the recording of the activity in the accounting records should be clearly described. The use of printed forms providing for proper authorizations and routing of the data is extremely useful in accomplishing this objective. In selling, for example, procedures should be provided to regulate all activities from the recording of receipt of the order to the recording of receipt of the cash for the merchandise sold.

A number of actions taken by a company may not at first glance appear to be a part of the internal control system when, in fact, they are. For example, customers are sometimes used as a part of the internal control system. What better way is there of insuring that the cashier records all sales than to convince customers that no exchanges or refunds will be made unless they have a sales ticket showing the purchase of the item?

Because of the nature of cash, it is most vulnerable to misappropriation. Therefore, the usual systems of internal control center around the control of cash. A good system of internal control of cash should include the following:

1.   All receipts should be deposited intact daily.

2. The collection of cash and the recording of cash receipts should be separated.

3. Cash payments should be made by check and only after such payments have been properly authorized by someone other than the person making the payment.

4. The firm's bank should be told not to cash any check made payable to the company. Such checks should be accepted for deposit only.

5. Frequent reviews of the control system by the internal auditing staff should also be performed.

A good system of internal control requires qualified, well-trained, and well-supervised personnel. Also, well-defined procedures being performed by qualified personnel are essential to an adequate system of internal control.

Budgetary Control

Nature of Budgets. Budgets are prepared as a part of management's planning function. The firm's objectives and goals are considered when budgets are being prepared. But budgeting is more than planning; it is a control device. A comprehensive operating budget presents a plan for the future expressed in dollars. Continuous comparisons between the budget and actual results are made and significant variances point to the need for corrective action. Thus, the budget becomes a yardstick or standard for measuring actual performance.

A comprehensive operating budget includes a sales budget, a production budget, an expense budget, a cash budget, and a capital expenditures budget.

The sales budget requires a forecast of the sales volume for the future period. The forecasted sales volume is based on past sales, anticipated firm activities (such as a change in prices or a new advertising program), economic and industry conditions, competition, and other factors.

Production and purchasing budgets, expense budgets, and cash budgets are directly related to the sales budget. To obtain the forecasted amount of sales, merchandise must be available to sell. Therefore production must be budgeted to insure the availability of products.

Purchases must be budgeted to insure the availability of materials for the production operation. Expenses must also be budgeted to correspond with forecasted sales and production. And finally, cash must be budgeted to insure the availability of cash when it is needed.

From the various budgets, a comprehensive operating budget can be prepared which estimates the firm's earnings and financial position in the future. The individual budgets and the comprehensive operating budget become the standard against which actual performance can be compared.

Budgets are frequently prepared for the following year. However, since conditions frequently change, a yearly budget often becomes outdated. Budgets for shorter time periods, a quarter or a month, are less likely to become outdated due to changing conditions.

Flexible Budgets. Since operating budgets, production budgets, expense budgets, and so forth, depend so much on the volume of sales or output of the firm, and output is an estimate and subject to variance, companies frequently use a flexible budget. A flexible budget provides a standard by which to measure performance at varying levels of output. Budgets are prepared for different levels of output and a means of interpolating among the various budgeted levels is determined; when actual output is known, a budget for that level is available. The preparation of a flexible budget centers around the division of costs between fixed costs and variable costs. Some costs will remain about the same, regardless of the firm's volume of output (such as the president's salary). Other costs vary with the volume of output (such as sales commissions). Still other costs vary with output but not necessarily in direct proportion with the volume of output. For example, the more electricity one uses the less per kilowatt hour it costs. In preparing a flexible budget, costs are budgeted for varying levels of output, considering what the different cost (fixed variable or semivariable) should be at each budgeted level of output. The use of flexible budgets enables management to control costs at different levels of output more effectively. Some functions, such as the purchase of raw materials, cannot wait for the level of actual output to be determined before they are budgeted, and therefore a single-volume budget is still required even if a flexible budget is being used.

Responsibility Accounting. To better enable management to control operations, responsibility accounting is frequently employed. In responsibility accounting, costs are budgeted for responsibility centers and actual costs are assigned to the responsibility centers. A distinction must be made between controllable and noncontrollable costs assigned to a responsibility center.

A responsibility center is a unit of the organization which is responsible for the performance of some specific function. The function of the unit is its output and the costs involved in producing the output are the units inputs. A given responsibility center may have a number of smaller responsibility centers within it. For example, the manufacturing function of a firm is a responsibility center, but included in the area may be a number of production departments which are also responsibility centers. A good organization chart will help in identifying the various responsibility centers within an organization. Subdivisions of responsibility centers may be desirable for such things as work shifts, so that individuals who are actually responsible for a particular function can obtain a report of the inputs and outputs identified with their scope of responsibility. Flexible budgets which include the probable range of the center's output should be prepared for each responsibility center.

Some companies charge only controllable costs to responsibility centers and other companies charge all costs of operating a responsibility center to the particular center. Since some of these costs are not controllable by the manager of the responsibility center, they should be shown separately. Each operating unit occupies a part of the firm's building, and cost associated with this part of the building will be assigned to a responsibility center, but the manager of the center cannot control this cost.

When controllable costs are associated with a responsibility function, management has a sound basis for evaluation of the center and for taking corrective action.

Standard Costs.   Flexible budgets are often difficult to devise for a manufacturing concern which makes a number of products. A different method of budgeting, known as *standard costs*, is frequently used in such cases. Standard costs are based on "what it should cost" to manufacture a product rather than what it actually cost. A standard cost system is of particular importance to the control system. The standard cost is the yardstick by which actual performance costs are measured.

In a standard cost system, the cost of manufacturing the various products of the firm are determined before production occurs. All elements of cost are included in the standard cost of a product. Actual cost of producing the product is determined and the two are compared. The comparison of standard and actual costs indicate areas which may require management attention. A detailed breakdown of the difference between standard and actual costs, which are called "variances," allows management to pinpoint the area requiring attention.

To illustrate, assume that the Head Company has established the following standard costs per unit for its Product X-2:

Materials–18 lb per unit at $1 per lb	$18.00
Direct labor–4 hr per unit at $3.50 per hr	14.00
Overhead–$2 per standard direct labor hr	8.00
Total standard cost per unit	40.00

During July, the Head Company produced 10,000 units of product X-2. The company used 190,000 lb of material costing $.95 per pound or a total material cost of $180,500. To produce the 10,000 units the company incurred 41,000 hr of direct labor at a cost of $3.60 per hour, or a total direct labor cost of $147,600. During July, the company incurred $85,000 of overhead costs.

Under these assumptions a comparison of standard and actual costs reveals the following.

	Standard		Actual	
Materials	(18 lb at $1 × 10,000)	$180,000	(190,000 at $.95)	$180,500
Direct labor	(4 hr at $3.50 × 10,000)	140,000	(41,000 hr at $3.60)	147,600
Overhead	(4 hr at $2 × 10,000)	80,000		85,000
Total	(10,000 units at $40)	$400,000	(10,000 units at $41.31)	$413,000

The total difference between standard and actual cost for July is $13,100, an unfavorable variance. Knowing this, however, does not help to pinpoint the person or persons responsible for the variance. A further breakdown of the variance is more helpful. Material and labor variances can be identified and broken down between quantity variance and price variance. A quantity variance is determined by calculating the difference between standard quantities which were used and multiplying this difference by the standard price. A price variance is determined by calculating the difference between standard and actual prices and multiplying this difference by the actual quantity used.

During July, the Head Company's material and direct labor variances would be calculated as shown below:

Material:

Quantity Variance–

Standard quantity (10,000 units × 18 lb)	180,000 lb
Actual quantity	190,000 lb
Excessive use of materials	10,000 lb
Standard material price	$ 1.00
Unfavorable material quantity variance	$ 10,000

Price Variance–

Standard material price per pound	$ 1.00
Actual material price per pound	.95
Favorable price variance per pound of material	.05
Actual pounds of materials used	190,000 lb
Favorable material price variance	$ 9,500

Direct Labor:

Quantity Variance–

Standard quantity (10,000 × 4 hr)	40,000 hr
Actual quantity	41,000 hr
Excessive use of direct labor	1,000 hr
Standard direct labor price	3.50
Unfavorable direct labor quantity variance	$ 3,500

Price Variance–

Standard direct labor price per hour	$ 3.50
Actual direct labor price per hour	3.60
Unfavorable direct labor price per hour	.10
Actual hours of direct labor used	41,000 hr
Unfavorable direct labor price variance	$4,100.00

In summary, the material and direct labor variances are as follows.

Material quantity variance (unfavorable)–	($10,000.00)
Material price variance (favorable)–	9,500.00
Excess of actual material cost over standard	$ (500.00)
Direct labor quantity variance (unfavorable)–	($ 3,500.00)
Direct labor price variance (unfavorable)–	(4,100.00)
Excess of actual direct labor cost over standard	($ 7,600.00)

With this breakdown, better control can be obtained over the use and prices paid for material and direct labor. The same individuals are not responsible for the quantities of materials used and the prices paid for materials used. Nor are the same individuals responsible for the use of direct labor and the hourly rate paid employees. The breakdown of material and direct labor variances enables management to locate problem areas and then take whatever corrective action is indicated.

Overhead variances are calculated somewhat differently than material and direct labor variances. When standard costs are used, overhead costs are charged to production by the use of a predetermined rate. The rate may be based on any one of a number of measures of production activity, such as direct labor cost, direct labor hours, machine time, or quantity of materials used. In the preceding illustration, the Head Company charged product X-2 with $2 overhead for each direct labor standard hour, or a total of $80,000 during July. Overhead was charged to production on the basis of standard hours, not actual hours. The application of overhead to production should not be affected by the efficiency of the basis of application. In other words, standard overhead per unit should not vary simply because the quantity of direct labor varied from standard.

The amount of overhead applied to production is determined by the use of a flexible budget for the anticipated level of operations. The amount of overhead at that level of operations is budgeted as well as the basis of applying the overhead. In the illustration the basis of application was standard direct labor hours. This predetermined rate is used to apply overhead to the units of product which the company produces. At the end of a cost period the actual amount of overhead is compared with the applied amount and the variances are determined to pinpoint the area responsible for the differences.

Overhead variances are frequently identified as volume variances and spending variances. To determine these variances, a calculation of the budgeted overhead at the actual level of operations attained is required.

ACCOUNTING AND FINANCIAL CONTROLS 489

In other words, what should the overhead cost have been for the actual quantity of production attained? In the illustration, the overhead rate of $2 per direct labor hour was obtained from a flexible budget at the anticipated level of production for July. The overhead application rate includes both fixed and variable overhead costs. When a firm operates at any level other than the level anticipated in determining the application rate, fixed overhead will be incorrectly applied. This is a volume variance. For example, assume that the $2 rate used by the Head Company to apply overhead had been determined as follows.

Budgeted Overhead Cost

	Production Level			
Capacity	70%	80%	90%	100%
Standard direct labor hours	35,000	40,000	45,000	50,000
Fixed overhead costs	$40,000	$40,000	$40,000	$40,000
Variable overhead costs	42,000	48,000	54,000	60,000
Total budgeted cost	$82,000	$88,000	$94,000	$100,000
Overhead application rate	$2.34	$2.20	$2.09	$2.00

NOTE: Overhead application rate is the total budgeted cost divided by standard direct labor at the same budgeted level.

The Head Company anticipated producing at 100 percent of capacity and therefore used an overhead application rate of $2 per standard direct labor hour. However, the company actually operated at 80 percent of capacity. The overhead volume variance is therefore $8000 unfavorable (standard overhead at the actual level of operations attained $80,000 [applied], less budgeted overhead at the actual level of operations attained $88,000 @ 80 percent of capacity). This variance is due to the fact that the company operated at a level other than the level anticipated when determining the overhead application rate.

The Head Company's overhead spending variance is the difference between the budgeted overhead at the actual level of operations attained, $88,000, and the actual amount of overhead cost $85,000, or $3,000. Since the company spent less at the level of operations attained than was budgeted for that level, the variance is favorable.

To summarize overhead variances:

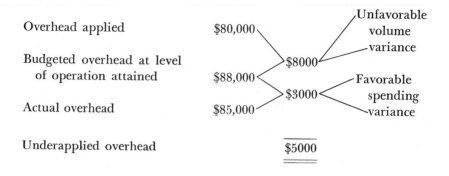

Underapplied overhead $5000

By breaking down the overhead variance into its component parts, management can obtain better control, directing their attention to the areas where significant variances are noted.

Other Financial Controls

Profit Analysis.   An analysis of a company's profit can be accomplished through a number of different methods. One method is to compare the firm's budgeted income statement for a period of time with actual amounts for the same period. The differences between budget and actual are determined, identified, and explained. Corrective action can then be taken if warranted.

The comparison of a firm's actual income statement with its budgeted income statement often presents differences, which require additional calculations to explain the cause of such differences. To illustrate, the following income statement will be used.

GLASSCO
Income Statement
for the Year Ended December 31, 19X2

	Budget	Actual	Variance
Sales	$500,000	$507,000	$ 7,000
Cost of sales	300,000	311,100	(11,100)
Gross margin	$200,000	$195,900	$(4,100)
Operating expenses	100,000	98,000	2,000
Net income before taxes	$100,000	$ 97,900	$(2,100)

The budget was prepared under the following assumptions.

		Sales			Costs		Gross Margin	
	Quantity	Unit Price	Total	Unit Cost	Total		Per Unit	Total
Product M	2,000	$ 90	$180,000	$50	$100,000		$40	$ 80,000
Product N	2,000	85	170,000	55	110,000		30	60,000
Product O	1,000	150	150,000	90	90,000		60	60,000
Total	5,000	$100	$500,000	$60	$300,000		$40	$200,000

Actual operating results were as follows.

		Sales			Costs		Gross Margin	
	Quantity	Price	Total	Unit Cost	Total		Per Unit	Total
Product M	2,100	$ 95.00	$199,500	$54	$113,400		$41.00	$ 86,100
Product N	2,100	80.00	168,000	56	117,600		24.00	50,400
Product O	900	155.00	138,500	89	80,100		66.00	59,400
Total	5,100	$ 99.41	$507,000	$61	$311,100		$38.41	$195,900

A comparison of budget and actual operations indicates a total un-favorable difference in the company's profit for the period of $2100. This difference can be explained as follows.

Volume Variance = (budgeted quantity − actual quantity) × budgeted sales price
$$(\quad 5,000 \text{ units} \quad - \quad 5,100 \quad) \times \quad \$100.00 =$$
$$\$10,000$$

Price Variance = (budget price − actual price) × actual quantity
$$(\quad \$100 \quad - \quad \$99.41 \quad) \times \quad 5100 = (3,000)$$

Total sales variances $\quad \underline{\$ 7,000}$

Cost of Sales Variances:

Volume Variance = (budget quantity − actual quantity) × budget cost
$$(\quad 5,000 \quad - \quad 5,100 \quad) \times \quad \$60 = (\$6,000)$$

Price Variance = (budget cost − actual cost) × actual quantity
$$(\quad \$60 \quad - \quad \$61 \quad) \times \quad 5,100 = (\ 5,100)$$

Total cost of sales variances − unfavorable $\underline{(\$11,100)}$

Gross Margin Variances:
Volume Variance—

(Budgeted quantity − Actual quantity) × Budgeted gross margin = Volume variance

(5,100 − 5,000) × $40 = $4,000

Price Variance—

(Budgeted gross margin − Actual gross margin) = Difference × Actual quantity = Price variance

Product

M ($40.00 − $41) = $1 × 2,100 = $ 2,100
N ($30.00 − $24) = ($6) × 2,100 = $(12,600)
O ($60.00 − $66) = $6 × 900 = $ 5,400

Total gross margin price variance $(5,100)

Mix Variance—
Quantities

Product	Budget	−	Actual	=	Difference	×	Budgeted Gross Margin	=	Mix Variance
M	2,040	−	2,100	=	60	×	$40	=	$ 2,400
N	2,040	−	2,100	=	60	×	$30	=	$ 1,800
O	1,020	−	900	=	(120)	×	$60	=	$(7,200)
	5,100		5,100						$(3,000)

Unfavorable − ( )

Total gross margin variances—	
Volume variance − favorable	$ 4,000
Price variance − unfavorable	(5,100)
Mix variance − unfavorable	(3,000)
Total gross margin variance − unfavorable	$(4,100)

Note: Budget is based on budget proportions of 2:2:1.

When combined, the total favorable sales variances of $7000 and the unfavorable cost of sales variances of $11,100 explain the $4100 unfavorable variance in gross margin. Another method of analyzing the variance in gross margin is shown below.

Combining the unfavorable gross margin variance of $4100 with the favorable variance in operating expense of $2000 explains the unfavorable variance in the company's profit for the year.

Knowing why actual results differ from budget enables management to direct their attention to the trouble spots.

Percentage Analysis.   Another method of analyzing a firm's profit, progress, and position is through the use of percentages and ratios. Many firms wish to compare current operations and position with the past. This type of comparison is often prepared to determine if the firm is progressing as planned.

In comparing a company's current operations with past performance, conventional financial statements are often reduced to percentages. There are two basic methods of analyzing financial statements on a percentage basis: *trend analysis* and *common-size analysis*.

In a *trend analysis* of financial statements, a base period or year is determined and later years' figures are determined as a percentage of the base year. Both the balance sheet and the income statement are shown as percentages of the base year's balance sheet and income statement. For example, assume you wish to compare the following income statements by using a trend analysis.

Hardrock Mining Co.
Comparative Income Statements
for the Years Ended December 31, 19X1, 19X2, and 19X3

	19X3	19X2	19X1
Gross sales	$1,450,000	$1,300,000	$1,040,000
Sales returns	75,000	60,000	50,000
Net sales	$1,375,000	$1,240,000	$1,000,000
Cost of sales	825,000	750,000	600,000
Gross margin	$ 550,000	$ 490,000	$ 400,000
Selling expenses	$ 140,000	$ 140,000	$ 100,000
General expenses	110,000	90,000	100,000
Total operating expenses	$ 250,000	$ 230,000	$ 200,000
Net income before taxes	$ 300,000	$ 260,000	$ 200,000
Income taxes	120,000	100,000	80,000
Net income	$ 180,000	$ 160,000	$ 120,000

Using 19X1 as our base year, a trend analysis for the preceding income statement would appear as follows.

Hardrock Mining Co.
Percentage Analysis of Income Statements
For the Years Ended December 31, 19X1, 19X2, and 19X3

	19X3	19X2	19X1
Gross sales	138.10%	123.81%	100.00%
Sales returns	150.00%	120.00%	100.00%
Net sales	137.50%	124.00%	100.00%
Cost of sales	137.50%	124.00%	100.00%
Gross Margin	137.50%	122.50%	100.00%
Selling expenses	140.00%	140.00%	100.00%
General expenses	110.00%	90.00%	100.00%
Total operating expenses	125.00%	115.00%	100.00%
Net income before taxes	150.00%	130.00%	100.00%
Income taxes	150.00%	125.00%	100.00%
Net income	150.00%	133.33%	100.00%

When using a trend analysis to analyze a firm's balance sheet, each item on the balance sheet is shown as a percentage of the same item on the base year's balance sheet. For example, cash for 19X2 and 19X3 would be reflected as a percentage of the 19X1 cash balance shown on the firm's comparative balance sheets.

When a *common-size* analysis of financial statements is prepared, each item shown on the firm's comparative income statements is shown as a percentage of the year's net sales, and each item on the comparative balance sheets is shown as a percentage of total assets for each year. Using the comparative income statement, presented earlier, of the Hardrock Mining Co., a common-size analysis would appear as follows.

Hardrock Mining Co.
Common-Size Income Statements
For the Years Ended December 31, 19X1, 19X2, and 19X3

	19X3	19X2	19X1
Gross sales	105.45%	104.83%	105.00%
Sales returns	5.45	4.83	5.00
Net sales	100.00%	100.00%	100.00%
Cost of sales	60.00	60.48	60.00
Gross margin	40.00%	39.52%	40.00%
Selling expenses	10.18%	11.29%	10.00%
General expenses	8.00	7.26	10.00
Total operating expenses	18.18%	18.55%	20.00%
Net income before taxes	21.82%	20.97%	20.00%
Income taxes	8.73	8.07	8.00
Net income	18.09%	12.90%	12.00%

Using either method of analyzing financial statements by the use of percentages is helpful in identifying changes in a company's operations or its financial position.

Ratio Analysis.   An additional tool used by management to interpret accounting data and pinpoint trouble spots is ratio analysis. The use of ratio analysis enables management to not only evaluate the company's progress from one period to another, but also to compare the firm with others or with industry averages. Ratios indicate to management the manner in which the company is operating. There are a great many ratios which may be used to evaluate a company's financial position and profitability. However, only a few of the more common ratios will be discussed here.

Profitability ratios are used to obtain an idea of how well the firm is employing its assets or the capital invested in the firm. A return on investment in assets can be calculated by dividing net income by the average total assets during the period. A similar ratio which may be of more importance to the firm's owners is the ratio of net income to average stockholders' investment during the period. The ratio of net income to sales for a given period is also used as a test of the firm's profitability.

In evaluating a firm's liquidity (the ability of a firm to meet its current obligations), ratios such as the current ratio, quick ratio, inventory turnover, and average collection period may be used. The current ratio is simply the relationship of a company's current assets to its current liabilities. If a firm has two or three times as many current assets as current liabilities, it probably can pay its obligations as they come due.

The *quick ratio*, sometimes called the acid-test ratio, is the relationship between a firm's quick assets and its current liabilities. Quick assets include cash, notes and accounts receivable, and temporary investments. These assets are either cash or can be converted into cash in a relatively short period of time. The quick ratio then indicates the relationship of cash and near-cash items to current liabilities.

Inventory turnover is calculated by dividing the firm's cost of sales by average inventory. This indicates the number of times the average amount of inventory passed through the business during the period. Inventory turnover, when high, may indicate that the firm is carrying too little inventory and not having available what the customer wishes to buy. A low turnover might indicate plans for expansion or possibly an accumulation of obsolete items in inventory.

If the inventory turnover is divided into the number of days in the period, you obtain the average number of days in each inventory turnover. If this number is less than the normal time required to order and receive merchandise, too little inventory is being carried. If the number of days in each turnover is much greater than the normal time required to obtain merchandise from suppliers, the amount of inventory being carried is probably too high.

A firm's *average collection period* is calculated by dividing the average of accounts receivable by net charge sales and multiplying the result times the number of days in the period. An indication of the firm's accounts receivable management can be obtained by comparing the average collection period with the firm's normal credit terms.

A firm's ability to meet its long-term payment schedules, such as interest costs, is referred to as solvency. Two common ratios used to test a company's solvency are "times interest earned" and "equity ratio."

The *times interest earned* ratio is calculated by dividing net income before interest and taxes by the annual interest charge. This ratio gives bond holders some idea of the level to which income can fall before the company's ability to meet interest payments will be impaired.

Equity ratio is simply a breakdown of the firm's equity in percentages. This is sometimes referred to as the debt-to-capital ratio. The ratio indicates the relationship between creditors' and owners' funds being used in the firm.

The use of ratios assists management in reducing raw numbers to understandable figures and are of great help in the control function.

The following illustration shows how the various ratios previously discussed are calculated.

Mini Press Sales
Balance Sheet
December 31, 19X1 and 19X2

Assets

	19X2	19X1
Current assets:		
Cash	$11,500	$ 8,000
Accounts receivable, net	24,800	25,200
Merchandise inventory	23,100	24,900
Prepaid expenses	1,200	900
Total current assets	$60,600	$59,000
Fixed assets:		
Machinery, net	$ 19,000	$ 20,000
Equipment, net	30,400	26,000
Land	40,000	40,000
Total fixed assets	$ 89,400	$ 86,000
Total assets	$150,000	$145,000

Liabilities

	19X2	19X1
Current liabilities:		
Accounts payable	$11,000	$14,000
Notes payable	5,000	4,000
Accrued expenses	4,000	5,000
Total current liabilities	$60,600	$59,000
Long-term debt:		
6% bonds payable, due 19X9	$20,000	$20,000
Total liabilities	$40,000	$43,000

Owners' Equity

	19X2	19X1
Common stock, $10 par value, 10,000 shares authorized, issued and outstanding	$100,000	$100,000
Retained earnings	10,000	2,000
Total owners equity	$110,000	$102,000
Total liabilities and owners equity	$150,000	$145,000

Mini Press Sales
Income Statement
For the Years Ended December 31, 19X1 and 19X2

	19X2		19X1	
Sales		$365,000		$328,500
Less cost of sales:				
Merchandise inventory, January 1	$ 24,900		$ 19,100	
Purchases	202,200		190,800	
Goods available for sale	$227,100		$209,900	
Merchandise inventory, December 31	23,100		24,900	
Cost of sales		204,000		185,000
Gross margin from sales		$161,000		$143,500
Operating expenses		141,800		126,300

Net income from operations	$ 19,200	$ 17,200
Interest on bonds	1,200	1,200
Net income before taxes	$ 18,000	$ 16,000
Income taxes	4,000	3,500
Net income	$ 14,000	$ 12,500

The following ratios are calculated for the year 19X2.

$$\text{Return on total assets} = \frac{\text{Net income}}{\text{Average total assets}} =$$

$$\frac{\$14,000}{\dfrac{\$150,000 + \$145,000}{2}} = \frac{\$14,000}{\$106,000} = 13.21\%$$

$$\text{Return on owners' equity} = \frac{\text{Net income}}{\text{Average owners' equity}} =$$

$$\frac{\$14,000}{\dfrac{\$110,000 + \$102,000}{2}} = \frac{\$14,000}{\$106,000} = 13.21\%$$

$$\text{Net income to sales} = \frac{\text{Net income}}{\text{Sales}} = \frac{\$14,000}{\$365,000} = 3.84\%$$

$$\text{Current ratio} = \frac{\text{Current assets}}{\text{Current liabilities}} = \frac{\$60,600}{\$20,000} = 3.03{:}1$$

$$\text{Quick ratio} = \frac{\text{Quick assets}}{\text{Current liabilities}} = \frac{\$36,300}{\$20,000} = 1.82{:}1$$

$$\text{Inventory turnover} = \frac{\text{Cost of sales}}{\text{Average inventory}} = \frac{\$204,000}{\$24,900 + \$23,100} =$$

$$\frac{\$204,000}{\$24,000} = 8.5 \text{ times}$$

$$\text{Average collection period} = \frac{\text{Average accounts receivable}}{\text{Net charge sales}} \times$$

(Total sales are used here since
charge sales are not shown.)

$$\text{Number of days} = \frac{\dfrac{\$24,800 + \$25,200}{2}}{\$365,000} \times 365 = \frac{\$25,000}{\$365,000} \times 365 =$$

25 days

$$\text{Times interest earned} = \frac{\text{Net income before interest and taxes}}{\text{Annual interest charge}} =$$

$$\frac{\$19,200}{\$1,200} = 16 \text{ times}$$

$$\text{Equity ratio} = \frac{\text{Total liabilities}}{\text{Total liabilities and owners' equity}} \quad \text{and}$$

$$\frac{\text{Total owners' equity}}{\text{Total liabilities and owners' equity}} = \frac{\$40,000}{150,000} \text{ and } \frac{\$110,000}{\$150,000} =$$

26.67% creditors equity and 73.33% owners' equity.

Financial controls are an integral part of managerial control. Some financial controls are established to safeguard the company's assets while others are used to measure performance. In the planning function, management sets certain goals and objectives. These goals and objectives are often reduced to figures and become the basis for comparison with actual results, which are also presented in figures. The measurement and evaluation of performance by management is greatly facilitated by the use of financial data.

Summary

This chapter was designed to provide the reader with some insight into control as it relates to the accounting and financial aspects of the organization. The initial portion of the chapter was devoted to a discussion of some of the conventional accounting statements and the subject of internal control. The remainder of the chapter focused on the areas of budgetary control and ratio analysis. The key concepts cited will serve to highlight the specific material.

Key Concepts

Balance Sheet.   Sets forth the assets and liabilities of the firm as of a given date. Comparing a firm's balance sheet from one period to another can show a change in the firm's assets from current liabilities to long-term debt.

Flow of Funds Statement.   This statement shows either the inflows or outflows of a firm's working capital or inflows and outflows of cash. It shows why the firm's cash or working capital position changes by more than the amount current period profits.

Income Statement.   This statement provides a summary of the firm's profit or loss position over a period of time. By comparing statements from previous periods, variations can be noted and areas such as selling expenses or gross margin on sales that may need management's attention can be pinpointed.

Internal Controls.   Employed by management to safeguard company assets. Internal controls may involve either accounting controls or they may be administrative in nature.

Budgets.   Budgets are a planning as well as a control tool. A comprehensive operating budget includes a sales budget and a capital expenditure budget.

Flexible Budgets.   Provides a standard by which to measure performance at varying levels of output.

Responsibility Accounting.   Accounting costs are budgeted for responsibility centers and actual costs are assigned to the centers. A responsibility center is a unit of the organization which is responsible for the performance of some specific function.

Controllable Costs.   Those over which the unit has direct control.

Standard Costs. Are based on what it should cost to manufacture a product based on past experience. The standard cost is a yardstick by which actual cost can be measured.

Variance. Variances represent the difference between standard costs and actual costs. When a variance occurs, it is a signal that an area requires attention.

Ratio Analysis. A ratio is a comparison between any two items on the income statement or balance sheet. Ratio analysis is used to form general guidelines for judging the efficiency of operation in any number of areas, such as inventory turnover or profitability.

Discussion Questions

1. Define the following terms.
   - (a) Standard costs.
   - (b) Flexible budgets.
   - (c) Accounting controls.
   - (d) Administrative controls.
   - (e) Responsibility accounting.
   - (f) Trend analysis.
   - (g) Common-size analysis.
   - (h) Ratio analysis (give three examples).

2. The Rojo Furniture Company employs five girls in the customer collections department. Each girl's job is to collect the customers' payments and record these payments in a cash receipts book. The receipt books are audited periodically by the accounting department.

   Does this represent a sound internal control system? If you feel a better control system is needed, what do you suggest?

3. Observe the standard costs given on page 489. Suppose the following figures were given for the month of August.

(a)   200,000 lb of material costing .90 per lb to produce 12,000 units.

(b)   45,000 hr of direct labor at a cost of $3.65 per hr.

(c)   Overhead costs of $85,000.

Prepare a statement showing which of the above three costs are favorable or unfavorable and show the favorable or unfavorable amounts in each case.

Selected Readings

Chris Argyris, "Human Problems With Budgets," *Harvard Business Review, XXXI* (1), pp. 97–110.

Bela Gold, and Ralph M. Kraus, "Integrating Physical With Financial Measures for Managerial Controls," *Academy of Management Journal, VII* (2), June 1964, pp. 109–127.

Charles L. Hughes, "Why Budgets Go Wrong," *Personnel, 42* (3), May–June 1965, pp. 19–26.

Rensis Likert, and Stanley E. Seashore, "Making Cost Control Work," *Harvard Business Review, 41* (6), 1963, pp. 98–108.

Rensis Likert, and Stanley E. Seashore, "Direct Costing To The Rescue," *Business Week*, March 24, 1962.

Burnard H. Sord, and Glenn A. Welsch, "Managerial Planning and Control as Viewed by Lower Levels of Supervision," Bureau of Business Research, The University of Texas, Austin, 1964.

Index

DATE DUE

RES			
JUN 6 1986 Nov. 1			

DEMCO 38-297